MOTTY

By the Same Author

Second to None: Great Teams of Post-war Soccer
The European Cup 1955–1980 (with John Rowlinson)
Match of the Day: The Complete Record
Motty's Diary: A Year in the Life
Motson's National Obsession
Motty's Year
Motson's FA Cup Odyssey
Motson's World Cup Extravaganza

MOTTY

Forty Years
in the Commentary Box

John Motson

Published by Virgin Books 2009

2 4 6 8 10 9 7 5 3 1

First published in Great Britain in 2009 by

Virgin Books
Random House,
20 Vauxhall Bridge Road,
London SW1V 2SA

www.virginbooks.com
www.rbooks.co.uk

Addresses for companies within The Random House Group Limited can be found at:
www.randomhouse.co.uk/offices.htm

The Random House Group Limited Reg. No. 954009

A CIP catalogue record for this book
is available from the British Library

Hardback ISBN 9781905264681
Trade Paperback ISBN 9780753518120

The Random House Group Limited supports The Forest Stewardship Council [FSC],
the leading international forest certification organisation. All our titles that are printed
on Greenpeace-approved FSC-certified paper carry the FSC logo.
Our paper procurement policy can be found at www.rbooks.co.uk/environment

974, 103/920/MOT

Mixed Sources

Product group from well-managed
forests and other controlled sources
www.fsc.org Cert no. TT-COC-2139
© 1996 Forest Stewardship Council

FSC

Typeset by Palimpsest Book Production Limited, Grangemouth, Stirlingshire
Printed and bound in Great Britain by
Clays Ltd, St Ives plc

To my dear wife Annie, who suffered my long absences, and to my son, Fred, who became my best mate. Also to David Jones and Bob Abrahams, two of my mentors who both passed away in 2009. Without them, I would not have made the grade.

'I couldn't consider retiring when there are still so many things I want to do.'

Paul Anka on BBC Breakfast Time – on his sixty-sixth birthday, July 2007

'The first and last appearances are the big ones. Everything in between is just your job.'

Michael Parkinson on his own retirement at seventy-two in 2007

'I like what I do and I'm getting better at it, why shouldn't I continue? Is there something wrong with that?'

Debbie Harry (Blondie) – aged sixty-two

'When I started in television there were only two channels, so if you were a success on one or the other you made quite an impact.'

Sir David Frost

'Never retire completely, Johnny. Don't even think about it.'

Doug Ellis, aged eighty-four – in the Aston Villa boardroom

ACKNOWLEDGEMENTS

My job was made a lot easier by the support of a number of people who read my manuscript thoroughly and suggested some sensible and worthwhile changes. They included Roger Ball, Rick George, Patricia Gregory, Duncan Hamilton, Roger Jones, Jane Morgan, Anne Motson, Fred Motson, Jennifer Plowman, John Rowlinson, Bob Sims, Bob Watson and Karen Watson. My heartfelt thanks also go out to my publishers, particularly to Ed Faulkner and my editor Tom Bromley.

CONTENTS

Prologue

'At the end . . .'

ON THE MORNING OF 29 June 2008, I was sitting in an outdoor café in the Stadt Park, Vienna, when a young boy came up and introduced himself. He was twelve-year-old Maxim Fillin from Moscow, and he'd come to Austria with his parents to watch the European Championships. Despite living in Russia, Maxim was extremely knowledgeable not only about English football, but also my own contribution. 'I don't like Russian football much so I download a lot of English games and listen to your commentary,' he explained.

To be honest, I was glad of the interruption. Preparation for that night's final between Germany and Spain was not going well. I'd been thinking about what Pierluigi Collina had said at the Referees' Association Centenary dinner, when he was asked about how he had felt walking down the tunnel to referee the World Cup final. 'You think of the good games you have had earlier in the tournament that have got you selected for the final,' Collina had said. 'Then you realise one single mistake would wipe all those away and be the only thing you are remembered for.'

At a BBC press call two days earlier I had announced that Euro 2008 would be my last major tournament – a ninth European Championship to go with nine World Cups. Would one mistake in the Ernst Happel Stadium, where the commentary position is farther from the pitch than anywhere else in Europe, spoil the memory of eighteen championships? Maybe even cast a shadow over thirty-seven years of television commentary?

It only needed me to call the wrong goalscorer, miss a yellow card, or misidentify a player at a key moment, and the viewers would be waving white handkerchiefs as a send-off. The thought was too frightening to contemplate.

I was so wound up that I can hardly remember anything at all about the actual game, other than the winning goal scored for Spain by Fernando Torres. But it must have gone quite well, because David Pleat, an old friend but at major tournaments a rival commentator with ITV, phoned me afterwards to congratulate me. He said he had watched the match at home and considered my partnership with Mark Lawrenson had been immaculate.

Gary Lineker also had something to say. At the airport the following morning, he confessed, 'I was a bit nervous for you last night. It would have been horrible if something had gone wrong for you on your last one.'

Lineker had taken it upon himself, before handing over to me at the start of the match, to list my portfolio of big games for the BBC: nine World Cup finals, with the final itself coming my way six times; nine European Championships, with eight finals; twenty-nine FA Cup finals with five replays. Talk about putting me under pressure! After the final whistle, though, he was kind enough to say I had 'played a blinder'.

I suspect not all the 12 million viewers would have agreed with that, but as such luminaries as David Coleman and Sir Peter O'Sullevan have said: 'Sports commentary is first and foremost about survival.' They couldn't be more right: all those big games look great on my record, but a critical mistake in any one of them could have made my career unrecoverable.

This, then, is the story of how I survived for the best part of forty years . . .

PART I

'Barry commentates from the grandstand, John is talking from the terraces'

Chapter 1

'Motson, that's your lot son'

Mugged in Manhattan

Rosie O'Grady's bar and restaurant is on Seventh Avenue in New York, more or less opposite the Sheraton Hotel and Towers. It has a perceptibly Irish feel to it, as well as a sporting one. There are framed baseball and American football memorabilia in the bar at street level, but downstairs, curiously for a steak and seafood house in the theatre district of the Big Apple, there is a collection of fine prints of celebrated cricketers.

There was nothing for me to celebrate when I took a call on my mobile in the upstairs bar during the World Cup of 1994. At the time I was enjoying a beer with David Davies, a former BBC colleague working for the FA, and Terry Venables, who was working with the BBC as a co-commentator. Terry had just taken the job as England coach following Graham Taylor's failure to qualify for the tournament.

The call came from Malcolm Kemp, the BBC team leader at the International Broadcast Centre in Dallas, and it was not good news. 'I'm ringing to tell you that Barry has got the final,' intoned Kemp in his thick New Zealand accent.

If I'm being honest, the call did not come as a complete surprise, since the BBC had played off Barry Davies and me in a neck-and-neck contest for nearly twenty years. Up to that point, I had enjoyed by far the best of it. Sixteen successive FA Cup finals had come my way, including the most recent one, while Barry was still waiting to commentate on his first (usually he had been awarded the European Cup final instead, which, not unreasonably, he saw as the second prize). It was much the same story with World Cups. After David Coleman handed over the microphone following the 1978 tournament in Argentina, I had broadcast the next three finals, culminating in Italy in 1990.

In 1994, though, it had been my understanding that some in the BBC hierarchy were putting pressure on the heads of my department to make a change. They preferred Barry's more restrained style to my own. I sensed that editor Brian Barwick had fought hard to keep me in the seat during Italia 90 when others had wanted him to make the switch. Four years later, having left the decision until after the quarter-finals, he went the other way.

Before Kemp could ring off I asked him where Barry Davies was. With the way this World Cup was working, he could have been in one of three time zones. 'He's right here in the office,' said Kemp.

'Let me speak to him,' I said, seizing the moment to offer congratulations before the news had sunk in. We had a convivial conversation, and Barry later dropped me a note saying that although it was his turn this time, he expected the keen competition to go on for years to come.

Terry Venables and David Davies could see by the look on my face that it wasn't good news. 'We had better do what we did when I got sacked at Barcelona,' said Venables. 'Have another beer.'

The word soon went round that I had lost the final. It had taken the BBC such a long time to make the decision that many people believed it would be a defining one. MOTSON – THAT'S YOUR LOT SON trumpeted one tabloid headline.

But I can say with hand on heart that once the feeling of being mugged died away, I was nowhere near as heartbroken as people seemed to think. For a start, I didn't find it the easiest of World Cups. Only Japan in 2002 was more difficult. Much as I admired the way the Americans put on a show, and despite enjoying most of the matches I was allocated, I had been limping around with a broken toe.

Admittedly, that was largely my fault. I had kicked the bedpost in frustration one night, after being told that our commentary positions would be several rows farther away from the pitch than expected. This was to accommodate a small camera so that the co-commentator or any other pundit at the ground could do a live interview with the studio at half-time or full-time.

The BBC sent me to hospital in Boston to have the damage assessed, but short of offering me a walking stick and telling me it would take six weeks to heal, there wasn't much that could be done by the American medics.

I was asked to hand in the air ticket that would have taken me back to Los Angeles, and instead stayed in New York for the semi-final between Italy and Bulgaria before flying home. John Rowlinson, a BBC colleague and firm friend, who had joined soon after me and had risen from assistant producer to Assistant Head of Sport, took my mind off the situation by taking me shopping. 'Rowly' had spent a lot of time in America and knew the big stores in Manhattan where I could buy some presents. My son, Frederick, was only eight, and I thought he might appreciate getting some toys a few days earlier than expected.

I received a number of supportive messages from home, including one from Mike Dillon, the face of Ladbrokes Racing. Other friends in the team, such as Des Lynam and Tony Gubba, rang to sympathise. I appreciated it but told them that it was hardly necessary – nobody had died.

As it happens Des and Tony were with me in Dallas at the start of the tournament when a group of us, including Liam Brady, who did some co-commentary with me, turned tourists and visited the Texas School Book Depository on Dealey Plaza from where Lee Harvey Oswald shot John F Kennedy in 1963.

I'll always remember Tony, who is quite useful with a rifle, expressing amazement when we looked down from the window of the room where Oswald had stood, on to the pavement below. 'Bloody hell, I could have shot him from here,' exclaimed Tony. He, like the rest of us, had always believed that Oswald had had to set his sights over a much greater distance.

Our headsets told us in great detail about the events that led up to the day the people of Dallas clearly didn't enjoy reliving. The conspiracy theories, the political climate of the time, and the conclusions of the Warren Commission made it a memorable morning.

Gubba was able to solve one mystery. 'I always wondered why Oswald was arrested in a cinema,' he said. 'If you had just shot the president of the United States, would you go to the cinema?' We discovered that Oswald was actually hiding in the cinema after going on the run. He had also shot a police officer, J D Tippit. 'You would have thought that Oswald would have gone back home and watched television,' added Tony.

Which is exactly what I did when I limped to the airport after the semi-final. Jonathan Martin, the BBC's Head of Sport, phoned to say I should not be disheartened. 'The pressure is on Barry now,' he said.

In fact the final between Brazil and Italy was a disappointing goalless draw, settled on penalties. My feelings were more of relief than rancour. I certainly did not miss being in the Rose Bowl at

Pasadena where the final was played. I had covered an earlier game there between Argentina and Romania and had never been so far from the pitch in my career. I never was again, until my last international, the European Championship final in Vienna fourteen years later!

Back in Britain, the time had come to consider my position. I had a decent contract at the BBC and had no real wish to leave, but clearly I needed to decide how bothered or desperate I was to regain my status as the perceived number-one commentator.

My agent at the time, John Hockey, went with me to see Jonathan Martin at the start of the following season. Jonathan had been a studio director when I joined the department in 1971, and ten years later rose to be Head of Sport, a position he kept until he retired in 1998. Apart from an encyclopedic knowledge of sport, and a brain that could work out television schedules months (sometimes years) ahead, Martin scrutinised every single sports programme in great detail. Nothing escaped his notice.

He was also a straight talker. He was making no promises about the FA Cup final the following year, and he pointed out a few incidents and matters of style that he felt I needed to address, and areas where I may have lost ground on Barry.

In the second round of the World Cup, Mexico had played Bulgaria in the Giants Stadium in New York and, believe it or not, a goalpost collapsed and had to be replaced. Martin thought I treated the incident with somewhat childish glee, and clearly felt the time had come for the occasionally incredulous, raucous Motson to hand over to the more mature Davies.

For the first and only time during the whole episode I felt upset. I had been hoping for a more encouraging prognosis, but Martin had told me in no uncertain terms that it was up to me to fight back. Had I been a golfer he would probably have said, 'Go away and adjust your swing.' That, eventually, was just what I did. But before things got better, they got decidedly worse.

In September I was chosen to do live commentary on both legs of Blackburn Rovers' first-round UEFA Cup tie against Trelleborg of Sweden. Blackburn were going great guns at the time under Kenny Dalglish and his coach, the late Ray Harford. Thanks to owner Jack Walker's largesse, they had acquired the likes of Alan Shearer, and the previous season had finished runners-up to an Eric Cantona-inspired Manchester United, who won the league and cup double.

This time it would be Blackburn's turn to lift the championship, but their entry into Europe was hardly an auspicious one, and neither, sadly, was my performance. The first leg at Ewood Park was a poor game which the part-timers of Trelleborg won by a single goal. But the live broadcast went smoothly, and Trevor Brooking and I travelled to Sweden two weeks later knowing we had already familiarised ourselves with the Trelleborg team. Or so I thought.

What we discovered when we got to their tiny 6,000-capacity stadium was not only that the Swedish producer had never directed a football match before, but he had built us a commentary platform where the view of one half of the field was obscured by a huge tarpaulin. We never expect conditions abroad to be as structured as our home-based production, but even by overseas standards this was starting to look like a makeshift job.

Things started all right with Chris Sutton scoring for Blackburn in a first half that ended one apiece. So Trelleborg were still ahead on aggregate. Then early in the second half Trelleborg's big, blond right back, Brorsson, brought down Blackburn's left-winger, Jason Wilcox, in full flight. Trevor and I waited to see the replay of the incident on our monitor. And waited. And waited.

We knew about slow motion and 'super slow', as it is known in the trade, but this replay seemed to go on for ever. When we looked up, Blackburn had taken the free kick and play had resumed, and it was a couple of minutes later that I had a sick feeling in the pit of my stomach – Trelleborg were playing with ten men.

Instantly I realised what must have happened. Brorsson, who was already on a yellow card from the first half, had been sent off by the referee. It was no good blaming the tarpaulin, the quality of the replay or any of my colleagues. Quite simply, I had missed the sending off. While Trevor had been watching the replay to analyse the tackle, I should have been keeping my eyes on the pitch and seen the referee show the red card.

The dilemma of when to watch the monitor and when to ignore it is one all commentators have to grapple with at some time. I know a couple who have actually thought a goal was scored, and looked up after the replay to see the ball was back in play. They assumed the defending team had kicked off when in fact that 'goal' was ruled out and a quick free kick had been taken. So for a few minutes they found themselves commentating with the wrong score. In those cases somebody in the studio or an outside broadcast production vehicle spotted what had happened and they were able to correct themselves, just as I did in Sweden, although it was an experience I don't ever want to go through again.

For me it couldn't have come at a worse time. When Trevor and I got back to Stansted the following morning I told him that was me finished as far as cup finals were concerned. To compound my misery, the first person I saw in the car park when I got back to the BBC was Jonathan Martin. He wound down the window and said how sorry he felt about what had happened. He did not need to say any more. Any lingering chance of me retaining the FA Cup final the following May had disappeared.

Strangely the rest of my season went quite well. By the time I covered Tottenham's victory over Liverpool at Anfield in the sixth round I had done nine FA Cup ties, including replays, without any complaints. I then set off for the National Hunt Festival at

Cheltenham – the first time I had gone for the whole week, although it was to become a regular pilgrimage in the years that followed. On the morning of the Gold Cup Brian Barwick phoned. 'I've got something to tell you, Mots.' Brian always called me that. 'You can either come into the office or we can do it on the phone.'

He didn't need to tell me what it was. Barry Davies was to get the Cup Final job he had coveted for so long. My consolation prize was to be the live semi-final between Tottenham and Everton at Elland Road.

The BBC put out a brief announcement on Ceefax, trying not to attract the same headlines as had greeted the World Cup decision nearly a year earlier. But the news soon got round, and now it really did look a bleak picture as far as I was concerned.

Jimmy Hill always said 'try to get a plus out of a minus'. It was one of his little homilies that I picked up. 'Always praise your enemies' was another, as was 'admit your mistakes openly, people will like you more for it'. How to get a plus out of my situation was not immediately apparent.

I know I shocked a few people when I decided to take a sabbatical. For the past twenty-five years I had recharged my batteries at the end of one football season, and then wound up ready for the next. But in 1995 I asked Jonathan Martin and Brian Barwick if I could go on holiday and miss the whole of August and September. I felt a complete break from the business would be in my and the BBC's long-term interest.

In hindsight they would have had every reason to say no. I was under contract and I was asking to be absent from the first six or seven Saturdays, not to mention midweek games. Even when they agreed, some others thought I was taking a gamble. 'Out of sight, out of mind,' they mused, suggesting that I was retreating at the wrong moment.

My wife, Annie, insisted that I did something positive and useful rather than moping around at home, so I booked a cruise on the Nile from Luxor to Aswan, and it proved to be just the therapy I needed. Sitting alone in my cabin one day, I looked at the season ahead. England was about to stage Euro 96 so there would be two big cup finals to be fought for. I decided there and then I would go hell for leather when I got back.

And when I did it was to a reception I never expected. Somehow or other my absence had made a few people's hearts grow fonder. I was told my commentaries had been missed, and suddenly all the doubts and deliberations that had clouded the previous twelve months turned into a flattering, warm affection.

To my great surprise my return to work received wide coverage in several newspapers. 'Where have you been, Motty?' was the general theme. My gamble seemed to have paid off.

By a quirk of fate my first game that October was in Scandinavia, where I had stumbled so badly a year earlier. It was an England friendly, which put me right back in touch with Terry Venables, who had bought the comforting beer at the start of my demise. A quiet 0–0 draw in Norway was probably the ideal way to kick-start the next phase of my career. There were no major incidents to contend with, and I flew home sipping champagne with the England manager in the front seat of the plane.

All the time I was fighting back I reminded myself of a favourite quote of Dave Sexton's, the former Chelsea and Manchester United manager and coaching guru, from one of the philosophers whose books he studied. 'Failure in itself is not important. It's what you learn from it that counts.'

I felt I had learned a lot. Getting away from the game for a while had refreshed my enthusiasm and made me think about my excitable style. After a match at Chelsea that autumn, Ken Bates came up to me and said, 'Motty, you have become a much more rounded commentator.' I wasn't entirely sure what he meant, but a compliment from Mr Bates was not to be treated lightly!

Jonathan Martin and Brian Barwick then came up with a judgement of Solomon. Barry Davies would keep the FA Cup final for a second year and I would do the European Championship final at Wembley, whether England were in it or not. As it turned out, it was the second occasion when my ambition to see England in a major final was thwarted by the narrowest of margins. In Turin in 1990, those agonising penalty misses were by Stuart Pearce and Chris Waddle. Now it was the turn of Gareth Southgate.

It was Barry who talked the viewers through this latest anguish. I commentated on only one England game in Euro 96, but that was the group match against Scotland in which Paul Gascoigne's goal confirmed my view that he was the most gifted English player during my time at the microphone.

From his days as a raw teenager at Newcastle, Gazza had the lot. The late Jackie Milburn, himself a Tyneside hero, said he had never seen such a talent. For a start, he was strong and determined on the ball, able to go past opponents using his body weight. But he was also nimble in his movement and could spot a pass that others just could not see.

Most of all, he came up with brilliant individual goals at critical moments in big games. Such as the one against Scotland, when he cheekily lobbed the ball over Colin Hendry before beating Andy Goram. Sadly, Gazza was a few inches away from putting England into the final of Euro 96. He just failed to reach a cross from Alan Shearer that would have won the semi-final against Germany.

As it was, my first Wembley final for over two years finished on the 'Golden Goal'. Germany's Oliver Bierhoff delivered that in extra time to see off the Czech Republic, although it was only after the match that it became clear that a linesman had been flagging for offside against the German forward, Stefan Kuntz, standing in the six-yard box. During the goal celebrations he lowered his flag again.

*   *   *

It was level pegging again between me and Barry. They say the better the game, the better the performance of the commentator – a generalisation with which I would largely go along. Unfortunately for Barry, his two FA Cup finals were hardly classics. I had sat squirming in the stand watching Everton beat Manchester United with a Paul Rideout goal. I was no more comfortable a year later when United returned to beat Liverpool. Eric Cantona's volleyed goal robbed the Merseysiders (and Barry for that matter) of what looked like a certain replay.

While Davies and I had been battling it out on the BBC, over on ITV the urbane Brian Moore had had things all his own way. Brian's mellifluous voice and easy armchair manner won him many admirers and kept him clear of the field of regional commentators who supported ITV's coverage of football. From the time he left BBC Radio, where he was football correspondent until 1968, to when he retired thirty years later, Brian often combined the roles of presenter and commentator with admirable professionalism.

As I got to know him better it turned out he was often more nervous than me. Brian suffered a lot of sleepless nights before commentaries – as I did in the early days – and would be hugely and unnecessarily worried about his performance, until somebody reassured him that it had gone well. So it did not come as a complete surprise when, just before Christmas 1996, he told his ITV bosses he would like to step down – either at the end of that season, or after the World Cup in France in 1998.

What did come as a bombshell was when they offered me his job. The first contact came from Jeff Farmer, ITV's Head of Football, who took me to lunch at Isolabella in Red Lion Street – a family-run Italian restaurant close to ITV headquarters which was to become a favourite of mine in later years.

ITV had just secured the rights to the FA Cup and England matches from 1997 onwards, so the Cup Final would be shown live by them and not by the BBC. They also had rights to the Champions League. Jeff said that they would like me to replace Brian as their principal football commentator from the start of the following season. After further discussions with him, the plan would be for Brian to go to the World Cup, but not as the number one.

I had two good friends at ITV. Gary Newbon and I had been at boarding school together in Suffolk, and had rekindled our friendship when we found ourselves in the same profession. I had also got to know Jim Rosenthal well when he joined BBC Radio in the seventies. I played with him in the commentators' Sunday football team as he made rapid strides as a presenter after joining ITV in 1980.

Gary and Jim gave me the best advice they could. Without laying it too much on the line they said how welcome I would be made on their channel, and emphasised that my position would be a lot more secure as the number-one voice than it appeared to be at the BBC. I then received a letter from Michael Southgate, ITV's Commercial Director, setting out the terms of a four-year contract. He said he felt their football portfolio, and the mass audiences it delivered, would provide the professional satisfaction to justify a major career move on my part.

The offer came just before Christmas, so I had some serious thinking to do before letting them have my answer early in the New Year. The promise of an unrivalled number-one position, considerably more money and benefits, together with a guarantee of big live matches across several competitions, was very tempting. Yet something was nagging at me about the BBC. Call it pride, ego or just plain stubbornness, but I couldn't get it out of my head how badly I wanted to turn the tables and get back to where I had been.

What swayed me in the end was a meeting with Brian Barwick, by now Head of Sports Production. The same man who had given me the bad news about the World Cup final and FA Cup finals over the previous two years. Barwick offered to rewrite my contract, beating ITV's offer. He and Jonathan Martin promised I would get the FA Cup final back in 1997 – the BBC's last before losing the contract – and implied that they saw me as the number-one man at the World Cup in France the following year.

As a sweetener, Brian also assured me I no longer had to race across the pitch at the end of my Saturday commentary to fight my way to the front of the queue waiting to do interviews. This had been a source of frustration for some time, partly because I never thought my mind was clear enough to ask sensible questions after ninety minutes at the microphone, and partly because there were younger reporters who were perfectly capable of getting the sound bites for *Match of the Day*.

One of them was Garth Crooks, whom I had known well as a player at Tottenham, and who had been keen to pursue a media career after guesting on a BBC teatime show during the 1982 World Cup. The decision was supported by the new editor of *Match of the Day*, Niall Sloane. Garth would come to the match I was covering and do the interviews. It was the start of four highly enjoyable years on the road with a man who could be as sociable or as serious as the moment demanded.

Now I had to tell ITV that my decision was to stay with the BBC. The first Saturday in January is traditionally set aside for the third round of the FA Cup, and I was scheduled to cover Birmingham City's tie against non-league Stevenage at St Andrews. The Hertfordshire club was a rising force under manager Paul Fairclough, and *Match of the Day* felt they could smell a shock result. As it turned out, however, Trevor Francis got his Birmingham team in the right frame of mind and they coasted to a 2–0 win.

When the game was over I met Jeff Farmer in the street, where he had parked his car so that we would not be overheard in the club car park. He was utterly gracious, although admitted he was disappointed that I was not coming. Michael Southgate wrote to say they both respected the reasons behind my decision. 'You never know, in four years time we might try again,' was how he signed off. As it turned out they did not need to. Clive Tyldesley, who had joined the BBC team after ten years with Radio City in Liverpool, moved across from *Match of the Day* to succeed Brian Moore.

All in all, it had been a remarkable turnaround in my fortunes. When I went to my old Cup Final seat to describe Chelsea's final against Middlesbrough, I could only smile at the events of the previous three years. Up until 1994 I had been getting on with my job with the minimum of fuss and publicity. Now I had been pushed into the limelight, first as a failure, then as a commentator in demand.

Not that I had much time to dwell on that when I picked up the microphone at Wembley. It took Roberto Di Matteo just forty-three seconds to score what was then the fastest goal in a Wembley FA Cup final. Every year since I had started, I had a note on my pad in case somebody beat Jackie Milburn's record of forty-five seconds in 1955. My homework had paid off at last.

So had my decision to go away and readdress my career. Getting the Cup Final back topped the recovery process, and that seemed somehow appropriate. Not only has there always been something special about the FA Cup, but the competition and my career have always been curiously interlinked. After all, it was the FA Cup that had set me on my way in television in the first place . . .

Chapter 2

The Giant-killers
How Ricky and Ronnie changed my life

O N A COLD, DARK Friday evening in February 1972, I took the 251 bus from Mill Hill, near my flat in North Finchley, to Edgware Station, where I was due to meet the Hereford United striker Billy Meadows. Billy was giving me a lift to Hereford, where his team were about to play an FA Cup replay against Newcastle United, and I was to make my FA Cup debut as a *Match of the Day* commentator.   974, 103 / 920 HOT

Billy turned up in a Vauxhall VX490: footballers in those days did not drive Ferraris or Hummers. He was one of those players who got signed up by a league club in the sixties – Arsenal in his case – but did not make the grade at top level. After playing for Dunstable and Hastings, he arrived at my local club, Barnet, where he made his name as a fearless centre forward.

In two seasons of Southern League football Billy scored seventy-eight goals. He wasn't particularly tall, and he certainly wasn't quick, but with his false teeth out and a nose so often broken that you didn't know which side of his face it was on, he cut an angry, aggressive figure ready to go to war with any centre half.

The previous season Meadows had moved from Barnet to Hereford United, another semi-professional club in the Southern

League. He was followed by his friend and fellow forward Ricky George. I had known Ricky since he walked into the office of the *Barnet Press* in 1964 and told me he was leaving Tottenham Hotspur to join Watford.

When Spurs manager Bill Nicholson saw George play for Hertfordshire Schoolboys at the age of fourteen, he told one of his coaching staff that this was the best boy he had ever seen at that age. Ricky was taken on to the Tottenham groundstaff the summer after they won the double in 1961, trained with the likes of Dave Mackay and John White, but graduated only as far as the A team.

George then became one of football's itinerants, moving on first to Watford, then to Bournemouth, Oxford United (playing in the Football League for all three), Hastings and Barnet, for whom he scored a hat-trick against Newport County in the first round of the FA Cup in 1970. The Southern League side beat their fourth-division opponents 6–1.

It was the great John Charles, who ended his illustrious career as player-manager at Hereford, who signed Meadows and George. They were immediately in awe of the 'gentle giant' who had been idolised at Juventus following his move to Italian football from Leeds United.

When Charles left Hereford after five years, he was succeeded as player-manager by thirty-one-year-old Colin Addison, who had played around four hundred league games for York City, Arsenal, Nottingham Forest and Sheffield United. Addison was a swift, imaginative inside forward with an eye for goal, but he also possessed obvious leadership qualities, and was keen to move on to the coaching and managing side of the game. Hereford, where he would make his home for the next thirty-five years and more, was a perfect breeding ground, especially now that they had drawn first-division Newcastle United in the FA Cup.

'I'll introduce you to Colin and the rest of the team at the pre-match lunch,' promised Billy Meadows as we drove to pick up Ricky George at the Oxford Moathouse, where he had been working at a shoe fair.

As a newcomer to television commentary, I was still very much in awe of the players, and flattered to be in their company. At the age of twenty-six, and just assuming the independence of a bachelor flat, I felt as though I was at the start of a great adventure. The fact that Ricky and Billy were part-timers did not detract from that one bit.

Having dropped out of the professional ranks, both players were supplementing their £25 per week wage as Hereford players with full-time employment outside the game. Meadows was a representative for a carpet cleaning company. George, meanwhile, worked for Adidas.

On the way from Oxford to Hereford, Ricky and Billy went through the rest of the team. Goalkeeper Fred Potter had played a handful of games for Aston Villa and more than a hundred for Doncaster Rovers. Roger Griffiths at right back was Hereford born and had never played in the league. But on the other flank the boisterous Ken Mallender had made 200 appearances for Sheffield United and Norwich City.

The two centre backs were ex-Newport County man Mick McLaughlin and Swansea-born Alan Jones, who had completed fifty games for his home-town club. In reserve was Billy Tucker, who was competing with Ricky George for the single substitute's shirt.

Colin Addison, as player-manager, patrolled the midfield, ably supported by the languid skills of Dudley Tyler, at twenty-seven a late developer who was still to have a future in league football. Captain Tony Gough was a busy influence, having had experience at Bristol Rovers and Swindon; then there was Ronnie Radford, born in Leeds but signed, without making the senior side at Elland Road, by Newport County for whom he had played in the humbling cup defeat at Barnet the previous season.

Meadows' partner up front was bustling Brian Owen, without whom this replay against Newcastle United, to which we were going, might never have happened.

The Hereford–Newcastle match took place during my first season covering football on television. The previous summer, it had been announced that Kenneth Wolstenholme was to leave the BBC after more than twenty years as the nation's leading football commentator. With David Coleman and Barry Davies established as regular Saturday and Wednesday commentators, the BBC needed a back-up contributor who could also go out and report stories for the *Football Preview* show on a Saturday lunchtime.

Sam Leitch, voted Sports Journalist of the Year during a highly successful career as a Fleet Street columnist, had the job, in his capacity as editor of *Match of the Day* and *Sportsnight*, the BBC's flagship football programmes, of replacing Wolstenholme.

At the time, I was a young BBC radio reporter. David Coleman had heard me on the air and recommended me to Sam. The result was a drink in the cocktail bar at the Royal Lancaster Hotel with Leitch and his wife Shirley. It was something of a shock to find myself being handed a glass of champagne: when my boss in radio bought me a drink, it was invariably a brown ale.

'We want you to go to Leeds and do a test commentary on the Fairs Cup [later the UEFA Cup] final against Juventus,' Leitch explained. 'You will go up anonymously as "Commentator X" and we will record you down a private line into a separate channel at TV Centre. We don't want to upset the radio people by letting them know we are after you at this early stage. The only thing you will notice straight away compared with radio is that you will hear the director talking in your ear, even when he is addressing his cameras. It's called talkback. Frank Bough is a master at it. There is somebody talking in his earpiece the whole time he is in front of the camera chairing *Grandstand*.'

At this point Shirley chipped in, 'That Frank Bough, if Sam told him in his ear that the laundry was coming at ten past four, Frank would promptly tell the nation the laundry would be arriving in a few minutes' time.'

My first few television broadcasts were mediocre to say the least. It was a completely different medium to radio, and I was less than comfortable when 'in vision' on the screen. In those early months, I quickly realised my future lay behind the microphone.

At first I was sent out with David Coleman to monitor his commentary, then moved in front of the camera to deliver a match report for *Grandstand* at the final whistle. Coleman was a great act from whom to learn, but he also protected me. The first time I went out with him was to a match at Anfield between Liverpool and Manchester United in September 1971. George Best, Bobby Charlton and Denis Law were playing for United. Best cheekily set up Charlton with a clever back-heel for him to strike a powerful equaliser in a 2–2 draw.

'We only want sixty seconds,' the *Grandstand* producer screamed at me as I sat nervously on the camera platform, waiting to do my first ever television report. Coleman heard the instruction and shouted across to me: 'Just do what you want, and let them sort it out.'

The BBC used to put on a private plane when Coleman travelled north, and I often went with him. We would assemble at Denham aerodrome on a Saturday morning and be flown north in a four-seater piloted by a man called Tony Trowbridge.

The two things I remember, apart from being terrified, were the sandwiches that Tony's wife provided for the journey, and his call sign as he taxied down the runway. 'Bumpetty bump, bumpetty bump, Tony Trowbridge bumpetty bump' is what it sounded like.

When we returned to Denham after the match David would be driven to his home in Buckinghamshire, have dinner, change his clothes, and then be driven back to the *Match of the Day* studio at Lime Grove to introduce the programme. He was a brilliant broadcaster who revelled in living on the edge. Many were the times when the titles were running as he took his seat.

Up in the production gallery above the studio floor at the old Lime Grove studios, as my learning curve continued, I would sit next to Sam Leitch, who seemed more nervous of the phone call he would get from his boss, Bryan Cowgill, at the end of the show than of anything that might go wrong on the air.

Cowgill used to dial as soon as the end titles were running. If he didn't like the show, or there weren't enough goals, he used to say, 'Always remember, Sam, the last name on the titles is the arse that I kick.' As the editor, Leitch's name always went up last.

Not everyone was as supportive as David and Sam in my early television days. The *Sun* had hit on the idea of sending Kenneth Wolstenholme to cover games I was doing, and had even started a campaign to bring him back.

To be fair to Ken, he resisted any direct comparisons, but the veteran *Daily Mail* reporter Ron Crowther took me to task after a match at Old Trafford between Manchester United and Tottenham.

It was only my third commentary for *Match of the Day* (the first had been a goalless draw between Liverpool and Chelsea) and it was a great thrill to be commentating on the United 'holy trinity' of Best, Law and Charlton. A great day too for seventeen-year-old Sammy McIlroy, who marked his home debut with the opening goal in a game United won 3–1.

Denis Law got the other two, but as he converted a cross from Willie Morgan I noticed that the Spurs left back, Cyril Knowles, was lying on the ground injured, unable to make a tackle. I pointed this out, but was criticised by Crowther for taking some of the gloss off the admittedly majestic finish by Law. It taught me to get used to my commentary being dissected from time to time. A thick skin was something I had to develop.

There was something else about those early days that, even now, people find hard to believe. We were in the early years of the 'action replay' – or the 'video disc', to give it the technical term.

This had been developed during the 1966 World Cup, but there was only one machine available at Television Centre on a Saturday, and that was used for horse racing on *Grandstand*, which was shown live, while the *Match of the Day* games were being recorded.

Therefore, when a goal was scored, David Coleman, Barry Davies and I had to reprise the move as best we could remember it, without seeing the pictures, while the players ran back to the centre circle.

You would desperately hope that you had the correct player crossing the ball, the right defender who had missed it, not blamed the goalkeeper unfairly, and then hold your breath until they put the slow-motion pictures in later in the evening.

What a difference to today, when commentators get so many replays that you run out of things to say!

Hereford's FA Cup journey that season had started in October 1971 with a 3–0 victory over Cheltenham Town in the fourth qualifying round. In the first round proper they had drawn 0–0 at King's Lynn, then won the replay at their own Edgar Street ground with a single goal by Gough.

League opposition loomed in the second round, when they were drawn at home to fourth-division Northampton Town. A goalless draw, with the prospect of a replay at the County Ground, suggested Hereford's brief cup dream would soon be over. A spirited perform-ance saw them force a 2–2 draw after extra time with goals by Tyler and Owen. There were no penalty shoot-outs in those days, so the teams had to meet again for a third time at The Hawthorns – home of West Bromwich Albion. Again the tie went into an extra thirty minutes with the scores level at 1–1, but then Tyler came up with the winning goal to send Hereford's vocal support in the 8,300 crowd into dreamland.

The winners had been drawn away to Newcastle United, who at the beginning of that season had broken their transfer record by signing 'Supermac', the brash, electrically charged centre forward Malcolm Macdonald, for £180,000 from Luton Town.

I reported on the original match for BBC Radio. I caught the train at King's Cross and travelled up to Newcastle to see the game. It was being played on a Monday because the match had been postponed twice owing to a waterlogged pitch. When I arrived at St James' Park, the first person I saw on the steps outside the main entrance was Ricky George.

When the game finally started many in the 39,000 crowd had not taken their seats when Brian Owen lashed Hereford into the lead in just seventeen seconds. Within a matter of minutes John Tudor had equalised and Malcolm Macdonald put the first-division side in front from a penalty. But Hereford had a shock in store. Colin Addison struck the sweetest of 25-yard shots past Ian McFaul in the Newcastle goal to make the score 2–2 at half-time.

And that was how it stayed, even though Billy Meadows went mighty close with a header in the second half. Ron Greenwood, whose West Ham side were to meet the winners, came into the Hereford dressing room afterwards. He said to Meadows, 'If you had just glanced that it would have gone in.'

In hindsight, one wonders whether a Hereford victory that night would have attracted the lasting romance created by the replay. But suffice to say, as I rushed to the BBC studio in Newcastle to do a radio report, I was as excited as the Hereford supporters.

Although I was officially still on trial at *Match of the Day*, I had been told that in the unlikely event of a draw that night I would be sent to the replay. What I didn't know, as I recorded my radio piece under the watchful eye of BBC North East producer Clive Page, was just what a life-changing experience that would be.

Page was an ardent Newcastle supporter himself and would become a good friend of mine when I later married a Geordie girl. That night he recounted how many times his team had been turned over by smaller clubs in the FA Cup. 'You could be on to a giant-killing,' he said.

I travelled back to London on the train the following day with Ricky George and Billy Meadows. Neither had moved from their London homes when they joined Hereford, so more often than not they made their own arrangements while the team coach made its tortuous journey back to the West Country.

'Never mind their pitch, what about ours?' said Billy. 'It's under water at the moment. God knows when they will be able to stage a replay.'

In fact the replay was postponed three times. The Newcastle party were marooned at their base in Worcester, unable to go home in case the game went ahead at short notice. It was finally rescheduled for the day of the fourth round.

That gave me a bit of a problem. My flatmates at the time were a lifelong friend called Jim Currie and the BBC news reporter Bill Hamilton, who would go on to greater things after a short stint in the sports news department at Radio Two.

Bill was due to get married to his fiancée, Veronica Lee, on Saturday, 5 February at Brampton, near Carlisle. Normally he would have expected both Jim and me to be there, but in the circumstances it was agreed that Jim would put on the kilt and be best man for our proud Scottish bridegroom. I would put on my overcoat (the sheepskin days were still ahead of me) and travel with Billy and Ricky to Hereford.

We were all booked into the Green Dragon Hotel in the centre of Hereford. When we arrived there were a number of journalists drinking in the bar, as well as my producer, John Shrewsbury. John had joined the Sports Department as a young production assistant and had just graduated to match directing. He was at the same apprentice stage as I was as a commentator.

We had a good chat about the match during dinner. I told 'Shrews' what I had learned from Billy and Ricky about the Hereford team, while he made a few notes for the benefit of his camera team, to whom the Southern League side were unknown faces. Not so Newcastle. Apart from Supermac there were household names in Frank Clark, Bobby Moncur, Tony Green, Terry Hibbitt and the on-loan Viv Busby.

The north-east press corps following the team included the legendary Jackie Milburn, then writing for the *News of the World*. One of the kindest men on the circuit, 'Wor Jackie', as he was known when he won three FA Cup medals with Newcastle in the fifties, joined us for a chat and a drink after dinner.

I made the introduction to Ricky George, whereupon Milburn gave him a long, searching look. 'It was lads like you that made me give up football management,' he said, shaking his head. 'You should be in bed!'

'I'm only the substitute, though, Jackie,' Ricky protested, 'and I haven't had a drink.'

Milburn replied, 'You never know, you might come on and score the winning goal!'

On the morning of the match Ricky drove me to two different hotels. The first stop was to meet two new Hereford signings, Ivan Hollett and Calvin Palmer, whom Addison had persuaded to drop out of the Football League to help Hereford try to gain admission themselves. Then it was on to the The Spread Eagle, where the Hereford team were having a pre-match lunch.

Manager Colin Addison gave me a warm welcome. 'I think a nice steak would suit you, John, with a fried egg on top,' he said.

Steak was very much the pre-match favourite for footballers in those days, and I was welcomed as though I were one of the squad. Years later Tony Gough would officially adopt me as the 'thirteenth man', when he and his wife Brenda came to my sixtieth birthday party.

But then I was just twenty-six and getting more fidgety by the minute as I prepared myself for the first major cup tie I had covered for BBC Television. Every commentary had to start with an 'intro' in which we featured a couple of players who might make an impact in the game or between whom there was some connection.

I told John Shrewsbury I would like to feature Macdonald and Meadows, who had, I discovered, played against each other when Malcolm was a full back at Tonbridge – before he was discovered by Fulham in 1968 and converted into a striker.

As I waited in the Edgar Street foyer for the teams to be announced, I overheard Billy explaining to Malcolm what I had in mind. It only involved a shot in the warm-up of which neither would be aware. But somehow the eagerness of Meadows' conversation – which seemed utterly lost on the England centre forward – summed up what was to be a surreal afternoon.

The atmosphere was everything an FA Cup tie should have. There were fifteen and a half thousand people somehow crammed into Edgar Street that afternoon, and that number did not include the many people watching from trees and floodlight pylons. Referee Dennis Turner from Cannock got the match started, with Newcastle in an all-red strip, as I sat on the temporary platform that the BBC had constructed especially for the occasion.

In the first few minutes Macdonald, who had been boasting in the days leading up to the game how many he would score, raced through the Hereford defence only to be foiled by a brave save from Fred Potter, diving at his feet.

Next Tony Green, exuding quality in the Newcastle midfield, broke away from Addison and found Busby, whose cross caused untold confusion in the Hereford penalty area before they scrambled it away for a corner. First-division class beginning to tell, was my assessment. But then Addison settled Hereford down, starting a move that ended when McFaul almost fumbled Tyler's shot.

Then Hereford had two amazing escapes. First a Macdonald header dropped into the net, only for Turner to pull Tudor up for a foul on Potter. Then, within minutes a clearance by McLaughlin hit Tudor, the ball looping over Potter and hitting the Hereford crossbar. Hibbitt, seizing on the rebound, promptly struck the bar again.

Hereford survived until half-time. Tyler forced a decent save from McFaul on the restart, then Ken Mallender hit the post with a header. Alan Jones shot inches wide from the rebound. Fred Potter continued to perform heroics in the Hereford goal. Even when Macdonald took the ball past him, he somehow contrived to shoot over the bar.

Then, eight minutes from the end, the Green/Busby combination on the right produced the cross from which Macdonald headed what any sane person would have thought was the winning goal. 'That's it,' I said. 'Eight minutes from the end, Newcastle break the deadlock.'

At that point the Match of the Day highlights were pencilled in to last four minutes. My FA Cup debut would have taken its proper place at the back end of the programme.

Then substitute Ricky George came on to replace Roger Griffiths, who was later found to have fractured his fibula. With five minutes to go, George showed a flash of the skill that once impressed Bill Nicholson. His trickery on the left wing forced Newcastle to clear hurriedly, and Ronnie Radford won a fifty–fifty tackle with John Tudor some forty-five yards out from goal.

Radford played a quick one-two with Brian Owen, and then, as the ball rose just slightly out of the mudbath that had once been a football pitch, propelled himself, his team and the match into FA Cup folklore. 'Oh, what a goal!' I said. 'What a goal!

Radford the scorer. Ronnie Radford. And the crowd are invading the pitch . . . Now it will take some time to clear the field.'

Even now, when I see the goal replayed, I half expect it to hit the bar. The bulge of the net and the pitch invasion that followed would forever be imprinted on my memory. Ironically Radford's wife, Ann, missed the goal because she was attending to one of their young sons in the stand. When she looked up, the celebrations were in full swing!

Now it was extra time, with the teams playing from the same ends. My recollection is that the part-timers looked the fitter side, although Macdonald's first touch let him down again when he was clean through.

Then Ronnie Radford found Tyler, who picked out George on the right-hand side of the Newcastle penalty area. Given space by Moncur, he controlled the ball with his left foot, moved it in an arc on to his right, then drove it through the Newcastle captain's legs wide of McFaul and into the bottom left-hand corner of the net: *'He's got it! Ricky George! Ricky George has done it! What a moment for Hereford!'* Hereford were leading 2–1 after 103 minutes.

Up in the stand George's wife, Patricia, never a great football fan, said to her sister Teresa, 'Do you know, I think he's done something famous!' In the second half of extra time the first-division side made a belated bid to save the game, but as one of their attacks petered out Turner blew the final whistle and the pitch was covered again with delirious supporters in their parkas. *'It's all over!'* I exclaimed. *'They've done it! Hereford have done it. Well, what a cup tie. What can you say?'*

I can't remember how I made my way round the ground to the dressing rooms on the opposite side to my commentary position. When I got there the place was in uproar.

One of the first into the Hereford dressing room was John

Charles, who had brought so many of their heroes to the club. I managed to get Addison, George and Radford to change quickly and get out on to the pitch for a *Match of the Day* interview.

We had no interview room or indoor facilities in those days. The trio walked calmly across the pitch – with Ronnie's two young sons – to tell the nation how it had happened. Ten million people watched *Match of the Day* that night.

Billy and Ricky drove back to London in convoy with their families. I squeezed into the back seat, and when we stopped for petrol George remembers me saying, 'Do you realise that you have just made history?'

His wife, Patricia, said to me, 'Try to get him as much publicity as you can, John, because he is the youngest player in the team.' George was twenty-five at the time.

We got some fish and chips and settled down to watch the programme in the Meadows' front room. When it was over we went on celebrating. Pat Meadows, Billy's wife, had just bought the chart-topping single 'American Pie' by Don McLean.

For me, it was far from being the day the music died. Perhaps the band had just started to play, but only faintly, because I often wonder, with good reason, what course my career would have taken if Hereford had not won that game.

Hereford United's cup journey did not end there. Just four days after the Newcastle match Edgar Street was packed again for the delayed fourth-round tie against West Ham United.

Hereford fielded the team that had finished the Newcastle replay, with Ricky George now in the starting line-up. The Hammers included Bobby Moore, Geoff Hurst, Trevor Brooking and Harry Redknapp. They say lightning doesn't strike twice, but the non-league side came mighty close to providing another upset. Ron Greenwood's team were relieved to escape with a 0–0 draw.

The replay at Upton Park was fixed for the following Monday, with an early afternoon kick-off owing to the country being in the throes of a miners' strike and power cuts.

By the time I got inside the ground the game had started with over 42,000 watching. I stood at the back of the paddock in front of the main stand and watched Geoff Hurst put an end to Hereford's fairytale with a hat-trick. Billy Meadows scored a consolation goal.

After the game I linked up with the Hereford party at their London hotel. For them it was the end of a chapter. For me, it was just the beginning.

Although I was left out in the closing rounds of the FA Cup – I went to the semi-finals and final as a reporter and interviewer – I made my international debut at the end of the season when I was entrusted with Scotland's match against Northern Ireland in the Home International Championship.

The game was played at Hampden Park, and enabled me to meet Jock Stein, the legendary Celtic manager who was working for the BBC as a pundit at that time. Denis Law and Peter Lorimer scored for Scotland in a 2–0 win, and I remember being in awe of Stein, who disarmed me by inviting me back to his house for a cup of tea.

Experiences like that meant that I didn't attach that much importance to the significance that the Hereford cup saga would assume in the years that followed. It was only much later, when the Hereford giant-killers started to hold regular reunions, that I fully appreciated what a momentous occasion I had been part of and what a launching pad it had been for my career.

In 1992, to mark the twentieth anniversary of the game, the club gave a well-deserved testimonial to their physiotherapist Peter Isaac. Alan Ball was the speaker, and the ovation the team got probably rivalled that given to John Major, who won the general election on the same night!

The last time the whole team were together was in March 2005, when I drove from an evening FA Cup tie in Southampton to join a dinner organised by Hereford supporters in conjunction with Colin Addison, just before midnight. This caused quite a stir, as I had already sent a video message apologising for not being there, but it was worth the effort to get a big hug from Ronnie Radford, who had made a great recovery from illness.

I say the last time, because Roger Griffiths, the right back who played on in pain against Newcastle that day, passed away in July 2006.

Ronnie and Ricky's contribution to FA Cup history was recognised again when they joined the parade of FA Cup heroes at the first final in the new Wembley Stadium the following year.

After Hereford, other cup shocks came my way on *Match of the Day*. Non-league Leatherhead led Leicester City 2–0 at Filbert Street thanks to Chris Kelly, the 'Leatherhead Lip', before losing 3–2. York City beat Arsenal with a last-minute Keith Houchen penalty in 1985. Four years later, Sutton United, under the pipe-smoking Barrie Williams, put out a Coventry side who had won the trophy eighteen months earlier.

There was a trip to Whitley Bay to see them beat Preston North End in 1979; I was at Chesterfield when they beat Premier League Nottingham Forest on their way to the semi-final in 1997. Then, in my last season before *Match of the Day* lost the rights to the competition in 2008, there was a dramatic day at Oakwell when homespun Barnsley, having already knocked out Liverpool, put paid to the billionaire high rollers, Chelsea.

Maybe it was because it came so late in my career, but in the closing minutes of that game I got the same tingle in the spine that I had experienced at Hereford all those years before.

So what made that Hereford victory over Newcastle stand out above all the other giant-killing acts down the years? Was it because the invasion of the pitch in pure exuberance marked the end of the age of innocence? Within two years, the ugly face of hooliganism started to replace such genuine euphoria.

Maybe it was because regular televised football was still in its infancy. Coverage in colour was only three or four years old, and the action replay was no more than a new toy.

Perhaps Newcastle United themselves, with the acquisition of 'Supermac', had been such a big FA Cup name in the past that the exploits of their non-league conquerors assumed national importance.

Or was it simply 'Ronnie's goal'? Over the next thirty-five years, that 35-yard shot was replayed every time the third round of the FA Cup came round.

Whatever the reason, being part of an event that touched so many people so unexpectedly is something I will always cherish. Fittingly perhaps, my love affair with football had started exactly twenty years earlier.

Chapter 3

From Woolwich to Wembley

How a clergyman's son became a commentator

O N 26 April 1952, when I was six years old, my father took me to watch my first ever Football League game. We went to The Valley to see Charlton Athletic draw 1–1 with Chelsea, both goals coming in the first half from Charlie Vaughan and Chelsea's Roy Bentley.

My main memory of that day concerns the Charlton captain, Benny Fenton, whom I later met in my professional life when he was manager of Millwall. In those days it was customary for a marching band to entertain spectators before the match. At The Valley, they would sit with their instruments on the track by the side of the pitch to watch the game. When Fenton came across to clear a Chelsea attack, and struck the ball with venomous force out of play, it landed smack in the middle of one of the drums. I can still hear that sound today.

It is my father I have to thank for my football education. The Reverend William Motson, 'Bill', as he liked to be known, served for forty years in the Methodist ministry, fourteen of those in mission work in inner London. He preached far and wide to raise money for the poor and needy in the deprived areas of Deptford and Stepney. He was also instrumental in cleaning up areas in the East End like Cable Street – notorious for prostitutes.

My father was born and brought up in Swineshead, a village just outside Boston, Lincolnshire. His twin brother, Frank, died as a child, but his two other brothers, Stan and Darwin, and two sisters, Mavis and Irene, were raised in a strict Methodist household. As a young man, Bill trained as a barber, but then felt a calling to be a preacher. He studied for the Methodist ministry at Didsbury College in Manchester, married a Boston girl, Gwendoline, in 1940, and was working in one of his first churches at Haydock when their only son was born in Hope Hospital, Salford, in 1945.

While in Lincolnshire, Bill had developed an affection for Derby County, his nearest first-division club. When they beat Charlton 4–1 in the first FA Cup final after the war, he listened to the match on the radio while keeping an eye on the gurgling baby in his pram.

Charlton Athletic was to play a major part in both our lives. I was a year old when Dad was appointed the minister at Plumstead Common Methodist Church, on the edge of Woolwich in south-east London. We moved into the manse – a rambling old house in Burrage Road. There was a bomb site between the church and our back garden. I remember my mother, in that period of post-war austerity, buying essential food items with her ration book.

The first time I remember watching football was when Arsenal played Liverpool in the 1950 FA Cup final. My father knew of a music shop in Woolwich called Drysdales, where they had a small black-and-white television. Soon afterwards, I was introduced to the real thing. Dad would take me down to The Valley on a midweek afternoon to see Charlton's reserves play in the Football Combination.

When Charlton were away, Dad and I would go to The Den to watch Millwall. The two goalkeepers – Sam Bartram at Charlton and Malcolm Finlayson at Millwall – were among my childhood football heroes. It wasn't long before I started keeping scrapbooks and collecting programmes.

My father would go anywhere to see a game. We went to all the London grounds, including Arsenal, Chelsea and Tottenham, before I was ten years old. Even when we took a holiday in the late summer, football was top of our agenda. One August we visited a Methodist family in the north-west of England, and Dad managed to cram in trips to Preston, Manchester City and Manchester United.

Tom Finney was still playing for Preston at the time, and when we visited Old Trafford it was just a few months after the Munich air disaster. One of the survivors, a young Bobby Charlton, scored a hat-trick in their 5–2 win over Chelsea. Jimmy Greaves scored both goals for the visitors.

A few days later, we were at Maine Road for a thrilling 3–3 draw between Manchester City and Bolton Wanderers, for whom the great Nat Lofthouse was among the scorers.

It was only much later that I was able to appreciate how much of my love for the game was down to my father. I also inherited something of his speaking voice, which he used to great effect delivering sermons from the pulpit. The combination of the two were to stand me in good stead in my eventual career.

When we left Plumstead Common, his new church, the Deptford Mission, was three miles away from our home in Lewisham. We did not own a car at first, and there were lots of bus journeys for my parents – especially on Sundays, when my father had two services.

On Sunday afternoons, I would meet a lady called Elsie Green at the bus stop in Lewisham, and she would take me on the bus to Sunday school. I was invited to speak at the Deptford Mission in 2005, when they celebrated their centenary. My father had been the minister there fifty years earlier. Now in her nineties, Elsie Green was in the congregation.

Although we didn't have a television in the early fifties, this was a luxury enjoyed by both our neighbours in Slaithwaite Road. On one side lived Ada Smith – I saw Jackie Milburn win the FA Cup for Newcastle on her flickering set in 1951 – and on the other, another Methodist minister called Walter Ridyard.

Walter had endeared himself to the members of Albion Road Methodist Church in Lewisham, where he was a minister before the war. During the Blitz in 1941 the church was destroyed, but after the war Walter returned and supervised its rebuilding, staying for seven years.

Walter and his wife were keen sports fans. They often offered lodgings to West Indian cricketers when they were playing in England. I remember having tea with Collie Smith, the Jamaican all-rounder killed in a car crash, and also having a conversation over the garden fence with Learie Constantine, the former West Indian captain and fast bowler, who later became Lord Constantine and was high commissioner for Trinidad and Tobago.

It was at Walter's house than I saw the second half of Hungary's historic 6–3 victory at Wembley in 1953 – the match that changed England's conception of football. I raced home from school to discover the half-time score was 4–2 to the magnificent Magyars, who played England off the park and became the first overseas team to win at Wembley.

There was a weekend in that same Coronation year that I will never forget. One Friday night, Dad took me to Highbury for the first time and we saw Arsenal clinch the first-division title on goal average with a 3–2 win over Burnley.

Saturday was Cup Final day, with the nation wondering whether thirty-eight-year-old Stanley Matthews could finally collect a cup-winner's medal. I had once queued up to get his autograph when he made an appearance in a Lewisham store. My father and I watched Blackpool beat Bolton 4–3 at the home of a family who lived a stone's throw from his church in Deptford.

After the game we walked to The Den and saw Millwall draw 4–4 in a friendly against Manchester United. Matt Busby's team had won an FA Cup tie at Millwall earlier in the season, and he brought them back as a gesture. I still have the programme.

With little or no televised football in the early fifties, household names like Finney, Matthews and Lawton were almost remote figures, unless or until you saw them in the flesh at your local ground. You would look at the fixtures to find out when, say, Newcastle were playing in London, so you could go and see Jackie Milburn. I count myself extremely fortunate to have grown up then: children today will never experience the thrill that came out of such rarity value.

I went to Ennersdale Primary School in Hither Green, where we would pretend we were Billy Wright or Tommy Lawton when we kicked a ball about in the playground.

One of my best friends was Barry Hart, who bought himself a guitar when rock and roll started and formed a group. Barry and his father George were keen Charlton fans. On Saturday mornings before we went to The Valley, George would take us up to Blackheath to play football. We were also hooked on the football game Newfooty, which was the fore-runner of Subbuteo. Joan Hart, Barry's mother, made us a pitch out of some old curtains, even sewing on the touchlines and penalty areas.

My days at Ennersdale were those of an innocent childhood spent soon after the war. We had no idea what the country had been through, and still less of what to expect when we grew up. We played simple games on the pavement on the way to and from school, went into the local sweet shop to buy chocolate drops and lemonade, and treated teachers and policemen with fear and respect.

In Coronation year, the school took us down to Lewisham town centre to see the new queen and Prince Philip drive along the main road in an open-top car. We all took little Union flags on sticks and waved them like mad when she went past.

When I passed the eleven-plus exam, my mother and father decided it would be better for my education if I went to boarding school. They were worried that if my father was moved around by the Methodist Church, it would mean interrupting my schooling. So I took a scholarship exam for Culford – a Methodist school near Bury St Edmunds in Suffolk. As I was the son of a minister, we got assistance with the fees.

I did not take too well to boarding school. The grounds at Culford were stunning and the education first class. It did the job, but socially I always felt inhibited. The rules were strict and we growing boys never came into contact with the opposite sex. Many years later Sir Clive Woodward told me he once ran away from school because they wouldn't let him play football. I knew how he felt, although it was ironic seeing him become an England player and then coach to the World Cup-winning rugby team.

Football was played only in my first term, when I made the school team and scored on my debut. After that it was rugby in the autumn term, hockey in the spring and cricket in the summer. That did not stop me or many other boys following the national game just as closely as if we were at home. In my year was a certain Gary Newbon, whose grandparents would send him the classified Saturday evening football paper from Leicester.

Newbon, whose qualities as a leader would come to the fore when he captained the first XV at rugby, would draw up a rota for us to borrow the paper. He was a big fellow, but a fine athlete. On sports day, he made up 60 yards on the last lap to win the relay for his house, filmed by his father on a cine camera. Newbon was always one step ahead of the rest.

George Zeleny was another friend with whom I kept in touch in later years. His father was from Czechoslovakia and serving in the Royal Air Force in Kenya. It was too far for George to go home in the school holidays, when he was supposed to stay with his legal guardian, a vicar living near Saffron Walden. Suffice it to say he preferred to go home with some of his school friends!

Zeleny later became a headmaster, and I met up with him about nine years after we had left Culford. George was a big boxing fan, and I bumped into him at a Joe Bugner fight at York Hall, Bethnal Green, deep in London's East End. He reminded me that when we were at school, I had written a report for the school magazine when George boxed in a tournament. His chief second was Gary Newbon.

My base now was in Stepney, where my father was superintendent minister at the East End Mission on Commercial Road. Mum and Dad were at Stepney for seven years, most of which I spent at Culford. Three times a term they were allowed to visit me on a Saturday and take me out for the day, usually to Portman Road to watch Ipswich Town.

We became friendly with an Ipswich family called Edwards, who owned an outfitters' shop in the town. Their son John was in my year at Culford and developed into a fine cricketer. Once a term we had what was called a 'whole day's holiday', and as it was too far for me to travel to London and back, Bernard and Delia Edwards would take John and me to their home in Ipswich.

The East End Mission was a tough assignment for my father, and not the easiest environment for my mother. My father was so committed to his ministry, and his daily routine so all consuming, that my mother must have been terribly lonely at times. She was a wonderful support to him, and although they had to manage on a minister's modest salary, we did not want for anything when it came to special treats and holidays.

Mum was used to being in the background, while Dad enjoyed being the centre of attention. She taught me valuable lessons in tidiness and punctuality – she was always smart and on time for everything. Letter writing was something of an art in those days, and the neatness of her handwriting left a big impression on me. My mother was so methodical that I'm sure that gave me the ground rules for my approach to my job, and the structured preparation for my commentaries in later years. She was so proud to hear me on television and radio.

One Saturday afternoon, when I was away at school, my mother went all the way to Chelsea on the bus to buy me a programme. She had no intention of going to the match, but she knew I was a keen collector and would like her to send me the programme for that particular match.

As a child, I had spent many happy holidays with my grandparents on her side of the family, William and Alice Harrison, in Boston. Dad's father, Arthur, had died when I was very small, but his mother, Caroline, together with his brothers Darwin and Stan, their wives Mary and Mabel, and his sister Mavis, all spoiled me and my cousin Jane when I spent time in Lincolnshire.

By the time I had taken my O-levels and passed in eight subjects, I was starting to think about a career in journalism. I started a school newspaper called *The Phoenix*, and after one term in the sixth form, at the age of sixteen, persuaded my parents that A-levels and university were not for me.

Getting a job on a local weekly newspaper proved harder than I expected. I must have written to nearly every one of them in the London area over a period of some eighteen months, without success.

For a time I worked at the Epworth Press, the Methodist

publishing house in City Road, where I met David Ray, who later became a Methodist minister. He took me to his home in Barnet and introduced me to Brookside Methodist Church, where there was a thriving youth club.

I was writing the odd article for the *Methodist Recorder*, and also editing a small football magazine started by a freelance journalist, Bryan Breed. It was called *Action*, and my job was to write captions for the photographs of players. Bryan had given me a start.

Tom Goodall, my boss at the Epworth Press, encouraged me to keep plugging away at searching for a newspaper job. My frequent trips to East Barnet provided the breakthrough when I found a vacancy on the *Barnet Press*. Mr Leonard Gayleard, the editor-in-chief of the newspaper, offered me a four-year apprenticeship starting at £7 10 shillings a week.

Taking the job meant two important changes in my life. First, the job entailed working Saturdays, which meant I could no longer watch football regularly with my father. For six years, Dad and I had been season ticket holders at Chelsea. That had come about thanks to a friend of my father, the Reverend Jimmy Butterworth, a minister who started a refuge for troubled youngsters in south-west London called Clubland.

In the days when football was played on Christmas Day, Jimmy had taken us to Stamford Bridge to see Chelsea play Portsmouth. A seventeen-year-old Jimmy Greaves scored four goals and Chelsea won 7–4. After that, we had become regular visitors to the Bridge.

The second change was that I could not commute from Stepney to Barnet, so I went into digs with a Methodist family called the Dangerfields. After being at boarding school, living away from home was not going to be too much of a problem. But having some money in my pocket to buy clothes, run a car and mix with my colleagues at the local pub meant I was starting to live the life of a sixties teenager.

Alfred and Joan Dangerfield had two sons, Malcolm and Kevin, who had been with me at Culford. Malcolm was a bit of a rebel, but we got on fine, and I always remember I had been living with them for only a few weeks when John F Kennedy was assassinated.

It was one of those defining moments where everybody remembers where they were on that particular day. I was in the bedroom when Malcolm breezed in.

'Have you heard about Kennedy?' he asked. 'Someone shot the bastard.'

My first scoop on the local weekly came courtesy of the Methodist youth club connection. Chris Brewer was a friend of mine at the club, and his father Bill was secretary of Barnet General Hospital.

Brewer senior rang the *Barnet Press* office one morning and asked to speak to me. 'I have an address in Totteridge that you ought to go to,' he explained. 'Two young children fell into the swimming pool and their father rescued them. They are being checked out in the hospital, but I think they will be all right.'

I jumped into my battered old car and drove to a secluded close in one of the affluent parts of Hertfordshire. I rang the front door-bell, and when it was answered nearly jumped out of my skin. The man with the horn-rimmed glasses was Hank Marvin, lead guitarist with the Shadows.

He was most cooperative. His two young children had been playing in the garden, just a few feet away from where he was composing some music in the back room. He heard their screams as both, presumably one pushed by the other, fell into the pool. Neither could swim. Marvin rushed into the garden, pulled out both kids, and as I recall administered the kiss of life to at least one of them. He then took them to hospital, where they recovered.

It made a front-page story with my first byline.

*   *   *

My four years on the *Barnet Press* were among the happiest of my life. I made friends with the other junior reporter on the paper, Roger Jones, and everything seemed in front of us.

Our training fell into two parts. For most of the week we reported on weddings, funerals, court cases, council meetings and traffic accidents. We also had a number of church ministers on whom we had to call for news.

Some of them had little to give us, so we mischievously started a competition to see who could make the shortest 'church call'. Roger had a Catholic priest on his list called Father P J Devins. 'Hello, Father, any news this week? No. Thank you' was timed at three seconds.

No wonder Father Devins had no news. When we watched the next FA Cup final on television and the cameras panned across the crowd, we saw him sitting at Wembley in his dog collar.

The local paper threw up some bizarre stories. Pirate radio stations were all the rage, and I was sent to interview a disc jockey who called himself Larry Pannell. When I got there, it turned out his real name was J Ross Barnard, but he made me promise not to use it. No doubt he had good reason for his alias.

The other part of our training was what was called a day-release scheme. Jones and I would go to the North-West London Polytechnic in Kentish Town every Friday to study shorthand, newspaper law, local government and English.

In many ways it was like going back to school. The class was made up of junior journalists like ourselves from weekly papers around London and the Home Counties. They included John Goodbody, who later made a big name for himself as a sports news reporter in Fleet Street; Jeremy Chapman, who became golf correspondent for the *Racing Post*; and Chris James, who worked on the *Liverpool Daily Post* and *Echo*.

The English course was something like the A-level I never took. We had three set books; *The Shetland Bus*, about wartime evacuation from Scandinavia by boat; Richard Hoggart's *The Uses of Literacy*, and my favourite – *Catcher in the Rye*, by J D Salinger.

John Goodbody and I virtually learned *Catcher* by heart. No wonder Salinger became a recluse, because he never wrote anything half as good again. I remember feeling bitterly short-changed when I read *Franny and Zooey* and *Raise High the Roofbeam Carpenter*. The Glass family just didn't do it for me.

At the end of the first year, we took exams in all the subjects on our course, and I won a prize for the best all-round performance. Life on the paper also got better. My mother and father had moved to nearby Potters Bar, where dad was preaching at St John's Methodist church. It meant I could say thank you to the Dangerfields and move back home.

By then, I had also bought myself my first car. That battered Hillman Minx, bought from a lady in East Barnet, cost the princely sum of £2. One wing was virtually dropping off, and I was stopped by the police and summonsed for 'dangerous parts'. I was fined a fiver at Highgate Magistrates' Court and the *Barnet Press* solemnly gave their reporter a one-paragraph rap over the knuckles.

Roger Jones had a pre-war Austin Eight, which was as temperamental as my vehicle. If one of our cars was working, we would go to the office together. If neither was, we took the bus. Our social life revolved very much around the Methodist Youth Club, where we both met our early girlfriends. Christine Smith and I went out for a year, and remain family friends to this day.

Away from work, Roger Jones and I were having the time of our lives. Roger had a passion for pop music, and studied the charts furiously when he bought the *New Musical Express* every week. I had a brief flirtation with a local girl in Barnet and wanted to take her to see the Beatles in concert. Roger made his way to Hammersmith Odeon and queued for hours to get us two tickets. To have seen the Merseyside group live on stage was like wearing a badge at the time, but Jones went one better and managed to interview them for the paper when they put in an appearance at nearby Elstree Studios.

On the sporting front, I helped form a table tennis team called Jardak – an amalgamation of the members' initials – and I won the Barnet and the Potters Bar youth championships in successive years. It remains my only sporting achievement.

Roger and I both passed the National Council for the Training of Journalists' Proficiency Certificate, the professional qualification to which our four-year indentures with the *Barnet Press* were geared. Again, I was lucky enough to win a national award.

We both had a lot to be thankful for. The paper, started in 1859 by the Cowing family, was still owned by Miss Gwyneth Cowing. As chairman of the directors, she made sure staff were well looked after. We used to queue up outside her office for our Christmas bonus.

The training of the junior reporters was seen as a benchmark of the paper's reputation. Editor Len Gayleard had an experienced team. The assistant editor, John Walton, was a pillar of the local community; the sports editor, Bill White, wrote under the pseudonym 'Argus'; the chief reporter, Bill Field, taught me how to structure a story and the importance of a contacts book, which stood me in good stead for the rest of my career.

My job on a Saturday afternoon was to report the fortunes of Finchley Football Club in the Athenian League. Amateur football was attracting big crowds in those days. A lot of players were drawing 'expenses' and the FA would soon abandon the distinction between amateur and professional.

It was customary for the local newspaper reporters to travel in the team coach. I was in good company, because there were three papers covering Finchley. Jonathan Lang of the *Finchley Press* and John Pollard of the *Hendon and Finchley Times* were my regular companions as we toured the Home Counties covering matches at grounds like Hounslow, Hayes, Carshalton and Maidenhead.

In 1965, Finchley reached the semi-final of the FA Amateur Cup. Their manager, Sid Prosser, was a product of the relatively new FA coaching scheme and took his part-time job very seriously.

When Finchley won away at Ferryhill in County Durham in the third round, it was quite an adventure for a young reporter to travel by train to the North-East. But that was nothing compared to the thrill of sitting in the press box at Highbury for the semi-final – only to see Finchley beaten 4–1 by Hendon.

It was my first experience of how the mood of managers can change. If Finchley had a good win, Prosser would turn to his assistant and say: 'Buy the boys a drink, Charlie.' If they lost, and we were waiting for his quotes, he would sometimes give Pollard, Lang and me short shrift. 'Tell the boys to clear off, Charlie' was not uncommon.

Jonathan Lang, Roger Jones and I were frustrated at not being able to play local football on a Saturday because of our work commitments, so we came up with a solution. Together with Jonathan's twin brother Jeremy, we formed our own Sunday team.

As we had no home ground, and three of us were journalists, we called the club 'Roving Reporters'. Our first season was a learning curve as we persuaded other teams to let us play friendlies on their pitches, but in 1966 we were a founder member of the Barnet Sunday League.

Forty-three years on, Roving Reporters are the only original members still playing in the league. I am club president and Roger is chairman. We still go on the club's annual tour together to Bournemouth.

At the start of the 1967/68 season, Bill White went on holiday, and for three weeks I was given the plum job of covering Barnet. One of the great names in amateur football, they had turned semi-professional two years earlier and joined the Southern League.

Not that I knew it then, but this was the start of a forty-year friendship with an immaculate football man called Dexter Adams. I knew he had been a formidable amateur international centre half, but discovered that it was his father who had stopped him turning professional and told him to get a trade.

Dexter was in the advertising department of the *Daily Mirror*, but all his spare time was spent managing Barnet. 'Do you work in the evenings?' was the first thing he asked me when I met him. I quickly learned that Dexter's evenings were invariably spent on the telephone, while his wife Sheila was busy washing the team kit.

When they read my reports on Barnet's opening games, Dexter and the captain, Dennis Roach, told me they thought I had a future as a sports journalist. I also received encouragement from the right back, Roger Thompson, who had joined Barnet from Nuneaton Borough and had once been on the books of Aston Villa.

Dexter Adams sought advice on my behalf from the *Mirror*'s sports desk, and suggested my next move might be to leave Barnet and set my sights on a provincial daily or evening paper. My early applications again bore no fruit. Letters to newspapers in thriving football cities like Liverpool, Manchester and Newcastle met with no response.

Then, rather like London buses, two jobs came along at once. The *Nottingham Evening Post* and the *Morning Telegraph* in Sheffield both had vacancies for a sports reporter and, following an interview, offered me a job.

The Sheffield opening seemed more attractive. The *Telegraph* had a good name in the business, having exposed police brutality in the city in 1963, when the then editor, David Hopkinson, was voted Journalist of the Year for revealing what became known as the 'rhino whip case'.

His successor, Michael Finley, wanted the paper to have a quality feel about it, modelling it more on the *Guardian* than the *Daily Mirror*. Sports editor David Jones welcomed me with the words: 'What you achieve with us will be entirely down to you. You will do what you want to do. All we can do is give you opportunity.'

As well as reporting, I also subbed copy on the sports desk. The hours were unsociable. We started at half past five in the afternoon and worked until two o'clock in the morning, when the last edition went to press.

My digs were in Hampton Road next to Firth Park Hospital, with Mrs Brown and her family – another Methodist connection. I soon made a number of good friends. The assistant sports editor, Benny Hill, knocked some rough edges off me and taught me a lot about accuracy; Keith Farnsworth, a highly respected writer in South Yorkshire, welcomed me into his home; and John Hughes was to make a big impression as a writer and broadcaster in Southampton. (When John's wife Pat went into hospital for the birth of their first child, he drove straight to the local squash court to join me for a prearranged game. How times change!)

Unlike its sister paper the *Star*, the *Telegraph* did not operate a 'one man one club' policy when it came to football reporting. I was soon covering not just Rotherham United, Chesterfield and Barnsley, but also getting a crack at Sheffield United and Sheffield Wednesday.

Sometimes the *Sunday Times* would want a freelance match report, so there was plenty of scope for me to spread my wings. Even though I stayed only for a year it proved to be an eventful time. Both Sheffield clubs changed their managers. John Harris handed over to Arthur Rowley at Bramall Lane, and Alan Brown left Sheffield Wednesday to join Sunderland. His successor was Jack Marshall. At Rotherham, Tommy Docherty was in charge when I arrived. At Barnsley I was on *Telegraph* duty in the press box when they clinched promotion under Johnny Steele.

David Jones sent me to Wembley for the FA Amateur Cup final, and to Wimbledon for an interview with Sheffield's Roger Taylor during the tennis championships. But it was when he was co-opted to start a sports programme on the fledgling BBC Radio Sheffield that he changed my life.

Chapter 4

'Saw you on the wireless'

The joy of radio

I STRUCK LUCKY IN my year in South Yorkshire. It coincided with the BBC launching their first raft of local radio stations, with Radio Sheffield one of the six chosen as part of the experiment.

There were few permanent staff and the budget was minimal. So as David Jones had a Saturday sports show to man, he turned to his *Telegraph* staff for help. I would go into the radio station in the morning to preview games to be played by local clubs, then cover a match for the paper in the afternoon before calling in to do a radio report on the way home.

After a mere handful of freelance broadcasts, I was working on the *Telegraph* sports desk one night when the assistant sports editor, Benny Hill, glared at a piece of copy I had written and said, 'Motson, I heard tha ont radio on Saturday, tha's better off goin' tha a way than tryin' to be a writer.'

At the time, the BBC were advertising for sports news assistants for Radio Two at Broadcasting House. I had no idea what that meant, but submitted my four-page application to the Appointments Department, and was thrilled to get an interview.

My 'board', as the BBC like to call it, took place in an upstairs room at 5 Portland Place, a building across the road from Broadcasting House. There were four grey-suited men on the other side of the table, including Angus Mackay, an irascible Scotsman and the authoritarian editor of BBC Radio Sports News.

When asked about my level of radio experience I replied, quite truthfully, that I had done a few match reports and previews for BBC Radio Sheffield. At this point, the sombre mood on the other side of the table evaporated. They burst out laughing.

Quite how closely they had studied my CV on the exhaustive application form I never knew, but their faces were enough to tell me that a lot more experience was needed for me to have a chance of landing the job. I went back to Sheffield feeling a little chastened. A letter arrived at my digs a few days later, stating that I did not meet the requirements for the job at this time, but my name would be kept on file.

A polite rejection, I thought. No more than two months later, another letter dropped on the mat bearing the BBC logo. 'You may recall coming to London for a board a few weeks ago,' it began. I could hardly forget. 'Two more jobs have now become available in the BBC Radio Sports Department, and we would like to offer you another chance to apply.'

Once again I caught the train to London, and found myself in exactly the same room in Portland Place. The board members even seemed to be in the same chairs.

Angus Mackay was watching me closely this time, moistening his upper lip below his moustache from a tin of Vaseline. He was badly burned in the Barnes rail crash of 1955 in which thirteen people died when a passenger train caught fire. Alongside him was his assistant editor, Vincent Duggleby, a businesslike figure who fired most of the questions. The two other members of the board, including the chairman, came from the BBC Appointments and Personnel departments.

Taking in more at my second board than I had at the first, I realised that Mackay and Duggleby were the two most likely to weigh up the claims of the candidates – some of whom were still downstairs waiting to be summoned.

Bearing in mind that the two interviews were just a few weeks apart, I doubt whether my qualifications had moved forward. It was now midsummer, and my football shift on Radio Sheffield was over until the new season. So what I said to make them change their minds I have no idea. But this time there was no laughter. A few days later I received a letter offering me the post of sports news assistant at the princely annual salary of £1,955.

And I do mean princely. I was just twenty-three and my pay at the *Morning Telegraph* had been around £23 per week. It did not take me long to work out that the BBC offer was not to be sniffed at, bearing in mind that I would be living at home again with my parents. But the job that went with it was what really excited me. I had little idea of what I would be doing, but maybe that was a good thing.

On the morning I arrived on the third floor of Broadcasting House, my initiation ceremony made me feel completely out of my depth. Vincent Duggleby brusquely introduced me to the other new boy – a confident lad with a high-pitched voice called Roger Macdonald.

'Where are you from?' he asked me.

'Sheffield *Morning Telegraph*,' I replied, sensing that didn't mean a great deal to him.

'Hmm. I have come from *The Times*, I've just been covering a big story in Europe,' said Roger.

I quickly realised that we would be seeing Angus Mackay only when he wanted us in his office. He rarely moved from there, even when other departmental heads needed to speak to him. It was Duggleby who was giving the orders.

'We see you as a potential producer, John,' he explained. 'Roger is an experienced journalist, and we think he is better equipped to go behind the microphone.'

That plan lasted about three days.

There was a little studio at the end of the Sports Room called 3H, which was used for short bulletins. The longer programmes, such as *Sports Report*, the flagship programme of the department, went out from a studio in the basement called B9. At the end of our first week, Vincent Duggleby and Bob Burrows, who was a senior producer working opposite me, took Roger and me into 3H with a sheaf of papers. 'We are going to try you both out at reading the racing results,' said Vincent, as Bob switched on a tape recorder. 'Pretend you are doing them for tonight's bulletin.'

The bulletin was what they called the '6.32'. That eight-minute segment up to 6.40 p.m. was the only daily output for which the sports newsroom was then responsible. It would consist of two minutes of football news, a brief round-up of other sports stories, and then all the day's racing results.

I found announcing 1-2-3 with the prices quite straightforward. I wasn't into racing then, but I had heard the results read over the air countless times. Rhythm and timing were everything. Roger, however, did not seem so confident. His world exclusive for *The Times* had not prepared him for this. Burrows switched off the tape, looked hard at Duggleby, and they left the room.

A few days later, I happened to see a memo sent by Angus Mackay to Bob Hudson, his opposite number in the Sports Outside Broadcast department. 'I think we may have got our two new recruits the wrong way round,' was its message. 'We think Motson might make a broadcaster and Macdonald's flair might be for production.'

So it proved. I was given scripts to read during the 6.32, as well as spending the earlier part of the day reading the sports news from the teleprinter, and writing some of the bulletins.

My next step forward was to present a programme, and I was given the regional south-east sports round-up on a Saturday night, called *Sports Session*. This went out at 6.30 p.m., half an hour after the end of *Sports Report*, in which I used to do a round up of games not covered by our reporters. But on *Sports Session* I was in the chair, with four match reporters at London games coming in to voice their summaries live in the studio.

One of these was W Barrington Dalby, who made his name as the 'other half' of the radio boxing commentary team in the fifties and early sixties alongside Raymond Glendenning and Eamonn Andrews. Listeners in those days, when there was little or no boxing on television, would get used to Eamonn always closing a round with the words 'come in, Barry'.

Eamonn had made his name as the presenter of television's *What's My Line* and front man for Angus on *Sports Report*, but had left by the time I joined. So, it was a thrill for me to say 'now with the details behind Chelsea's victory over Arsenal at Stamford Bridge, here's Barrington Dalby'.

Another regular on *Sports Session* was a Congregational minister from Brighton, the Reverend Emrys Walters. A versatile Welshman, who seemed to be able to combine his church duties with a broadcasting career, Emrys seemed to bullishly surmount any problem. He quickly took on a self-appointed role as guide and mentor to me and another new recruit, Desmond Lynam, who arrived from Radio Brighton just a year or so after me.

What my dad would have made of Emrys, I don't know. Des had a young baby called Patrick, and Emrys was forever offering to christen him. 'But I'm a Catholic,' Des would protest. 'No matter, no matter, I can do it,' insisted the Welsh multitasker.

When Emrys had a fall-out with Angus Mackay – by no means the only one – he got his own back by staying in the office on

Saturday afternoon digesting the details of the match he was supposed to be covering from the teleprinter, and then coming on to *Sports Session* and pretending he had been at the game. With a huge slice of journalistic licence, and a conviction in his voice that must have wowed them from the pulpit, Emrys got away with it for nearly a season.

Then one day Des was at a match where Emrys was carded to be the reporter. 'Never saw you in the press box, Emrys,' said Lynam, smiling, when they next met. Walters replied instantly, 'Directors' Box, boyo, I was in the Directors' Box.'

It was clear from moment one that Lynam was going to be a big number. Mackay quickly established him in the *Sports Report* hot seat, which until then had been shared between Peter Jones and the BBC football correspondent, Bryon Butler, who both doubled up as commentators.

Peter Jones, who died after collapsing at the Boat Race in 1990, had a voice and delivery admired by many. But I had a greater regard for Butler, whose one-minute set pieces, delivered in his rich Somerset accent, were a work of art.

I had been in the department less than a year when word came up from Bob Hudson that the Outside Broadcast department would like me to do a 'test' commentary.

They sent me to Wembley, where the FA Amateur Cup final of 1969 was between Sutton United and North Shields. My effort was not broadcast, but recorded on tape for Hudson and his producers to assess. I must have passed the test because at the end of the year I was given my first live commentary, when I was sent in December 1969 with the experienced Maurice Edelston to cover Everton's match with Derby County at Goodison Park.

Everton were in the race for the championship under Harry Catterick. But as far as the press were concerned the club was a closed shop compared with their neighbours, Liverpool, when it came to media access. But if Goodison was like Fort Knox, Maurice Edelston was just the man to spring the lock. He had been a fine player for Reading, and won many amateur international caps for England. But for the war, he would almost certainly have played at the highest level.

Thanks to his relationship with Catterick, we were able to meet the manager before the game. I was at the microphone when Alan Ball, wearing a pair of revolutionary white boots, scored the only goal.

When my train got to Euston, I followed two blind lads out of the station and struck up a conversation.

'We were listening to the match on the radio this afternoon,' one said. 'It's the only way we can follow our football.'

It was a reminder of the part radio played in the life of the nation, and the Radio Two Sports News department was growing all the time. They seem small steps compared to the twenty-four-hour broadcasting of today, but a sports bulletin was incorporated into BBC Radio's *Late Night Extra*, and then into the early morning *Today* programme, which meant one of us staying overnight.

When it came to the World Cup in Mexico in the summer of 1970, commentators Maurice Edelston, Bryon Butler and Peter Jones went out to cover England's bid to retain the trophy. Bob Burrows and I were assigned the 'home shift', which meant staying in Broadcasting House for days and nights on end, monitoring the news from Mexico and preparing bulletins for the early morning.

What I was *not* prepared for was the sound line from Mexico 'going down' during one of England's early matches, and listeners losing commentary. I picked up a microphone in the bowels of Broadcasting House and worked off a small monitor until the fault was repaired. I still have a memo from Bob Hudson thanking me for my efforts in 'exceptional' circumstances. I guess I could say that my first World Cup commentary was actually in 1970, not 1974.

I'll always remember, when England lost 3–2 to West Germany in the quarter-final, having to present the *Today* bulletin the following morning in a state of shock. Ramsey's team had been leading 2–0 and I assumed the nation would, like me, be devastated. That obviously didn't apply to John Timpson, one of the *Today* presenters. As I handed back to him, he said somewhat sarcastically, 'Well, thank goodness that's over, and we can move on to something else.'

One of the things I was moving on to was boxing. I had stood in a couple of times for the regular commentator, Simon Smith, but my main role was as a ringside reporter. Armed with a portable tape recorder – known then as a 'Uher' – I would also do interviews after the fight.

That was my role on the unforgettable night that Henry Cooper defended his British and European heavyweight titles against the bright young hope Joe Bugner at Wembley in March 1971. I scored the fight on my programme, and like many others (including Harry Carpenter), I had Cooper two rounds in front when they went into the last three minutes.

I can still picture the scene now when the bell went. Cooper walked across the ring towards the referee, Harry Gibbs, who swerved past him. Cooper's expression was one of resignation even before Gibbs reached Bugner to raise his hand.

As all hell broke loose ringside, I raced for the dressing rooms, Uher in hand and tape at the ready, to catch the two fighters for an interview. I got into Cooper's room and somehow got the tape recorder in front of Henry and his manager, Jim Wicks. No sooner had I asked the first question than Cooper said that was it, he was going to retire.

While I was absorbing the fact that I had the news ahead of anybody else, the door burst open and in rushed Mickey Duff, the matchmaker.

'Why aren't you talking to winners?' he demanded. 'It's Joe Bugner you should be interviewing.'

Jim Wicks gave Duff a look that spoke volumes. I managed to finish the interview with Henry, and eventually found the new champion in exultant mood in his dressing room along the corridor.

These days, interviews like that and Cooper's retirement announcement would have been live on air, or at worse recorded and used within minutes. But back in 1971, there was no direct line out of Wembley. I had to take the tape back on the Tube, edit it myself, and hope the *Today* programme would use it before most people had seen their morning paper.

Another sport I tried my hand at on radio in later years was tennis. I spent six years as a Radio Two commentator at the Wimbledon championships. I was fortunate to be on Centre Court to watch Björn Borg win his five successive titles, and as a support commentator to Max Robertson. I was starting to get some good reviews as a ball-by-ball broadcaster.

I really enjoyed the experience, especially when executive producer Bob Burrows paired me with Fred Perry. We seemed to hit it off together, and I made up for my lack of technical know-ledge with enthusiastic attempts to describe every shot. Fred came in with his dry, deliberate delivery and vast experience – dating back to his three Wimbledon victories before the war.

Towards the end of my six-year spell, a number of friends and colleagues were pointing out that Max Robertson would soon be retiring. They believed I would be a candidate to replace him as the radio voice at Wimbledon.

It was very flattering, but I believed the same about tennis as I did about boxing. I felt I could handle both sports capably, but not to the extent that I could devote the time to do justice to them, as well as football.

* * *

Back at the start of the 1970s, my priority was gaining a foothold on the regular commentary rota. More games came my way as the 1970/71 season developed, and Angus Mackay was pleased with my progress.

Bob Burrows succeeded Vincent Duggleby as Mackay's deputy, and many was the time in the BBC Club on a Saturday night, after all the programmes were finished, that the pair of them dissected the performance of Bill Hamilton, Lynam, Christopher Martin-Jenkins, Motson and the other young broadcasters in the team.

Angus would be sipping a large whisky with Bob at one shoulder and his driver, whom we only ever knew as Mr Smith, at the other. We were all expected to buy Angus a drink at some stage before Mr Smith took him home. But when we went to the bar in what is now the Langham Hotel, it seemed impolite not to include Mr Smith in the round. These were the pre-breathalyser days of 1971.

'That's very kind of you, John,' he would say. 'Mine's a brown ale.'

By the time the session was over and Angus was ready to be driven home to Teddington, there would be seven or eight empty brown ale bottles lined up on the shelf.

We were a group of eager, young professionals, keen to get on in the industry. Bill Hamilton went on to become an outstanding BBC Television News correspondent, working in some of the world's most threatening trouble spots. Chris Martin-Jenkins completed a unique 'treble', serving as cricket correspondent at the BBC, the *Daily Telegraph* and *The Times*.

Even though my test commentary for television was initially kept away from Angus, once *Match of the Day* wanted to sign me, he was quick to encourage me and clearly felt my switch was a feather in his own cap. He was a hard taskmaster, but his stand-ards and strict discipline gave many of the broadcasters who worked under him a training that proved invaluable. Those before me, such as Brian Moore, and those who joined later, such as Alan Parry, were part of a radio conveyor belt that provided a string of television commentators in the future.

Although he rarely socialised, Mackay's eye for a broadcaster meant those of us working under him had a lot in common, and there was great camaraderie between us. I was lucky to be part of the last team he assembled. A year after I left for *Match of the Day*, Angus Mackay retired and started a new life.

He learnt to drive and spent all his time with his family. His legacy was there for his successors to build on, for in many ways he embodied the spirit and soul of radio, which had sustained the nation during wartime and entertained it afterwards. It was very much *his* medium.

Mackay had been suspicious of television since its influence grew in the fifties and sixties. Alan Parry, who joined the department soon after I left, discovered that when he attended his board. 'What ambitions do you have in the long term, Alan?' growled Mackay, with Bob Burrows sitting next to him.

'Well, I suppose if I was successful in radio, Mr Mackay, I would like to think I might get into television,' replied Alan.

'Television? Television?' yelled Angus. 'Don't you think if television was important Mr Burrows and I would be in television?'

That's exactly where Bob Burrows eventually went when he left BBC Radio to join Thames in 1980. After Mackay's retirement in 1972, Bob had led the development of radio sport in a big way, including creating the structure for the blanket coverage of Wimbledon which exists today. Alongside Cliff Morgan, who became the Head of Radio Outside Broadcasts, he modernised the department and built a platform from which Five Live would later be launched.

After Bob and I left the Wimbledon team and went our separate ways, I was occasionally called back to front *Soccer Special* and never lost my feel for radio. So although I was disappointed when BBC Television lost the Premiership highlights package to ITV in 2001, I was pleased when Bob Shennan, as Controller of Five Live, asked me to join his team of commentators.

I did not find switching back to radio commentary insurmountable. Many years earlier, Bob Hudson had emphasised the three main priorities: geography (where the ball is on the pitch); the score (could not be repeated often enough for those constantly switching on) and the elapsed time.

One or two of the younger commentators must have wondered whether I was overdoing it at times. 'The play is on the far side of the field, that's West Ham's left, halfway inside the Newcastle half' can sound a bit repetitive. But I was conscious that having addressed a television audience who could see all this, together with the score and the time in the corner of the screen, I needed to be aware of those who could see nothing. The radio commentator is their eyes, as well as their ears.

I couldn't have wished for a better start to my second radio career. In one of my first matches, Newcastle beat Manchester United 4–3 at St James' Park, and two weeks later United beat Tottenham 5–3 at White Hart Lane after being three down at half-time. Five Live were delighted that I managed to persuade Sir Alex Ferguson to come live on to *Sports Report* after that game. We were on good terms at that time, and Bob Shennan made it clear to me that my contacts were a major reason why he wanted my voice on the channel.

In 2001, Bob created a Saturday morning vehicle called *Matchday with Motty*. This was a ninety-minute chat show with studio guests looking ahead to the afternoon's fixtures. I drafted in my old Barnet mate, Ricky George, as a co-host, and we had three months of great fun before we were replaced by Ian Wright and Mark Bright. Even then the Motson family weren't off the air. My son, Fred, then fifteen years old, was hired to deliver a 'mini Motty minute' which Wright and Bright thought was hilarious.

I was lucky enough to enjoy both mediums, and my radio career picked up again after BBC Television lost the rights to the FA contract in 2008. With no England matches or FA Cup ties for me to cover, Five Live again came to my rescue with a package of live Premier League commentaries and a regular slot on the *Monday Night Club*, where I was free to offer a few opinions.

Cliff Morgan always used to say, when he heard me on the radio: 'Saw you on the wireless last night.' But on a more serious note, he said the one thing any of us in television or radio would do well never to forget – 'it is a privilege to broadcast'.

If I was to compare television and radio, I guess I would say radio can be more fun. The scrutiny is not quite as severe, since nobody can actually see what you are describing, but on the other hand the television commentator has more aids than his radio counterpart, who often works without a monitor and therefore has no access to replays. A bit like television in the seventies . . .

Chapter 5

It Was Tough in Those Days

Life with Coleman, Carpenter and Cowgill

'IF YOU TWO don't get Bugner in the ring exactly on nine twenty, I'll blast the pair of you so far into orbit you'll never bloody well come down.'

It was an abrasive David Coleman speaking in the autumn of 1971. The two young men he was addressing were myself and Martin Hopkins, a young assistant producer who had been in the BBC Sports Department just a little longer than me.

The atmosphere in the *Sportsnight with Coleman* meeting on Monday morning was always lively, sometimes intimidating and occasionally downright hostile. Which sums up exactly what life was like in the BBC Sports Department in the early seventies.

Sam Leitch would chair the meeting, but it was Coleman who would bark most of the instructions. Jonathan Martin, then the studio director, would be busy scribbling notes about the running order in his big diary, but rarely escaped Coleman's withering glance or the rough edge of his tongue.

Leitch had cut his teeth in the highly competitive world of Fleet

Street, but in television terms he was a beginner compared to Coleman. He was, however, supremely gifted editorially and had a flair for getting the best out of people. 'Football and boxing, contacts and contracts, that's what we're about,' he said when I joined.

Bearing in mind he was responsible for *Match of the Day* and *Sportsnight*, his simplicity was not misplaced. Boxing was second only to football on the BBC's sports agenda at the time. There were any number of home-bred fighters winning titles – men like Alan Rudkin, Ken Buchanan, John H Stracey, Alan Minter, Chris Finnegan, John Conteh and Tony Sibson. All found fame thanks to fighting regularly in front of the BBC cameras.

Our two big contracts were with Harry Levene, who promoted at Wembley Arena, and Mike Barrett, who put on shows at the Royal Albert Hall. *Sportsnight* would show most of the big fights midweek – while *Grandstand* would sweep up the rest of the bill with *Fight of the Week* after Sam Leitch's *Football Preview* at Saturday lunchtime.

Joe Bugner had won the British and European heavyweight titles in controversial circumstances from the lovable Henry Cooper just a few months before I moved into television. But that summer, Bugner had stumbled embarrassingly to Jack Bodell, the Derbyshire pig farmer from Swadlincote who knocked him down and beat him on points. In a bid to get Bugner back on track, matchmaker Mickey Duff organised a fight at Nottingham Ice Rink against a decent American opponent called Larry Middleton.

It was to be the main event on *Sportsnight* that Wednesday in November. Hopkins and I were sent purely to make sure it happened precisely in the right time slot. Coleman had left us in no doubt of the consequences if anything went wrong.

I was sharing a flat in Finchley at the time, and had just purchased my first sports car, an open-top Austin Healey Sprite, from Brian Pitts, a dear friend who later died during his BBC career. Not that

Hopkins and I felt like a couple of joyriders on our way to Nottingham. Fortunately Mickey Duff had things well in hand with the timing. Bugner entered the ring at exactly 9.20 p.m. Not so fortunately he went and lost on points!

Harry Carpenter was doing the commentary, and it gave me the opportunity to study at close quarters another of the broadcasters who had helped to establish the BBC's reputation in sports television.

'One of the early homework men', was how Leitch described him to me once. But Harry was a great deal more than that. His preparation was impeccable and his delivery faultless. He had a nice, concise turn of phrase, and away from the microphone a little chuckle and a twinkle in his eye that would appeal to, among others, Muhammad Ali.

Although videotape was now used to record the main events, some items were still shot on film. If that was the case, and a commentary was required to be laid on later, we would be cocooned in the 'dubbing theatre' at Lime Grove and told to record our words to fit the small picture on a black-and-white monitor.

In the very early days, once they started to run the film you could not stop and go back. If you made a slip in delivering one of your links, the dubbing mixer had to wind back the tape to the start and you had to begin all over again. Bob Abrahams, an outstanding film editor who had been in the department almost since its inception, taught me how to write to film. My newspaper days proved a useful tool in finding words to fit the pictures.

Mind you, I watched in awe one day as Harry Carpenter put half an hour of dubbed commentary on to the highlights of a Formula One event. He did it in one take, and from that day on I set that as a target whenever I was asked to post-record a commentary.

Most weeks in my first few seasons, Bob Abrahams and I would go and shoot a story for Leitch's *Football Preview*. We went out with a three-man film crew: Roy Gladish, cameraman; Ian Kennedy, assistant cameraman; and Fred Clark, the sound recordist who'd worked on Roger Bannister's four-minute mile back in 1954. The filming was a good way for me to make contacts in the football world and to get to know some of the managers and players, as well as watching Bob expertly cut the piece to the length required. He had directed the cameraman in the first place with a keen eye for a good shot, but to see him with a razor blade attacking the tape in the cutting room was an education in itself. You have to remember that colour television had come in only two or three years before I joined, and many of the techniques that now entail merely the push of a button had not been developed.

Sometimes Bob and I would be accompanied on our midweek football journey by Peter Lorenzo, like Sam Leitch a former Fleet Street reporter who had moved to television. Peter was highly regarded as the best contacts man in the business. He taught me a lot about acquiring the trust and telephone numbers of key people in the game, such as the leading managers of the time, like Bill Shankly, Don Revie and Bertie Mee. As well as other contacts, such as club secretaries, chairmen and even physiotherapists, who would offer useful information. 'Always make a point of thanking the man on the door,' said Peter.

Lorenzo was especially close to Sir Alf Ramsey. He had culti-vated a relationship with the England manager before, during and after the 1970 World Cup in Mexico. Many was the time at the *Sportsnight* meeting that Coleman would demand, 'Peter, have we got Alf for Wednesday?' if a Ramsey interview had been planned in the programme running order.

One morning Lorenzo hesitated.

'There might be a slight problem this time, David,' he muttered.

Peter was as smooth and debonair as they come, but under Coleman's gaze even he could falter.

'What problem?' growled Coleman.

'Well, Lady Ramsey says the colour television hasn't arrived yet,' Peter replied.

Nobody was ever quite sure what arrangements went on between Sam, Peter and the managers we used as experts, but these were the early days of the television pundit, and the likes of Don Revie, Joe Mercer, Brian Clough and Malcolm Allison all played their parts in BBC coverage.

I also met Peter Dimmock, who had fronted the first midweek BBC sports programme – *Sportsview* – in the fifties. Having been a keen viewer when I was at school, it was quite an honour to be in the presence of such a distinguished figure.

Dimmock held the title of General Manager, BBC Television Outside Broadcast Group, which meant he was responsible for the events side of BBC Television, including royal occasions. With his elegant white moustache he was certainly at home in such elevated company.

By far the most formidable figure in the department was Bryan 'Ginger' Cowgill – the Head of Sport. An intimidating Lancastrian with a rich Blackburn accent, Cowgill was something of a television stormtrooper. He was quite fearless when it came to fighting his corner against other departmental heads, and he could be quite ruthless with his own staff when they fell below the high standards he, and Coleman in particular, were setting.

This was still BBC Sport in its formative years, breaking down frontiers and establishing a worldwide reputation for innovative coverage and sharp television reporting. Many was the time senior members of the department were almost brought to tears by some of the hurtful criticism that would follow any lapse in standards. I saw Cowgill personally sack people on the spot with a total disregard for their feelings, usually to reinstate them within twenty-four hours. Such behaviour in the BBC today would result in the

Human Resources department intervening within minutes, but political correctness was several years away, as I felt myself moving through this minefield in the early seventies.

What an education though, and what an eye-opening experience. As Coleman would affirm in later years, 'We just wanted to make you better,' and in most cases that is what they did.

Any commentator or producer who had slipped up on *Match of the Day* on a Saturday night would be summoned to the first-floor bar in the BBC's Kensington House at Monday lunchtime and given a dressing down. Humiliating it could be, but character-building it certainly was.

Bryan Cowgill was particularly proud of the action-replay machine, which was an innovation in his time as a producer. In its early days it was used for cricket, when Brian Johnston was a television commentator before he became a fixture on radio. During one over a delivery came off the bat and lodged in the top of the batsman's pad. A fielder ran in, collected the ball and appealed for a catch. Nobody seemed sure what the umpire's decision should be, so Cowgill immediately decided to replay the incident.

'I'm showing that again, Brian,' he boomed from the gallery.

Unfortunately Johnston did not have his headphones on. When he saw the same thing happen again on his monitor he shouted, 'I don't believe it. Twice in two balls!'

Not that Cowgill would have seen the funny side of that. One of the reasons tempers flared so often in those days was that producers and editors were coming to terms with new technology. Sports coverage was still in its formative years.

Even the careers of young commentators like myself were far from mapped out. Although I was taken on primarily to do football, the scrutiny applied to every commentary I did meant nothing was cast in stone. At one point, when David Coleman was absent for a time, Cowgill even suggested I might try athletics. It never came to that, but such was the competitive nature of the department, where reputations were ripped apart during heavy drinking sessions in the BBC Club, that I took nothing for granted.

Cowgill's flair and leadership qualities earned him promotion to Controller of BBC1, where his combative style and competitive instinct hugely improved BBC audience ratings. When he moved to Thames Television as managing director he had major successes there too, making striking acquisitions in the light entertainment field.

I was privileged to speak at his funeral in July 2008.

Bryan Cowgill followed the same trail as Paul Fox, who, when I joined, was Controller of BBC1. He later left to join Yorkshire Television as managing director, before returning to the BBC as Managing Director of Network Television from 1988 to 1991.

Word was passed down to me that Fox was not a big fan of the new young commentator, and had expressed doubts about whether I would make the grade.

In the season after the Hereford match, Brighton and Hove Albion played at home to Chelsea in the third round of the FA Cup, and London Weekend Television screened the highlights. Their regular commentator, Brian Moore – who also presented the Sunday afternoon *Big Match* programme in the London area – was taken ill at the last minute and Jimmy Hill, who was making waves as the first television football analyst, stepped in as emergency commentator.

Hill was a great innovator, as he proved when he introduced new ideas as manager of Coventry City, and a fierce competitor, as he showed when forcing the abolition of the maximum wage in his previous role as chairman of the Professional Footballers' Association. Later he would become a director of Charlton Athletic, chairman of Coventry and the best known of all the television football pundits.

As I found when I worked with him in the BBC commentary box, Jimmy enjoyed grabbing the microphone. But the roles of commentator and analyst are distinctly different, and need to be treated as such. My job is to identify the players, inject some excitement into the game if the occasion merits, and amplify what may be happening – what the Americans call 'play by play'. My co-commentator (the 'colour man', they would call it) is there to analyse specific incidents, especially over the replays, as well as comment about the performance of individual players and the two teams.

Brilliant though his analysis was, Jimmy's commentary at Brighton sounded exactly as you would expect – a rather jumbled stand-in job.

'Even John Motson sounds better than that,' Paul Fox said to Sam Leitch.

Many years later Fox wrote a vigorous column on television sport for the *Daily Telegraph* and was not particularly complimentary either to Jimmy or me, but although he had made no secret of the fact that he preferred Barry Davies's style, he mellowed towards me before he finally put down his pen.

A few months after his Brighton effort, Jimmy Hill left ITV to join BBC Sport in a highly publicised transfer. He came over to us not so much as an analyst, where he had made such an impact, but as a presenter. David Coleman was out of the picture temporarily. There were stories of a contract dispute, and rumours he had been offered a job in America. So Jimmy was the host on *Match of the Day* from the start of the 1973/74 season, although Coleman returned a few months later.

The BBC were still using the private plane to sweep the presenter to matches in the North, although Jimmy would sit in the stand and watch the game while I did the commentary. In January, we flew to Merseyside for a first-division match between Everton and Leeds United, who were gunning for the title under Don Revie.

It turned out to be an uneventful 0–0 draw, but our journey was anything but. The plane was buffeted from side to side by heavy winds as we flew across the Mersey, and by the time we landed at Speke Airport our stomachs were turning over.

Jimmy pulled me into the bar and ordered two port and lemons before we got in the car to go to the ground. Having recovered, I did the commentary and we had an uneventful flight back. In the studio that night, Jimmy introduced the programme by saying that he was still feeling queasy after a bumpy journey in a four-seater aircraft.

Unfortunately, this incident took place during an energy crisis, caused by another miners' strike, when petrol was at a premium. We even had coupons in case things got worse. Hundreds of viewers stormed the BBC duty office with complaints about our waste of petrol. Needless to say, producer Alec Weeks put a stop to the plane from then on.

The two things I found most difficult to contend with, as I tried to adapt from radio to television, both concerned the way the BBC Outside Broadcast producers, talented thought many of them were, went about their side of the job.

'Talkback', which Sam Leitch had warned me about, often consisted of the producer or his assistant talking to the cameramen, directions that went straight into my ear while I was desperately trying to concentrate on the game. I found this a persistent and irritating distraction. It was only when I assumed a more permanent role that I persuaded the producers to take their 'dirty talkback' out of my ear, and speak directly to me only when necessary by pressing a button. This is called 'switch talkback'.

Having worked in a one-dimensional medium like radio, I often felt there were two ends playing against the middle when it came to television sport. The Outside Broadcast directors seemed concerned only with the delivery and quality of their pictures, which was largely understandable considering that this was, after all, television.

But for the commentator or reporter trying to get his story across, the technical requirements far too often outweighed the editorial message he was trying to convey. I developed a reputation for being irritable and impatient with some of the people I worked with. But I held the view, and still do, that the commentator is the last man on the line with no safety net. If his concentration is allowed to slip for any reason, he is the one left with egg on his face, and the output suffers accordingly. Having said that, I was fiercely self-critical and demanded of other people only the standards I had set for myself.

I got a lot of help from the Arsenal goalkeeper, Bob Wilson, who put together a number of feature items and voiced them himself while still a player. He also had one of the first VHS video recorders I had seen. Many was the afternoon I spent at Bob's home in Brookmans Park watching my commentary from the previous weekend and asking for his comments.

I was anxious to find out more about how professionals viewed the game, and to that end I enrolled on the Football Association's preliminary coaching badge course at Lilleshall in 1973. I passed my 'prelim', which was really a commonsense examination on the basics of the game, such as passing, shooting and general team play. We each had to demonstrate to our group the techniques involved, and I was proud to be one of only three out of thirty students on the course to gain my certificate.

It was a different story, however, when I attempted the 'full badge' at Durham two years later. Here, the demands were far more functional, and trying to work out where players should be on the pitch and how to get them there proved to be beyond me. In some ways that might have been a blessing in disguise. There was never any danger of my commentaries becoming too technical!

Those courses, and the hours spent in the Wilson living room while Bob's wife, Megs, served endless cups of tea, proved useful to me in learning just enough not to make sweeping judgements that would alienate the professionals.

It was clear to me at the outset that the television commentator treads a very thin line. You have to talk less than on radio, but when you do speak, you need to add to the picture without sounding as though you are telling the player what he should have done. Achieving that balance was one of my first big tests.

When Bob Wilson retired through injury in 1974, he was immediately employed by the BBC on a full-time basis. Sam Leitch was finding fronting the *Football Preview* too demanding alongside his main editorial and negotiating role. So it was decided to put Bob in front of the camera on a Saturday lunchtime.

We had a meeting when he first arrived and it was decided to give the programme a remake with a new title. I can modestly take the credit for coming up with *Football Focus*, a name that has stuck for well over thirty years!

At the end of my 'attachment', word came through from the BBC Personnel Department that I was to be offered a contract. From memory I think it was for three years at approximately five thousand pounds a year.

But if I had passed my examination as far as football was concerned, there were two other big obstacles to overcome in that summer of 1972.

First, Harry Carpenter was unavailable to commentate on a European featherweight title fight in Birmingham between Tommy Glencross and Jose Legra. I had had a stab at boxing commentary on radio but wasn't at all sure that I was sufficiently briefed on the fight game to go fifteen rounds on live television.

I felt I just about got away with it – Legra won on points thanks to a flash finish – although Bryan Cowgill said to Sam Leitch, 'I think you have found a boxing commentator, Sam.' I would stand in again from time to time on radio and television, and as a reporter I was regularly at ringside at Wembley and the Royal Albert Hall.

Whitewater canoeing though, was something else. That was the sport I was assigned to cover at Augsburg, just outside Munich, at the Olympic Games in 1972. All I can remember about it is sitting in a cabin with the British team, poring over a map of the course and trying to master the order and significance of the various obstacles.

Unfortunately, or perhaps fortunately in my case, they never looked like winning any medals. In fact, one competitor ended up in the water, upside down with his kayak on his head.

'I don't want to be pessimistic, but I think British hopes of a medal are fading fast,' was the only thing I could say. It got a few laughs on the after-dinner speaking circuit though!

As if that wasn't enough to keep me concentrating on football, four years later in Montreal I was sent to cover Greco-Roman wrestling. The only wrestling I had ever seen was Jackie Pallo at the Ritz Cinema in Potters Bar, but this was serious stuff. There was a range of gold medals at stake in the various weight categories.

I made a beeline for David Vine, the BBC's most versatile sports commentator, although Alan Weeks, who shared an office with Peter Lorenzo and myself, ran him mighty close. Vine gave me a thick volume covering the rules of Greco-Roman wrestling and told me to study it as closely as I could. It was a good job he did, because when I got to Canada it became clear that the Greco-Roman wrestling hall would be my home for the opening six mornings of competition.

For the first five I need not have bothered. Too many events were going on elsewhere for the BBC to worry about mine. On day six, though, my big moment arrived.

'There's been a big storm at the equestrian centre,' said the producer's voice in my ear. 'We have nothing else to go to. You are live in three minutes.'

At that moment a Soviet and a Bulgarian wrestler were wiping their hands ready to do battle down in the ring. As Frank Bough handed over to me, I must have blurted out all I had been preparing about the rules of the sport in the first thirty seconds. Once the bout started, though, I grew in confidence. I had learnt a lot of the moves and holds from the David Vine manual, and I was able to keep quite a close track on the score.

Sitting close to me, thank goodness, was John Goodbody, a newspaper journalist whom I had met at college and who had an expert knowledge of judo, karate and this range of sports. Come the end of the contest the winner's name was announced, and I mentioned who his next opponent would be before handing back to the studio.

It was only then I realised I had got the two wrestlers the wrong way round. The Soviet competitor had been in a *blue* leotard and the Bulgarian in *red*.

I felt a sinking sensation when John Goodbody asked how it went.

'All right on the holds, I suppose, but John, you won't believe this, I think I've got the two guys completely mixed up.'

I shouldn't worry about it too much if I were you,' said Goodbody, smiling. 'Only three people back in Britain know anything at all about Greco-Roman wrestling, and two of them will be out training.'

Which is one of the main reasons why, from then on, I tried to stick to football. Doing the second match on a Saturday while David Coleman or Barry Davies had the lead game meant I was making some headway at getting to know people at some of the less fashionable clubs.

It seems strange, all these years later, to think that at that time, well into the eighties, the BBC were only allowed to show excerpts from two matches. Not even the goals from elsewhere were screened.

The contract with the Football League – BBC and ITV had negotiated a joint deal, which was often called a 'cartel', to keep the price down – also stipulated that fourteen games a season had to come from the second division, with seven of them the main feature on *Match of the Day*. Furthermore, we had to televise highlights from four games in divisions three or four, with two of those leading the programme.

It was through watching Grimsby Town in this period that I first got to know a giant of a man called Lawrie McMenemy.

'You'll get to know me better when I get to a bigger club, bonny lad,' was one of his opening salvos.

I told Bob Abrahams I thought the ex-guardsman was going places, so off we went to Grimsby for a *Football Preview* feature.

'Don't worry about a hotel, you can stay with me and my family in Cleethorpes,' said Lawrie.

We did, and there started a friendship that has lasted until today.

'He's going to be a natural on the telly,' said Bob as we made our way home clutching parcels of fresh fish that Lawrie had given us. 'I'll have a word with Sam.'

Actually, McMenemy was perfectly capable of selling himself. Within a year he had been appointed Southampton's manager on the retirement of Ted Bates; a year later he was on the BBC studio panel for the 1974 World Cup.

Another manager who gave me a lot of help at the start was Ron Saunders at Norwich City. As they won promotion to the first division and then reached the final of the Football League Cup, I made friends with him and several of his players. David Cross, the big centre forward who bettered himself at a number of clubs including West Ham, made me welcome at the team hotel, and I still have handwritten letters exchanged with some of the

Norwich players. Imagine a commentator getting a pen-and-ink offering from Wayne Rooney today!

And then there was Bobby Robson and Ipswich Town. Here I had something of an emotional attachment. During my days as a boarder at Culford School, my father and I made the journey from Bury St Edmunds to Portman Road each time I was allowed a Saturday afternoon out – roughly three times a term.

Alf Ramsey was manager then, taking Ipswich from the old Third Division South to the first-division championship in just five years. I would travel back to Culford, to seek out other football fans and regale them with stories about Ted Phillips, Ray Crawford and John Elsworthy. So when Bobby Robson took over and steered Ipswich back towards the top of the pile, I found myself getting a valuable insight every time I went there for *Match of the Day*.

'This is my home telephone number. Ring me any time. This club needs publicity,' was the end of our first conversation.

I didn't need asking twice, and was soon captivated by Robson's passion and enthusiasm for the game. Many was the time I sat in his office at Portman Road, listening to endless stories about his own career as a player and his burning ambition as a manager. When he wanted to portray the strength of his own players, he would get up out of his chair and demonstrate their technique, their style and sometimes their fallibility.

He also had a warm sense of humour. Just before a fixture against Leeds United one December, the club press officer, Mel Henderson, had persuaded Ipswich's giant defender, Kevin Beattie, to dress up as Santa Claus for a charity photo shoot. Beattie was a bit slow in getting changed, and when I saw Robson an hour before kick-off he exploded: 'I'm trying to give a team talk and I've got my centre half pretending he's bloody Father Christmas.'

That was typical of the Ipswich atmosphere at the time. They punched way above their weight in the old first division, always finishing in the top six, and were unlucky on two occasions not to win the championship.

But the homeliness and humility the club projected off the field were best exemplified by the two brothers who owned the club, Johnny and Patrick Cobbold. I just wish the young commentators of today, who have to try to tread a path towards billionaire chairmen and overseas investors, could have a time machine to enable them to meet these two old Etonian eccentrics.

Brian Scovell has written a book about the pair in which their irreverent humour comes through. It was an era before the breathalyser, and any journalist invited into their boardroom after a match knew it would be a shaky drive home. It was not unknown for Johnny Cobbold, the more extrovert of the two, to jump in his Jaguar and personally drive a sozzled reporter all the way back to London. Not that Johnny was sober himself!

Alan Parry, who came from Radio Merseyside to take a post in the BBC Radio Sports Department when I moved to *Match of the Day*, once came with me to Johnny's house at Trimley near Ipswich. The grounds extended as far as the human eye could see. 'Tell me, Mr John, how much of this do you actually own?' asked Alan. 'All of it, you c***.' was the reply.

On the sideboard there was a black-and-white photograph of a shooting party out on the moors before the war. One of the men with a gun was Johnny and Patrick's father, Captain Ivan Cobbold, who was responsible for turning Ipswich Town into a professional club.

'Who's that guy with your father?' I ventured.

'That's the king, you wanker,' said Johnny.

Even though they came from aristocratic stock, they were as down to earth as you could imagine. They loved their club, but they never had to make a decision – they left that to Bobby Robson. It proved a good idea, because the Cobbolds drank their way through Europe nine years out of ten.

My next decision was a bad one. Just before the All England Championship at Wimbledon in 1973 there was a professional boycott, and two of the main BBC commentators, Jack Kramer and Donald Dell, had to withdraw because of their association with the striking players.

I was pressed into service for BBC Television and came off far worse than when I had attempted boxing, canoeing or wrestling. I was later to return to Wimbledon as a radio commentator, but as a budding Dan Maskell they picked the wrong man.

My first World Cup was now a year away and two things were uppermost in my mind. Would I not be better sticking exclusively to football, and how was I to progress up the ladder and make a significant challenge to David Coleman and Barry Davies?

Chapter 6

The Battle with Barry

Who's doing the Cup Final this year?

O N A SPRING day in 1991, I found myself sitting alone in my car in Regent's Park. It was the year that Paul Gascoigne was almost single-handedly steering Tottenham towards the FA Cup final at Wembley, and I was anxious to know whether I would be doing the commentary. Even though I had been selected for the previous ten, it never made the waiting any easier. When it came to commentating on the FA Cup final, there were no guarantees.

It was BBC policy to keep Barry Davies and myself on tenterhooks until the decision was announced. It caused plenty of speculation within the Sports Department, not to mention a nagging uncertainty in our household, and probably chez Davies too.

That day in the park I was getting frustrated. We were already past the sixth-round stage of the competition and the final was barely eight weeks away. I rang the Head of Sport, Jonathan Martin, and asked him outright. 'Who is doing the Cup Final?'

'Haven't decided yet,' he replied tartly. 'I've got two very capable commentators and there are also the live semi-finals to consider.'

In previous years, when the BBC screened the highlights of one semi-final and neither was shown live, the package of semi-final and final went together. I usually did both. But under the FA contract, from 1990 both semi-finals were shown live on the BBC. In the first season, they produced thirteen goals; Crystal Palace beat Liverpool 4–3 in a thriller at Villa Park, and a few hours later Manchester United and Oldham Athletic drew 3–3 at Maine Road.

Finally, Jonathan made his decision. Barry was given the more appealing of the two semi-finals – the North London collision between Arsenal and Tottenham at Wembley. I would go to Villa Park and cover Nottingham Forest against West Ham – and, I was relieved to hear, would keep the final.

The competition between Barry and myself, both for the Cup Final and the big international games, went far wider than the three-year period covered in the first chapter. It started soon after I joined the department in 1971, and did not finish until Barry completed his last major tournament – the European Championship of 2004.

The first time it came to public prominence was in 1977. For the second time since I joined, David Coleman dropped out of the BBC scene for a few months, which meant he would not be the commentator on the FA Cup final between Liverpool and Manchester United.

At that stage, I had never been entrusted with a live match. I was on the team for the 1974 World Cup, but only doing highlights. It was only two years later that I was given a Wednesday night extended highlights match for *Sportsnight* – Manchester City's UEFA Cup tie against Juventus.

So, once Coleman's absence was confirmed, Sam Leitch had what seemed a straightforward decision to make. Barry had been in the department two years longer than me, he was eight years older, more experienced and a more versatile broadcaster. He had also frequently stood in for Coleman in the *Match of the Day* presenter's seat.

Barry made his name as a football commentator while working for ITV in the 1966 World Cup. He was commentating when North Korea beat Italy in that famous match at Ayresome Park, and was able to identify their players without referring to their shirt numbers. So when *Match of the Day* adopted a two-match format in 1969, Bryan Cowgill decided to sign Barry from Granada Television in the North.

I first caught sight of him at Vienna airport the following year. He was covering the European Cup Winners' Cup final between Manchester City and Gornik. I was doing reports and interviews for Radio Two. We didn't get introduced properly for over a year. I was coming back on a train from the Watney Cup final, a short-lived tournament that ran for four seasons in the early 1970s, in which Colchester had beaten West Brom on penalties after a 4–4 draw. There, in the same compartment, I spotted a familiar face.

'I hear you are coming to join us,' said Barry.

He made some telling points about the differences between television and radio – he had done a few months' work experience in Radio Two prior to getting his break in TV – and struck me as confident in his ability and quite ambitious to compete for the top games with David Coleman.

Barry did the commentary when Poland ended England's World Cup hopes in 1973. It was generally agreed to be one of his best. I was downstairs doing the interviews, asking Alf Ramsey whether he was going to resign,

'I've no idea. What else would I do? Would you walk away from this job?' is how Ramsey somewhat ambiguously ended the interview.

'I'm not sure if that means John Motson is a candidate for the England job or not,' joked Jimmy Hill when I handed back to the studio.

In my first six years the pecking order was clearly established. David Coleman was the undisputed number one – both as presenter and commentator – Davies was next in line, and I was trying to improve after my shaky start, but still firmly in third place.

The first crack in the wall was evident in the summer of 1976 when I was selected to go to the European Championship finals in the then Yugoslavia. England, under Don Revie, had been knocked out in the group stage by Czechoslovakia, who were one of only four teams in the finals. Maybe my view is coloured by the fact that it was my first European Championship, but I still believe it was the finest football I ever saw, witnessed by very few Englishmen.

The Czechs had already shown in beating England the previous year that they had a side with flair and vitality. Any thoughts that this tournament would produce a repeat of the West Germany–Holland World Cup final of two years earlier were laid to rest when Czechoslovakia defeated the Dutch 3–1 in the first semi-final.

It was a fiercely contested encounter played at a furious pace, but the quality of the football stood out. Welsh referee Clive Thomas, never one to shirk controversy, sent off three players, and even though the game went into extra time, Czechoslovakia were worthy winners.

But the drama of this game was nothing compared to the semi-final I covered for the BBC the following day in Belgrade. Although the match between hosts Yugoslavia and the World Cup holders West Germany was billed as recorded highlights, the game was shown almost immediately after the final whistle, and it was therefore the nearest I had yet come to doing a live match for television.

A dazzling first-half performance, inspired by their celebrated forward Dragan Dzajic, saw Yugoslavia establish a two-goal lead. Even Franz Beckenbauer, at the heart of the German defence, seemed unable to hold them back. But the Germans showed their fabled Teutonic tenacity in clawing their way back. Once it was Gerd Müller whose goals turned games; now it was his namesake Dieter, no relation, who came on as a second-half substitute and ripped apart the Yugoslav defence. The Germans came back to 2–2, and in extra time Müller completed a hat-trick to send them into the final.

On the final whistle, for the only time in my career, I slumped on to the front of the commentary box with my head in my hands. There was a good reason why I felt absolutely drained. Owing to the travel arrangements in getting from one semi-final to the other, I had not seen either team train. With video recordings of overseas teams few and far between in those days, the whole exercise had me terrified of making a mistake in what was the biggest assignment I had yet been given. Not that I had much time to catch my breath: it was back to Zagreb for the third-place match, in which Holland beat Yugoslavia 3–2 in another thriller which went to extra time.

The final in Belgrade was covered live by ITV, but as a spectator I had the pleasure of watching a game that surpassed even the previous three. Again, the Germans went two goals down. Svehlik and Dobias, who had both figured against England in the group stage, rocked the holders, only for Müller to pull a goal back before half-time. There was barely a minute left, with the Czechs still leading 2–1, when Holzenbein completed a recovery for which the Germans were now renowned, heading in a corner to force extra time.

As there was no further scoring, this became the first major final to be decided on penalty kicks. It was also the only shoot-out the Germans have ever lost. Uli Hoeness blazed one of their penalties over the bar, enabling Antonin Panenka to win the title with his famous disguised fading shot – for many people the only memory of what was for me an eye-opening football experience.

Most of all, I remember it for two reasons: the extraordinary influence Franz Beckenbauer exerted on both German matches from his position as sweeper, often moving forward to initiate attacks; and the fact that I was one of a mere handful of Englishmen present. I was lucky to be in the company of Jeff Powell, of the *Daily Mail*, and Frank Clough of the *Sun* – the only two print journalists to cover the tournament. Two home-based coaches, Ian McFarlane and John Docherty, were also present, but that was about it. I realised then how insular the outlook back home was, when England were not involved.

As it was, Don Revie then set about trying to qualify for the 1978 World Cup, and the pivotal match in England's group was their visit to Rome to play Italy in November 1976. I was sent along with David Coleman, ostensibly to do the interview with Revie at the end of the game. But this was the start of Coleman's second period of uncertainty at the BBC, and Jonathan Martin, who accompanied us on the trip, warned me that if David felt unable to handle the commentary, I would need to step in.

Coleman was fine, which was more than could be said for England. Revie picked a negative side which included Trevor Cherry as an extra defender, and succumbed to a press campaign to include Stan Bowles. Italy won comfortably 2–0, and England failed to qualify for the second successive World Cup.

Belgrade and Rome had convinced me that I was now farther up in Sam Leitch's thoughts. Even so, when he called me in to tell me I would be doing the 1977 FA Cup final, it still came as a major surprise. It sent most of the department into shock as I was still short of my thirty-second birthday, had only been with *Match of the Day* for less than six years, and had never done a live game.

Barry made no attempt to hide his disappointment. To be honest he was pretty devastated, and I could understand why. He, like many others, had seen himself as the natural replacement – successor even – to David Coleman. It didn't take long for the newspapers to spot a story. One of them solemnly reported that Barry would be going on holiday – 'unheard of for a football commentator during the season', said an editorial. In fact, when the dust settled, he was given the considerable consolation prize of the European Cup Final, in which Liverpool would play Borussia Mönchengladbach in Rome.

Meanwhile, I had to try to ignore all the media speculation and concentrate instead on the semi-final between Liverpool and Everton at Maine Road. I knew my performance would be closely scrutinised as the final was only a month away.

I had already covered a couple of Merseyside derbies in the old first division, so I knew something about the rivalry between the two clubs. I had also experienced standing on the Kop at Anfield as a teenager. I met a group of lads from Liverpool on holiday in the early sixties, and visited them on three occasions in the 1964/65 season when Bill Shankly's team were defending champions. The intensity of the support for Liverpool which cascaded down from that famous terrace was something I would never forget. It was a mass of humanity with one voice.

Not that Everton supporters were any less passionate. After all, they had been champions under Harry Catterick in 1963 and regained the title in 1970, with an FA Cup success in between. But by the time the clubs met in that 1977 semi-final, Liverpool had established themselves as top dogs on Merseyside. They were not just gunning for Everton, but had their sights set on an unprecedented treble of league, FA Cup and European Cup.

My first FA Cup semi-final ebbed and flowed the way a commentator would want. Terry McDermott and Jimmy Case each put Liverpool in front; Duncan McKenzie and then Bruce Rioch pulled Everton level. With three minutes to go and the score 2–2, Everton winger Ronnie Goodlass crossed for Bryan Hamilton to steer the ball past Ray Clemence for what everybody – including the Liverpool players – thought was the winning goal.

This was where the absence of any replay facility made me realise how the commentator was living on a knife-edge. Referee Clive Thomas, who in terms of profile could reasonably be described as the Graham Poll of his day, controversially disallowed the goal. I never heard him reveal why.

Nowadays I would have three or four replays from different angles to come up with an explanation. Back then, I had to make an instinctive decision on what I had just seen. My first reaction was offside, because Hamilton was standing alongside or just ahead of Liverpool's Joey Jones when the ball was crossed. Others were convinced that Thomas had mistakenly given handball. The ball actually went in off Hamilton's hip.

Everton supporters argue about it until this day, but my commentary was accepted without criticism. The replay a few days later was won 3–0 by Liverpool and passed without incident.

In order to keep me in touch with the club, *Sportsnight* sent John Rowlinson and me to Merseyside for a few days to film part of the build-up to Liverpool's FA Cup final. We were given decent access at Anfield, one of the highlights being a scene in the car park where a supporter trying to buy tickets blocked in Tommy Smith's car. 'Do you mind, mate, I work here,' complained Smith in his thick Scouse accent. He then re-enacted the incident in the Liverpool dressing room with our camera still rolling.

We also went to see Eddie Braben, the brilliant scriptwriter who was the inspiration behind Morecambe and Wise. He took us to his local pub, where we filmed him with some of the regulars.

'Who do you think will win, Eddie?' one piped up.

'It will be three each. Toshack three, Keegan three and Case three,' was the reply.

John Rowlinson asked Eddie whether he went to all the games at Anfield, even if Liverpool weren't playing well.

'Oh no,' he said, 'Bob Paisley doesn't come to see me when I'm poorly.'

The nearer the FA Cup final got, the more of an ordeal it seemed. Not only was it my first live game, it was one of only two or three out of the whole season that both BBC and ITV televised in those days, and on the day the performance of each channel was analysed down to the smallest detail.

Having spent some time with Liverpool, I knew I would need to familiarise myself with their opponents. Manchester United were staying at the Selsdon Park Hotel in Croydon. After losing to Southampton the year before, they had moved from the Sopwell House at St Albans.

Tommy Docherty could not have been kinder. He rattled off his team line-up from one to eleven in that clipped, rasping Scottish voice, which made him one of the most recognisable personalities of his day. His regular left back, Stewart Houston, had broken his leg, so young Arthur Albiston was to deputise.

After a sleepless night I arrived at the television compound at Wembley not really knowing what to expect. *Cup Final Grandstand* was on the air already, with others doing the job I was given in previous years, of interviewing the teams at their hotel and on the coach en route to the stadium.

Julie Welch – one of the first women football writers to break into a male domain – was doing a background piece for the *Observer*. She remarked on how cool and unperturbed I seemed. Little did she know how I felt underneath. Bob Wilson, who had experienced a few Wembley nerves himself as an Arsenal player, walked me round the gantry and the compound a few times to keep me focused. *Grandstand* let me join the panel voting 'Goal of the Season', because I had commentated on Terry McDermott's exquisite chip over Everton goalkeeper David Lawson in that semi-final.

When the game started I felt very much the same as I did on my television debut – hesitant, inhibited and worried about saying something that would be seized upon and ridiculed. Fortunately half-time arrived without incident and with no score.

John Toshack, the Liverpool forward who was injured and sitting in the BBC studio just a few yards away, kindly referred to my closing remarks. I said it was 0–0 when Liverpool had played Newcastle in the final three years earlier, but all the excitement had come in the second half.

Well, it certainly did this time, and with mixed results for me. Stuart Pearson gave United the lead with a shot inside Ray Clemence's near post. An easy goal to call. Then, barely two minutes later, I reminded the audience of an old adage: *'There's a saying in football that Liverpool are at their most dangerous when they're behind.'* Right on cue Jimmy Case crashed Joey Jones' cross past Alex Stepney for the equaliser.

Any satisfaction that gave me was wiped out three minutes later by one of the strangest ever Cup Final goals. Tommy Smith was robbed by Jimmy Greenhoff on the edge of the Liverpool penalty area. The ball ran on to Lou Macari, whose shot was going wide of the post until it deflected off Greenhoff's chest and looped into the net.

Easy to say that now. At the time I was unsure what had happened. *'Macari, was it?'* I shouted uncertainly, but Jimmy Hill, next to me in the commentary box, came to the rescue. 'Watch the replay,' he mouthed, 'I think it's Greenhoff.'

It was a brilliant spot by Jimmy. Because we were live we had the replay machine to show us the incident again in slow motion, and I was able to identify the deflection and award the goal to Greenhoff: *'Tommy Smith got himself into a bit of a tangle with Jimmy Greenhoff. He seemed to have got the ball away but he hadn't and Macari, possibly off Greenhoff in the end. Macari had the shot but it probably deflected off his own player. Anyway it's in the net.'*

I got through the rest of the match relatively unscathed, and enjoyed my first opportunity to commentate on the closing scenes and the presentation of the trophy. I suddenly remembered something I had read in a magazine a week earlier – that there were thirty-nine steps from the pitch to the Royal Box at Wembley. The link with the Manchester United captain and his namesake John was one not to miss. *'How fitting,'* I said, *'that a man named Buchan should be the first to climb the thirty-nine steps that lead from the pitch to the Royal Box.'* Whenever I see Martin Buchan now, he always says, 'Remember me? I'm Buchan who climbed the thirty-nine steps.'

Looking back now, it was not a great final by any means. Maybe Liverpool had their minds on their European Cup final in Rome the following Wednesday, but I got the feeling that, on the day, Manchester United wanted it that little bit more. After losing to Southampton the year before, their elation at winning was understandable. Tommy Docherty cavorting with the lid of the FA Cup on his head remains a memorable image.

As for my own performance, my first Cup Final commentary was received with a deathly silence. I remember sitting at home all weekend hoping somebody would ring and tell me I had at least not let the BBC down. But nobody did, not even Sam Leitch. I wondered whether he was regretting his decision not to give the Cup Final to Barry Davies.

A year later David Coleman was back in his usual seat, and the battle between Motson and Davies was on the back burner. I did the Ipswich Town interviews at their hotel on the morning of the 1978 final, and watched Allan Hunter and Kevin Beattie take fitness tests on the lawn. With my Suffolk connections I was pleased to see them win.

It was Barry's job that day to do the interviews afterwards and mine to grab various managers and players as they left the pitch, and take them to the interview room down the tunnel (cameras were not allowed on the pitch in those days). It was a job that wasn't without its hazards. Two years earlier, when Southampton won the cup, I was walking down the tunnel with Lawrie McMenemy when someone threw a can and knocked my glasses off the end of my nose. Lawrie stopped, put down the FA Cup he was carrying, picked up my glasses, replaced them and then carried the trophy into the interview room.

In 1978, Lawrie was part of the BBC team for the World Cup finals in Argentina along with Coleman, Davies and myself. This time I was given plenty of live action. If I was to single out my most scary moment as a television commentator, it would be in the River Plate stadium in Buenos Aires when Argentina came out for their opening match against Hungary.

Remember, this World Cup was played in a highly charged political atmosphere, with the country under the ruthless control of General Jorge Videla and his military junta. Security was intense, and any attempt to get near the Argentinian camp was resisted. Bob Abrahams and I somehow managed to get permission to interview the Argentine midfield player Osvaldo Ardiles, little knowing how he would figure in our lives in the future. But even so, we were not allowed to watch Cesar Menotti's team training.

Ron Greenwood, who had taken over from Don Revie as England manager, was my co-commentator for the match, and we had a double shock before a ball was kicked. Our commentary position was low in the stadium, a long way from the pitch and behind glass – something I have always hated. Worse still, not only had I not been able to see the team train, but the numbers on the Argentine blue and white striped shirts were virtually indecipherable.

How we got through that night I'll never know, but if survival is the name of the game as a live commentator, then I moved on and did well enough to be selected for two key matches – the game in the second group phase in which Holland beat Italy to reach their second successive final; then the third-place match between Brazil and Italy. That was memorable for an amazing goal by the Brazilian right back Nelinho, who swerved the ball over Dino Zoff from almost out on the touchline.

My first experience of a World Cup in South America had been a vivid and challenging one. Buenos Aires was a vibrant city despite the military rule, and provincial venues like Córdoba, Mendoza, Mar del Plata and Rosario all embraced the competition with a fervour that transmitted itself to a young broadcaster still feeling his way. The fact that England were not there, and Scotland flopped so badly, did not detract from my enjoyment. Not when there were players to watch like Kempes, Luque and Ardiles of Argentina; Zico and Dirceu of Brazil; Bettega and a young Paolo Rossi of Italy; Neeskens and Haan of Holland.

I was also pleased with the matches I was allocated. Although my first FA Cup final the year before had not brought any bouquets, I felt I grew up as a commentator in the 1978 World Cup and was pleased when columnist Norman Giller, in the *London Evening News*, pinpointed my performance as that of a leading commentator for the future.

Although all this suggested I had edged ahead of Barry again, I was still astounded by a conversation with the new Head of Sport, Alan Hart, as I sat on a sofa in the foyer of the El Dorado Hotel in Buenos Aires.

'Just want to tell you that David will be doing the final,' said Alan. 'There wasn't much in it, but he has the experience, and there will be many finals ahead for you in the years to come.'

It had never occurred to me that there was the slightest possibility of my being considered in preference to Coleman. But it made me feel that I had had a good World Cup, and Alan's words were a big boost to my confidence.

*   *   *

A year later, David Coleman decided to go back inside and take over the studio presentation of *Grandstand*. Which meant he was leaving the field open again, and Hart decided I should do the FA Cup final between Arsenal and Manchester United.

Again, my performance could have been better. Producer Alec Weeks and I got our lines crossed in the build-up, and I had another messy goal to deal with when Brian Talbot and Alan Sunderland seemed to arrive at the same moment to stab in Arsenal's first goal.

To be honest, it was another mundane final until a crazy last five minutes in which United came from 2–0 down to 2–2, only to concede a last-minute goal by Alan Sunderland. I made the most of Liam Brady's cultured first-half performance, in which he figured in Arsenal's two goals, and of United's recovery, when Gordon McQueen and Sammy McIlroy momentarily turned the match on its head. But I squirm a bit when I hear my commentary on Arsenal's winner. It happened so quickly after United's equaliser that I never gave Graham Rix credit for the cross, which led to Alan Sunderland's dramatic, last-minute lunge at the far post.

The jury was still out on me as the Cup Final commentator. That summer, when I went on tour with England to Bulgaria, Sweden and Austria, I was still conscious of not having got anywhere near proving myself as a worthy successor to the likes of Kenneth Wolstenholme and David Coleman. Bearing in mind I was still in my early thirties, perhaps that was not surprising. Maybe I was expecting too much of myself, or else too conscious of the questions others were asking about me. Commentator's insecurity, I suppose.

The following March I came face to face with Alan Hart in the BBC box at Cheltenham racecourse. He must have known I was worried because he took me to one side and said quietly, 'Just to let you know you will be doing the Cup Final.' It set the trend for all those late decisions in subsequent years.

When most of them went my way Barry became more disgruntled, although he never took it out on me and his manner towards me was always dignified. We were, after all, two completely different animals. Jonathan Martin once said, 'Barry commentates from the grandstand, John is talking from the terraces.'

Our two different approaches were no bad thing for the programme when *Match of the Day* televised highlights of two games every Saturday. Barry's style was more restrained, more considered, his words more selective; I was more exuberant by comparison, and I was getting a reputation for using too many statistics.

As time passed, and maybe because the football vote went my way so often, Barry chose to diversify into other sports. No commentator has turned his hand so competently to so many. I'll always remember one of our most friendly and talented producers, Fred Viner, who worked with both of us, expressing surprise at how many things Barry was keen to try.

'The only one I wouldn't want to attempt is golf,' Barry told Fred.

Viner, who had a dry, waspish sense of humour, replied, 'Why stop at golf, Barry?'

Right up to the summer of 2008 Davies was still a member of the commentary team at Wimbledon and, at the age of seventy, worked at the Olympic Games in Beijing.

In the meantime, I had gone completely the other way. Having cut my teeth on some tennis and boxing in both radio and television, I saw the way the football season was expanding and decided I wanted to be a specialist commentator in that field. Trying to cover my favourite sport thoroughly for eleven months a year, before racing home from a World Cup or European Championship to work for a fortnight at Wimbledon, was something I had attempted in the late seventies and early eighties. I decided then it was not for me.

One reason was that I saw myself as a football fan as well as a commentator. I wanted to be at matches two or three times a week, even when I wasn't working, and even today I would rather go to a game than settle for the settee. These days, young commentators can watch live football seven nights a week without leaving the house. Back then, to see a match relevant to my next commentary, I often made a 400-mile round trip on a Tuesday or Wednesday night.

Not that I found it a chore. My passion for the game, instilled all those years earlier by my father, never wavered. Friends who said I was so lucky to be paid for my hobby were not far wrong. It was by making the effort to go to matches, not always in the first division, that I got to know managers, players and club officials who became close contacts over many years. Getting their telephone numbers became something of a mission. As Brian Clough once said, I didn't want the day to come when I couldn't get a ticket!

In total, Barry and I worked together at eight World Cups (he did two before me and I did one after he moved away from football) and six European Championships (again he did one before I started, and I was present at two he missed). We also alternated for many years on England games. Bearing in mind I totted up around 150 of these, Barry must have been close on a century himself.

As we shall see, we also shared the tragic side of football in the dark days of the eighties. He had to deal with the horror of Heysel; I was in the commentary box at Hillsborough. To deal with unfolding events such as these, you need to be a decent broadcaster as well as a commentator. I would like to think we both were.

PART II

'And still Ricky Villa . . .'

Chapter 7

A Ticket to Ride with England, Part One

A dozen times to the wishing well

I N JUNE 1977, when the nation was celebrating Her Majesty the Queen's Silver Jubilee, I was in South America for the first time, having been sent on my first England tour as a BBC commentator. I was not to know it then, but it was the start of a great adventure. Over the next thirty years, I would be at the microphone for over 150 England games in World Cups, European Championships and friendlies, covering the national team for the BBC in nearly fifty countries.

I would also work alongside fourteen different managers – three of them only in temporary charge – but when we flew out to Brazil for the start of that 1977 tour, the man in charge was not with the party. Don Revie, who had succeeded Alf Ramsey three years earlier, was allegedly in Finland watching England's main group opponents, Italy, as they tried to qualify for the 1978 World Cup. England had already lost in Rome, but the

Italians were due at Wembley for the return in the autumn.

Little did we know, as we stood on the steps outside Rio airport for the first press conference of the tour, that Revie was nowhere near Finland. What transpired later was that he had slipped off in disguise to the United Arab Emirates to secure a four-year deal as coach there at £60,000 a year, plus bonuses. Dick Wragg, the chairman of the Football Association International Committee, was also in the dark as to Revie's real whereabouts when he addressed the assembled press corps on the pavement outside the arrivals lounge. 'What I want to say to you guys is let's get off the back of Don Revie,' said Wragg in his broad Yorkshire accent. 'It's time you were fair to him. He is doing a decent job for us.'

That was debatable. England had failed to qualify for the final stages of the 1976 European Championships – Revie's first target – and the defeat in Rome had put their World Cup hopes in jeopardy. Before leaving for South America they had lost twice in five days at Wembley to Wales and Scotland.

The three-match tour was to take in friendlies against Brazil, Argentina and Uruguay. In Revie's absence, his assistant Les Cocker was to take charge for the first game. It was my first long-haul trip as a broadcaster, and sleeping on the plane had proved difficult. Revie had arranged a contract for the FA with kit manufacturer Admiral, and throughout the flight their representative sat in front of me, his seat pushed firmly back in my chest. Wasn't travelling with the England team supposed to be glamorous?

When we got to our hotel the English journalists were greeted by Jose Werneck, one of our Brazilian counterparts, who was married to an English girl. He said he would arrange a trip to the Brazilian training camp the following day. I have never been able to sleep off jet lag until day turns to night, so that afternoon I found myself running along Copacabana Beach, where so many young Brazilian footballers perfected their skills. My companion was Steve Coppell, at twenty-one an uncapped member of the England party.

I had got to know Coppell over the course of the last two FA Cup finals. When he joined Manchester United from Tranmere Rovers he was still studying at Liverpool University. He played at Wembley when United lost to Southampton in 1976, and collected a winner's medal when they beat Liverpool in my first final as commentator, a year later.

That game was followed by the Home International Championship, in which I was chosen to commentate on England's matches against Northern Ireland in Belfast, and Scotland at Wembley. The first was a scary experience. The troubles in Ulster were just starting in earnest, and soldiers paraded on the concourse of Windsor Park, where the match was played. Revie was flanked on the England bench by two security men.

Security of a different kind was needed at Wembley the following week, where Scotland's 2–1 victory prompted a wild display of euphoria by their supporters. *'The fans have climbed over the barriers,'* I reported from the commentary box. *'You are really divided between appreciating the delight of the Scottish fans but not happy to see the ground pulled apart like this. They've even knocked the goal down and broken the crossbar.'* It was quite an introduction to international football for a young commentator.

The BBC was due to cover only the match against Argentina on the tour that followed, so I had a watching brief for the opening game in Rio. Seeing the Maracana Stadium for the first time was something I had really been looking forward to, but it came as something of an anticlimax. It looked shabby and dilapidated, a poor legacy of the spanking new stadium in which 200,000 people had seen Uruguay snatch the World Cup from Brazil in 1950. Neither was the match one to remember. Brazil and England played out an uneventful 0–0 draw. It would be another seven years before John Barnes left his indelible footprint on the pitch at the Maracana when he ran through the entire Brazilian team to score one of England's best ever goals.

As we prepared to leave Rio for Buenos Aires, I thought I was starting to see the world as a football reporter. Unfortunately it was then that I committed my first faux pas as an England camp follower. The run with Coppell had left my training shoes caked in sand, and to avoid soiling the clothes in my suitcase I asked Norman Medhurst, one of the England medical team whom I knew well from Chelsea, whether he would mind packing them in one of the huge skips carrying the team kit.

Norman was happy to oblige, but when we reached Argentina I received a severe reprimand from Les Cocker, who said my request was completely out of order, and it was not England's job to transport my running gear. Cocker was no longer in charge of the team because Revie had returned to the England camp, but I was about to learn an even tougher lesson – just how different and difficult it can be for a football commentator working abroad.

The main stadium in Buenos Aires – River Plate – was being renovated for the World Cup finals the following year, so England's friendly was scheduled for the Boca Juniors ground in the rough area of the city that spawned, among others, Diego Maradona.

The stadium was nicknamed *La Bombonera*, meaning the 'chocolate box'. When I went to inspect our commentary position I saw what that meant. The pitch was hemmed in on all four sides, with the written press well positioned at the front of one stand, close to the touchline. My commentary box was on the other side of the ground, high up at the back of the stand and behind glass. It was, to say the least, a testing position from which to make my live debut as an international commentator.

Stuart Pearson's early goal for England was answered by a curling free kick from Daniel Bertoni. With eight minutes to go the game seemed to be drifting into a 1–1 draw. Then, in an incident on the far side of the field from me, Trevor Cherry tackled Bertoni from behind. *'The linesman saw something on the far side there. There was a bit of an altercation which involved Trevor Cherry, I feel.'* I could not see clearly what happened next, and the small black-and-white monitor in the commentary box was not much help. Argentina did not embrace colour television until the World Cup the following year.

My eyes were firmly on the pitch, where there was a lot of scuffling and confusion between the players around the referee and the linesman. When I saw the referee show a red card to the disbelieving Cherry, I knew I had a story. *'And the referee is showing the red card!'* I exclaimed. An England player had been sent off – only the third time this had happened in their international history.

Then Sam Leitch, watching in London, came across the line and shouted, 'The Argentine number seven has gone off too.' I managed to piece together the fact that Bertoni had punched Cherry in the mouth, and the referee had dismissed both players. *'It looks like the Argentinians are down to ten men . . . Cherry is being led off and they've both been sent off! A fist was raised and the referee has sent both players off.'* As Cherry made his way round the touchline to his dressing room, the local fans made their opinions more than clear. *'Cherry is still walking around the pitch in front of a very hostile crowd . . . they're throwing missiles from behind the barriers . . . he looks to be holding his head.'* It was not an auspicious end to my first overseas broadcast, but I made a mental note of the name Bertoni, and it proved useful the following year.

What I remember most about that early trip was how easy it was to mix freely with the players. I spent the following morning in the hotel bar with Mike Channon discussing Revie's team selection in a frank, relaxed fashion. There was total trust between the players and the media in those days. Now I would be lucky to get a nod of recognition from some of them.

The tour ended with another draw, this time 0–0 with Uruguay in Montevideo. It was good to see the Centenario Stadium, where the first World Cup final was played in 1930, but as in the Maracana, the match petered out in a 0–0 stalemate. All I remember about it was Steve Coppell telling me that Don Revie had promised to put him on as a substitute for his first cap. Coppell had excitedly rung home to tell his family, only to find he never got off the bench.

Don Revie's trip to the Middle East had still not been exposed, so when we got home he presented a short report on the tour to his FA International Committee. It was a few weeks later that Jeff Powell, in the *Daily Mail*, reported the shock news of his resignation. It was front-page headlines. 'The job is no longer worth the aggravation,' Revie said. 'Nearly everyone in the country seems to want me out, so I'm giving them what they want. I know people will accuse me of running away, and it sickens me that I can't finish the job of taking England to the World Cup.'

It was no secret that Revie had fallen foul of the FA's autocratic chairman, Sir Harold Thompson, who responded to the news of Revie's clandestine deal with the Arabs by threatening to sue him for breach of contract. In fact an FA hearing banned him from any involvement with domestic football for ten years, which was turned over on appeal in the High Court. That did not stop the judge from making some disparaging remarks about Revie.

So my first few months as an England commentator were scarcely memorable for the right reasons. Revie had been kind to me in my early days when he was at Leeds United, so I had no personal axe to grind. Ron Greenwood took over, but could not rescue England's bid to qualify, and so my first two World Cups took place without England being present.

I could say, somewhat cynically, that things did not get an awful lot better over the next thirty years. Although England missed out on only three of the next fifteen tournaments, I never saw them go farther than a semi-final.

Some of the reasons are obvious and have never changed. Even before the Hungarians came to Wembley in 1953 and showed how far England were behind in technique, tactics and teamwork, the Continentals had been catching up by virtue of importing British coaches and concentrating on movement with and without the ball. More significantly, they had now learned how to shoot.

Even before the war, when England did not deign to enter the World Cup, they lost friendlies in Spain, France, Hungary, Czechoslovakia and Austria. And in the period when football resumed, a generation that included Stanley Matthews, Tom Finney, Billy Wright and Wilf Mannion swept aside most of the opposition in friendlies, but stumbled in England's first World Cup in 1950.

After the Hungarians beat England 6–3 and 7–1 in the 1953/54 season, and Uruguay knocked them out of the 1954 World Cup in the quarter-finals, there was a cry for more and better coaching. Walter Winterbottom, England's first full-time manager from 1946, put structured coaching schemes in place which produced leading managers of the future such as Bill Nicholson, Malcolm Allison and Ron Greenwood.

Young players like Don Howe and Dave Sexton immersed themselves in courses that brought the English game a greater understanding of coaching methods and systems of play. But the first touch of the overseas player still seemed more assured, his intelligence in the heat of battle sharper, and his ability to spot a pass more astute. That was clearly illustrated even in the modern era when the likes of Dennis Bergkamp, Ossie Ardiles and Eric Cantona helped transform some of our top clubs.

As for the national team, Winterbottom's hands were tied. He was answerable to a selection committee, an outdated concept that survived until Alf Ramsey took over in 1963 and insisted on picking the team himself. Despite winning the World Cup in 1966, and rated unlucky not to defend it successfully four years later,

Ramsey was plagued by a club-versus-country conflict that has never gone away.

Certain club managers, then and since, were perfectly prepared to withdraw players from international squads with fictitious or exaggerated injuries. Self-interest prevailed. The demands of club football, especially today with the growth of the Champions League, have clouded what should be a simple truth. England and its football will be judged by their performance in major international tournaments, and priority should be given to the availability of their players. As Malcolm Allison once said: 'The England team does not belong to the clubs or the managers. It belongs to you and me.'

Even when the England manager *did* get his best team on the pitch – and that happened all too rarely – his players faced not just top-class opposition, but also an additional barrier – that of expectancy. I remember talking to Graham Taylor as England prepared for a vital World Cup qualifier against Norway in Oslo in 1993. His press conference that morning had been all about whether Paul Gascoigne was 'refuelling' in the right way. But Taylor had spotted a wider problem. 'These players may be earning big money and be self-important at their clubs,' he said, 'but they find it hard to cope with the pressure of playing for England. There are those who are not mentally strong enough.'

They certainly weren't in Oslo, where England lost 2–0 – a result that, in my view, did Taylor's hopes of qualifying for the 1994 World Cup more damage than the points dropped against Holland.

Now fast-forward to a private members' club in London's West End thirteen years later. Steve McClaren and his assistant Terry Venables were meeting a group of England players to discuss how they felt the 2008 European Championship campaign was going. Venables was there early, and I asked him whether these meetings with the players, held across the country, were proving fruitful.

'It gives us a chance to find out how they feel. I believe some are finding it hard to cope with the expectancy when they pull on the England shirt. They find it a massive step up from playing for their clubs,' he said.

By now, most of the England regulars were multimillionaires, but that doesn't buy mental toughness. The views of Taylor and Venables, though years apart, were echoed by Fabio Capello when he took over as England coach in 2008. Capello had been in the job only a few months and still had to play his first competitive game when he started talking about 'mental fragility'. 'My biggest problem is getting individuals to play for England like they do for their clubs,' Capello explained. 'There has been a lack of confidence, and it's my job to rebuild that. There's a lot of pressure playing for your country, and this has weighed down too heavily on some players.'

My own feeling is that an awful lot of this has to do with the way young professionals are brought up in this country. They are taken straight out of school, often with the most basic education, and, if they make it as professionals, they enter a totally protected and cosseted world. Most of the decisions other people make for themselves, a young footballer can leave to his family, his agent or his club. By and large all his needs are catered for. Every door is opened for him. Even at club level most of the decisions he makes on the pitch are in the company of players he knows well, and trains with every day. He can usually cope with what is expected of him, as the coach will have given him detailed instructions as to what to do and when to do it.

Now he is selected for a big England game. Days of build-up, training sessions and press conferences have made him realise that there is no hiding place. He may be up against opponents as good or better than him. Who has to make the big decisions then? The player – maybe for the first time in his career.

Revie tried to prepare his teams with huge dossiers on the opposition. But the average attention span of most professional footballers would suggest they would rather pick up a men's magazine or, these days, listen to their iPod. Revie even brought Elton John on one England trip to entertain the team the night before the game. 'You know Elton, John, don't you?' he said to me at the airport. I never knew whether the John applied to me or Elton!

Ron Greenwood's solution, when he took over from Revie, was to base his first selection on England's most successful club side – Liverpool. He picked seven of their players for his first international against Switzerland, and although too much ground had been lost under Revie for England to qualify for the 1978 World Cup in Argentina, Greenwood steered them through the next two tournaments.

Sadly the first of those, the European Championships in Italy in 1980, saw the first serious outbreak of what became known as the 'English disease' – hooliganism in overseas cities on a grotesque, frightening scale. When police had to use tear gas to quell a riot during England's opening match against Belgium in Turin, it marked the start of a grim decade.

Travelling abroad with England became a gruesome game for the troublemakers. Johnny Foreigner was their opponent, his towns and cities a ready-made target. The bile and frustrations of a disenfranchised section of society were taken out not just on their own kind, but on unsuspecting and well-mannered European citizens.

What should have been an enjoyable exercise, watching or reporting England abroad, became a game of hide-and-seek, trying to avoid the bars, restaurants, shops and hotels that were on the hooligans' hit list. Sometimes it was a relief to get into my seat at the stadium and concentrate on the football.

Although England failed to get past the group stage in that 1980 tournament, hopes were high that Greenwood's team, led by the attacking tandem of Kevin Keegan and his midfield room-mate Trevor Brooking, would prosper in the 1982 World Cup in Spain.

This was my first World Cup as the BBC's lead commentator, and I always remember the colourful scene at the San Mames Stadium in Bilbao when England came out for their first match against France. Sadly, I was unable to share it with the viewers because a BBC producer had decided to play in a recording of the team coaches arriving an hour earlier! Even in the early eighties, we were still learning how to be flexible with live television.

It was a good job we caught the kick-off, because Bryan Robson put England ahead in twenty-seven seconds – a then record for the World Cup finals. Even though Keegan and Brooking were both ruled out with injuries, Greenwood's team took maximum points in their group from France, Czechoslovakia and Kuwait.

But it was one of the other group matches between Kuwait and France which gave me another unique incident to deal with. France were leading 3–1 when Alain Giresse had the ball in the net for what they thought was their fourth goal: *'Platini. And offside here, oh no, he's not. It's Alain Giresse and that one counts. Kuwait are appealing but the goal stands and Giresse makes it 4–1.'* A whistle had been blown from the crowd and the Kuwait defenders had stopped. When the referee, Miroslav Stupar of the Soviet Union, gave a goal, Kuwait's general manager, Sheikh al-Sabah, came down to the pitch and ordered his team off. *'Anarchy here of a sort,'* I commentated. *'A World Cup team refuses to resume . . . the general manager of the Kuwait team has come down. The head of the delegation is there in full regalia and the police are being called in to get people away from the pitch . . . the situation here is completely out of control.'*

Now the referee decided to disallow the goal and restart the game with a dropped ball. So then the French team refused to continue until their manager, Michel Hidalgo, persuaded them to accept the decision: *'Now the French won't play . . . The best thing the French can do is get on with the game and make sure they win it and I feel that's what Genghini is saying. Number nine Genghini has clearly said, "We may as well go through with it and just finish the match and make sure we don't concede two goals." What an extraordinary scene here.'* They later added a fourth goal anyway, but I was grateful for the assistance of my producer in the commentary box, Jimmy Dumighan, who was convinced he heard the 'phantom whistler' above the noise of the crowd.

England, meantime, were through to the second group stage and facing a three-cornered contest with West Germany and hosts Spain. The big question was – would Keegan and Brooking be fit?

Keegan had secretly driven through the night in a borrowed car from the England hotel in Bilbao, to Madrid, where he caught a flight to Hamburg and received treatment on his back injury from the German specialist he had always trusted. Brooking needed a deep-seated cortisone injection in his troublesome groin, and the FA flew out the West Ham surgeon, Brian Roper, who had treated the injury before at club level.

Neither was fit for the first match in the group against West Germany, which ended in a 0–0 draw. When the Germans beat Spain 2–1 in their second game, it left England needing to beat the hosts 2–0 in Madrid to qualify for the semi-finals.

The day before the game Keegan and Brooking took part in a practice match, and both were hopeful of being selected – especially as Keegan had played for the first team. But overnight Ron Greenwood, possibly advised by his assistant Don Howe, decided to put them both on the bench. With the score 0–0 after sixty-three minutes, he sent the pair on in place of Tony Woodcock and Graham Rix.

They had been on just seven minutes when Bryan Robson crossed from the right, and Keegan put a great heading chance wide. Then the ball fell just right for Brooking, whose left-footed effort was blocked by the Spanish goalkeeper Arconada.

England went out of the tournament without losing a match and conceding just one goal in five games. It is my firm belief that, had they gambled with Keegan and Brooking earlier, they would have had a team good enough to reach the final of that World Cup.

Ron Greenwood had already announced his intention to retire and, after England were knocked out of the World Cup, Bobby Robson took over after a decade of success at Ipswich Town. In terms of their coaching credentials, their passion and pride in wearing the Three Lions on the blazer, and their popular image, both men were indisputably proper choices as England manager.

But around that time opinion was polarised. Some wanted a more radical figure like Brian Clough or Jack Charlton. Both had been successful at club level, both had great motivating qualities, but both were outspoken and did not suffer fools, and would have given short shrift to some of the mandarins on FA committees. Neither got the job.

The public debate continued, especially after Robson failed to qualify for the 1984 European Championships and made a disastrous start to the 1986 World Cup finals in Mexico. Defeat to Portugal in the shadow of Saddleback Mountain in Monterrey was followed by a 0–0 draw against Morocco, in which Bryan Robson was put out of the tournament by a shoulder injury and his vice-captain, Ray Wilkins, was sent off for dissent.

Robson and Wilkins were two of England's most influential players, winning 174 caps between them. They also shared a room, and I remember being invited in to talk to them about the mood in the camp. Access to the players was still fairly easy, and Bobby Robson had no problem with it if he trusted you. Today a commentator would be lucky to get inside the foyer of the England hotel, never mind a player's bedroom.

It was also my first chance to get to know Gary Lineker, who rescued England with a hat-trick against Poland and then scored two more when they beat Paraguay 3–0 in the first knockout round. This match was played in the Azteca Stadium in Mexico City, then the biggest stadium in the world with its 120,000 capacity. I had a decent commentary position looking down on the near touchline, where some thoughtful horticulturalist had planted some nice flower beds on the grass surround.

After the match I raced down there to interview Bobby Robson. Peter Shilton had formed an impenetrable shield in goal, so I asked the England manager how influential he had been in keeping a clean sheet.

'What can I say about Peter Shilton?' gasped a breathless Robson. 'Peter Shilton is Peter Shilton and he's been Peter Shilton since the year dot.'

It was another quote for the 'Colemanballs' book of clangers, and one for the after-dinner circuit.

England were through to the quarter-finals to face Diego Maradona and Argentina. But sadly I would not be there to witness it. The BBC base was at the Maria Isabel hotel in Mexico City, and it was there Jonathan Martin informed me that I would not be covering what was England's biggest game since they had lost to West Germany in the quarter-finals, also in Mexico, sixteen years earlier. Barry Davies had been selected for England v. Argentina instead.

The BBC doctor, John Newman, who became my personal physician and a great friend over thirty years, took the brunt of my dismay. 'Don't overreact,' he sympathised. 'They are probably keeping you back for the semi-final and final if England get through.'

As things turned out, there was quite a consolation prize. The day before the England match, Brazil were paired with France in the first quarter-final in the Jalisco Stadium in Guadalajara – where Gordon Banks had made his amazing save from Pele in the World Cup of 1970.

It was a gripping match, and one for my all-time list. Careca put Brazil ahead, Michel Platini, on his thirty-first birthday, equalised for France. In the second half, Zico came on for Brazil to the biggest roar I have ever heard greeting a substitute. He promptly missed a penalty.

Then the Brazilian goalkeeper, Carlos, appeared to bring down the French substitute Bruno Bellone when he was clean through. The Romanian referee waved play on, and Jimmy Hill – incensed by the decision – grabbed the microphone. Suddenly I realised that Brazil's right back, Josimar, was racing down the wing inside the French half. I wrestled the mike back from Jimmy just to shout 'Socrates' as the Brazilian captain hit the post at the other end. It was scintillating stuff, even without the penalty shoot-out that followed, in which Zico scored and Platini missed. France won that 4–3 to advance to the semi-finals.

So watching Maradona dismantling England on television the following day, in the company of Ron Atkinson, was not such a bitter pill to swallow. Much as I would have liked my voice to be covering his 'hand of God' goal and the divine winner that followed. And I got my chance to extol the virtues of the world's best player when Maradona executed two more breathtaking goals in the semi-final against Belgium.

By now I had been selected to do the final and felt I was in good form, but my attention to detail still needed a little fine tuning. After the semi-final, my friend and producer John Shrewsbury took me to one side and whispered: 'Motty, I know those substitutions are a nightmare, but five minutes from the end you identified a player who had already gone off the pitch.'

The final between Argentina and West Germany was played at noon local time, with the sun glinting on the players' shirts and the numbers not easy to identify. I felt at a slight advantage over my ITV counterpart Brian Moore, who had flown out for the final after presenting most of the World Cup from the studio in London.

In my preamble before the kick-off, I referred in some detail to the earthquake that had ravaged Mexico City a few months earlier, and how the poverty had been eased temporarily for a beleaguered population by the football. *'As we wait for the teams to make their entrance,'* I said, *'perhaps what's sociologically more significant is that it's being played in a city of nineteen million people – the largest convocation on the globe – that only nine months ago was devastated by a colossal earthquake which rendered hundreds of thousands homeless. And if they still seek their temporary accommodation among the ruins and the rubble of a tormented capital, they take solace in their football. The luckier ones making a pilgrimage to the Azteca to worship Diego Maradona or maybe watching on a shared television set.'*

After the game, which Argentina won 3–2 after leading 2–0 and being pegged back to 2–2, I was told that David Coleman had sent a message to the studio in Mexico to say my opening words had been brilliant, though nobody passed it on. Compliments to commentators were hard to come by in those days.

The 1986 World Cup marked a real turning point in Gary Lineker's glittering career. He won the Golden Boot as the tournament's top scorer with six goals and this, combined with his form for Everton, for whom he scored forty goals that season, brought him a lucrative move to Barcelona. The tournament also saw the start of his broadcasting career, when he joined the BBC studio panel back in London for the final.

Lineker was not the most spectacular goal scorer I ever saw. He didn't blast shots from a distance like Bobby Charlton, and he didn't run past a string of defenders like Jimmy Greaves. Neither was he a great header of the ball. But for being in the right place at the right moment, he had an instinct I have never seen bettered.

What a pity, from his and England's perspective, that he was suffering from the early effects of hepatitis when Robson's team went to Germany for the 1988 European Championships. He missed chances he would normally have swallowed up, and England lost all three group matches.

One of those was to Holland, for whom Marco Van Basten hit a devastating hat-trick. He was the most complete centre forward I ever saw, and proved his pedigree by scoring a late winner against West Germany in the semi-final and a sumptuous volley to settle the final against the Soviet Union.

Bobby Robson was so deflated by England's performance that he offered his resignation, which was turned down by the FA chairman, Bert Millichip. Instead, England went through their qualifying campaign for the 1990 World Cup unbeaten, in a season that saw Robson give a chance to a young midfield player called Paul Gascoigne.

Gazza's tears are an iconic image of Italia 90, and there is a theory that his and England's performance in that World Cup – when they lost on a penalty shoot-out to the eventual winners – turned the game in this country around after the dismal decade that had gone before.

Forgive me, but having covered the 1990 World Cup from start to finish, I consider this a load of tosh. But don't just take my word for that. Gerald Sinstadt, the senior commentator of my generation, who was covering World Cups when I was at primary school, is in agreement with me on this one.

Sinstadt's World Cup portfolio went back to 1954, when he worked for British Forces Broadcasting in Switzerland. When Gerald was the Granada commentator in my early days with the BBC, he lived in London, and many was the time I sat at his home in Highgate and marvelled at the meticulous way he kept his records. So I sat up and paid attention when he described the 1990 World Cup as the poorest he had covered.

With my more limited experience, I have to agree with him. Leaving England on one side for a moment, there was too much negative football, too many teams playing for extra time and penalties, and precious little pleasure travelling around Italy. The legacy of hooliganism hanging over from the eighties meant no alcohol was served in the city on the day of the game. That summed up the austere atmosphere in which this World Cup was played.

As I was not covering England all the time, I have to confess that my negative view of the 1990 World Cup is coloured by my own schedule. Owing to some poor planning by the BBC I had to cover twelve matches in seventeen days, travelling to and from venues at the crack of dawn most days and trying to catch up with other matches on television whenever I could.

Naturally, most fans would have loved to swap places with me. How can you complain about being paid to watch the world's best tournament? I take that argument on board, but as a commentator you need to be at your brightest when you pick up the microphone, and in Italy I never felt I was.

England fans may remember Terry Butcher and Chris Waddle dancing with delight as they look back wistfully on how close Robson's team came to reaching the final. But the facts tell a different story. The 1–1 draw against the Republic of Ireland in England's opening game was ridiculed across Europe for the paucity of good football. A 0–0 draw against a Dutch team riddled with internal strife followed; and it needed a headed goal by defender Mark Wright against Egypt for England to reach the second round.

Towards the end of the match against Belgium in Bologna, most of us had settled for penalties before Gascoigne floated a free kick forward and David Platt scored with an acrobatic volley. It is worth recalling, too, that they were 2–1 down to Cameroon in the quarter-finals with just eight minutes to play.

'Had it stayed like that,' Bobby Charlton said to me in the hotel the following day, 'it would have been England's biggest humiliation since we lost to the United States in the 1950 World Cup.'

The unthinkable was avoided largely because the Africans, who had beaten holders Argentina in the opening game, had not learned how to tackle properly. They conceded two penalties, both nerve-lessly dispatched by Lineker, and England were through to the semi-finals.

England's hotel was on the outskirts of Turin, and the mood was like that at the end of term at school. Everyone seemed to be of the opinion that we had already met or exceeded expectations, and that anything we did now would be a bonus. Out on the lawn, Bobby Robson's hairdresser, who had flown over from Ipswich, was giving the England manager a haircut, much to the amusement of all concerned. In a corner of the bar Steve McMahon was sitting alone, having lost his place in the side after playing against Egypt and Belgium.

When I got to the stadium, the first person I met in the media centre (we used to call it the press room) was Gordon Taylor, the chief executive of the PFA. 'All the boys are tired out, John,' he said, pointing to the assembled journalists, 'they just want to go home.'

I didn't tell Gordon, but I had seen a few packed suitcases discreetly placed around the foyer of the England hotel earlier that day.

My mood did not improve when I got to the commentary pos-ition. The Stadio delle Alpi was not commentator friendly. There was a steep, considerable distance to the pitch, and for some reason a number of journalists without assigned seats had positioned themselves on the concrete steps immediately behind our row of broadcasting positions, which was quite distracting.

I decided that this was a night to play it safe. Much as I would have liked to expand my commentary to meet the occasion (I would never again commentate on England in a semi-final) I knew one mistake would stay in the archives for ever.

England's performance that night was a significant improvement from the matches that had gone before. After a goalless first half, they were unlucky to go behind when Paul Parker deflected an Andreas Brehme free kick over Shilton's head. Parker then made amends when he crossed for Gary Lineker to equalise with nine minutes of normal time to go. In extra time, there was little to separate the two sides: both teams hit the post but neither could score the decisive winning goal. It meant that penalties would decide who would win a place in the World Cup final.

This isn't the place to discuss the merits of penalty shoot-outs, but for all the pressure on the players and the anxiety of the watching fans, they are certainly no easier for commentators, especially after two hours of live television. With no helpful diagram on the screen in those days, I had to summon up all my concentration just to keep track of the sequence in the shoot-out. That is why, when I am asked how emotional I felt when Chris Waddle and Stuart Pearce missed those vital penalties, I answer honestly, 'Not at all.' Imagine me shouting 'England are in the World Cup final', when the Germans still had one kick to take. Even when I had to utter the words 'England are out of the World Cup', one bright spark stopped me afterwards and said, 'Oh no they are not, they are only out of the final. They still have to play for third place.'

It was only after the match, when I was standing alone in the television compound waiting for some transport back to the hotel, that the BBC office in Rome told me I would be doing the final. It was said with an air of reluctance, and it was made clear to me that it had been a close call between Barry and myself.

I went back to the England hotel to say my farewells. Bobby Robson was in jovial mood.

'I'm not retiring, John,' he joked. He was fifty-seven at the time and had already agreed to take over as coach at PSV Eindhoven. 'Come and see me in Holland,' he shouted above the hubbub. Little did any of us know he still had half a career in front of him, in Holland, Portugal, Spain and back home with Newcastle

United. Latterly Sir Bobby has fought cancer on five occasions. What a hero.

Don't ask me why, but when I left him I remembered him taking me to the South East Counties League dinner with his inimitable chairman John Cobbold, soon after I started. We got there early and they told us the bar was closed. 'Can we have a drink while we wait?' asked Mr John.

We had also made a film with Robson for *Sportsnight*, soon after he took over as England manager. Producer Brian Barwick and I virtually lived with him for a week, and the highlight was when he spotted a lady with a shopping bag while he was travelling on the Tube from Liverpool Street to Lancaster Gate. 'Where have you been, love, Marks and Spencer?' enquired Bobby. That is one of the reasons why people think of him so fondly: he has the common touch. There was never any danger of Sven-Göran Eriksson travelling on the Underground – his chauffeur wouldn't have let him!

Bobby Robson's successor as England manager was the Aston Villa boss Graham Taylor. His appointment meant that for the fourth time in a row, one of the greatest English managers was not given his chance with the national team. But while the FA ignored this charismatic and idiosyncratic character, I have no intention of following suit. Indeed, such were my encounters with this remarkable man that I have given him and his sparring partner their own chapter.

Chapter 8

Brian Clough and Peter Taylor

'Don't tell Brian I told you'

'SHITHOUSE!' YELLED BRIAN Clough, and his jabbing forefinger was pointing in only one direction. Mine.

It was early 1987. Nottingham Forest were in London to play Arsenal in a League Cup quarter-final. Clough had been walking through the main entrance at Highbury into Arsenal's marble foyer, when he spotted me near the bust of Herbert Chapman.

'Shithouse,' he repeated, storming towards me now.

I backed off even farther, fearing that the statue of Arsenal's famous pre-war manager would take a battering at any moment.

'I pay my licence fee because I expect the BBC to be fair,' he snarled. 'Not biased like you were at Tottenham on Sunday.'

I should point out straight away that the match he was referring to was a North London derby at White Hart Lane. It was Arsenal whom Clough believed I had favoured in my commentary.

'Bloody disgrace,' he boomed.

All this time, his embarrassed Nottingham Forest players were trying to get past him into the dressing-room corridor. Just as shocked were a handful of people standing near the ticket window on the far side of the hall. The mascots and their parents couldn't help hearing his outburst either.

Eventually Clough's coaching staff coaxed him away, and I moved sheepishly through the door to the players' tunnel, where the teams for that night's League Cup quarter-final between Arsenal and Forest would be announced.

The previous Sunday, Arsenal had beaten Tottenham 2–1 to extend their lead at the top of the first division. George Graham was in his first season as Arsenal manager, and was assembling a vibrant young team including David Rocastle, Michael Thomas, Tony Adams and Niall Quinn. It was a performance in which I detected a spirit and a character that were going to take Arsenal places.

I was shaking slightly at the unexpected tirade from Clough, but determined not to let it affect my commentary. As Duncan Hamilton revealed in his award-winning book *Provided You Don't Kiss Me*, 'Brian Clough used the word shithouse like other people said please and thank you.'

Nottingham Forest lost that night to goals from Charlie Nicholas and Martin Hayes, but that didn't stop *Sportsnight* wanting an interview with Clough. As one of my early editors said: 'Get him to read the telephone directory and people will still listen.' The man was pure box office.

I made my way gingerly round the frozen track at Highbury that January night. The temperature had dropped significantly during the game, and by the time I spotted Clough waiting by the interview camera I was frozen. I was probably shivering over the reception I expected to get.

'Are yer cawld, John?'

The familiar Middlesbrough accent cut deep into the night. As I got closer to Clough I could see he was holding a paper cup. Rather like the finger earlier, it was for me.

''Ere, get this down yer, young man,' he shouted.

I was over forty at the time, but compared with his earlier fury, 'young man' was almost a term of endearment. I took the cup of kindness from Clough, expecting it to be either tea or coffee. I should have known better. It was full to the brim with whisky.

And there, on one cold evening in North London, you had the contradiction that was Brian Howard Clough. Chairmen, players, supporters, newspapermen, commentators – none of us ever knew which side of his unpredictable nature we were going to encounter next.

I had first met Clough when he was the young, brash manager of Derby County in 1969. It was my first year in BBC Radio, and Derby had just been promoted from the second division. They had beaten Crystal Palace 1–0 at Selhurst Park – Dave Mackay had been awesome for Derby – and I was detailed to interview Clough for *Sports Report*.

He came in wearing a grey checked overcoat. I told him there would be a short delay while they read the football results. He smiled and said he was happy to wait. The results took longer than I expected, and I was worried that Clough would walk away. He detected my anxiety. 'Just relax, young man,' he said. 'You can't do anything unless you are relaxed.'

It was the first of many interviews I did with him over the next twenty years. The sheer magnetism of the man means he merits a chapter to himself, but it should be linked to the man who helped make him what he was – Peter Taylor.

My first season with *Match of the Day* saw Derby win the first-division championship. Clough and Taylor had built a team around Roy McFarland and Colin Todd at the back; Archie Gemmill and Alan Durban in midfield; John O'Hare and Kevin Hector up front; and Alan Hinton providing inch-perfect crosses from the left wing. It was a pattern they would later repeat at Nottingham Forest.

Clough, meanwhile, was already making a name for himself as a television pundit and, still in his mid-thirties, knew exactly how to play to the camera. After one game at the Baseball Ground, Sam Leitch passed a message telling me to ask Clough about George Best, who had gone missing. 'Has Frank found him yet?' jeered Clough, targeting the beleaguered United manager, Frank O'Farrell. He could be mischievous as well as outspoken.

From their little office at Derby – which later became the board-room – Clough and Taylor could access the press room within seconds. 'What are we going to do about Toddy?' asked Clough of the journalists one day, after Sir Alf Ramsey had ignored Colin Todd because he had refused to go on a summer tour. Todd later won twenty-seven caps as an accomplished defender.

The more I saw of the partnership, the more I realised that the route to Clough, for a young commentator, was via Taylor.

'There's one player we need here,' said Peter, who had a habit of sticking his tongue into his cheek when he told you something relevant. 'I'm not saying who it is.'

We all knew it was Peter Shilton, who had replaced Gordon Banks in goal at Leicester and in the national side. They finally got him from Stoke when they teamed up again at Nottingham Forest.

I was working on the camera platform in the Ley Stand in October 1973 when Derby faced Leicester City, after Clough and Taylor had resigned following a prolonged dispute with chairman Sam Longson. Just three days earlier, Poland had knocked England out of the World Cup, and Clough on ITV had famously called the Poland goalkeeper, Jan Tomaszewski, 'a clown'.

Now Clough appeared in a front section of the main stand waving to the supporters, while Longson stood in the directors' box, only a few feet away. When the game started, Clough slipped away, to appear later that evening on *Parkinson*.

The following Monday, the Derby players, who at one stage

threatened to go on strike, handed Longson a letter asking for the reinstatement of Clough and Taylor. Their protest fell on deaf ears. The following day, the board announced that Dave Mackay – a key figure in the Derby side that Clough had established in the first division – would succeed him as manager.

A week later, the Brighton and Hove Albion chairman, Mike Bamber, appointed Clough and Taylor as his new managerial partnership. Brighton were nineteenth in the third division.

Just a couple of weeks on, Italy defeated England 1–0 at Wembley with a goal from a certain Fabio Capello. Following England's failure to qualify for the World Cup, Sir Alf Ramsey's future was now called into question.

How quickly things can change in football. Had Clough stayed at Derby, he would have been a lively outsider in the race to become the next England manager. Having won the first-division championship and taken Derby to the semi-final of the European Cup, his stock was high until his resignation.

But not now. At the end of November, Brighton lost 4–0 at home to non-league Walton and Hersham in an FA Cup replay. Three days later they were again humiliated on their own Goldstone Ground – this time 8–2 by Bristol Rovers.

My father was preaching just outside Brighton at the time and had a season ticket there. He met Clough briefly. 'I need to talk to someone like you,' said Brian. But he was never in Brighton long enough to meet anybody. He kept his home in Derby.

The nearest Clough got to the England post was succeeding at club level the man who got it. Don Revie, after his success at Leeds, seemed a logical choice for England, but few people expected Clough to turn up at Elland Road. When he did, it was straight from a family holiday in Majorca. He agreed to take the job and flew straight back to rejoin his wife Barbara and sons Nigel and Simon.

When Clough left Brighton they were just one place higher in the third division than when he had arrived six months earlier. Peter Taylor, though, stayed on as Brighton manager rather than joining Clough at Leeds. He made his home in the town, where his daughter was working on the local newspaper.

It seemed like the first schism in the partnership. I went down to interview Taylor one day, and he spoke of his discontent with the way their salaries had been structured when he and Clough were together. 'Brian always got most of the money. I don't think I got what I deserved,' he said.

Clough's forty-four days at Leeds United have been well documented, and were the subject of *The Damned United*, a novel by David Peace that was made into a film, released in spring 2009. Clough was clearly not made welcome by Don Revie's players, and the only match I covered when he was there made me think he looked out of place.

I went into his office, which had been Revie's for thirteen years, before a game against Birmingham City. Michael Keeling, a former Derby director who became a close friend of Clough's, walked in and gave him a clean shirt. Clearly, keeping his home in Derby and staying in a Leeds hotel were not to Clough's liking. They beat Birmingham 1–0, their only league victory while he was there.

The next time I saw him was on the day he took over at Nottingham Forest. They won an FA Cup replay against Tottenham at White Hart Lane, and he was sitting in the stand not far from me. 'Welcome back to football, Mr Clough,' said the Tottenham commissionaire.

Nobody could have foreseen what Forest would achieve in the next five years. But I do not believe they would have scaled those heights had Clough not been rejoined by Taylor. In the only season they were apart, Forest finished eighth in the second division, and Taylor's Brighton missed out on promotion from division three by one place. That summer, Taylor, who had been born in Nottingham, went back to his home city to resume his partnership with Clough. The double act was back in business – and how.

Yet things could have worked out very differently. In February 1977, just as they got things moving at Forest, Clough and Taylor were invited to go back to Derby. It was such a big story that *Sportsnight* sent me and their chief reporter, Kevin Cosgrove, to Derby on the day Clough went back to the Baseball Ground to give the then vice-chairman, George Hardy, his decision.

The street outside was packed with supporters cheering Clough's arrival, and pleading with him to return. Under the acting management of Colin Murphy, who had succeeded Dave Mackay, Derby were struggling just outside the first-division relegation zone. It was the middle of February, and Derby had won only four league games all season. Forest, meanwhile, were fifth in the second division and candidates for promotion.

Inside the Baseball Ground, Clough was ensconced in the tiny boardroom that had once been his office, with Hardy and the Derby directors. Just across the corridor in a crowded press room, I was one of a throng of newspaper and television reporters waiting for the outcome. It was almost as though we expected a plume of white smoke to blow out of the boardroom.

Colin Murphy put his head round the door and said: 'Let me know if I am still in a job.' He and his assistant Dario Gradi – later to spend a near-lifetime at Crewe – were only in charge on a temporary basis.

Finally, Clough came out and walked into the street. Derby fans gathered round him, only to be told he would not be returning. 'This is a sad day for me,' he said later.

For all he and Taylor went on to achieve at Forest, it remained a source of regret to Clough that he never went back to finish the job he had started at Derby. All sorts of reasons were put forward for his decision not to return. Sam Longson, the chairman with whom Clough had fallen out so badly, was still on the board, although Hardy was about to replace him. Longson was made president. Before we put our piece together for *Sportsnight*, I asked Clough what part Taylor had played in their decision. 'A big part,' he said, but refused to elaborate.

The history of the two East Midlands clubs probably changed from that day. Derby were to go into decline, sliding into the third division, while changing their manager six times. Nottingham Forest were to conquer Europe twice. Although when Clough and Taylor returned to their adjacent offices at the City Ground that February, the first item on the agenda was to win promotion from the second division.

They managed it by just one point, but took the first division by storm the following season. They won the championship at the first attempt, losing only three matches, and going on an unbeaten run which lasted more than a year and a total of forty-two league games.

After Don Revie's defection in the summer of 1977, the Football Association asked Ron Greenwood to take over as temporary manager until December. A 2–0 victory against Italy in the last World Cup qualifier at Wembley in November made Greenwood favourite to take over permanently, although it came too late for England to reach the World Cup finals in Argentina the following summer.

In December, with Forest storming away at the top of the first division, Clough was interviewed at Lancaster Gate. He gave the International Committee a typically forthright outline of his attitude towards the England job, but felt it was all a cosmetic exercise. A week later, the FA gave Greenwood a two-year contract. When he announced his back-up team, he asked Clough and Taylor to take responsibility for the England Youth Team. That didn't last very long. Their style of management did not lend itself to playing a minor role.

'The People's Choice' had been passed over. His cavalier approach may not have suited the blazers at the FA, who probably feared he would embarrass them, but Clough and Taylor were running things exactly as they liked at the City Ground. They sometimes gave players four days off in a row. The next time they saw them would be on Saturday at a quarter to three when Clough walked in to give the team talk.

Unpredictability was his trademark. John McGovern, who was with him at Derby, Leeds and Forest, recalled a team talk when they were 3–0 down at half-time. 'Same again, please, gentlemen,' was all Clough said in the dressing room. Forest went out and won 4–3.

When I used to phone him for his team on a Friday, he would put players down like no other manager. 'Nice lad. Pity he can't play,' he once said of Viv Anderson, who went on to become the first black player to win a full England cap.

'If we're lucky we might get a performance out of him,' he said of Martin O'Neill, whose own style of management owes much to what he gleaned from working under Clough.

It was the same with the media. One day you would be invited into his office for a bottle of champagne; on another he would be uncontactable. Sometimes I would hang around in the corridor for hours having arranged to interview him. Then he would bound in waving his squash racket. 'I'm fat and forty,' he said as he challenged me to a game.

More often than not, I got my information from Peter Taylor. He had a conspiratorial air on the telephone. 'I'll mark your card,' he would say at the beginning of the conversation. And he always ended it the same way. 'Don't tell Brian I told you.'

This, of course, was part of their act. It was good cop, bad cop. But it certainly worked in the dressing room and the press room. Following Forest in Europe was now an eagerly sought-after assignment by those of us who, up to now, assumed that Liverpool would be our representatives in the European Cup.

As there was no seeding then, the two clubs met in the first round in the 1978/79 competition, Forest as league champions and Liverpool as holders. Clough's team won the first leg 2–0 at the City Ground, and I was at Anfield when they held Liverpool 0–0 in the return. By now, Clough and Taylor had the goalkeeper they had always wanted. Peter Shilton was outstanding in the second leg, and Clough was in typically bombastic mood when I interviewed him after the game.

'Perhaps now, John, people like you will realise we are a good side,' he barked.

Those of us in the media were never privileged to see quite how the partnership worked behind the scenes. Both men were stubborn and could be volatile, and there were stories of blazing rows and slammed doors. But as a professional partnership, it worked perfectly. Put simply, Clough was the motivator, Taylor the talent spotter.

Whether it was Garry Birtles, whom they picked up for next to nothing from Long Eaton, or Trevor Francis, whom they made the first million-pound player, Taylor could tell at first glance if they would fit the bill. Only a few months after joining Forest from Birmingham, Francis scored the winning goal in the European Cup final against Malmö.

When they defended the trophy the following season, Forest were drawn against the East German champions, Dinamo Berlin, in the quarter-finals. Forest lost the first leg at the City Ground 1–0, and things looked ominous when we arrived in Berlin for the return. The cold war was at its height, and the hotel in the eastern sector was grim to say the least.

Taylor gave me the team and said Francis would line up wide on the right. But to my surprise, as soon as they kicked off he was playing up front. He scored twice; Forest won 3–1, and went through 3–2 on aggregate. On the final whistle, *Sportsnight* wanted an interview with Clough. John Shrewsbury, my producer, left the commentary box five minutes from the end, and persuaded Brian to wait for me to get round the pitch before he went into the dressing room.

This he did, and when I had finished the interview Taylor came out of the tunnel and grabbed me. 'Sorry about that,' he whispered. 'We saw how frightened the East Germans looked when they came out of their dressing room and changed our tactics. Trevor was only told then to play up front.'

This seat-of-the-pants stuff was typical of Clough and Taylor. Nobody knew what to expect from one moment to the next – least of all the players. One Friday night at the Hendon Hall Hotel in north-west London, before they played in the League Cup final at Wembley the following day, Clough walked into the lounge with a crate of beer and insisted all the players had a drink until it was empty.

I was sitting on the other side of the room with Taylor, who asked me whether I thought he should write a book.

'If you do, you will have to link it with Brian somehow,' I said. Although I knew how much of a part Taylor played in the partnership, the public at large identified only with Clough.

'What should I call it, then?' asked Taylor.

'Well, something like *With Clough, by Taylor*,' I suggested.

When Taylor brought out his autobiography later, that was what it was called. Clough was not at all pleased at its publication, though at least he didn't know the title was my idea.

At that time my BBC colleague John Rowlinson and I collaborated on a book about the history of the European Cup, from its inception in 1955 to 1980, the year Forest won it for the second time, beating Hamburg in the final. We set about interviewing the key figures who had shaped the competition, and I arranged to sit down with Clough and Taylor.

'Compared with some of the other managers who have won it, you don't seem to spend much time coaching on the training ground,' I ventured.

Clough took a large gulp of champagne and gave me a look of pity. 'John, I coach every time I open my mouth,' he said.

Less than two years after Forest won the European Cup for the second time, Taylor announced his retirement. He said he was worn out after thirty-six years in the game. The lustre of those successful seasons had started to fade. Clough and Taylor had always insisted on taking holidays during the season to recharge their batteries. They often referred to the stress factor in management.

Forest now finished a modest seventh in 1981 and twelfth in the table in 1982, and in the same season were knocked out of the FA Cup at home to Wrexham. There was a match I covered at Aston Villa when Clough did not turn up. When I asked Taylor where he was, he replied, 'I have no idea.'

The pair fell out when Taylor returned to Derby County as manager just six months after his 'retirement'. The rift widened when he persuaded John Robertson, the winger who had played the Hinton role, to leave Forest and join him at Derby.

When Ron Greenwood retired after taking England through the 1982 World Cup finals unbeaten, Clough's name came up again. But the FA were far more comfortable with Bobby Robson, who had just taken Ipswich Town to second place in the first division for the second year running. He had won the UEFA Cup the year before, and took Ipswich into Europe nine years out of ten. Robson was a distinguished England player in his time, whereas Clough had won only two caps – something he always resented. If he was seen as rebellious, Robson was the respectable, reliable face of management.

Clough never succeeded in Europe again, although without Taylor at his side he came mighty close in 1984. Forest beat Anderlecht 2–0 in the first leg of the UEFA Cup semi-final, but then lost 3–0 in Brussels. An inquiry found that the referee, who awarded the Belgians an inexplicable penalty, had been bribed.

It is sometimes overlooked that Clough went to Wembley more often without Taylor than with him. The pair had reached the League Cup final three years running together, but from 1989 to 1992 Forest, under Clough, were there four times – winning two more League Cups and losing to Tottenham in the 1991 FA Cup final, and to Manchester United in the League Cup final the following year.

So Clough and Forest were still high profile when Bobby Robson stepped down from the England post after the 1990 World Cup. By now, Graham Taylor had made his mark as a successful manager with Watford and Aston Villa. There was the usual public debate, and Clough's name figured in the polls, but by now his claims to the job were not nearly as strong as they had been in 1978 and 1982.

He did get offered an international post – by Wales. But after insisting he could combine it with looking after Forest, that never came to fruition either. Clough just seemed destined not to manage his or any other country.

By now Clough's health was deteriorating fast. He was still capable of the compelling interview, but he was well on the way to becoming an alcoholic. There had always been whisky on the desk in his office, but when Forest turned up for matches in the late eighties, Clough's crimson features gave away his worsening condition.

His loyal assistants, Alan Hill, Ronnie Fenton and Liam O'Kane, would walk closely by his side as he made his way down the corridor to the dressing room. Once, before an FA Cup tie with Watford, I saw him on the pitch and asked him for his team. 'Liam will give you the team,' he said quietly. It was almost as though he couldn't remember it.

Lawrie McMenemy and his wife Anne suggested to Clough's wife, Barbara, that the four of them should take a 'holiday' in America, where Brian should go privately to rehab in the Betty

Ford clinic. But it seemed not even those close to him could stop his decline. His behaviour at the 1991 FA Cup final, when he came out of the tunnel holding hands with Terry Venables, and never got off the bench to talk to the team before extra time, was especially sad, since this was the one major honour he had never won.

Before the semi-final that year, his old friend Michael Keeling arranged for me to interview Clough at Twickenham Studios, where he was filming a commercial with Cherie Lunghi, the actress who starred in *The Manageress*. It was tactfully suggested I should do the interview in the morning, when Brian would be at his best. He was actually quite brilliant, but by the time I went to Nottingham to talk to him again two years later, his answers had become such a rant that *Sportsnight* could not transmit the whole interview.

It is one of my biggest regrets that I lost touch with Brian Clough after his retirement in 1993, the year Forest were relegated. The only time I spoke to him was in May 2000, when I hosted a lunch at the National Sporting Club in London. The guests were Alan Curbishley, David Mellor and Clough. I had to compère a question-and-answer session on the stage.

When Clough arrived with Ronnie Fenton at his side, Ronnie whispered to me that Brian was not too well. He posed for photographs but looked very much the worse for wear. His behaviour onstage was eccentric to say the least. He even tore my tie off at one point. The situation was not helped by one of the guests asking Clough what had happened to his old sparring partner Peter Taylor, who had died in 1990.

The last time I saw Clough, after he had been in hospital for a liver transplant, was in the corridor at Derby's new ground at Pride Park. He was busy talking to somebody about Middlesbrough, and I missed the chance to say hello.

The lounge he was in that day has since been named after him.

So has the road between Derby and Nottingham – Brian Clough Way. He was made a freeman of both cities. His son Nigel carried on the family tradition as manager of Burton Albion for ten years, before succeeding Paul Jewell at Derby County – his father's old club – in January 2009.

When BBC Radio 4's *Brief Lives* programme asked me to select as a subject someone who was no longer with us, there was only one name that came to mind. I enlisted the help of Duncan Hamilton, the former *Nottingham Evening Post* reporter, whose daily jousts with the Forest manager made for such absorbing reading in his book. Hamilton was the perfect guest to complement and embellish my memories of the most fascinating manager of my time. Presenter Matthew Parris also put in a lot of homework, and between the three of us, I like to feel we did justice to Brian.

Brian Clough's family remained proud, loyal and resolute throughout his success and his later tribulations. His wife Barbara was a great shield and support, even though she remained in the background until she emerged as the star turn in an ITV documentary *Clough* screened in April 2009.

Brian's sons Nigel – by then following in his father's footsteps as manager of Derby County – and Simon also figured in the programme. They have inherited the same family values and brought up their own children with the same care and attention they were given by their mother and father.

Two unanswered questions remain. Should Clough and Taylor have managed England? And what would have happened if, in 1977, they had gone back to Derby? It was, after all, Clough's spiritual home, and I have every reason to believe they could have finished the job they started there by taking Derby every bit as far as they took Nottingham Forest.

On the England issue, I am not so sure. Certainly Clough and

Taylor would have challenged the establishment, and would never have compromised their fearless style of management. Diplomacy was not in their vocabulary. Whether their powers of motivation and simple pattern of play would have worked with top international players – some less likely than those at his club to conform to Clough's belligerent approach – we shall never know.

I prefer to remember them as they were – Clough in his green goalkeeper's jersey, insisting his players never argue with a referee; Taylor walking into his office with his dog, his tongue pressed against the inside of his cheek as he weighed up Forest's next signing; the pair of them, in pullovers and slacks, sitting on chairs on the touchline as Nottingham Forest, late of second-division anonymity, twice won Europe's top prize.

Clough and Taylor didn't do it with a Manchester United, a Liverpool or an Arsenal. They did it with a team of so-called rejects, has-beens and novices who they turned into winners. It will never happen again. That's why they deserve a chapter to themselves. Even one written by a shithouse.

Chapter 9

Ticket to Ride, Part Two

Taylor to Capello

Bobby Robson's successor as England manager, Graham Taylor, was a thoroughly decent man. He came from a working-class background, having played in the lower divisions for Grimsby Town and Lincoln City, where he became the youngest manager in the country at the age of twenty-eight. But it was on the back of his success at Watford and Aston Villa that he was given his chance with the national team.

I knew Graham well from his time as a club manager, just as I did his assistant, Lawrie McMenemy. I quickly organised a *Sportsnight* feature early in their tenure, after England had beaten Hungary in their first game in charge. 'I should resign now,' joked Graham, 'with a hundred per cent record.'

The piece we made included Graham urging Gary Lineker to improve his lap time round the running track at Tottenham's training ground, and sitting on the grass talking to Paul Gascoigne about how to handle his new-found fame. Poignant moments, bearing in mind what came later.

Taylor's record as manager was not as wretched as is often thought. England remained unbeaten until his thirteenth match in charge, a 1–0 defeat by world champions Germany, and when the team were knocked out of the European Championships in Sweden (the match in which Taylor substituted Lineker) it was only their second defeat in twenty-four games. But I felt he lost confidence in himself and others after that, pulling in people to protect him from the media when things turned sour.

Like Robson before him, Taylor was the victim of a savage hate campaign in the tabloid press. The football writers were mostly England fans who told it how it was, but the news reporters who now followed the team not only targeted Taylor – they pilloried him. Some of the treatment he received was brutal. He was not helped by the documentary he allowed to be filmed during the World Cup qualifying competition. The access he gave the film crew rebounded on him horribly when England lost in Norway and Holland. England had failed to qualify for the World Cup finals for the first time since 1978, and Taylor paid the price.

'We needed each other' is how Terry Venables summed up his appointment when he was made England coach in 1994. Bruised by his fall-out with Alan Sugar after winning the FA Cup with Tottenham, Venables needed to rebuild his reputation as badly as England did theirs. Euro 96 gave them both the perfect platform. As host nation, there were no qualifiers to worry about. And just as they had been for Alf Ramsey thirty years earlier, all of England's games would be at Wembley.

Frank Skinner and David Baddiel, with whom I had worked on their *Fantasy Football* show, got the nation singing to 'Three Lions', which they turned into a number-one hit with Ian Broudie of the Lightning Seeds. 'Football's Coming Home' seemed to sum up the mood of the nation as I drove around the country covering the tournament. There were flags everywhere, and with Scotland also involved, it was easy to get caught up in the atmosphere. The BBC hired a bus to transport the studio team around. Ruud Gullit, now with Chelsea, became a popular member of the panel with Des Lynam, Jimmy Hill and Alan Hansen.

After England were held to a 1–1 draw by Switzerland in their opening game, I went to see Venables at their Thameside hotel near Marlow. The next game was against Scotland, and Terry said of one England star: 'If he plays like that again I've told him he'll be sitting next to me on the bench after twenty minutes.' Venables had always struck me as the most innovative coach of his generation, and I knew he would come up with something fresh. His use of Darren Anderton and Steve McManaman as mobile wide players (not, as some have suggested, as wing backs) was typical of his thinking.

Having said that, he was a restless spirit, always coming up with business ideas outside football. One of these was a board game called *The Manager*, which he asked me to test out with some friends one Friday afternoon at one of his favourite London haunts – the Carlton Tower Hotel in Knightsbridge. Four of us played the game all afternoon, but in the end it was a bit like *Monopoly*. You had to make good decisions in order to finish with the most money.

The following day I bumped into Terry's old friend Malcolm Allison, and told him about the game. 'So the player with the most money wins,' I explained.

Malcolm looked at me as though I was stupid. 'It's like life,' he said simply.

Allison had been Venables' mentor in their Crystal Palace days, and he would have warmed to England's performance against Holland. The 4–1 win, with the Shearer–Sheringham combination, finely tuned by Venables, rates as one of England's best performances since 1966. The way they took an experienced Dutch team apart compares with two games that came later – the 5–1 victory in Munich under Sven-Göran Eriksson in 2001, and another

World Cup qualifier seven years later, when Fabio Capello inspired a 4–1 triumph in Croatia.

I had the pleasure of commentating on Paul Gascoigne's magical goal against Scotland, but in the end Venables' dreams went the same way as Robson's and, as we shall see, those of Glenn Hoddle and Eriksson. England couldn't get the hang of penalties when it came to a shoot-out.

The Euro 96 semi-final was Venables' last match as England manager. The previous January, he had announced he would be leaving at the end of the tournament, after the FA refused to offer him a longer contract. So another talented product from the east side of the London tracks stepped into the England coach's job.

I had known Glenn Hoddle since he was a seventeen-year-old prodigy at Tottenham. Quite apart from his exquisite skills on the pitch, I saw him as one of the lads off it. An Essex boy, he was always first off the coach for a beer. But in his time as an England player, I saw his personality change. He developed a deep interest in religion and, by the time he left his job as Chelsea manager to take over as England coach, he was careful to the point of being withdrawn in his dealings with the media.

Denying the access offered by his predecessors, Hoddle stopped the press pack travelling with the England team, and was reluctant to give out any information before the game. He had been in enough television studios to see captions going up on screens with the suggested line-up, and was not prepared to give anything away. 'Surely, John, you must know the players by now,' he would say with a smile. It was a fair point, but in terms of information before a game I found him the most guarded of his breed.

Yet he was tactically astute and utterly focused, losing only one of his first ten matches on the way to qualifying for the 1998 World Cup in France. That one early defeat had been at the hands of Italy at Wembley – Gianfranco Zola scored the goal – so when

England went to Rome for the return in 1997, it was paramount they did not lose.

I wasn't working as the match was on Sky, so I went as a guest of Ladbrokes, and watched one of England's most heroic performances from the stands. Paul Ince went off to have a cut stitched and returned with his head heavily bandaged. He and Paul Gascoigne were immense in midfield. The point gained made qualification certain for England, and condemned the Italians, as runners-up in the group, to a play-off.

Although he was under forty when he was appointed, Hoddle was no respecter of reputations. Having already decided not to include Paul Gascoigne in his World Cup squad, Hoddle then left both David Beckham and Michael Owen out of the first two games against Tunisia and Romania. Owen, still only eighteen, came on as a substitute with England 1–0 down to the Romanians, and promptly equalised. But a late defensive error meant they lost the game, and Hoddle's team faced their third group encounter against Colombia in Lens, needing a draw to qualify for the knock-out stages.

This was my first England match in the 1998 finals, and the atmosphere was terrific. I remember a shot of Mick Jagger in the stand, clapping his hands and chanting 'England, England'. The World Cup experience had also spread to the Royal Family, and Prince Charles was present with Prince Harry. Later I learned that the match had been watched by 24 million viewers. Darren Anderton put England in front, and David Beckham's free kick – his first England goal – secured victory and a second-round meeting with Argentina in St Etienne.

Just as in 1986, I was destined not to be present at this summit meeting. The BBC policy was for Barry Davies and me to commentate on the live games for our channel, and for our colleagues to cover the ITV matches with a recorded commentary.

I watched England's penalty defeat by Argentina with Craig Brown, the Scotland manager, in a bar in Bordeaux. Jon Champion did the BBC commentary, his words reflecting the wonderful goal by Owen, and the sending-off of Beckham after a petulant flick of the foot at Diego Simeone.

Eight months later, it was Hoddle who got the red card. His resignation followed two errors of judgement that had nothing to do with England's performances, even though they had started their Euro 2000 qualifying campaign by losing in Sweden and only drawing with Bulgaria at Wembley.

I was baffled by the decision of Hoddle and the FA's David Davies to bring out a book about the 1998 campaign so soon after the World Cup, especially as he was critical of certain players whose wounds would not have healed (Davies, to be fair to him, has since acknowledged the book was a mistake).

But what finally brought Hoddle down was an interview in *The Times* the following February. Hoddle expressed some radical views on reincarnation – karma, he called it – suggesting disabled people were being punished for sins committed in an earlier life. It was heavy stuff for a football manager, and Hoddle maintained his views were 'misconstrued, misinterpreted and misunderstood'. The opportunistic journalist who reported them, however, effectively ended the coach's England career.

If Hoddle was taciturn, his successor started off being just the opposite. Kevin Keegan took on the England job on a temporary basis while still employed as the Chief Operating Officer at Fulham. As manager of Newcastle, Keegan had returned after eight years away from the game to inspire a brand of thrilling, attacking football that took them close to the championship for the first time since 1927. He was not likely to moderate his cavalier style with England.

I was in Vancouver working with Electronic Arts on the *FIFA* computer game when Keegan walked out at Wembley for England's European Championship qualifier against Poland. Even watching from there on television, the welcome was so effusive you almost thought he was a cheerleader rather than a manager. Paul Scholes responded with a hat-trick in a 3–1 win.

After two matches, Keegan took the job permanently and led England to Euro 2000. His three results in Holland and Belgium rather summed up his heart-on-the-sleeve style of management. There was a 3–2 defeat by Portugal after England had led 2–0; a passionate performance against old rivals Germany, in which Alan Shearer scored the only goal; then another 3–2 reverse, this time against Romania, when England were within two minutes of qualifying for the quarter-finals before Phil Neville gave away a penalty.

From his time as a player, I knew Keegan to be a stubborn, impulsive character: hugely inspirational one minute, likely to turn on his heel the next. I always felt his tenure as England coach would be brave, but brief. And so it proved.

The day the old Wembley Stadium closed in October 2000 was the most miserable I can remember for an England supporter, save possibly for the defeat by Croatia in the new stadium seven years later. I took my son Fred to the World Cup qualifier against Germany, because the BBC did not have access to the game. I'm glad we didn't. In pouring rain, the stadium looked more dilapidated than ever, and England's performance was not much better. A free kick from Dietmar Hamann slipped through David Seaman's grasp, and World Cup hopes were up in the air again.

As we sat in traffic after the final whistle, we heard Keegan's resignation on the radio. He had apparently told the FA's chief executive, Adam Crozier, in the undignified surroundings of the dressing-room toilets. Four days later England were in Helsinki for another qualifier. Howard Wilkinson, for the second time in two years, took over as caretaker and speculation was rife about Keegan's successor.

After a 0–0 draw in Finland, Garth Crooks and I collared Crozier and pressed him on the direction the FA would now take. 'Look at the top four or five clubs in our Premier League and you won't find an English manager,' mused Crozier.

The message was clear – they were looking abroad.

Later that night at our hotel, Crooks and I went through the likely list of candidates. I settled on Sven-Göran Eriksson, based on his success at Lazio, and put out a few feelers. When I suggested on *Football Focus* the following Saturday that Eriksson would be first choice, those in the studio shot me down. But less than three weeks later he was appointed.

Like most England managers he got off to a good start, winning his first four games, before losing to a bright Dutch team in a friendly at White Hart Lane in August.

Everybody knew the first acid test for Eriksson was the return with Germany on 1 September 2001. I was down to commentate live for the BBC, as well as presenting my *Matchday with Motty* programme on Five Live from Munich on the Saturday morning.

My co-host Ricky George and I went out for a quiet meal the night before the game and fell into the company of some convivial England supporters. I awoke on my bed in the early hours of the morning, fully dressed. We ploughed through the radio show, and I spent the rest of the day trying to keep my concentration on the game ahead. Not the perfect preparation, and not something I have allowed to happen either before or since.

Come the match, England's performance would have jolted anybody out of a trance. Going one behind to an early goal by Carsten Jancker, they terrified the Germans and their erratic goal-keeper, Oliver Kahn, and inflicted their biggest defeat on home soil in living memory. Michael Owen's hat-trick in the Olympic Stadium, now no longer used for football, was a demolition job in itself. When he scored his third goal, I could think of only one thing to say: '*This is getting better, and better, and better.*'

Just as we were celebrating England's 5–1 victory, the news

came through that my old sparring partner, Brian Moore, had died earlier in the day. It was a sad postscript to a memorable occasion, but I'm sure Brian would have enjoyed it as much as we did. Moore was a gentle, principled individual with a flair for both the studio and the commentary box. His voice was always controlled, pitched at just the right level – a thoroughly rounded broadcaster. He was much missed by colleagues on both major channels, and his funeral service and the family occasion that followed drew together many who had enjoyed his companionship in far-flung parts of the football world.

When we assembled at the airport in Munich the morning after England's five-star show, I fell into conversation with Greg Dyke, who had succeeded John Birt as the BBC's director general, and who had come over for the game. 'Great, wasn't it?' enthused Dyke.

'Yes, it was so good we ought to show the whole match again in case there were some people who missed it,' I suggested.

'Good idea,' said Dyke, and bellowed across to Mark Thompson, then managing director of BBC Television, who was checking in his bags. 'Mark, how do we get rid of *Panorama*?'

They quickly rescheduled that evening's line up on BBC1, and the repeat drew an audience of several million. In my forty years in broadcasting, I never knew the nation so thrilled by an England display.

There was an amusing sequel to the match, and to my commentary, when I went to watch a game at West Ham a few weeks later. As I walked back to my seat for the start of the second half, a quiet voice behind me muttered: 'This is getting better, and better, and better.' I turned round to see Sven-Göran Eriksson, who had just caught up with the BBC recording.

Whatever Sven got up to with Nancy, Ulrika, Faria or the 'Fake Sheikh', I always found him approachable, if in a sterile sort of way. He agreed to give me the England team the day before every game, a promise he kept right up to the World Cup quarter-final in 2006 – his last game as coach. He would ring me on my mobile as he left the press conference on the way back to the England hotel. 'Here is the team, John,' he would say, giving me the names in formation. 'I will name the substitutes tomorrow.'

There was no point in drawing Sven into further conversation. He did not invite any discussion about tactics, the weather or whether he preferred Abba to Mungo Jerry. The information had been passed on as promised, and the conversation was politely closed.

I could forgive him for that. The media conference he had just attended would have involved around three hundred people, including up to a dozen television crews, and at least five radio stations. The print press would include many overseas journalists. What a contrast with the first England press call I ever attended. That was in Malta in 1971, when I was a young radio reporter. I was just one of eight crammed outside Sir Alf Ramsey's bedroom. From what I can remember he was even less forthcoming than Eriksson.

My chief criticism of Eriksson's reign was his use of substitutes. He liked to make eleven changes in friendlies, but when it came to the permitted three in key games, I often thought he seemed unsure of plan B, especially when he had to react to an unforeseen injury.

That was the case when Wayne Rooney was injured in the 2004 European Championship quarter-final against Portugal. Until that happened England looked capable of going all the way, but once the Rooney–Owen partnership was broken, the team lost their way. You could say the same about Owen's injury in the 2006 World Cup.

Those two quarter-finals both went to penalties, but in his first – the World Cup of 2002 against Brazil in Shizuoka – Eriksson faced a different charge. He was accused of giving a less than inspired team talk at half-time. Here I have some sympathy with him. Brazil had equalised almost on the whistle, and he could hardly have catered for the free kick from which Ronaldinho fooled David Seaman early in the second half.

That goal created quite a storm in the BBC studio afterwards. Ian Wright and I thought Ronaldinho had meant to shoot, while Gary Lineker and Alan Hansen insisted it was a freak. As it was, Ronaldinho was sent off seven minutes later, and England played the last half-hour against ten men. It looked like a lost opportunity, with England lacklustre in attack, but Brazil kept the ball so well that scoring opportunities were few and far between.

And don't forget who went on to win the World Cup.

Four years later, just before the 2006 tournament in Germany, I saw Eriksson's indecision at first hand. Unless he was trying to fool everybody.

Adrian Bevington, the FA's Director of Communications, asked the BBC to prepare a tape for the announcement of the twenty-three-man squad to the media. I had to read the list of names, with their clubs and number of caps, to add a bit of spice to the press conference. Stephen Booth and Stefano Bozzi, our England producers, booked a studio one Thursday afternoon and showed me a list of some forty players. 'Why are there so many?' I asked. 'Some of these have got no chance of being in the squad.'

'We can't take any chances,' said Stephen. 'Adrian is going to let us have the final twenty-three at the last minute on Monday morning. Then we have to edit the tape quickly for the announcement at noon.'

I duly recorded the names and thought no more about it over the weekend. Then on the Monday morning Stefano phoned me in a panic. 'You will have to come into the studio immediately,' he said. 'Sven has added a name none of us ever thought of.'

For the life of me, I could not think who that might be. All the possible selections, I was convinced, were covered on the original list.

'It's Theo Walcott,' Stefano gasped when I got to the studio. 'But we won't know whether he will get the final spot for another hour.'

Above: Gwen and Bill Motson with their young son John © JOHN MOTSON ARCHIVE

Left: Bill Motson outside his barber's shop in Boston before he was called to the Methodist ministry © JOHN MOTSON ARCHIVE

Below: Ennersdale School in the early fifties. The author is fourth from the right on the back row © JOHN MOTSON ARCHIVE

Above: My twenty-first birthday party in 1966. The group includes several players from my Sunday team Roving Reporters © JOHN MOTSON ARCHIVE

Above: Hereford's Ronnie Radford celebrates the goal that changed my career. Ricky George and Billy Meadows are about to swamp him with congratulations © POPPERFOTO/GETTY IMAGES

Above: My early days at the *Barnet Press* were spent in front of a portable typewriter. I still use one! © JOHN MOTSON ARCHIVE

Above: Meeting Kenny Dalglish, who was then twenty-three, before the 1974 World Cup. The first of his three for Scotland © JOHN MOTSON ARCHIVE

Above: Lou Macari's shot deflects off Jimmy Greenhoff for Manchester United's winning goal in my first FA Cup final in 1977 © GETTY IMAGES

Above: Another tough one to call! Brian Talbot and Alan Sunderland both claiming Arsenal's first goal against Manchester United during the 1979 FA Cup final © BOB THOMAS/GETTY IMAGES

Above: Bobby Charlton was still playing when I started. Later he joined me in the commentary box © JOHN MOTSON ARCHIVE

Above: Just one will do! A single goal was enough for Nottingham Forest to win two European Cup finals under Brian Clough and Peter Taylor © BOB THOMAS/ GETTY IMAGES

Right: I could never get very close to Glenn Hoddle © JOHN MOTSON ARCHIVE

Above: 'And still Ricky Villa!' © BOB THOMAS/GETTY IMAGES

Above: Jimmy Hill and a bloke in a sheepskin © JOHN MOTSON ARCHIVE

Left: Paolo Rossi and Falcão both scored in the greatest game I ever covered, the 1982 World Cup meeting between Italy and Brazil © BOB THOMAS/ GETTY IMAGES

Above: 'Tigana! Tigana! Platini! Goal!' © STAFF/AFP/GETTY IMAGES

Above: In the commentary box at the 1986 World Cup in Mexico … © JOHN MOTSON ARCHIVE

Right: … where a future *Match of the Day* presenter won the Golden Boot with six England goals © BOB THOMAS/GETTY IMAGES

The 11 England managers I interviewed. Not forgetting three caretakers! From the top left: Alf Ramsey © GETTY IMAGES, Don Revie © POPPERFOTO/GETTY IMAGES, Ron Greenwood © GETTY IMAGES, Bobby Robson © JOHN MOTSON ARCHIVE, Graham Taylor © BOB THOMAS/GETTY IMAGES, Terry Venables © SUSAN GREENHILL, Glenn Hoddle © ROSS KINNAIRD /ALLSPORT/ GETTY IMAGES, Kevin Keegan © PHIL COLE/ALLSPORT, Sven-Göran Eriksson © ROSS KINNAIRD/ GETTY IMAGES, Steve McClaren © PAUL ELLIS/AFP/GETTY IMAGES, Fabio Capello © IAN KINGTON/AFP/GETTY IMAGES.

I recorded Walcott's name and details, but now Stefano was really sweating. It appeared Eriksson had still not decided between Walcott and Jermain Defoe. Time was ticking away. At the last minute Adrian Bevington phoned the studio to say that Walcott – who was just seventeen at the time and had yet to make his Premier League debut for Arsenal – had been selected.

You never knew what to expect next from Sven. I was driving home from my mother-in-law Marion's eightieth-birthday party in January 2006 when the *News of the World* sting effectively brought his five-year stint as England coach to an end. The interview with the 'Fake Sheikh', in which Eriksson criticised certain England players and suggested bungs were being paid to managers, tested the FA's patience to breaking point.

He had already flirted with Chelsea and Manchester United, not to mention FA secretary Faria Alam, and now the game was up. Later that month Eriksson agreed a staged pay-off on his contract, to leave England after the World Cup that summer.

He never had to worry about money. Sven took over as manager of Manchester City for the 2007/08 season – they finished ninth after being fourth at Christmas – then moved out with the change of ownership to become coach of Mexico. 'How's Sven?' I asked his agent, Athole Still, when I bumped into him at Reading early the next season.

'He's fine. He's got the biggest and best apartment in Mexico City. It has a balcony on all four sides.'

But in March 2009, with Mexico struggling in their World Cup qualifying group, Eriksson was sacked and found himself back in the marketplace.

The FA's search for his replacement after the 2006 World Cup was made all too public. Martin O'Neill, Sam Allardyce, Alan Curbishley and Stuart Pearce were all interviewed – the press found out when and where – until the FA appeared to settle on Luis Felipe Scolari, who had been in charge of Brazil when they won the 2002 World Cup and had also knocked out England as manager of Portugal in the 2004 European Championship.

Television cameras caught up with chief executive Brian Barwick as he flew to Lisbon to close the deal. I was told Scolari had promised to ring Barwick the following Saturday morning to finalise the details. As I left Sandown Park racecourse on the Friday afternoon, my mind was on the Chelsea v. Manchester United match I was due to cover at Stamford Bridge the following day.

Then I heard on the radio that Scolari had told the Portuguese media that he would not be taking the England job. *Football Focus* would now want a very different piece from me. I spent most of the night telephoning FA contacts, one of whom summed up the situation best when he said: 'Let's be honest. Scolari has bottled it.'

The following morning a tabloid newspaper broke a story about Steve McClaren, Eriksson's coach, having an affair with an employee of Middlesbrough Football Club. I wondered whether that had come out in order not to embarrass McClaren later, should he now be a candidate for the England job.

But something else happened at Stamford Bridge that afternoon which put my conspiracy theory out of my mind. Wayne Rooney broke the fourth metatarsal on his right foot as Manchester United conceded the Premier League title to Chelsea in a 3–0 defeat. Rooney's involvement in the forthcoming World Cup was now touch and go, and would dominate the headlines between now and then. In the meantime, McClaren was appointed to succeed Eriksson. 'He was a unanimous second choice,' one FA councillor told me. Bearing in mind what's happened at Middlesbrough since, McClaren's record at club level was a good one. He took them to seventh in the Premier League, won the League Cup and reached a European final. When he moved to Holland in 2008, he took Twente Enschede into the Champions League.

But I never quite understood why the FA had to commit themselves *before* the World Cup. Had they appointed Scolari, they would have found their new coach trying to knock England out just before he took over.

Rooney was not fit for England's first match against Paraguay, and neither was I, to tell the truth. Having never missed a match through illness in my thirty-five years with BBC Television, I went down with a bout of food poisoning when I arrived in Germany. For a few days I could hardly sleep or eat. I went out for a run with Mark Lawrenson and Gavin Peacock, and was embarrassingly ill at the roadside. At our hotel in Frankfurt I managed to get some tablets, and thanks to my producer Karen Graham, made my way to the stadium on Saturday, 10 June.

The first person I saw in the television compound was the BBC chairman, Michael Grade. Twenty years earlier he and I had taken a private plane to get from one venue to another during the World Cup in Mexico. How quickly the years had passed.

'We've been very worried about you,' said Grade.

'Don't worry, I'll be fine,' I said, and then dashed to the nearest toilet.

The stomach bug finally subsided, and in the end England's biggest casualty of that World Cup was not Wayne Rooney, but Michael Owen. His injury, in England's third group match against Sweden, meant his partnership with the now recovered Rooney was broken up just as it had been two years earlier in Portugal.

The fact that Rooney now found himself playing on his own up front led to the frustration that brought him a red card in the quarter-final against Portugal. Had England won the penalty shoot-out – and if Steven Gerrard had converted his kick, I believe they would – they would have faced France in the semi-final without Rooney, Owen and the suspended John Terry.

England's 'Golden Generation' had failed to deliver. And I now knew I would never commentate on my own country in the World Cup final.

* * *

Steve McClaren's reign began with the decision to drop David Beckham. He had tearfully relinquished the captaincy before leaving Germany and was left out of the squad that started the 2008 European Championship qualifiers.

Beckham's omission didn't last for long. Goalless draws against Macedonia and Israel, together with defeats in Croatia and Russia, left England sweating on qualification. Just as the media were turning on McClaren, he was thrown an unexpected lifeline. Israel beat Russia in Tel Aviv. Now England only had to draw against Croatia at Wembley to get through.

If only it had been that simple. There was a nervousness in the England camp. McClaren was without his two first-choice centre backs, Rio Ferdinand and John Terry, as well as left back Ashley Cole. His front two, Wayne Rooney and Michael Owen, were also out. On top of that, McClaren decided to gamble on a young goalkeeper, Scott Carson, who was virtually untried at this level. At training the day before the game, he looked a worried man.

So was Brian Barwick. The FA's chief executive knew what failure to qualify would mean. He phoned Bill Beswick, the psychologist whom McClaren had brought into the England set-up, and told him to 'get the manager's head up'.

I had commentated on enough England cliff-hangers not to write their obituary when they went 2–0 down on that rainswept night at Wembley. 'We always make it difficult for ourselves,' I said to Mark Lawrenson at half-time.

Rejuvenated by the now recalled Beckham, brought on at half-time in place of Shaun Wright-Phillips, England got back to 2–2 – a score that would have put them through and allowed Croatia to leave Wembley with respect intact as group winners: *'Here's Beckham, Crouch waiting in the centre . . . Crouch, surely. Yes! Peter Crouch has done it for England! . . . The big man adds to his phenomenal scoring record and guess who supplied the cross? David Beckham. Is this the goal that saves them from humiliation?'*

As McClaren sheltered under his umbrella, those close to the England bench reported he was urged by his staff to send on Owen Hargreaves to close down the midfield. But that change was never made. So with just thirteen minutes to go, Mladan Petric was allowed the space by a retreating defence to plant a routine shot inside Carson's left-hand post. England had failed to qualify for the European Championships for the first time since 1984: *'England are out of the European Championships . . . England players standing, lying in disbelief. Steve McClaren shepherded away . . . Wembley is stunned. There are sounds of disbelief, a bit of booing. There are people standing, trying to take in what has happened . . . the scene is one of desolation at Wembley.'*

In thirty years of covering England I had never felt so angry. When we came off the air I spent as little time as possible in the BBC studio and the hospitality areas, where I normally took my time in winding down. On my way out of the stadium to meet my son Fred and his friend, whom I knew would be suffering too, I was stopped by two Irishmen wanting a photograph and auto-graph. I swore under my breath and they heard me. I went back to apologise and have the picture taken, but it was not a happy incident. I had let myself down because I felt let down by England, in company with the rest of the nation.

Brian Barwick left Wembley and hardly slept before assembling the FA International Committee at daybreak. The dismissal of McClaren was a formality. Barwick took on personal responsibility for the next appointment. He knew they couldn't afford to get it wrong again.

When Fabio Capello accepted the job, England hired a coach whose honours board outstripped that of most of his predecessors put together. But that was at club level. We were curious to see what he would make of a national appointment.

I first met him in the Aston Villa boardroom before their third-round FA Cup tie against Manchester United in January 2008. He spoke little English, and it was his first public appearance since taking the job. 'Videos,' he said, as I gave him the teamsheet. 'Must see videos.'

According to those in an adjacent office at Soho Square, that is largely what he did in his first months in charge – watched recordings of all England's matches prior to his appointment.

'What did you need against Croatia, remind me, Brian?' he said to Barwick.

'A draw, Fabio, that's all we wanted.'

'Yes, so at 2–2 you were through. Why was Beckham racing to take a throw-in? In Italy we kill the game.'

I had another opportunity to find out the way he was thinking when we met at Portsmouth after an encounter with Manchester United early the following season.

Capello and his assistant, Franco Baldini, were clearly concerned about playing at Wembley, which they saw as a handicap more than an advantage. 'The players are finding it hard to cope with the expectation of the crowd,' Capello said. 'I am pleased our first two qualifying games are both away from home.'

We had just got on to the subject of Jimmy Bullard, whom we had both seen playing for Fulham against Arsenal the previous weekend, when Harry Redknapp came in. The Portsmouth manager and the England coach had an issue to sort out. Redknapp had accused Capello of playing Steven Gerrard on the left wing against the Czechs, a comment that Capello refuted. I moved away while they sorted out their differences. It wasn't to be their last disagreement, as it turned out.

I attended some of Capello's early training sessions and they were very different from what I had seen before. There was less shadow play and formations. It was all about ball retention. That took me back to the start of my association with the England team.

Alf Ramsey's team rarely gave the ball away. Yet in the years that followed, it was England's distribution which most annoyed my co-commentators Jimmy Hill, Trevor Brooking and Mark

Lawrenson. In international football, if you lose the ball it takes a long time to get it back – a lesson that seemed to escape England teams, which, when they ran out of ideas, either settled for the long, hopeful ball upfield or played in straight lines.

With Capello I sense it is going to be different. The 4–1 victory in Croatia, with Theo Walcott now justifying Eriksson's original faith with a hat-trick, was compared to the 5–1 triumph in Germany seven years earlier. And when England won 2–1 in a friendly in Berlin, Capello had engineered a run of seven wins and a draw in his first nine games. More important, he seemed to have got the players, the press and the public on his side. That would last, of course, as long as he kept winning. Which he did, with seven straight victories in the 2010 World Cup qualifiers.

So, in summary, who was the best England manager? In all I have dealt with fourteen of them down the years, although three – Joe Mercer, Howard Wilkinson (twice) and Peter Taylor – were there only briefly as caretakers. Putting those three to one side – and leaving judgement of Capello to a later date – this, not to be taken too seriously, is how I'd grade my top ten of England managers:

1. Alf Ramsey
    Still the only England manager to win the World Cup, but he also finished third in the European Championship and took England to two other quarter-finals. Hard to please and difficult to interview, but loved by his players in whom he inspired great loyalty.

2. Bobby Robson
    His eight-year spell in charge included a World Cup semi-final and a quarter-final. Not so successful in the European Championship, where he failed to qualify and later went out at the group stage. A proud, patriotic Englishman

who survived some merciless treatment from the press to become popular with the public and the players.

3. Sven-Göran Eriksson

England qualified for each of the three tournaments under his tenure, and got to the quarter-finals every time. Unlucky to lose on two penalty shoot-outs, he went about the job in a systematic, Scandinavian way. Only found wanting when it came to the later stages of competition.

4. Ron Greenwood

One of the early coaching disciples and a fine, honest individual who could be very warm and sometimes quite caustic. Was in charge only for two tournaments, but took England to the European Championship finals in 1980 and to the second group stage of the 1982 World Cup, coming home unbeaten.

5. Glenn Hoddle

Difficult to assess how well he would have done had he not left the job for non-footballing reasons. He qualified bravely for his only tournament in charge, going out of the 1998 World Cup on penalties to three-times finalists Argentina.

6. Terry Venables

Went farther than Greenwood and Hoddle in taking England to a semi-final, but in Euro 96 all the games were at Wembley, and he did not have to qualify. Was also Steve McClaren's assistant in 2007. An excellent coach, appreciated by the players.

7. Kevin Keegan

Revived a flagging England after Hoddle's departure, and took them to the final of Euro 2000. On his own admission not the best tactician, but his enthusiasm was paramount until he admitted he was not up to the job.

8. Graham Taylor

   Even more reviled in the press than Robson, but despite failing to qualify for the 1994 World Cup and losing to Sweden in the 1992 European Championships, he came from a modest playing background to earn the right to lead his country.

9. Steve McClaren

   Took some credit for his work as Eriksson's coach, and then became his successor as second choice in difficult circumstances. He was thirteen minutes away from qualifying for the finals of his only tournament.

10. Don Revie

    Sadly, never got close to matching his achievements at Leeds United. A sad and superstitious man who was brilliant at club level but whose methods were sometimes questioned. They did not work with England, where he failed to qualify in 1976 and abdicated when the 1978 campaign faltered.

Where Fabio Capello will fit into this list can only really be assessed once his England have played in the finals of a major tournament. But his start has certainly been promising: he overcame the early disadvantage of speaking little English, and overhauled the structure in the England camp to command great respect. If he wins the World Cup he will join Ramsey at the top of the list. Even a semi-final in the modern era will put him second.

So how do I reflect on thirty years of covering England? I saw them play around two hundred times in fifty different countries. I travelled at somebody else's expense, stayed in some top hotels, and watched international football on the world's finest stadia.

My only regret is that I never saw my country play in a major final. But, oh my word, what a gripping, maddening, privileged experience it was, watching them try.

Chapter 10

'We know you are a Tottenham fan'

Trying to remain unbiased

STEVE PERRYMAN, CAPTAIN of Tottenham Hotspur from 1975 to 1986, often used to say that John Motson was the man who brought Ossie Ardiles to Tottenham.

Certainly, I had been back from the 1978 World Cup in Argentina only for a couple of days when I received a call from the Spurs manager, Keith Burkinshaw. 'What can you tell me about these fellers Ardiles and Luque?' he asked.

I had known Keith since I had started in television. He was coach to Joe Harvey at Newcastle and, ironically, had been on the other end of that FA Cup defeat at Hereford. When he came down to Tottenham, first as coach when Terry Neill was manager, we got to know each other pretty well. Burkinshaw succeeded Neill as manager and, after suffering relegation in his first season, brought Spurs back to the first division at the first attempt.

But it was a close call. They went up in third place, finishing ahead of Brighton on goal difference, and Burkinshaw knew he had to strengthen his team. Harry Haslam, the manager of

Sheffield United, alerted him that some of Argentina's World Cup winners were available for transfer. When Keith rang, he was due to fly to Buenos Aires with Harry the following day. I gave him what details I had about Osvaldo Ardiles and Leopoldo Luque, who had both played a major part in their country's success.

Keith, armed with my information, made Ardiles his main target when he and Haslam arrived in Argentina. Their contact over there was Antonio Rattin, who had been infamously sent off when playing for Argentina against England in the 1966 World Cup quarter-final at Wembley. The deal with Ardiles was done in a couple of days. Keith acted for Tottenham on his own, as nobody else from the club had flown out with him. But he discovered that Luque was not so keen to sign.

'What about my friend Ricky Villa?' asked Ardiles.

Burkinshaw did not know much about the bearded midfield player, since Villa had made just two substitute appearances during the World Cup campaign. What was more, he was under the impression that Terry Neill – by then manager of Arsenal – was negotiating to take Villa to Highbury. Then he learned that the Arsenal board had blocked the deal. 'They did not want foreign players then,' Burkinshaw told me later. So before returning to England, and with Rattin proving an invaluable middleman, the Tottenham boss made his second signing.

The arrival of Ardiles and Villa was the start of overseas players parading their skills in English football. And Spurs were far from alone in looking abroad. Lawrie McMenemy had signed the Yugoslav full back Ivan Golac for Southampton; Bobby Robson acquired the Dutch pair Arnold Muhren and Frans Thijssen.

When the new season started, Ardiles and Villa were in the Spurs line-up at Nottingham Forest – Villa scored in a 1–1 draw. I was at White Hart Lane for their home debut against Aston Villa. Spurs fans gave them a ticker-tape welcome in true Argentine tradition, but they seemed completely out of touch with the game, which Spurs lost 4–1.

'What about those two?' the Villa manager Ron Saunders asked me after the game. 'They won't find it easy over here.'

The following week, Spurs crashed 7–0 to Liverpool at Anfield. Four days later they lost a League Cup replay to third-division Swansea at White Hart Lane. Things got better for the pair after that. Ardiles, with his cute passing game, became the midfield foil for Glenn Hoddle. Villa was more fitful, but possessed a majestic left foot. Spurs finished eleventh in the first division, and reached the sixth round of the FA Cup.

Burkinshaw still had to win over the Tottenham fans, though. Just before Christmas I commentated on the North London derby at White Hart Lane and saw Arsenal destroy their rivals 5–0. The best goal was a screamer from Liam Brady, which had me shouting, 'Look at that. Just look at that.' I always used to join Keith and his family for a drink in his office after a game. I remember that that day his wife Joyce, and their daughters Tracy and Lynn, were almost in tears.

Partly thanks to that family connection, I was sometimes allowed to travel on the team coach when I was covering a Spurs match in the North. It was both a privilege and an insight, but by no means restricted to me. Many clubs in those days took along the local reporter. I also hitched a lift at times with Arsenal, Liverpool and even the Republic of Ireland when I went to Dublin.

Having said that, by the time Burkinshaw led Tottenham to two consecutive FA Cup finals, my commentary was becoming synonymous with some memorable Spurs moments. It led some fans to question how neutral my standpoint really was, and whether beneath my sheepskin coat there was a secret Spurs fan waiting to get out.

I suppose it started with that one season they spent in the second division. *Match of the Day* saw Tottenham as an ideal way to meet their quota of second-division games, and sent me to cover a home match against Bristol Rovers in October 1977.

Burkinshaw was away scouting, but in the car park before the game one of his staff introduced me to Colin Lee, who had just been signed from Torquay United for £60,000. The twenty-one-year-old striker marked his debut by scoring four goals. His partner, Ian Moores, playing his second game after signing from Stoke City, weighed in with a hat-trick in Spurs' 9–0 win – a *Match of the Day* record.

By the time Tottenham reached the 100th Cup Final in 1981, Burkinshaw had overhauled the team. Players such as Lee, Moores, John Pratt, Peter Taylor, John Duncan, Terry Yorath and Gerry Armstrong all moved on. Firing the bullets ahead of Ardiles, Hoddle and Villa now were Steve Archibald and Garth Crooks, a striking partnership that had gelled immediately.

Tottenham's opponents in the FA Cup semi-final were Wolves, and after a 2–2 draw at Hillsborough, the replay took place at Highbury. I can remember the cheer that went up from the Spurs dressing room when they saw the Wolves team sheet and noted that Andy Gray was not in the side.

It seemed strange to see Spurs playing a semi-final on the ground of their avowed enemies, but 52,000 packed into Highbury that night, and it was a commentary I could not help but enjoy. Garth Crooks scored twice, and Villa topped off a 3–0 win with a stunning curling shot. Perhaps we should have known then that he would play a key role in the final.

The other semi-final, which I had covered the previous Saturday, was between Ipswich Town and Manchester City at Villa Park. I had spent the Friday night at the Ipswich team hotel just outside Birmingham, and remember their chairman, John Cobbold, buying the BBC team dinner. 'Let's all get absolutely pissed,' he said as we sat down.

Ipswich were chasing a treble. They were well placed in the

championship race and on the verge of a final spot in the UEFA Cup, which they later won. Bobby Robson told me he was taking a gamble on the fitness of Kevin Beattie. It backfired when the giant England defender broke his arm.

'*Somewhere his luck took a wrong turning*,' I said as he left the pitch, sensing it could be the end of his career.

Manchester City won with a free kick from Paul Power. It was the first occasion extra time had been adopted in the semi-finals.

To offset any accusations of Tottenham bias, I made a point of going down to City's Cup Final hotel. They were at Selsdon Park in Croydon, where I had been to see Tommy Docherty and Manchester United four years earlier. The City manager was John Bond. He had turned the club around in a few short months and was another manager who was easy to work with. 'You want to get it right, don't you?' he said when I arrived, and gave me all the help I needed.

Perhaps that was why the 1981 final was the first in which I felt comfortable with my commentary. Both clubs were totally open about their plans, and determined to mark the centenary FA Cup final in the right fashion.

Mind you, City put in a few tasty tackles. Tommy Hutchison scored at both ends in a 1–1 draw. Even though I had been in my pram at the time, I was aware that Bert Turner had done the same thing in the Derby–Charlton final of 1946.

In between the first match and the replay, I had gone down to White Hart Lane to update myself on Tottenham's injuries and likely line-up. I was wandering round the pitch when the Spurs groundsman, Colin White, stopped me. 'You know who will be the star on Thursday night?' he asked me. 'Ricky Villa.'

I was surprised. Villa had been substituted by Burkinshaw in the first game, and wandered disconsolately to the dressing room. Some believed he would not start the replay.

The first FA Cup final replay at Wembley was played on a balmy Thursday night that year. It takes its place in my top five matches, but that had nothing to do with my Tottenham connections.

Colin White's tip about Ricky Villa turned out to be an excellent one. Not only did he start, but he put Spurs in front after eight minutes: *'Here's Archibald with the touch. A good save but Ricky Villa! Ricky Villa has scored and it was made by his fellow Argentine Ossie Ardiles.'* Three minutes later came one of the best Cup Final goals, but one that is often forgotten. Nineteen-year-old Steve Mackenzie, who City's previous manager, Malcolm Allison, had signed from Crystal Palace, equalised with a breathtaking volley from outside the penalty area: *'Oh, a tremendous goal! Steve Mackenzie! Fabulous shot. An absolutely outstanding volley!'* Eleven minutes gone, and we were into the best Cup Final for years.

City looked the more likely winners when Kevin Reeves put them ahead from a second-half penalty. It took a typically opportunist goal from Garth Crooks to equalise. The match recording clearly shows Crooks and his strike partner, Steve Archibald, laughing at each other as they ran back to the centre circle. Thereby hangs a tale.

As young players who had arrived at White Hart Lane the previous summer, they often went up to London socialising. Crooks became tired of Archibald calling himself 'The King of the Shelf' – which was where the hardcore Spurs fans used to congregate in front of the East Stand.

'Wait and see, one day I will be King of the West End,' Crooks used to say. As they walked through Piccadilly, he would taunt Archibald. 'One day you will see my name up in lights.'

As they celebrated his goal at Wembley that night, Crooks looked up and saw the scoreboard flashing: 'Spurs 2, Manchester City 2. Crooks.'

'There you are,' he shouted to Archibald. 'I told you I would have my name up in lights.'

Then came the goal that very nearly gave me a title for this book.

I am still not quite sure how many players Ricky Villa beat on that twisting run that took him into FA Cup folklore. Garth Crooks and I have often joked that even he was one! Villa's meandering path seemed to go on for ever before he stabbed the ball underneath Joe Corrigan, the City goalkeeper.

'*Villa. And still Ricky Villa. What a fantastic run,*' I bellowed, before finally gasping, '*He's scored! Amazing goal!*'

It is a moment etched for ever in the memory of all Spurs fans of that generation. None more so than Jeffrey Zemmel, a corpulent North London business friend of Ricky George. The first time I was introduced to Jeffrey, he shouted at me across the restaurant: 'And still Ricky Villa.' It was his calling card whenever we met.

Contrary to what many people think, I was never a Tottenham supporter. One reason, perhaps, why I resisted the book being entitled *And Still Ricky Villa*. Also younger readers would have found it mystifying.

I have explained how I had a boyhood affection for Charlton and Chelsea, and how Ipswich Town touched my life. From my childhood holidays in Lincolnshire, I still have a soft spot for Boston United. The first result I look for, though, is Barnet's.

I was unwittingly responsible for Fred's allegiance to Derby County. When he was a baby, I brought home from the Baseball Ground a pencil case bearing the ram motif – a gift from the sponsors. Fred grew attached to it, and became a Derby supporter from that day.

So, although my father and I had purred with pleasure when watching the Spurs 'double' team of 1960/61, they meant no more to me than any other club. But the fact that I commentated on Tottenham in four FA Cup finals in eleven years means that an awful lot of people assumed they were always my team.

When they reached the 1982 final to face Queens Park Rangers, Villa and Ardiles were in the news for very different reasons. Mrs Thatcher's taskforce was fighting the Argentines for control of the Falkland Islands.

Even before the war had started, Burkinshaw gave Ardiles permission to leave Tottenham after the FA Cup semi-final and travel home to join the Argentina squad, who were defending the World Cup in Spain. But on the night before Tottenham and Leicester City were due to meet at Villa Park, the conflict started. Ardiles and Villa were up all night taking telephone calls from friends and relatives in Argentina.

Burkinshaw told Ardiles he wanted him to play, although he omitted Villa. Spurs beat a Leicester team including Gary Lineker 2–0, with Crooks scoring the first goal. Ardiles went off as planned, but after the World Cup rang Burkinshaw to say that because of the way the war was developing, he could not possibly return to Tottenham. The Spurs manager was also feeling the heat of the Falklands conflict. He and his family were given police protection after receiving death threats.

Burkinshaw gave Ardiles permission to go on loan to Paris St Germain after the World Cup, but he continued to pick Villa, who scored in consecutive matches against Notts County and Birmingham, and played in Spurs' last three league games prior to the Cup Final.

Tottenham used the same Ponsbourne Hotel in Hertfordshire where they had stayed on the Friday night the previous year. But this time the mood was decidedly more sombre.

Two high-ranking government officials arrived just as I was about to join Burkinshaw for dinner. They took him into a private room and a long conversation ensued about the wisdom of selecting Villa for the final. The player's safety was clearly one issue, but the decision was left to the manager. Burkinshaw slept on it and made an announcement at the Spurs training ground at Cheshunt on the morning of the game. 'I have decided it would not be fair on Ricky to pick him,' he said. 'I think with the war going on, there would be too much pressure on him.'

This final also went to a replay. Glenn Hoddle scored in both games, his penalty in the second match securing the cup for Spurs for the second successive year.

When the Falklands War ended, Ricky Villa stayed at Tottenham and figured in their side the following season. Ardiles returned from Paris but was injured in his second game. He made a handful of appearances before coming on as a substitute in Spurs' UEFA Cup success against Anderlecht in 1984.

That summer I covered the European Championship finals in France, and even though England were not there I was to see another match that makes my top five.

By the time France met Portugal in the semi-final in Marseilles, their talisman, Michel Platini, had scored seven goals in three games – including two hat-tricks. But this was to be his finest hour. The scores were level at 1–1 after ninety minutes, but eight minutes into extra time Jordão put Portugal 2–1 ahead. Five minutes from the end, left back Domergue scored his second goal of the game to equalise for France.

I am forever reminded about the dying seconds, since my commentary was probably one of my most emotional and over-stated. Jean Tigana got away on the right, and I went with his run. *'Tigana, Tigana . . . Platini . . . goal! . . . I've not seen a match like this in years.'* It was some time before I saw another one.

Back at our hotel that night, Keith Burkinshaw and Peter Shreeves were in the bar. They were not only excited about the match, but also about seeing the tunnel in Marseille where the car chase was filmed for *The Italian Job*.

But their jobs were changing. Burkinshaw was moving out of the manager's chair, and Shreeves was about to replace him. A new regime had swept through White Hart Lane. Until then, the board had been a conservative group led by the families of Sidney Wale and then Arthur Richardson. Now the thrusting Irving Scholar – a lifelong Tottenham supporter – and his sidekick Paul Bobroff were trying to revolutionise the club.

In hindsight, some of Scholar's ideas were commercially sound. Ten years later, they might have worked in the Premier League. But at the time, he overstepped the mark and Tottenham were plunged into a debt of £20 million, which could have bankrupted the club.

'There used to be a football club here,' was Burkinshaw's famous comment as he left Spurs to pursue a career in Bahrain and Portugal. He also worked with Ardiles at West Bromwich Albion, and Adrian Boothroyd at Watford.

When Spurs reached the FA Cup final in 1987, they lost 3–2 to Coventry City in the most fluent final since that against Manchester City six years earlier. David Pleat was then the Tottenham manager, and had tilted them at a treble. In the end they were beaten by Arsenal in the semi-final of the League Cup and finished third in the league.

But something else happened in that final that neither I, nor the ITV commentator Brian Moore, spotted. Half the Spurs team had the name of their sponsor, Holsten, on their shirts, while the other half were blank. It caused a right furore in the press the following morning. My first call at daybreak was from Brian Moore.

'Motty, did you spot the thing about the shirts?' hissed Brian. He was clearly wound up.

'Never noticed it, Mooro,' I said. 'They were too far away and I was concentrating on the game.'

Brian sighed. 'Thank God for that. Now I can relax and go to church.' He knew that if one of us had made a story out of it the other would have been hung out to dry.

It was in the same year that Mike Rollo, the Spurs commercial manager, came to me with an idea. He wanted to start a telephone interview service called 'Spursline' which fans could dial and hear their players talking before and after matches. A lot of other clubs had pooled their resources and started a joint service called 'Clubcall', but Scholar and Rollo had realised they could make more money going it alone.

'The players will respond better to a trained journalist than they will to me,' insisted Rollo. I took the job on a temporary basis, and when the BBC lost league football to ITV the following year, it seemed the perfect vehicle to keep a handle on a big club. I made two trips a week to the Spurs' training ground, delivering a tape to Rollo's office at lunchtime which he then put straight on to Spursline. Scholar paid me well for my efforts, and over the next four years I enjoyed talking to Glenn Hoddle, Chris Waddle, Gary Lineker, Paul Gascoigne and Gary Mabbutt.

But there was a downside. More and more people were saying that my relationship with Tottenham implied some kind of bias. Not least when the BBC appointed me to three consecutive FA Cup ties – against Oxford, Portsmouth and Notts County – on Spurs' route to Wembley in 1991. When Tottenham reached the semi-final, I told Rollo I had to resign. If they got to the final and I was the BBC commentator, it would be hugely unprofessional for me to be doing Spursline interviews.

So I went into the final between Tottenham and Nottingham Forest strictly neutral. But I had to deal almost at once with one of the most dramatic and regrettable Cup Final incidents. Paul Gascoigne, having already committed one untidy challenge, lunged at Forest's Gary Charles. *'If that had been any other player than Paul Gascoigne . . .'* I said. *'With his second offence of the match should he have had the yellow card or will Roger Milford speak to him when he gets up?'* Gascoigne, though, had torn his cruciate knee ligaments. It was to put on hold his transfer to Lazio, which was part of Spurs' financial survival package.

I did not think I was as hard on Gazza in the commentary as I might have been, but he must have thought differently when he heard it later. Before a match the following season, he made it clear he was unhappy with my remarks. He later retracted his comments and we were back on terms.

The final continued without him, and went to extra time. I was as perplexed as the rest of Wembley as to why Brian Clough did not get off the bench to talk to his Forest team: *'And now will Brian Clough get some words across to his team? But perversely he sits on the bench. Does not move. Feels no need to go over and say anything . . . I'm just wondering where the Forest manager has gone now. I'm told he's having a conversation with a policeman. Yes, exactly that. Well, there you are. Supercool, eh? Would rather talk to the policeman than talk to his players.'* I am sure Terry Venables' animated words had a lot to do with Tottenham winning the game in extra time.

I was invited to the club's banquet, and remember it starting late because the team coach had called in at the Princess Grace Hospital to show crocked Gascoigne the trophy. On the way out of the dinner, I stopped by a small table where Bill Nicholson was sitting quietly with Dave Mackay. You didn't need to be a Spurs supporter to realise that those two men did as much as anybody else to make the club such a force.

I had met Bill Nicholson in my first season as a television commentator. Along with Ron Greenwood I found him to be the most honest of managers. When Nicholson died in 2004, I went to his memorial service at White Hart Lane one Sunday morning. All the players appeared soberly dressed to say farewell to a legend. The framed memorabilia of that day are in my house today.

That still doesn't make me a Tottenham supporter, although Burkinshaw and Peter Day, secretary in those exuberant times, are still close friends. The post of club secretary then was not like that of the high-profile chief executive of today on a handsome salary. He was normally never seen outside his office, but ran the club like clockwork on a day-to-day basis.

Guys like Peter Day, Steve Stride at Aston Villa, Graham Hover at Coventry, Bernard Halford at Manchester City, Des McBain at Bolton and Brian Truscott at Southampton became good friends. They all made my job easier.

I finally got the Tottenham monkey off my back when Liverpool and Manchester United dominated the next twenty years of English football. Not that the accusations of bias were buried – if anything, they got worse!

After I had covered a game between the two rival North-West clubs, my postbag could be divided neatly into two piles. Those with a Merseyside postmark were guaranteed to contain some bile about me being a 'Red', and those from the Manchester conurbation insisted I had always been a closet Scouser.

With due respect to all the other clubs I have mentioned, I decided to nominate Barnet, where I started on the local paper, as my favourite team. It got me out of so much trouble.

There was a time, back in 1993, when for the only time in my life I could have become a director. Chairman Stan Flashman had hit hard times and left Barnet's future in the balance. Two of their creditors were threatening to close the club down. Ricky George and Stephen Glynne roused enough public support to keep the club in the Football League. I contributed the wages of goalkeeper/manager Gary Phillips – but only for one week!

In the 2003/04 season, the last before *Match of the Day* regained the Premiership highlight rights, I decided to visit all the league grounds to which I had never been. I thoroughly enjoyed the tour. It took me to Doncaster, Scunthorpe, Hull, Cheltenham, Northampton, Hartlepool, Macclesfield and Rochdale, as well as to new grounds at Brighton, Swansea, Bristol Rovers, Huddersfield and Darlington.

Thanks to Chris Hull of Nationwide, then Football League sponsors, I managed a whirlwind journey which ended at Bury's Gigg Lane, where I was presented with a souvenir shirt with 'Motson 92' on the back. It is proudly framed at home.

Now let me tell you why commentators are not biased. Simply, they do not have the time to be. I can speak for most, if not all, of my colleagues and contemporaries when I say that the concentration required to deliver an acceptable commentary does not allow a moment's thought to dwell on who you want to win. The commentator has got quite enough on his plate without worrying about any emotional involvement he may have with either team. You might be driving home afterwards and feel particularly pleased for someone involved with the winning team, or genuinely disappointed for one of the losers. But at the time, you are there to do a job.

So, having dispelled the urban myth about Tottenham and Motson, I now have to close by admitting they played a major part in the way my career progressed. On the team coach on the way back from Middlesbrough in 1979, Steve Perryman came up to me and said: 'It disappoints me to hear you doing tennis.' That thought remained with me until I gave up my radio role at Wimbledon two years later. Had I not done so, I doubt whether I would have been selected for as many big football occasions as I was.

Bertie Vogts, the former Germany and Scotland manager, once said: 'You meet everybody in your life twice.' He was referring to drawing the same opponents in successive competitions. I was reminded of that quote when Exeter City of the Conference held holders Manchester United to a draw at Old Trafford in the third round of the FA Cup in 2005. I was detailed to commentate on the replay in Devon.

There was not time to see Exeter play or familiarise myself with their players, but thanks to their Director of Football, I was invited to have tea with him and the team before the match. So thank you, Steve Perryman.

Chapter 11

Hillsborough, Heysel and Hooliganism

The dark days of the eighties

I WAS SURPRISED TO see John Smith, executive director of Luton Town Football Club, walking towards me outside the club's Kenilworth Road ground. It was March 1985 and their sixth-round FA Cup tie with Millwall was still four hours away.

'We've heard there are going to be a lot more Millwall fans than we originally expected,' he explained. 'I'm just checking on our entrances and the various access routes to the ground.'

In 1985, Luton were enjoying life in the old first division under David Pleat, whose dash across the pitch when they survived relegation at Maine Road two years earlier had been one of the iconic football television images of the time.

Millwall, meanwhile, were pushing for promotion from the third division under George Graham. It was his first job as manager, and he was clearly destined to go places. His team had knocked out two first-division sides – Chelsea and Leicester

City – and Crystal Palace from the second division to reach the sixth round.

The quarter-final should have taken place the previous Saturday, but there were no penalty shoot-outs in the FA Cup then, and Luton's fifth-round second replay with neighbours Watford took place on the day of the other sixth-round ties. Luton won that 1–0 with a goal by Wayne Turner before a crowd of 15,000, but that attendance was comfortably exceeded when Millwall arrived four days later.

I was there to commentate for BBC *Sportsnight*'s highlights. As referee David Hutchinson started the match, I remember thinking I had never seen Kenilworth Road so packed. What should have been a night of celebration for Luton, who went through to the semi-final, thanks to a goal by Brian Stein, was tarnished by one of the worst outbreaks of domestic football hooliganism ever seen on English television.

Millwall followers provoked a riot, which forced Hutchinson to take the teams off the field for twenty-five minutes, while mob rule took over on the pitch. I looked on as fans fought freely with the police: *'Supporters, or so they would call themselves – they're not – have gone across and started to throw seats out of the stand, adding to the scene of devastation and unrest, which the police are trying to control . . . sooner or later something has got to be done to try to prevent people like this spoiling the football for others. It's getting uglier and uglier out there.'*

Eventually, some semblance of order was restored. The referee restarted the match and, in a hostile atmosphere, managed to finish it. But then the fans went on the rampage again – at the ground, in the streets, and on trains back to London. Inside the ground snooker balls were hurled at guests in the directors' box, the players' tunnel was packed with supporters suffering from cuts and bruises, and at any moment I was expecting the mob to attack the television gantry, suspended below the roof of the main stand.

I was absolutely terrified. There was nothing I could do but sit and wait for the carnage to subside. Later, in the Luton boardroom, their manager David Pleat said he thought I still looked as white as a sheet.

Thirty-one policemen were injured that night, including one officer who was seen lying prostrate on the pitch being repeatedly kicked in the head by a youth wearing a white anorak. As part of their investigation the police spent hours at BBC Television Centre watching videotape of the riot and trying to identify the culprits. Inevitably, many were never caught.

Luton were ordered to erect fences around the pitch, but John Smith said after the FA verdict, 'It was not our fans who wrecked our town and our stadium.' David Evans, Luton's autocratic chairman, who would go on to become a Member of Parliament, was more outspoken: 'I don't care if they shut our ground. We will not fence in our family enclosure and season-ticket holders.'

Evans took his own action by slapping a ban on all away supporters unless they produced an identity card. Manchester City's directors boycotted their next league game at Luton in protest. I ended up sitting in the seat normally reserved for the visiting chairman.

It later transpired that trouble had started on trains out of St Pancras, which is why Millwall – whose hardcore fringe were already labelled with a bad reputation after a series of incidents down the years – took most of the blame. That is not to say others did not contribute to a horrible stain on the FA Cup.

That night at Kenilworth Road was by no means the start of football hooliganism, which had been with us since the late sixties and early seventies. When Tottenham reached the final of the UEFA Cup in 1974, their manager, Bill Nicholson, had to go on the public address system in the stadium in Rotterdam when fans rioted during the match. There were 70 arrests and 200 were injured.

The following year, Leeds United supporters smashed seats and caused mayhem in Paris when their team lost to Bayern Munich in the final of the European Cup. The government set up a working party designed to combat hooliganism and the then minister for sport, Denis Howell, wrote to the FA and the Football League, insisting that all ninety-two clubs implement recommendations.

Ten years later, the events at Luton showed the problem had anything but gone away. 'Somebody is going to get killed soon' was the prediction we were hearing constantly, and those of us in a state of shock that night were only thankful that it had not happened at Kenilworth Road.

What we did not know was that within two months we would be witnessing two of the worst disasters to befall football, and that an even bigger one was but four years away.

On the last day of the 1984/85 season, I was driving home from Southampton, where the club had beaten Coventry City in what proved to be Lawrie McMenemy's last match as Saints' manager. He moved on that summer to Sunderland. It was a bright, sunny afternoon and all seemed well with the world until the news came over the radio about what had happened at Valley Parade, where Bradford City were playing Lincoln City.

It was supposed to be a day of celebration. Bradford had just won the third-division championship – their first piece of domestic silverware for fifty-six years. Half an hour before the game, the City team did a lap of honour, and captain Peter Jackson was presented with the trophy.

The first forty minutes of the match passed without incident. Then five minutes before half-time, white smoke was seen rising from the rear of the seventy-seven-year-old wooden main stand. Three minutes later flames emerged from beneath the stand, and referee Don Shaw stopped the match. Within another two minutes the entire stand had been engulfed in flames.

It was later established that the fire had been started by a discarded cigarette which had been dropped behind a seat and fallen into an empty space below the stand, where rubbish had accumulated for some twenty years. As there were no fences at Valley Parade, many spectators escaped by running on to the pitch, but for some it was too late.

Fifty-six people lost their lives, and a further two hundred needed hospital treatment for burns. Most of the fatalities occurred at the rear of the stand, where many were trapped in a narrow corridor. Only countless acts of heroism by police and supporters prevented the death toll from being much higher. Yorkshire Television's cameras – there to reflect Bradford City's celebrations – showed the tragedy unfolding instead.

A public inquiry was set up under Mr Justice Popplewell, and new legislation was introduced to improve safety at football grounds in the United Kingdom. The construction of new wooden stands was prohibited.

The Bradford fire was not directly connected with what had happened at Luton, nor with what was to come at Heysel and Hillsborough, but the dilapidated state of stadia had for some time been a serious cause for concern. Many grounds had been largely untouched since the war, save for the odd new stand here and there at the more profitable clubs. Fans were still jammed shoulder to shoulder on crumbling terraces. Even in my privileged position as a commentator, I often found myself squeezing through narrow doorways and exits which would have no place under the health and safety rules of today.

My BBC colleague Alan Hansen has since given a graphic account of how worried Liverpool Football Club were about the way tickets were distributed before their European Cup final against Juventus in Brussels – eighteen days after the Bradford disaster.

It was Barry Davies who, as usual, was the BBC commentator

at the European Cup final. I had been commentating on the FA Cup final at Wembley the previous Saturday, when Norman Whiteside's goal gave Ron Atkinson his second FA Cup success with Manchester United and robbed Everton of a 'treble'. So I watched events unfold on television, along with millions of other horrified BBC viewers.

The outdated Heysel stadium, built in 1930, was hardly equipped to stage such a major final. I had been there two or three times to see Belgium play, usually in a friendly before a major championship. Those matches attracted only 4,000 spectators, and with the stadium largely empty, there was no threat of a large-scale accident.

But on the night Liverpool met Juventus there were more than 25,000 supporters from each team in the crowd of 58,000. Liverpool supporters in sections Y and Z on the all-standing terraces were only yards away from their Italian rivals. Trouble started when missiles were thrown half an hour before kick-off. A group of Liverpool fans then charged across the terrace, over the wire fence into section Z, and ran at the Juventus supporters.

As the Italians retreated, a perimeter wall collapsed. It was at this point that thirty-nine people – mostly Juventus supporters – lost their lives. A further 600 were injured.

Juventus fans tried to retaliate, but were stopped by police, with whom they clashed both before and during the game. UEFA decided that to abandon the match would cause further distress, so Juventus and Liverpool went through the motions of playing a European Cup final with piles of corpses lying outside the stadium.

The consequences for English football were severe. The official UEFA observer at Heysel, Gunter Schneider, said, 'only the English fans were responsible. Of that there is no doubt'. Two days later, the British prime minister, Margaret Thatcher, put pressure on the FA to withdraw English clubs from European competition. UEFA did it for them. They banned English clubs 'indefinitely', with

Liverpool to serve a further three-year exclusion order after the ban on other clubs had been lifted.

In the event, English clubs were banned for five years. Seventeen clubs missed out on the chance to play in the three European club competitions, including the then champions Everton, and the likes of Norwich City, Luton Town, Coventry City, Derby County and Wimbledon.

Even after the ban was lifted in 1990, English clubs had to wait a further five seasons before earning back all the European places they had held before Heysel. Liverpool eventually served only one year of their extra three, and were readmitted to Europe in 1991.

There was another heavy blow coming the way of English clubs in the wake of Luton, Bradford and especially Heysel. Television had fallen out of love with football.

BBC and ITV, still working together in negotiations with the Football League, were not prepared to pay the price they were being asked to renew the contract. Football was soiled goods. Even the national newspapers trimmed their coverage. Attendances at the start of the following season reflected a mood of anger and apathy in the country.

I remember going to see West Ham play Leicester in front of 12,000 at Upton Park; Aston Villa drew a crowd of just 11,000 for a home match against Queens Park Rangers; Coventry's home gate sometimes dropped below 10,000. First-division football was no longer a mandatory Saturday fix.

Those of us who had witnessed hooliganism at first hand saw it as a cancer rather than just a sore. The constant outbreaks of bad behaviour were not just tarnishing the game we loved, but were making it difficult for decent supporters to travel and watch football in safety. Fights were often arranged by rival gangs, and took place outside the ground or at a predetermined venue either before or after matches. In some ways, football's ills reflected a general breakdown in society. Rebels without a cause found one in and around football.

Judging by the number of books on the subject written since, some by gang members themselves, hooliganism became almost an industry in itself, with badges for the bravest. No wonder television executives turned their backs on the national sport.

As a result of the stand-off between the Football League and the BBC and ITV, no league football was shown on terrestrial television in England between August and Christmas 1985. And since satellite had yet to come on stream, that meant a total blackout. At one stage the BBC were showing basketball on a Saturday night.

I spent my Saturdays sitting in the stands watching games, waiting for somebody to give me my job back. My wife, Annie, was pregnant, and when a photographer captured me in the stand at Oxford United's Manor Ground, they captioned the picture 'Oh baby, look at him now'.

It was a highly unsatisfactory situation, and it was partially resolved at the BBC's *Sports Review of the Year* celebration in December. Head of Sport Jonathan Martin and Philip Carter of the Football League Management Committee got together and decided it would be carrying things too far not to show the FA Cup from the third-round stage.

Televised football was back after an absence of eight months. The first match chosen to be broadcast was an all-London affair: Charlton Athletic, who were sharing Selhurst Park at the time, were drawn at home to West Ham United in the third round. As I walked round to my commentary position I was aware of cameras focusing not just on the ground, but on our BBC vehicles and the commentator himself.

Frank McAvennie, signed from St Mirren, had rattled in eighteen goals for the Hammers in the first half of that season. But hardly anybody, apart from their own fans, knew what he looked like until he appeared in front of the television cameras for the first time that day. He made the winning goal against Charlton for Tony Cottee, and the two strike partners grabbed fifty-three goals between them in total as West Ham, under John Lyall, finished a best ever third in the top division.

Gary Lineker scored forty goals for Everton that season, but they had to settle for a runners-up spot behind Liverpool in both the league and FA Cup. Kenny Dalglish, in his first season as manager (Joe Fagan had resigned after Heysel), led them to 'the double'.

What with England then going off to Mexico and reaching the World Cup quarter-final, only to be robbed by Diego Maradona's 'Hand of God', the tide seemed to be turning. A year on, football was starting to look respectable again.

Sadly, the worst of the eighties was yet to come.

The FA Cup semi-final I was chosen to cover on 15 April 1989 was an exact repeat of the one I had covered a year earlier, where Liverpool had won 2–1 with two goals by John Aldridge. Same teams – Liverpool and Nottingham Forest. Same venue – Hillsborough. And the same fences round the stadium to deter unruly spectators.

Even though the BBC were now showing one FA Cup tie live in rounds three to six on a Sunday afternoon, the FA wanted to preserve the semi-final tradition and play both matches on Saturday. The cup was now of even greater importance to the BBC. Under a new television contract, ITV had bought exclusive rights to a given number of Football League matches, and a new satellite channel – British Satellite Broadcasting – was sharing the FA Cup and England matches with the BBC.

Des Lynam was coming to Hillsborough with Jimmy Hill, and then the pair of them were going back to London to present the highlights on *Match of the Day*. Before the match, Des and I had decided we would get out of the city and stay at a country hotel north of Sheffield. On the Friday night I phoned the Liverpool manager, Kenny Dalglish, who was guarded, as usual, about his team selection, but keen to fire some questions at me from the football quiz they had on the team coach.

Although my commentary would be recorded, I always felt semi-final days were special, and when Lynam and I walked round the grounds of the hotel in the morning the sun was shining. How could we ever have envisaged it would be the blackest day in English football history? A day when ninety-six people went to a football match and never came home.

When we arrived at Hillsborough, I was given a parking space near the BBC vans at the Leppings Lane end of the ground, which, as the year before, would be the stand and terrace where the Liverpool supporters would be situated.

Peter Robinson, the Liverpool chief executive and general secretary, was mindful of what had happened at Heysel. There, he had pleaded with UEFA to change the ticket arrangements so that Liverpool and Juventus supporters were kept well apart. Now, he asked the FA to give the Forest fans the Leppings Lane end since they would be outnumbered by the Liverpool support, and allocate the opposite end of the ground to his own club. That request was turned down. The police believed the Liverpool supporters, approaching the ground from the M62 motorway, would get there more easily if they were sited at the Leppings Lane end.

I went through my usual pre-match routine with producer John Shrewsbury. We agreed we would build up the atmosphere at the start with words and pictures reflecting the packed, expectant crowd.

It has always been my custom to knock on the door of the referee's room before a match. I like to double-check the names of his assistants, and on which side of the pitch they will operate. The referee that day, Ray Lewis from Great Bookham in Surrey, had been on the league list for fifteen years. His two assistants were David Axcell and John Brandwood, who both later went on to become Football League referees.

While I was in Ray's room there was another knock on the door. In came two police officers, one of whom I later learned was Chief Superintendent David Duckenfield, taking charge of his first football match. The briefing he gave to Lewis and his team was the one the referees expect every week. I was rarely allowed to hear it, although on this occasion nobody asked me to leave. I can recall Duckenfield saying something about an emergency alarm sounding if the ground had to be evacuated.

I made my way up to the commentary position, high on the roof of the main stand. Jimmy Hill and I sat in a small box with the BBC cameras positioned on a platform outside. John Shrewsbury wanted me to rehearse my opening words, but as I looked to my left at the Leppings Lane end, I saw a problem. Although the two central pens on the terrace were packed, the two wing sections were so sparsely populated that I could see steps where nobody was standing.

'Have to change some words here, John,' I said. 'Can't really talk about a capacity crowd when there are all those gaps.'

The time was about a quarter to three – fifteen minutes before kick-off. In a few hours' time the significance of what I had just seen would hit me.

The game had been in progress only for about four minutes when Ray Lewis noticed a commotion behind the goal at the Leppings Lane end. 'From where I was on the pitch it looked as though people were trying to move from one pen to another,' he said later.

As we were to discover, it was much worse than that. At six minutes past three a police officer ran on to the pitch and tapped Lewis on the shoulder. 'We have a crowd problem,' he said, 'you must take the teams off the field.'

Since the Leppings Lane end was occupied only by Liverpool supporters, Jimmy Hill and I dismissed any suggestion of misbehaviour and could see from where we were sitting that there was an overspill. It took a few minutes for it to sink in that people were being crushed, but we had no way of knowing how serious it was. After what seemed a long delay, one ambulance made its way slowly round the track. It was later reported that plenty of ambulances were parked outside the ground but not alerted in time to be of help.

By now my recorded *Match of the Day* responsibilities were obsolete as there was no match. Instead, *Grandstand* was on the line wanting a live report as to why the game had been stopped. It was the first of many inserts I gave them during the afternoon.

I became a news reporter, but with precious little hard information to go on. When Hill and I saw advertising boards being ripped out and used as emergency stretchers, we knew we had a tragedy on our hands. Down on the pitch below, a policeman was giving a supporter the kiss of life.

'People are dying,' hissed Jimmy, as more prone figures were carried away towards hurriedly assembled first-aid points. Ray Lewis vacated his dressing room so that it could be used to treat the injured.

BBC rules about reporting death had been instilled in me years earlier. I had been in the *Match of the Day* studio the night Graham Hill was reported dead in an air crash, but the editor insisted on having the news doubly confirmed before breaking the story. I was also conscious of friends and relatives watching at home. It was my responsibility to convey the enormity of what was happening, but not to speculate on what might later prove to be false information.

And false information was the very thing I got next. John Shrewsbury passed me a message from the police to say that Liverpool supporters had broken down a gate to gain access to the Leppings Lane End, which was how they said the crush had happened. In good faith, I read out the details of the message on the air.

In his subsequent report on the events of the day, Lord Justice Taylor was highly critical of senior officers for giving out this false information. 'This was not only untruthful,' Taylor said, '[but] set off a widely reported allegation against the supporters which caused grave offence and distress.' Taylor's report confirmed that it was the police themselves who had opened the gate, because there were security concerns outside the ground with some five thousand supporters still trying to get in.

One of those who had walked through the gate quite calmly was a banker from St Albans, Roger Ball, with his sixteen-year-old son Kester, and two friends. Once inside, they were drawn towards the tunnel that led to the two central pens.

'There was no signage,' was the first thing Roger Ball said when I met him in the wake of the disaster. 'We had no way of knowing how much room there was at either end.'

In the heaving mass of bodies in the overcrowded central pen, Roger and Kester were separated. His father passed out and was carried out unconscious. Once he had come round, he spent the rest of the afternoon and evening searching for Kester. Eventually, at 10.30 p.m., he identified his son's body in the gymnasium at the ground, which was being used as a makeshift morgue.

When *Grandstand* came off the air at five o'clock and the news programmes took over reporting the disaster, I went downstairs to the dressing rooms. Brian Clough, looking dazed, was leading his Nottingham Forest team back to their coach. The match had long since been abandoned. The conversation in the FA guest room revolved around the police, and their reluctance to open the fences at the front of the terrace when the crush started.

Even then, the full extent of the tragedy was still emerging. It was not until I drove home later in the evening that I learned that a total of 94 supporters had lost their lives; 760 fans had been injured, and 300 were taken to hospital. Two more died later.

I was asked to make a statement to the public inquiry. Two officers from the West Midlands force came to see me at a hotel in Liverpool, and to save their time and mine I gave them five typewritten pages of evidence. At the inquest in Sheffield I had to appear in person, along with John Shrewsbury. There was a model of the stadium in front of the coroner, and he asked me to point out exactly where my position had been.

When I was asked how good a view I had of the Leppings Lane end, I told the story of seeing huge gaps in the wing sections on the terrace. Four lawyers leapt up at once to protest. A number of different groups, as well as the families, were legally represented at the hearing.

'We claim Mr Motson's evidence to be inadmissible,' said one. 'He is a football commentator and has no knowledge or experience of crowd control.'

The coroner asked me to leave the room while they debated whether my statement should stand or not. I waited in the corridor for a few minutes before they called me back in. The rest of the coroner's questions centred on other matters, and we never came back to the empty pens.

So much has been said and written about the Hillsborough disaster in the twenty years that have followed, and I can add little of any comfort here to bereaved families such as those of Roger and Brenda Ball, with whom I became firm friends in the aftermath. I had the privilege of speaking at Kester's memorial service.

One of the first calls I had the day after the tragedy came from Barry Davies. He had been through something similar at Heysel and wanted to know whether I was all right. We shared a few private thoughts about how we each dealt with something both unforeseen and utterly appalling.

It was then that the size of the tragedy really came home to me. I had felt guilty on the day, inasmuch as my broadcasting responsibilities had left me partially immune to the size of the disaster. Once the dreadful truth and the number of fatalities sank in, I found it hard to comprehend the scale of what had happened. Hundreds of thousands went to football every week, but they expected to return safely.

I did not feel much enthusiasm for the delayed and rearranged semi-final in which Liverpool beat Nottingham Forest. The weeks in between had been dominated by funerals, many of them attended by Kenny Dalglish and Liverpool players.

On the same day as the tragedy, Everton had beaten Norwich City in the other semi-final, so the final at Wembley was bound to be a highly charged and emotional occasion. I agonised over what tone I should take in the commentary. Would the outpouring of grief simply overwhelm the match and the occasion?

We decided the pre-match build-up should be low key and respectful – hype was out of the question. Some of the relatives of the victims were sensitively shown on the screen. The grief of the bereaved was my main theme as the cameras swept around the stadium.

Then, there was a football match. Rightly or wrongly, I treated this in the normal way. Liverpool won an exciting game 3–2 in extra time. The Everton supporters were magnanimous in their respect and behaviour towards their heartbroken neighbours.

The aftermath, during which one half of Merseyside tried to put their lives back together, has gone on for more than twenty years. Roger and Brenda Ball were just one couple who sought justice through the Hillsborough Support Group. Whatever the rights and wrongs of what happened that day, the Taylor Report, with its insistence on all-seater stadia, ensured that such a disaster would never be repeated.

It may seem insensitive to link Hillsborough with a chapter that started with hooliganism. But I believe there *was* a link. Not, I should stress, between what happened and the behaviour of the Liverpool fans on the day, but because of how some troublemakers had carried on over the previous decade and a half. The sad truth is that the fences at the Leppings Lane end were there because of persistent misbehaviour at English grounds. If there had been no hooliganism, there would have been no fences. And if there had been no fences, those poor victims would almost certainly never have died.

Chapter 12

Tournament Football

How I managed without England

I COVERED SIX INTERNATIONAL tournaments without England, and once I got there I did not miss them. In terms of football spectacles, I don't think the quality suffered. And sad to say, the atmosphere was better than when it was poisoned by a section of so-called England followers.

Having watched the 1966 World Cup as a spectator, and worked at the London end of the radio operation in 1970, I was hoping to get my first taste of the real action in 1974. What I had not bargained for was that it would be with Scotland.

Once England's participation was laid to rest by Poland at Wembley in October 1973, the BBC had to revise their plans. Scotland under Willie Ormond had qualified by beating Czechoslovakia in front of a 100,000 crowd at Hampden Park. The Scots were now carrying the flag for Britain, and my boss Sam Leitch – himself a proud Scotsman – set about covering their exploits by sending me on a pre-World Cup tour to Belgium and Norway.

It was an eye-opener in more ways than one. Even before we set out, Celtic's diminutive winger Jimmy Johnstone had to be rescued from the sea when he drifted out off the coast at Largs in a fishing boat. Travelling with the Scottish press party was also something of an initiation. They were boisterous, to say the least, and the coach from the airport to the hotel had to make several stops when some well-known scribes from north of the border needed to relieve themselves.

Scotland lost 2–1 to Belgium in Bruges, and also lost the services of the Leeds United centre half, Gordon McQueen, through injury. Manchester United's Jim Holton was his replacement. But it was when we got to Oslo that the fun really started. The players were billeted on a university campus, and my producer Bob Abrahams and I were sitting in the bar surrounded by students when Billy Bremner and Jimmy Johnstone came in arm in arm.

Perhaps 'swayed in' would be a better description. They were singing a tuneless version of 'The Most Beautiful Girl in the World', which Charlie Rich had recorded earlier in the year and which peaked at number two in the hit parade. They were clearly in no fit state to make the team curfew that Ormond had set. They escaped with a warning about their future conduct, but the fact that they could have been sent home made for a great story.

Not surprisingly, Ormond banned the whole team from the bar and Bob Abrahams felt sorry for them. We knew some of the English-based players quite well, so he bought a crate of beer and decided to take it up to their floor. As the lift doors opened, standing there in front of Bob was Willie Ormond. 'I think I had better take care of that,' he said.

There was also a dispute over the Scottish players' pool. Their agent, Bill Bain, had been appointed by the Scottish FA, who had decided they would take ten per cent of the players' perks themselves. Those were early days for agents. Among the spectators in Germany for the World Cup was Dennis Roach, whom I had got to know well when he was captain of Barnet. He and his brother had a carpet company and Dennis fitted the carpets in Annie's and my first house in St Albans.

Roach gave the Scottish boys some unofficial advice, but his big break came when he went on holiday after the tournament and met Johan Cruyff and his family on the beach. Cruyff gave Roach approval to act as his agent in England, and off the back of that Dennis seized the opportunity to build one of the most successful agencies in football, with contacts and deals all over the world.

Even though his Dutch team lost the final to West Germany, Cruyff was the biggest name in the World Cup. Having piloted Ajax to three successive European Cup triumphs, he had moved to Barcelona in 1973, and in his first season at the Nou Camp had led them to the La Liga championship by eight clear points. His innate skills were much in evidence when Holland lit up the 1974 finals with their 'total football'. There were times when Cruyff, in particular, seemed to be in two or three different positions at once. He could score goals, make them, influence the way others played, and generally dominate the opposition.

Going to interview him at the Dutch team camp was one of the abiding memories of my first World Cup, when I doubled up as a reporter alongside my commentating duties. Thanks to Eddy Poelmann, a Dutch commentator who became a close friend over the next thirty-five years, Cruyff agreed to a one-to-one interview for the BBC in English. That would be nothing special today, but back in 1974 an overseas player speaking fluently in pefect English was still something of a rarity.

When I arrived at the hotel, Cruyff was standing on the edge of a jetty surrounded by television cameras, radio microphones and journalists from several countries. 'He has five interviews to do in different languages. Yours will be the last,' I was told.

That proved to be a blessing. By the time we got Cruyff in front of our camera, most of the others had gone. When we finished, he introduced me to his teammate, Ruud Krol, who also spoke good English. I finished up in their bedroom discussing the respective merits of our first division and the modest Dutch league in which Krol was still playing. 'Can you get me a transfer to Arsenal?' he asked me.

Following the debacle of Don Revie's reign, England were again absent from the next World Cup in Argentina. But again Scotland qualified, and were drawn in a group that included the then hardly known footballers of Iran.

Bob Abrahams and I were sent out to Tehran to film a preview – not the easiest assignment. It was the year before the Iranian Revolution, and though the Shah was still on his 'Peacock Throne', tension was rising in the capital, and we really had no idea what to expect. So we co-opted Frank O'Farrell, the former Manchester United manager, to come with us. Frank had coached in Iran, and knew a lot about the country and the players.

When we arrived in Tehran, the BBC had failed to book us a hotel. We went to the best one we could find. With Frank acting as an interpreter, Bob had to bribe the receptionist to give us a room. The three of us had to share. Frank volunteered to sleep on the floor. It didn't seem to worry him. He snored all night.

Iran were about to play a friendly against Wales, which we were filming, but the centrepiece of our trip was a visit to the Royal Palace to interview Crown Prince Reza, the Shah's son, who was a keen footballer. He had his own football pitch, and Frank took him through a few functional practice routines while Bob directed the film crew. I was more worried about the number of firearms in the hands of the surrounding soldiers.

When we arrived at the stadium for the match against Wales, we were introduced to the Iranian team. One player who spoke good English was the midfielder Hassan Nayebagha, who later came to university in England and whom I helped to find a local non-league club.

'They are quite good footballers,' said Frank, 'but their heads go down very easily. They haven't acquired any mental toughness.'

Wales beat Iran 1–0 in front of a 45,000 crowd, but the Iranians must have learned something. They had a shock in store for Scotland when the teams met in Argentina.

On paper, it was a talented Scotland team that went to the 1978 World Cup. It included not just Archie Gemmill but Lou Macari, Asa Hartford, Kenny Dalglish, Joe Jordan and John Robertson. Graeme Souness and Bruce Rioch were also in the squad. Their first match in Argentina was against Peru in Córdoba. David Coleman was commentating as Joe Jordan put them ahead, but Don Masson missed a penalty and Peru came back to win 3–1 with two goals from Teofilo Cubillas.

Holland, meanwhile, had comfortably seen off Iran with a 3–0 win in Mendoza. Scotland's next match, against Iran, therefore, was going to be crucial if they were going to progress. But before the game, their West Bromwich Albion winger, Willie Johnston, was sent home after a drugs test revealed he had taken an illegal stimulant. The scene in the Scottish camp was chaotic. It was similar at Heathrow when Johnston arrived to be whisked away by his club manager, Ron Atkinson, for an interview with Frank Bough at BBC Television Centre.

England manager Ron Greenwood was my co-commentator and constant companion in the early part of the tournament. I suggested we went to meet the Iran coach and his players before they faced Scotland. When I introduced Ron, they could not wait to pick his brains. 'What do we do to contain Archie Gemmill?' the coach demanded.

Greenwood was one of the most generous football people you could wish to meet. He felt the simple truths about the game were there to be shared, but he did admit to me, after his hour-long chat with the Iranians, that he might have been a shade disloyal to Scotland.

Frankly, Scottish morale was so low it wouldn't have made a great deal of difference. An own goal by Andranik Eskandarian put them in front just before half-time, but on the hour Iraj Danaifar equalised for Iran. Scotland made a brave attempt to rescue their campaign when they beat Holland 3–2 in their third match but it came too late. Archie Gemmill scored one of the best individual goals seen in the World Cup to show what might have been.

The Dutch team for the 1978 World Cup was missing Johan Cruyff, who had elected not to travel. But despite his absence, and the defeat by Scotland, they were good value in reaching their second successive World Cup final. I was in the River Plate stadium in Buenos Aires for their second-round group match against Italy, which would determine which of the two nations reached the final.

Holland lost their goalkeeper, Piet Schrijvers, after twenty-one minutes. His injury came from a collision with his own defender, Erny Brandts, who also nudged the ball into his own goal to put Italy in the lead. Schrijvers' replacement was Jan Jongbloed, who had played unconvincingly in the final in Munich four years earlier, and had since lost his number-one position. I was astounded to see him running up and down on the touchline, waving to the crowd. He appeared to have no sympathy for Schrijvers, whom he was about to replace.

At half-time the Dutch coach, Ernst Happel, gave Johan Neeskens a more advanced role, and the game changed. Within five minutes, Brandts made amends when he fired a first-time shot past Dino Zoff from the edge of the penalty area. Zoff must have thought he was on a shooting range. Fifteen minutes from the end, Arie Haan beat him with a wonderful 35-yard effort. Holland were through to the final.

Here, I have a confession to make. I walked out of the 1978

World Cup final halfway through the second half with Argentina leading 1–0. And I hadn't even seen their goal, scored by the tournament's Golden Boot winner Mario Kempes.

Having been on duty in the same River Plate stadium the previous day, when Brazil beat Italy 2–1 to claim third place, I had hoped to be a spectator at the final, as in Germany four years earlier. For some reason, the BBC decided they needed a stand-by commentator in the Broadcast Centre in case David Coleman's sound line broke down. The stadium was only a couple of miles away, so we reached a compromise. I would sit in the studio until the start of the second half. If all was well I would then be released to go to the stadium with my precious observer's ticket.

Once I took my seat I suddenly realised that if the match went to extra time, I had no chance of getting my flight back to London. I was due at Wimbledon the following afternoon to start my shift for BBC Radio. So ten minutes from the end I jumped in a taxi, just in time to hear the Spanish radio commentator describe Holland's equaliser from Dirk Nanninga. We were halfway to the airport when Kempes' second goal restored Argentina's lead. Just as the driver dropped me at Departures, Daniel Bertoni clinched the World Cup with the third goal.

I wasn't the only one to leave early. Enzo Bearzot, manager of the Italian team, who would go on to greater things four years later, sat near me on the Varig flight back to London. My wife Annie met me at Gatwick, thrusting some Wimbledon passes into my hand. Within two hours of landing I was beside Court 14, then an outpost for the junior commentator!

Funnily enough, my lasting memory of the 1978 World Cup had nothing, to with football. The military junta had a firm hold on the country, and their excesses with thousands of 'disappeared' people were causing huge condemnation. President Jorge Videla was at the head of this murderous government, and the BBC News reporter Vincent Hanna managed to get a one-to-one interview with him. He pressed him on their miserable human rights record, and I remember sitting transfixed in the BBC office in Buenos Aires watching the uncut version of the interview. Somehow football seemed a long way away.

After Argentina I was conscious that the more I was sent away, especially for six successive weeks as had happened that summer, the less my wife was seeing of me and the world. So I arranged to take Annie along when FIFA decided to stage the World Champions' Gold Cup – a tournament to mark the fiftieth anniversary of the first World Cup in Uruguay.

The teams invited to the tournament were the then six winners of the World Cup. The FA, however, decided not to take part, and England's place was taken by Holland. Once the FA had declined the invitation, the domestic season went on unhindered, which meant I had to get permission to miss a month of *Match of the Day* to go. Annie and I flew out on Christmas Day in 1980, and saw in the New Year in Montevideo. We also added a few days in Buenos Aires and Rio de Janeiro to make the trip more of a holiday.

Rather as with Yugoslavia in 1976, few English journalists or managers bothered to travel. Jeff Powell of the *Daily Mail* and Mike Langley of the *Sunday People* persuaded their editors that the tournament merited coverage. Robin Russell of the Football Association coaching staff also made it his business to be there.

One of the highlights for me was meeting Ronnie Biggs, who by now was something of a tourist attraction in himself. He came down from his home in the mountains to meet us at a restaurant just outside Rio. He wasn't supposed to go into the city, where he had been the target of a kidnap attempt a few months earlier. Biggs spoke openly about the Great Train Robbery of 1963, and debated the veracity of the book Piers Paul Read wrote about the subject. He also spoke fondly of West Ham and said that football was one of the things he missed most about his home country.

Another chance meeting I always treasured was that with Sir Stanley Rous, who was president of FIFA until João Havelange commandeered the African vote at my first World Cup in 1974. I had read a lot about the vast contribution Rous had made to football. A former schoolteacher, he had refereed the 1934 FA Cup final between Manchester City and Portsmouth, and during his time as secretary of the Football Association had completely rewritten and modernised the laws of the game.

He was eighty-five by the time Annie and I met him at the British ambassador's residence in Montevideo, but we kept in close touch with him. He and his companion, Rosemary Breitenstein, came to our house for dinner, and just before Sir Stanley's ninetieth birthday, we had tea at his home in Ladbroke Grove.

He showed me his souvenirs and mementoes of a life in football, including a notebook recording details of his first international match as a referee. It was Belgium against Holland in 1927, and his expenses to and from Brussels were £6.11 shillings.

The Gold Cup was won by Uruguay, who, in an echo of the 1950 World Cup, beat Brazil 2–1 to lift the trophy. I picked up some freelance commentary work at the tournament, which helped to pay for the trip, and it proved a valuable experience when I went to Spain the following year for the 1982 World Cup. It was during that tournament that I watched the finest game I have seen anywhere: the second-round group match between Brazil and Italy in Barcelona.

Italy had started the World Cup poorly, drawing all three group matches and qualifying for the second phase on goal difference ahead of Cameroon. Paolo Rossi, returning after a suspension for match-fixing allegations, had made an inauspicious start to the tournament. But when the second group phase started, Italy thumbed their noses at their critical press corps – which they had boycotted – with a 2–1 win over Argentina. Brazil, though, had gone one better, and beat their fellow South Americans 3–1 in a game during which a young Diego Maradona was sent off. It meant Brazil and Italy would meet in the final game of the three-cornered contest, with the South Americans needing just a draw to reach the semi-finals.

The game was played in the compact Sarria Stadium, now a car park, but it was then home to Espagnol. Had it been in the vast Nou Camp across the city, I don't think the drama and intimacy of the occasion would have left quite such a legacy. As I took my seat in the stadium next to Bobby Charlton, who was my co-commentator, our BBC colleague John Rowlinson bounded up the steps. 'The Italian journalists are all saying this could be Rossi's renaissance,' he said.

Was it not! A wonderful game ensued, the near touchline a handshake away from our commentary position. Rossi headed Italy in front after just five minutes, only for Socrates to beat Dino Zoff at his near post seven minutes later. Rossi restored the lead after twenty-five minutes following a howler in the Brazilian defence: *'Terrible mistake by Cerezo. And Italy are in front for the second time. Rossi didn't need to be asked twice, he was through the centre and he's returned to the world stage now in proper fashion.'*

But twenty-two minutes from the end Falcão conjured a brilliant equaliser to make it 2–2: *'Falcão over to the right and in a good position. Still Falcão. Still Falcão! What a drive! It's there! Falcão, who plays for an Italian club, wipes out Italy's lead . . . Now the flags come out and the Brazilians show their sheer relief!'* To qualify for the semi-finals Brazil just had to keep things as they were. But when had their magical interpretation of the game ever had anything to do with defence? The full backs, Leandro and Junior, were still seizing every chance to attack. Suddenly, Italy countered and forced a corner. The ball was half cleared, but Junior stayed on the left-hand post. Tardelli sent it back into the penalty area and Rossi, played onside, stabbed in Italy's winning goal. *'Unbelievable,'* I exclaimed. *'It's 3–2 to Italy.'*

With barely a minute to go, it was Brazil's turn to force a corner. Eder, the left winger, had to move an advertising board to take it. His whipped delivery went to the far post, where centre back Oscar rose to meet the ball with a firm header. Zoff, captain of the Italian team at the age of forty, pounced on the ball right on the line: *'Oh, and Zoff did brilliantly!'* The referee, Abraham Klein of Israel, blew the final whistle and the Brazilian players looked at one another in disbelief: *'Brazil, the great artists from South America, who came back twice, couldn't come back a third time and so it is the Italian players that celebrate,'* I exclaimed. *'Rossi, who I said at the beginning was having to sing for his supper, well, he can have the champagne now.'*

Some of the Brazilian players left the field in tears. Bobby Charlton was also crying through sheer emotion. John Helm, the ITV commentator in the row in front of us, turned round and looked at me. Neither of us could speak. Then a voice in my ear said: 'Hand back to London for the news.' How insensitive I thought. This *is* the news.

What made this particular match so special? Mainly the fact that this Brazilian team was rated alongside their magnificent winning side of 1970. Every time they won a game, one of their staff would come out of the dressing room and say to the press: 'Same team for the next match.' Such confidence and class made most of us think they would go on to win the World Cup.

The mood in Barcelona changed dramatically after Brazil's defeat. Italians aside, it was as though there had been some sort of fatality.

'Football is dead,' I remember one journalist saying.

'Long live football,' was my reply. The Brazilians had been fabulous, but they had only lost a football match. The World Cup was still alive and well.

Rossi scored twice more in the semi-final, when Italy beat Poland in the Nou Camp stadium, then opened the scoring against West Germany in the final in Madrid, as Italy went on to win 3–1. But it is Italy's second goal I remember most from my first World Cup as a commentator. The glazed look on Marco Tardelli's face as he raced towards the touchline having just put the Italians 2–0 up will stay with me for ever: *'This is Conti, it's Rossi, it's Scirea, it's Bergomi, it's Scirea, they're appealing for offside and it's not being given, it's Scirea right across to Marco Tardelli! 2–0 to Italy! Tardelli the scorer. A brilliant move and the Germans torn to pieces . . .'*

If I was starting to think that I would never see England in a World Cup final, the same could be said of Brazil. I had marvelled from afar when they won their third world title in 1970, but in my first six World Cups as a commentator they never got farther than the semi-final, and then, as I have explained, I was replaced for the 1994 final against Italy in Los Angeles.

The World Cup in France four years later was the most enjoyable I have covered. It was a case of right time, right place. The French had invented the idea of a World Cup (through Jules Rimet), had pioneered the European Championship (Henri Delaunay), and came up with the idea and format for the European Champions Cup (Gabriel Hanot). They also boasted the best football magazine in the world – *France Football* – which I took twice a week. They played their football in traditional stadiums, with the crowd and commentators close to the pitch – not having to peer across an eight-lane running track.

France and Brazil seemed destined to meet in the final, especially after two dramatic semi-finals. In Marseilles, Brazil beat Holland on penalties after Patrick Kluivert forced extra time with just four minutes on the clock. Trevor Brooking and I, meanwhile, were in Paris to see France play Croatia, who were enjoying their first World Cup since achieving independence, and took the lead through Davor Suker. Then the French right back, Lilian Thuram, came up with two goals in twenty minutes – the only two he ever scored for his country in 142 appearances.

When Trevor and I arrived at the commentary position in the Stade de France for the final, we got the sort of news that turns commentators into instant reporters. The team sheet, timed at 7.48 – just over an hour before kick-off – did not include the name of Ronaldo, Brazil's figurehead and centre forward.

The whole media stand went into a frenzy. What had happened? Was he injured? Had he been dropped? Had they saved the biggest story of the World Cup until just before the final? I was walking across from wishing Brian Moore of ITV all the best for his last commentary when I caught sight of our reporter Ray Stubbs. 'I've had a word with Pele,' he said. 'He's no wiser than the rest of us.'

While frantically trying to get the studio to interrupt their discussion and come live to the stadium, I saw one of the young stewards racing towards the commentary positions with another sheaf of papers in his hand. The time was now 8.18. A new team sheet had been distributed – and now Ronaldo *was* in the starting line-up. The BBC came 'live' to the stadium and I tried to make sense of the sequence of events, speaking into a camera that seemed a million miles away behind one goal.

After that the match was almost an anticlimax, with Ronaldo clearly out of touch after his 'collapse' and subsequent visit to the hospital on the afternoon of the game. Nobody expected Zinedine Zidane to score with two headers, and it wasn't the first time I was grateful for Trevor Brooking's confirmatory nod as I announced the goalscorer. My wait to see Brazil lift the World Cup trophy would go on for another four years.

Trevor and I were together again four years later for by far the most unusual World Cup I covered. FIFA's decision to split the

2002 tournament between Japan and South Korea threw up logistical problems for all broadcasters – some of which I had never encountered before. Japan and South Korea were not neighbouring countries, as Holland and Belgium had been in Euro 2000. They were approximately three hours' flying time apart.

Trevor and I started in Seoul, covering Senegal's shock victory over holders France in the opening game, before flying to Japan for the next series of group matches. Brooking always seemed to sense what lay ahead. He had been the first one to warn me I would not be doing the final in 1994. 'I've looked at the way things will work out,' Trevor said on the plane to Japan, 'and I don't think we will be going back to Korea.'

He was right. Just to give the reader some idea of a typical commentator's schedule at a World Cup, here's how our commitments unfolded.

31 May	France v. Senegal	(Seoul)
2 June	Argentina v. Nigeria	(Ibaraki)
3 June	Mexico v. Croatia	(Niigata)
5 June	Ireland v. Germany	(Ibaraki)
7 June	England v. Argentina	(Sapporo)
9 June	Mexico v. Ecuador	(Miyagi)
12 June	England v. Nigeria	(Osaka)
13 June	Mexico v. Italy	(Ouita)
15 June	England v. Denmark	(Niigata)
17 June	Brazil v. Belgium	(Kobe)
21 June	Brazil v. England	(Shizuoka) Quarter-final
26 June	Brazil v. Turkey	(Saitama) Semi-final
30 June	Brazil v. Germany	(Yokohama) Final

It is not uncommon for television commentators to cover thirteen matches in a month at a major championship. But in Japan, where we worked in ten different venues, the cities were a long way apart. Brooking and I were rarely in the same hotel for more than one night, and were lugging all our belongings from one station or airport to another virtually every other day.

What was particularly frustrating was that some of the matches played in South Korea were not shown on a main television channel in Japan. Since there was no time to reach any of the teams' training headquarters, we were struggling to see, in action, some of the teams with which we had to be familiar for our next game.

Much to Trevor's amusement, I once persuaded an old lady to open her café in the afternoon, so that we could watch an Ireland game on her small black-and-white television. She seemed utterly bemused as to why these two Englishmen were knocking urgently on her window. She told us in sign language to remove our shoes and sit on a small platform at the front of the café. As she struggled desperately with the aerial and the channel controller, I was shouting the word 'football'. Eventually she found it, and gave us tea and biscuits.

On another occasion in Osaka, I looked up Michael Kitchen, son of the former Orient and Doncaster striker Peter, who was a good friend. Michael had been living in Japan for some years, and we enjoyed two days in his company. When South Korea's next match was not transmitted on Japanese television, our lady interpreter took us to a Korean bank in the city, where the manager had arranged a private feed. We were taken down to the basement, where Trevor and I found ourselves surrounded by two hundred schoolchildren shouting for Korea. They certainly didn't need a commentary from the two of us.

For me, the highlight of the first phase was the match between England and Argentina, played indoors in Sapporo. After missing out on the 1986 and 1998 encounters, I was delighted to get the chance to commentate on my first match between these old rivals since my first England tour twenty-five years earlier. And if I was exorcising a ghost, so too was David Beckham. He wiped out the anguish of his red card in St Etienne by scoring England's winning goal from a penalty.

The Republic of Ireland were also having a good go, despite the absence of Roy Keane following his fall-out with manager Mick McCarthy. Their match against Germany in Ibaraki had a great feel to it, mostly provided by the Irish supporters. And it had the kind of finish commentators like, with Robbie Keane equalising in the ninety-third minute.

I then had two uneventful matches with England. A 0–0 draw with Nigeria meant a second-round match against Denmark. Eriksson's team were three up at half-time, and the game was over. The following day, the Irish unluckily went out on penalties to Spain.

The other feature in the 2002 World Cup, which brought a lot of criticism my way, was the time difference. A lot of the matches played in Japan were shown live in the early morning at home. I remembered being told after Italia 90 how the nation had been gripped by England's performance, and how difficult it was at the time to appreciate what the atmosphere was like back home.

This time, I made up my mind that I would try harder to identify with the British audience, and with what they might be doing around the time of the game. It was breakfast time in England when a number of my early matches in Japan were broadcast, and I suggested you could watch Argentina having croissants with Crespo and bacon with Batistuta.

Those weren't the only examples. In trying too hard to minimise the difference in time between the audience and myself, I was apparently getting on some people's nerves – including my bosses'. Niall Sloane, one of the finest of the many editors and department heads I have worked for at the BBC (including producers, there have been well over a hundred), cautioned me about the 'breakfast run', and we later had our only disagreement in the twenty-five years we worked together. 'The younger generation don't have breakfast, John, they have coffee,' said Niall. Although I had letters from more than one friendly lady saying things like: 'I was just putting the eggs on when you said that, Motty.'

I must say, the internal organisation in Japan was first class. They even had a lane reserved for the media when it came to driving from the stadium. I was also grateful for the company of Ricky George, who was penning a series of articles from a fan's perspective for the *Daily Telegraph*.

But in terms of the demands on commentators, it was by far the hardest job I ever did. I was relieved to get to Yokahama for the final without a major pitfall, although the distance from the commentary position to the pitch at some of the stadia made identification in matches such as Mexico against Ecuador a trifle difficult.

In the *Daily Telegraph* just before the final, Giles Smith revealed I would be surpassing Kenneth Wolstenholme's record of four World Cup finals for the BBC. I worried more about the World Cup final than any other match, simply because if you get it wrong, you have to wait four years to put it right. Thankfully, my fifth final was a pretty straightforward affair. Ronaldo, the cause of all the fuss four years earlier, made amends by scoring the two goals that beat an ordinary German side. Yes, the team England had beaten 5–1 in Munich ten months earlier finished up in the World Cup final!

The Germans were down to host the next World Cup, which I believed would be my last as a commentator. By now, Trevor Brooking had vacated the co-commentator's role to take up his new post as Director of Football Development at the Football Association. Graeme Le Saux initially replaced Trevor for England matches. We got along fine as he started to master the difficult transition from playing to commentating.

Mark Lawrenson, who had been working with the BBC as a

co-commentator prior to Euro 2000, had never been selected for England matches, simply because he had been a Republic of Ireland international. But when Roger Mosey took over from Peter Salmon as Director of Sport at the BBC, he saw this distinction as somewhat unfounded. One night at Stamford Bridge, where Chelsea were playing Newcastle in the FA Cup, Roger turned up unannounced and sat alongside Mark and me wearing a pair of headphones. He listened to the whole commentary, and later told me he thought the chemistry between us was just right.

A few days later, Niall Sloane rang me to say it had been decided that Lawrenson, and not Le Saux, would be sitting beside me when England took to the field in Germany. 'We think Mark makes you a better commentator,' he said. 'Nothing against Graeme, whom we still want to go to the World Cup.'

Graeme Le Saux saw it differently. He rang me to say he felt let down, having been promised Trevor's role, and told the BBC he did not now want to go to the World Cup.

It was not the first time the role of co-commentator came up for debate. Back in Euro 2000, when Trevor had been working with me for several seasons, Mark was chosen for the final in Rotterdam. Then in 2004, with Brooking at Soho Square and Le Saux still to come on board, Joe Royle filled in enthusiastically on the England games in the European Championships.

I felt I got on well with all of them, on and off the microphone, and from what they said afterwards, I think they felt I gave them a fair share of airtime. But Mosey had a point. Lawrenson's succinct summaries, his dry sense of humour, his ability to make his points clearly without ever embarrassing his commentator, gave him the edge over his competitors. It also helps if you get on away from the microphone. I have heard of broadcasters on other channels who hardly speak to each other when they come off the air. It could not be more different with Mark.

Lawrenson, Ray Stubbs and I have shared many great times

together when we have been 'on tour'. Mark brought something of the football dressing-room humour to the party, which made sure I never took myself too seriously.

Not before time, some might say.

Looking back, what these World Cups did for me was to put on the field in front of me some of the finest players it has been my privilege to watch.

They don't come much better than the two captains, Franz Beckenbauer and Johan Cruyff, who graced the 1974 tournament and came face to face in the final. It doesn't get more exciting than watching the flair and the pace of Mario Kempes and Leopoldo Luque as Argentina stormed to their first title in their own country in 1978.

Paolo Rossi commandeered the 1982 finals with his predatory six goals in the last three games, thereby ensuring a place in World Cup folklore for an Italian generation that included seasoned campaigners like Gentile, Scirea, Tardelli and Causio.

Nobody defined a World Cup like Diego Maradona in 1986. I doubt whether Argentina would have come close to winning without him. Anyone who saw him at his peak would struggle to argue there has ever been a better footballer in this generation. To Paul Gascoigne goes the accolade of dominating a World Cup like no other English player, the victorious 1966 team apart. He embodied the spirit and tenacity of Robson's team in Italia 90 – the nearest England has come to the final since Moore, Charlton and Hurst lifted the trophy.

America in 1994 was an experience in itself, characterised by the ponytailed Roberto Baggio for Italy and the effervescent Romario for Brazil. Zinedine Zidane did most to bring the trophy to the country that invented the World Cup when he inspired the French to victory on their own soil in 1998 – disgraced though he was by his sending off in the final eight years later.

The gap-toothed Ronaldo had been laid low on the day of that final, but four years later he got the monkey off his back with those two goals that beat Germany in the final in Yokohama. And maybe it says something about the game that the outstanding performer in 2006 was a defender – Fabio Cannavaro lifted the trophy for Italy, who won it for the fourth time.

Soon it will be 2010. If only an Englishman was leading a team on a lap of honour in South Africa. If only . . .

PART III

'Give 'em the score, Johnny . . .'

Chapter 13

From Lynam to Lineker

The changing face of sports broadcasting

I NEVER HAD ANY ambitions to become, or pretensions about becoming, a presenter. Still less so after the first time I appeared on television and a correspondent on a London evening newspaper said I needed a screen test. It wasn't just that the camera did not like me. Back in my radio days, shortly before Des Lynam joined, they asked me to front the Saturday five o' clock show *Sports Report*. I couldn't face it.

At that point it was clear that I was going in the direction of reporting, and later commentating. Lynam, however, showed he was a natural the moment he walked into Broadcasting House. Our different paths were mapped out.

Some in television thought sports presenting came so naturally to Des that he didn't have to work at it. Having known him a lot longer, I knew nothing was farther from the truth. In those early days, he used to drag me to football matches on our night off. I remember standing with him on the old North Bank at Highbury watching Arsenal play Huddersfield Town, who were then in the first division.

We also had a Brighton connection. Des was living in the town, and my father had moved to Southwick, just a few miles away, as Methodist minister. Later, my mother and father moved to Worthing, where he married Annie and me in Steyne Gardens Methodist church in 1976.

Lynam remained a firm supporter of Brighton and Hove Albion, where Dad had a season ticket. During one commentary at the old Goldstone Ground, my father's picture came up on my monitor as he took his seat for the second half. 'That gentleman in the clerical collar happens to be the father of the commentator' was all I could think of saying. I was reminded of it many times in subsequent years.

When I left radio to move into television, Lynam followed soon afterwards. But he continued to cover boxing for Radio Two, a role he enjoyed and which demanded the usual round of weigh-ins, interviews and homework.

One of the fighters whose rise to world champion he followed closely was Alan Minter. I remember before he fought Kevin Finnegan he was interviewed by Des at the lunchtime weigh-in. Why the story amused me so much I don't know, but I was driving in Barnet later that day when their conversation was broadcast.

'What do you think about Finnegan, Alan?' asked Lynam.

Minter replied in typical boxing parlance, 'Des, he ain't goin' nowhere.'

Unlike Lynam, who was going right to the top.

When he began to assume the main presenter's role on *Grandstand*, we maintained our friendship and our radio roots. We were still in Bob Burrows' team for the Wimbledon championships.

One morning Des went to interview Teddy Tinling, the fashion guru who had dressed many Wimbledon champions, and designed some daring outfits for the ladies. Tinling was in his late seventies and had some good stories to tell about Wimbledon, going back to pre-war days. When Lynam finished the interview, Tinling said: 'You've asked me about my past, but you haven't mentioned my future.'

Des came back to the radio studio chuckling. 'At his age, I nearly said to him, "What future?"'

This sense of humour, which became apparent on screen as he hosted the BBC's major sports events, was one of his great qualities. There was one commentator whose opinion of himself was somewhat higher than that of his producers. 'He wants to do Wimbledon badly,' I said to Des.

'Oh yes,' replied Lynam. 'He will do it. Badly.'

Following his years on *Grandstand*, Des then switched to *Sportsnight* and *Match of the Day*. We shared some good and bad nights with England at Wembley, in the company of Terry Venables and Jimmy Hill, who were Lynam's two pundits. At the end of the post-match discussion, Des would ask them to give England a mark out of ten. Venables would usually settle for seven or eight, but Jimmy always wanted to split hairs. 'Seven and a half,' he would reply. One night he decided it was 'six and three quarters'.

Sport on television has changed beyond all recognition since I started commentating. One factor that has become a contentious issue – and often a source of anguish – is the competition for rights with rival broadcasters. Lynam and I had to swallow the disappointment of the BBC losing an important football contract three times in our years in television.

In November 1978, ITV thought they had secured exclusive rights to Football League highlights in what was dubbed the 'Snatch of the Day'. Michael Grade, London Weekend Television's Director of Programmes at the time, was pictured with Football League secretary Alan Hardaker trumpeting a new deal that would exclude the BBC.

David Coleman got us all to write a letter to Members of Parliament, the Office of Fair Trading and any other bodies that came to mind. Though that deal was thrown out by the Monopolies and Mergers Commission, in two of the next four years ITV were given the Saturday night highlights spot, and the BBC had to move to Sunday afternoon.

In 1983 things changed again. Both channels were now allowed to show a selected number of live matches. But ITV struck a more permanent blow in 1988 when the top clubs negotiated a contract for live games on Sunday afternoons, and highlights virtually went out of the window.

It was temporarily the end of a regular *Match of the Day* programme, but the BBC countered by obtaining exclusive rights to the FA Cup and England games. Four years later, when Sky came on the scene, they narrowly defeated ITV in the fight for rights to the new Premier League. But they needed a terrestrial partner so back came *Match of the Day* every Saturday.

This contract in 1992 marked a huge turning point in the televised coverage of football. Sky brought to the table a lavish range of fresh production techniques, as well as wall-to-wall coverage and instant reaction from players and managers. But the BBC got access to the goals from all the Premiership games.

And how the game changed in the years that followed. Some of the younger generation, brought up on Sky's pictures and BBC Five Live coverage, won't remember what it was like in the days of the old first division. The Premier League opened doors not just to a galaxy of overseas players, but to a new range of corporate sponsors and, eventually, investors from all over the world. The game itself got faster, the players more athletic, clubs brought in fitness coaches, nutritionists and medical staff, the like of which were unheard of when I started.

As contracts continued to swing backwards and forwards, the next blow for the BBC was losing the FA contract in 1998. This meant the Cup Final off the BBC for the first time since it was televised in 1938, and for the next four years we were allowed to show only the highlights.

An even bigger shock for the BBC came a year after Des left to join ITV. We were covering the Euro 2000 finals in Holland and Belgium, when news came through that the Premier League had decided to change terrestrial partners. Their highlights would switch to ITV and *Match of the Day* – now hosted by Gary Lineker – was once again off the air.

There were those in our team who took the blow badly. One or two may have thought I was over-sanguine, assuming that with my contract I did not feel the same threat to my job. It was not the case. Rather, having been through the experience before, I was certain the FA would now put their England and FA Cup package the way of the BBC. Which is precisely what happened a few days later.

Nobody in the BBC football unit lost their job, and there were compensations. The arrangement from 2001 meant the FA Cup final – now being played in Cardiff's Millennium Stadium – returned to the BBC after a four-year break. Lineker was able to take our production team on the road to cover England matches abroad as well as at home.

Lineker certainly had the right pedigree to front international coverage. He and his agent, Jon Holmes, had met with the BBC to discuss his ambitions to be a broadcaster after the 1986 World Cup in Mexico, where, as I mentioned earlier, he appeared on the BBC panel for the final when he got home. For the next few years he made intermittent appearances on BBC and ITV while playing for Barcelona and Tottenham Hotspur. He was first involved in a major tournament when the 1992 Olympic Games were held in the Catalan capital.

By the time he came back from a short spell in Japan, Lineker had had offers from several media outlets. At first, he spent some time in BBC Radio, and wrote his own column for the *Observer*. Then, when he joined the BBC full time, he spent many hours in studios practising the role of presenter. These 'dummy' programmes were part of an apprenticeship that was to serve him well when he fronted *Football Focus* and later, in succession to Lynam, *Match of the Day*.

I have some sympathy with the view that sports stars should not expect to slide effortlessly into a media role just because of what they achieved on the pitch. But in Lineker's case his training and preparation exceeded even that of some established journalists who have moved into television.

I often wonder what previous England stars would have made of a media career had the opportunities been around at their peak. Television technology was still in its infancy when England won the World Cup in 1966. Twenty years later, just before the finals in Mexico, I was sent to interview each and every one of Alf Ramsey's winning team.

The series was called *The Summer of '66* and my two producers, Alan Griffiths and Graham Wellham, devised a way of combining each of the player profiles with segments of action from the tournament. As I was still on the local weekly paper when England won the World Cup, I had not met any of our heroes at close quarters. So this series was one of my most treasured experiences as a television reporter.

Appropriately we started with goalkeeper Gordon Banks, and I was struck instantly by the gap between his generation and the players of twenty years later. Banks was openly bitter about not making more money out of being a World Cup winner. 'We never made the most of it commercially,' he told me. 'We achieved something nobody else had done before or since, but all we got was a bonus of one thousand pounds. We even had to pay tax on that.'

Banks's views were in direct contrast to those of left back Ray Wilson. He was an undertaker and I visited him at his business just outside Halifax. Ray and his wife Pat took me to their local pub. He anticipated what Gordon Banks had said about cashing in on their fame. 'It just wasn't there then. The only thing I remember was signing a ball for ten quid,' said Ray.

Mind you, as a player with Huddersfield Town, he used to travel to the ground by bus with the supporters. I had never met a more down-to-earth footballer.

Wilson's fellow full back in 1966 was George Cohen. When I went to see him and his wife Daphne, he was just glad to be alive. George had survived a tough battle with cancer. 'I thought the lights were going out, John,' he said.

A good twenty years and more after that interview George was still hosting guests of Fulham in his lounge at Craven Cottage. After making over 450 appearances for his only club, he had been successful in the property business.

John Rowlinson, who suggested and edited *The Summer of '66*, had the awkward job of offering and agreeing fees with the players. For what amounted to a day out of their lives, the BBC paid £500. The Charlton brothers, now comfortably self-sufficient, happily gave us their time. Nobby Stiles, Roger Hunt and the late Alan Ball did the same, and I had a great day with each of them.

Nobby still seemed like a kid who could not believe he had played for Manchester United, let alone England. Roger was driving a lorry in his brother's haulage business. Alan, who we interviewed at the stables of a racing trainer, confessed: 'When I retired I just wanted to go racing every day.'

The West Ham trio were an entirely different matter. Geoff Hurst, who always knew his value, represented himself, along with Bobby Moore and Martin Peters. Without England's hat-trick hero, we did not have a series. In the end, I seem to recall a marginally more lucrative offer went their way. I spent some time in Southend with Moore and his second wife Stephanie, then working as an air hostess. Bobby was most anxious about her getting permission from her employers to appear in our film. After his premature death from cancer in 1993, Stephanie has raised millions of pounds for the Bobby Moore Fund for Cancer Research.

Rowlinson and I tried in vain to get Sir Alf Ramsey to take part in the programme. I even knocked on his front door in Ipswich to try to persuade him to take part. Lady Ramsey was courtesy itself, asking me in for a cup of tea. Alf was out playing golf. She promised to ask him again, but the answer was still no.

The series was transmitted just before Bobby Robson took England to Mexico, where Lineker in the penalty box, Motson in the commentary box and Lynam in the London studio could only reflect on how close England came to emulating the 1966 heroes.

Even after Maradona's two goals against England in the quarter-final, Gary not only pulled one back for England, but missed a cross by inches that could have brought an equaliser.

He also finished on the losing side in the FA Cup final that year. And that was despite putting Everton ahead when he got the better of a certain Alan Hansen. Little did they realise then how many FA Cup finals they would be working on together in the future.

One FA Cup final Hansen probably remembers less fondly, but of which I have great memories, happened two years later. Liverpool were poised to secure the double when they won the first-division championship for the seventeenth time and faced Wimbledon in the FA Cup final.

Liverpool that season had produced some of the finest football seen in this country. Their acquisitions of John Barnes, Peter Beardsley and John Aldridge made them an attacking delight, culminating in a 5–0 demolition of Nottingham Forest at Anfield, which the great Tom Finney described as the best performance he had ever seen. It was a privilege to be the commentator on that night.

As for Wimbledon, they had been in the Football League just eleven years, and it was only their second season in the top division. Three weeks before they faced Liverpool at Wembley, I went to Plough Lane to watch them play Chelsea. Wimbledon's first goal in a 2–2 draw was a near-post header by Lawrie Sanchez. I made a mental note of their set pieces, knowing that Don Howe, the coach alongside Bobby Gould, would have identified that as one way they might surprise Liverpool.

The Tuesday before the final, I was in a meeting at the BBC, planning *Cup Final Grandstand*. I asked a packed room whether anyone thought Wimbledon had a chance of winning. Nobody raised their hand.

That evening I rang Dave Beasant, the Wimbledon goalkeeper. He could see the Wembley floodlights from his home in northwest London. I was interested to know what he would do if Liverpool were awarded a penalty. John Aldridge had been pausing in his run-ups to fool the opposing goalkeeper. It had been deemed as gamesmanship in some quarters.

'I won't be put off by that,' said Beasant. 'I know where he likes to place his shot, and whatever happens I will dive to my left.'

My homework paid off on two counts. After thirty-six minutes, Dennis Wise took a corner on the Wimbledon left, and Sanchez got to the ball first at the near post to head it past Bruce Grobbelaar: *'Well, what a typical Wimbledon goal,'* I said. *'The unfashionable [side] from South London have taken the lead from the league champions and the team chasing the double.'*

In the second half, referee Brian Hill awarded Liverpool a penalty – harshly, I thought – for a tackle by the Wimbledon right back, Clive Goodyear: *'Here we have high drama because Aldridge, who*

I think might have been replaced a moment later, is the penalty taker.' I remembered the conversation I'd had with the Wimbledon goalkeeper. *'Beasant in the week told me that he's been watching where Aldridge puts his kicks . . . Beasant thinks that a kick might go to his left or to the right as we look, if Aldridge decides to go the same way as the semi-final . . . He did and he saved it! And made history. The first time ever that a penalty kick has been saved in the FA Cup final.'* What is more, Beasant was the first goalkeeper to go up and collect the trophy on behalf of the cup-winners at Wembley.

'The Crazy Gang have beaten the Culture Club' was one of my better lines. No sooner had I covered the presentation of the trophy and medals, than Desmond Lynam was hammering on the door of the commentary box. He had closed the programme only seconds earlier, but was keen to drag me off the television gantry.

'Let's go down to the Wimbledon dressing room,' he shouted above the chaos.

The BBC had had a good relationship with Wimbledon's owner Sam Hammam, and one of our producers, Chris Lewis, had worked closely with their former manager, Dave Bassett. That was all well and good, but I figured it was going to be well nigh impossible to get into the dressing room, even assuming we got through the crowd.

Lynam, though, was not to be deterred. As we walked down the players' tunnel, pushing our way past reporters who were already queuing for quotes, he forced his way past two security guards and knocked urgently on the dressing-room door. To my amazement it was opened by Chris Lewis, who had been in charge of interviews with the Wimbledon team for the BBC. 'Come in and have a photograph taken,' he said.

I had never been in a Cup Final dressing room so soon after the match. Vinnie Jones and John Fashanu were lying on the floor with towels over their heads. Bobby Gould was urging the players not to get carried away when they went outside to meet the press. 'Don't get big time. Don't be arrogant,' he exhorted.

Lynam persuaded Jones to get off the floor and have his photograph taken with him, Lewis, myself and, of course, the FA Cup. I still have the picture.

It is too easy to say that Wimbledon were a one-dimensional outfit who intimidated Liverpool. The Crazy Gang finished seventh in the first division that season. They were in the top flight for fourteen years before their relegation in 2000.

I recognised Lawrie Sanchez as the most cerebral member of the team. It was no surprise to me when he went into management, and I had good reason to look back on that day when he became manager of Northern Ireland. They were drawn in the same qualifying group as England for the 2006 World Cup. I went to cover the match in Belfast, where Northern Ireland had not beaten England for seventy-eight years.

The day before the game, Sanchez allowed me to watch his final training session. His tactics came over loud and clear. 'We've got to make them play this like a Football League match,' he said.

As a club manager, he had taken Wycombe Wanderers to the semi-final of the FA Cup with the same style and motivation. David Healy's goal put paid to England on the night, the first and only time Sven-Göran Eriksson lost a qualifying match.

England got off the hook by defeating Austria and Poland at Old Trafford. Sanchez looked as though he might get Ireland to the European Championship finals in 2008, but resigned to take the manager's job at Fulham. He saved them from relegation but the following season his reign lasted only seventeen league games before he was dismissed.

Sanchez was not alone in feeling cruelly rejected in 2007. The BBC suffered perhaps the most wounding of all the contractual changes I have mentioned when they lost the FA contract from 2008.

England matches and FA Cup ties had been pulling audiences of up to twelve million. It was generally agreed that the BBC's sensitive coverage of the cup from the early rounds had played a big part in reviving the competition. But not for the first time, ITV's opportunism was a factor in the negotiations, and ironically their executive chairman was the same Michael Grade who had attempted the 'Snatch of the Day' thirty years before. Only a few months earlier, Grade had been BBC chairman, playing a part in the settlement of the new licence fee. Now he garnered ITV's resources to outbid the BBC for all the live football they possessed.

I played no part in the process, and neither, strangely, did the Head of Football, Niall Sloane. Director of Sport Roger Mosey and the BBC's Director of Sports Rights, Dominic Coles, were the BBC team. Gary Lineker was called in to make a presentation when the bidding reached the third round. By then, it would appear Grade's more aggressive bid in the first two rounds had won the day. Even the considerable resources of Sky, who also lost out, came too late to salvage the bid in partnership with the BBC.

There was some consolation for the BBC in picking up the Formula One deal, which maybe ITV conceded in their determination to keep the Champions League. But that did nothing to alter the fact that the BBC's television football portfolio was at its weakest since extensive live coverage started.

It wasn't until the 2008/09 season kicked off that the impact was really felt by viewers. The first three England matches that season, and all their World Cup qualifiers away from home, were exclusive to Setanta.

At the same time, the BBC was criticised for not bidding for the Test cricket contract. While some questioned the core value of the licence fee and public service broadcasting, the corporation was caught in a classic dilemma. How much is sport worth? Can the BBC justify devoting a huge slice of its cake purely to sports rights when the cost of one live match can escalate to beyond five million pounds?

It is history now, but I believe the BBC – maybe hidebound by its charter – missed the boat twenty years ago. I remember John Rowlinson, then Assistant Head of Sport, sending a memo to Bob Phillis, the Deputy Director General, urging the BBC to consider setting up a dedicated sports channel. Plenty of sponsors would have backed the plan, although how the government would have viewed that is debatable. One thing is for sure – they would have been there to compete with Sky.

The BBC's commitment to events such as the Commonwealth and Olympic Games is an obligation that means it has to cater for sports other than just football and cricket. Then again, when Sky first hit the airwaves in the early nineties, their Head of Sport, the Australian David Hill, was quoted as saying: 'I have identified the three most important sports in the UK. Football, football and football.'

In my experience, even the most expensive television contracts tend to be cyclical. I have no doubt that, at some point, the FA Cup and the England rights will return to the BBC. Some live football returned to the corporation in the 2009/10 season. The BBC took over the Football League contract, showing ten live matches with highlights every weekend, while also inheriting live coverage of the Carling Cup semi-final and final.

I well remember sitting with Gary Lineker in a bar in Amsterdam in the early hours of the morning in 2000. We had just returned from the final between France and Italy in Rotterdam, and were debating the impact of losing the rights to Premiership highlights. 'It's about time we went to bed,' I said, but Lineker would have none of it.

'The boys and girls on the production team are having their end-of-tournament party in the city,' he said. 'We've got to go and join them.'

That sort of teamwork has been the hallmark of BBC Sport since I joined, and I can't think of many members of the team who have bettered themselves by leaving.

Among the memorabilia I value most are four *Radio Times* covers, framed on the wall in our bar at home.

One is from 1977, with Jimmy Hill, Barry Davies and myself standing under the scoreboard at Wembley celebrating the 500th edition of *Match of the Day*. The three others all relate to World Cups. In 1998, Lynam and Lineker are seated together, with Hansen, Davies, Hill and me. Behind us are the shirts of the countries we fancied to win the tournament. Believe it or not, I was the only one who went for France.

Four years later, before the World Cup in Japan, the cover picture also included Trevor Brooking and Mark Lawrenson, along with two young ladies in kimonos helping us to head a ball. Lineker, Hansen and I all survive on the 2006 cover before the World Cup in Germany. This time we are accompanied by Ian Wright.

It is something of an honour to be featured on the *Radio Times* cover, not least because you are invited to a party at which the framed souvenirs are presented. Among the celebrities I met at those functions were Jill Dando and Dawn French. The covers are a permanent reminder of how lucky I was to figure in an event that drew millions of viewers to BBC1.

I have been fortunate to have worked closely with stars like Lynam and Lineker, as well as many others who became household names thanks to the BBC's sports coverage across half a century. Lucky, too, that my work has allowed me to cross paths with so many other fascinating and talented celebrities. And they don't come much more fascinating or talented than one particular Hollywood legend.

Chapter 14

'Give 'em the score, Johnny'

Trapped by Edmonds and Aspel

NOBODY QUITE KNEW how Jack Nicholson had wandered into the eyrie that serves as a radio commentary box overlooking Court 3 at the All England Club, during Wimbledon fortnight. It wasn't as if it was easy to find. Working on the outside courts meant locating the narrow, spiral stairway that led into a commentary position just about wide enough for two people. How the engineers even got the equipment in there was a mystery.

Nicholson was searching for a vantage point from which to watch a young American player in whom he had a particular interest when he somehow stumbled across where I was perched. Quite where my co-commentator was at the moment Hollywood's iconic figure appeared, I cannot remember. He or she must have gone to the toilet, or maybe moved out of the way, because the first thing I remember was Nicholson planting his considerable frame alongside me.

Down in the control room beneath Centre Court, producer Geoff Dobson was alarmed to hear that an "intruder" had climbed unannounced into the radio position above Court 3. In my head-phones I heard the commotion while I was commentating. 'Who is he, and how did he get up there?' seemed to be the concern.

During a break for the players to change ends, the programme left me to go to a traffic report. It gave me the chance to explain to Bryan Tremble, the executive producer, that the guy next to me was . . . well, unless I was terribly mistaken, Jack Nicholson. I had seen enough of his films – *Five Easy Pieces* and *One Flew over the Cuckoo's Nest* were my favourites – to be absolutely sure, unless it was some uncanny lookalike.

'Jack Nicholson, did you say?' exclaimed Tremble. 'If you're sure, Motty, you must do an interview with him while the game is going on. Bring him into the commentary if you have to.'

By now Geoff Dobson had calmed down, and one or two people who had spotted Nicholson wandering around the outside courts, looking for the match he wanted to see, confirmed that he had been observed clambering up the staircase.

Nicholson seemed quite relaxed about joining me on the air. I managed to mumble a few questions about his interest in tennis, his reasons for being at Wimbledon, and what his next movie was going to be. 'Star-struck commentator loses the plot,' somebody might have said, because I had taken my eye off the match completely. Nicholson was applauding his man one moment, then answering my questions the next.

After about five minutes, a clearly delighted Bryan Tremble came over on the talkback. 'John, this is fantastic, but don't forget to give the score when you get a pause in the conversation.'

Bryan's instructions were meant for me, but Nicholson, the ultim-ate professional, had placed the spare pair of headphones over his ears when he first started talking to me, so he heard Tremble loud and clear. The eyes were bulging slightly as he turned to look at me, and his receding hairline reminded me of so many nights in the cinema.

'Give 'em the score, Johnny,' he intoned.

I promptly did. At the end of the set I noticed that Nicholson had seen enough of his young American protégé, and was ready to leave. I managed to thank him profusely on behalf of the Radio Two audience, and after shaking my hand in a vice-like grip, he made a slow exit behind me. I was praying he wouldn't lose his footing on the stairway.

Pleased though I was by this chance encounter, I forgot what he had said about the score. Until Des Lynam got hold of me. He was tickled pink by the episode and reminded me of it on many occasions afterwards. It was a nice way to remember my brief career as a tennis commentator.

Jack Nicholson's sudden appearance wasn't the only time in my career when a celebrity has appeared out of nowhere. In the late afternoon of 30 September 1996, Michael Aspel walked out of a cupboard at the Bayswater Families Centre, run by the charity Action for Children, carrying a red book and coming in my direction. Friends said later I didn't look terribly surprised.

The truth was I thought I was caught in a trap. I had been brought to the centre from Stansted, having just got back from Edinburgh, where I had completed the Great Caledonian 10-kilometre run. It was part of the BUPA Great Run series organised by Brendan Foster's company Nova International. In 1996 I committed to a series of runs, totalling 100 miles, to raise money for Action for Children. The National Children's Home, to use its original name, had been close to my heart since I had sold pictures of homeless children called 'Sunny Smiles' at the Sunday school in my father's Methodist Mission in Deptford.

Whereas the Methodist preacher who started the home saw it as a residential sanctuary for deprived children, the charity had now moved their work into other areas, including day centres where children could be accommodated until their parents or carers called to take them home. Visiting the centre in Bayswater seemed a logical step, as I knew that, if I reached my target of £90,000, a local-authority-assisted scheme would mean the charity would receive a total of £550,000 towards their work.

The first sign of something amiss as I played in a sandpit with some young children was a group of footballers running up and down outside the window. I vaguely recognised the gold-and-black colours of my old Sunday League team, Roving Reporters in Barnet, of which I was club president.

When I saw Aspel my heart sank. Quite simply I was expecting Noel Edmonds to jump out of an adjacent cupboard. Just a few months earlier he had caught me hook, line and sinker in a 'Gotcha' for his *House Party* programme – but as I shall now explain, a technical problem meant that the episode never went out on television.

Noel's people had been in cahoots with my then agent, John Hockey. Jane Morgan, who worked with him at the time, booked me a taxi outside the BBC to go to a lunch with John. Nothing unusual in that.

But within a couple of miles the driver pulled up sharply in a side street in West London. A policeman was standing in the middle of the road flagging down the cab.

When the driver stopped, the policeman opened the back door of the cab and jumped in. He was carrying what looked like a portable microphone.

'We're chasing a criminal in the car ahead,' he explained breathlessly. 'He's got a gun and we've got to catch him before he breaks in anywhere or causes any damage to people or property.'

Before I had a chance to reason with him, the cabbie jammed his foot on the accelerator and we were off in pursuit of what looked like a white Peugeot.

'Hold on a minute,' I remonstrated, 'I don't want to be involved in this. I'm on my way to a lunch appointment.'

'We'll get you there later,' said the constable. 'This is vital, we can't lose this guy. He will stop at nothing unless we catch him.'

'Did you say he had a gun?' I asked, the sweat now forming on my forehead, and in a few other places. 'You can't expect me to get involved in chasing a dangerous criminal.'

The policeman was too busy talking into his microphone, obviously briefing his control room. 'We've got him in our sights, he's just turning into a car wash. We will have to follow him.'

And so it went on. In and out of numerous turnings, through a shopping centre, up a one-way street in the wrong direction, matching his every manoeuvre, including a three-point turn. The more frightened I became, the less sympathy I was getting from the man beside me.

'This is an important investigation, Mr Motson. I'm sorry you'll be late for your lunch, but believe me, we have to intercept that car.'

Suddenly there was a screeching of wheels ahead, and the driver of the Peugeot roared away to our left, accelerated through the narrowest of gaps, and looked behind to check whether he was still being followed. He was. Our gallant taxi driver made exactly the same move, and it felt as though the back wheels of the cab were off the ground. He squeezed through the barrier ahead with inches to spare, and within seconds we had all the room we needed. The two cars were now marooned on a disused airfield.

The driver ahead now started to show off, turning his vehicle this way and that as though he was looking for an exit.

'Here, grab this,' insisted the policeman, passing me his microphone. 'I am going to apprehend this guy and I want you to tell my base exactly what I am doing.'

Feebly, I took the microphone as he dived out of the door.

'The officer is running across the tarmac towards the car.' I stumbled through the words as best I could with my heart pounding.

'He is within a few yards of it now, I can see the driver's face through the window.'

My commentary did not need to go any farther. The unmistakable figure of Noel Edmonds appeared from the other car and stood in the middle of the airfield with a trophy in his hand.

The cab driver was in stitches. It was only then I realised that he and the 'officer' were actors.

'What a great commentary, Motty,' he said, 'they really got you there, didn't they?'

My hands were still shaking when a delighted Noel Edmonds presented my 'Gotcha'. 'We've organised a cab to take you back to the Beeb,' he assured me.

'But I was going to lunch,' I protested.

He chuckled. 'I don't think so, John, not today. That was part of the wind-up.'

Job done, so Edmonds thought. Been had good and proper, *I* thought. But funny things happen when you're chasing criminals. A couple of weeks later, just before Christmas, I took a surreptitious telephone call in the *Match of the Day* office from Jon Beazley, the producer of *Noel's House Party*.

'John, I don't want you to think that this is another gag,' he said earnestly, 'but we have a problem with your "Gotcha". The sound did not come out in the cab.'

Blimey, I could be off the hook here, I thought, but Beazley had other ideas.

'Noel is livid. We have never had one go wrong before. If we can get the actors together on the same day, do you think you could go through it again and pretend you don't know?'

They had already sent me a fee of £500 for the original filming, so I could hardly refuse.

'All right, I'll have a go,' I said, 'but I can't act as shocked as I was last time.'

Jon said, 'Just do the best you can, and please don't say a word to anyone. Noel will go berserk if this gets into the press.'

I bet he will, I thought, but kept my word and waited for the date.

It was only a week before the Christmas holiday, and a seriously harassed Jon Beazley was on the phone again.

'John, this is getting impossible. We just can't get the same actors on the same day. We're going to have to scrap it. Noel is fuming.'

I was starting to wonder just how furious Edmonds could become when Beazley said, 'Look, we must keep this out of the papers. Noel is wondering if there is anything he can offer just to thank you for your support.'

'You've already paid me a fee,' I reasoned.

He said, 'Yes, but he wants to do a bit more than that.'

I replied, 'Well, I've got my Christmas party coming up. I always pay for a bash for some of my friends.'

'How much does that cost you?' Beazley asked

'I don't know exactly, maybe around £500 with all the drinks and that.'

'John,' Beazley said, 'the cheque is on its way, but don't say a word to anyone.'

A cheque from Noel Edmonds was in the post the next day and our Christmas lunch in 1994 was one of the best!

A month or two into the new year I was waiting for a lift in what is known as Stage Door Reception at BBC Television Centre. When the doors opened, out popped Noel Edmonds. He grimaced, then he grinned. 'Thanks for that, Motty,' he said, 'but don't think you are off the hook. I'll bloody well get you next time!'

I sat on the story as I said I would, but had to explain how I felt when Michael Aspel and his red book came my way. Even while I was being whisked away to Thames Television studios in Teddington, I still did not believe this was a real *This Is Your*

Life. They kept me in a room on my own well beyond the time the programme should have started. I wasn't to know that the audience was in place, but Jimmy Hill was late in arriving at the studio.

Others who have been the subject of the programme will know my sense of shock when the studio doors opened, and I saw a vast collection of family and friends applauding from all sides. Gradually I started to piece it together as I squinted into the studio lights. My wife Annie in the front row with my cousin Jane and two aunties, Mary and Enid from Boston (how the hell did they get here? I wondered) and colleagues from my newspaper days, as well as an array of BBC types.

Before you get a chance to gather your thoughts, the surprise guests are tumbling on to the stage. The fourteen Roving Reporters players had been brought to the studio in an old coach from the centre in Bayswater. Two of the first guests to be announced were Derek Ufton and Roy Bentley, who had played for Charlton and Chelsea respectively in the first league match I saw – as a six-year-old – at The Valley in 1952.

Then my ten-year-old son, Fred, came on in his Derby County kit. Gary Lineker and my old school friend Gary Newbon were next up.

My former flatmate Bill Hamilton came on to recount stories of us playing Subbuteo until three in the morning, and me commentating! This was back in the days when we shared a flat in North Finchley. The table was spread out in the dining room, and we used to solemnly play a cup competition between all the clubs in England and Scotland.

Talking of Scots, I was particularly delighted to see Tommy Docherty, manager of Manchester United in my first Cup Final. Then came the final moment of an unforgettable night.

The Hereford duo Ronnie Radford and Ricky George appeared to present me with a Carling No. 1 Award from the then sponsors of the Premiership, which was only four years old. Altogether there must have been sixty or seventy people in the audience who had touched my life in some way. It made for a terrific party after the show. Even Michael Aspel stayed for ages, which producers told me was very rare.

Besides being a very humbling experience, it was an insight into how television worked outside the sports sector. The amount of effort that went into one episode of *This Is Your Life* left me gasping, particularly as the producers reserved the right to scrap the programme if anybody blew the secret to the recipient.

I can reveal years later that it nearly happened to me. Just a few days before Aspel shoved his red book in my direction, David Pleat had come up to me at a function and said, 'Sorry I can't come to your whats-a-thing.' Fortunately, I never attached any importance to it at the time.

The red book originally contained the script from which Aspel was working. At the end of the night he presented it to me with a selection of photographs taken during the evening. A wonderful souvenir.

Around the same time, I could have taken a positive step into the light entertainment division myself. I was auditioned for the job of presenting *They Think It's All Over*, and initially selected to be the first chairman of the television version. The programme had started on BBC Radio with Desmond Lynam as the host. I was once a guest with Brian Johnston and Rory Bremner, who later incorporated me into his range of imitations.

Des decided he did not fancy the television show, and I went to the ITV studios on the South Bank to line up against David Gower, John Inverdale and Nick Hancock. The independent producer, Peter Fincham, decided Motson was his choice. Alan Yentob, then Controller of BBC1 was also in favour, but Jonathan Martin, the Head of Sport, was dead against.

He reasoned that the flippancy of the show might compromise a presenter whose day job was to take his subject seriously. He also wanted to protect the sensitivity of contracts the BBC had with sporting bodies. There was quite a tug of war over me between Yentob and Martin, but serious sport won. Nick Hancock became a very capable host.

There were, however, other compensations. Just before the 1998 World Cup in France, I was the subject of an irreverent but affectionate programme entitled *The Full Motty* (the film *The Full Monty* was all the rage at the time).

With Jimmy Hill as the presenter, there was a collection of characters such as Chas and Dave, Craig Charles and Vinnie Jones, performing tricks and treats in front of a studio audience that included Johnny Vaughan, Davina McCall and a number of other television and radio celebrities. Goodness knows what Jonathan Martin thought when he heard them singing 'Motty for the World Cup Final'.

One of the most bizarre commentary jobs I ever did was voicing the BBC's *Animal Games* and *Winter Animal Games*. Scheduled to coincide with the Olympic Games in 2004 and 2005, computer wizardry was used to scale all the creatures to human size and then compete in teams against each other in Olympic style events. Jonathan Pearce and I had our tongues firmly in our cheeks as we delivered such memorable phrases as 'that's one giant leap for frogkind' and 'the fish are struggling in the track and field events'. The programmes were very well received – and I learned that if all animals were the same size, a cheetah would lose a 100m sprint to a collared lizard . . .

Many years earlier, my football knowledge was the basis of another programme that I briefly had delusions of presenting. Before the 1978 FA Cup final between Arsenal and Ipswich Town, I recorded a one-off version of *Cup Final Mastermind*.

Taking Magnus Magnusson's famous black chair, and with his

assistant Mary Craig alongside, I put questions about their clubs to two teams of supporters. I always remember Mary saying to me afterwards, 'That was word perfect, you could do this show, you know.' Again it was not to be.

Other one-offs in which I found myself involved included *Through the Keyhole*, when Loyd Grossman came to our house in Harpenden. He seemed shocked by what he found, so much so that he had to sit down and ask for a glass of water. He seemed particularly taken by my grandfather clock, which has come down four generations. Maybe its loud strike was what made him feel faint.

Then there was *Hairdressing in Las Vegas*. Yes, I am serious, although I wasn't at all sure about it when the producer, Ruth Jackson, decided my voice was the one she wanted on a programme she had filmed in America. It was basically a world hairdressing competition, but sadly I didn't get the chance to go to the States. My task was to adapt her script to my style, and then put the words to the finished product back in London.

I was also privileged to work, however briefly, with two of my broadcasting heroes, Michael Parkinson and David Frost.

Not that I aspired to appear on Parky's long-running chat show, which for years used to follow *Match of the Day* on a Saturday night. My appearance was on a Friday night radio show that Parkinson hosted for a time. His untarnished love of sport came through loud and clear. Parkinson's success as a television chat show host, right up to his retirement at the age of seventy-two, tended to deflect attention from his magnificent sports writing. Cricket was his particular forte – in the *Daily Telegraph* and the *Sunday Times*. A proper journalist who later became a brilliant broadcaster.

You could use the same description for David Frost, whose father, like mine, was a Methodist minister. Back in the early sixties, after watching *Sports Special* (the football highlights fore-runner to *Match of the Day*), my dad and I would never miss *That Was the Week That Was*, the programme that really set the agenda for television satire.

Again, I could only brush shoulders with Frost in a working capacity. I bumped into him at a reception given by John Birt in the director general's suite at Broadcasting House.

Frost's love of football, like Parkinson's, was widely known. He was offered a contract by Nottingham Forest but turned it down to go to Cambridge University. 'You must come in on a Sunday morning and review the papers,' he said.

I found the task quite an ordeal. You would need to be up at about three in the morning to study all the papers and do them justice. Although I never gave it that dedication, he said I did a decent job, and the breakfast was the best meal I ever had inside a BBC building.

Another broadcaster I hold in great esteem but have never met is Alan Whicker. His research, sense of timing and delivery were a major reason why *Whicker's World* was such a compelling programme. The fact that he is one of the outstanding broadcasters of his generation was amply illustrated when, at the age of eighty-three, he embarked on a new series for BBC2 called *Alan Whicker's Journey of a Lifetime* in the Spring of 2009. It was compelling stuff and his delivery was as flawless as ever.

Hero, giant – there must be hundreds of epithets to sum up Muhammad Ali. By chance, I met him on more than one occasion in the BBC studios.

In the days when he was heavyweight champion and fighting in such far-flung places as Manila and Zaire, BBC technology was not nearly as infallible as it is today. When Harry Carpenter was flown out to cover the big championship fights on the other side of the world, there was no guarantee his commentary would come down the line with perfect, uninterrupted sound.

I was summoned to sit in the old Lime Grove studio, my notes as prepared as they would be were I actually doing the fight, and be the stand-by man in case anything went wrong. This never happened during an Ali fight, although his relationship with the BBC, and in particular with Harry Carpenter, meant he would sometimes pay a visit to the *Sportsnight* studio when he was in London.

On 3 October 1976 I was sitting in the curtained area just outside the studio floor when Ali came in with his posse of minders. I had bought a copy of his book *The Greatest – My Own Story*, published earlier that year. He signed it in clear handwriting – 'To John from Muhammad Ali. Enjoy life. It's later than we think. Peace'.

It is still one of my most treasured possessions. Do you know what that publication cost in 1976, all 413 pages of it? It was £3.95. To me it is priceless. Ali's message, too, is something I always try to remember – especially when faced with what my job can sometimes throw up.

Chapter 15

Setbacks and Soulmates

Racing, running and restaurants

O N THE FIRST Sunday morning in January 1998, the radio presenter Eleanor Oldroyd came to my house in Hertfordshire to do a live interview for Radio Five's *Sportsweek*. Just a few hours later I was in hot water, and for a while my BBC career was in the balance.

Eleanor had asked me quite innocently whether commentating was harder than when I had started. Almost without thinking, I said it was often difficult to identify one player from another, 'especially with so many black players now coming into the game'.

The wording was injudicious and clumsy, but was never meant to be racist. By lunchtime, however, two Members of Parliament were on the radio complaining, and the vilification continued in the newspapers the following day. Ron Neil, the BBC's Head of Production, phoned me to say he understood what I had been trying to say, but my comments had stirred a vigorous debate which did not reflect well on either me or on the BBC.

Without hesitation I issued an apology, directed specifically at any black footballers I had offended. I was also asked to explain myself in the *Daily Telegraph* letters column and on BBC Radio Four. To my relief, those who responded were on my side. Garth Crooks, Ian Wright, Mark Bright and Mitchell Thomas all phoned to assure me they knew I was not racist. Two newspaper editorials then followed up by taking my side.

Despite these supportive articles, the row did not die down. Alan Hubbard, the sports editor of the *Observer*, telephoned me to ask whether I would meet one of his reporters and be interviewed for the following Sunday's paper.

I had met Hubbard many years earlier when I was working on the *Sheffield Morning Telegraph* and he was the group's leading sports writer in London. I had enjoyed subbing his copy from major sporting events, and when I was sent to Wimbledon as a junior reporter, he took me under his wing at the London office of United Newspapers and gave me sound advice.

We initially tried to fix the interview at Wembley Stadium before a match, but could not find a suitable room. Hubbard then suggested it could be done at the home of Colin Hart, the *Sun*'s boxing correspondent, who was a good friend of his and lived near Wembley. When I rang Colin to get his address he did not mince his words. 'You realise that in America you would have been sacked for this,' he said.

He mentioned that a year earlier the seasoned golf correspondent Ben Wright had lost his job on the CBS channel over sexist remarks. By now I was getting nervous about doing the interview, and extending the debate. Alan Hubbard rang again and said sharply: 'I think we had better drop this, John. You don't seem happy about cooperating.' He was probably right, although it was only later that I discovered the reporter he would have sent was a black girl. A good angle, no doubt, for the *Observer*.

Working for a public service broadcasting organisation had put me in the spotlight, and I was held responsible for behaving inappropriately. There were no further repercussions, but I might well have had to face more severe consequences if the incident had occurred in today's climate.

I also believe there is an added scrutiny when and where the BBC is involved. To take a simple example, if a newsreader commits a gaffe on air during a prime-time bulletin, the chances are it will be on page one the following morning. Were it to happen on ITV, it might be on an inside page. Should there be a howler on a less watched channel, it might not make the papers at all.

I had my fingers burned in a completely different context three years later, when I was invited to the launch of a holiday website in an East London nightspot in Brick Lane. It was a Saturday evening, and I decided to go straight from a match at Tottenham. Ricky George and his wife had also been invited, and since Annie was not with me, the three of us met up in London and went together. At some point in the evening, after a few glasses of wine, one or two of the guests got busy with their cameras. I was asked to pose for a few pictures in a number of groups. I thought no more about it until I got a surprise call from Ned Kelly, the Manchester United security chief.

'I was in the press room at Blackburn last night and overheard a conversation between a couple of journalists,' he told me. 'They've got some pictures of you with a blonde woman which are not very flattering, and they are going to publish them on Sunday.'

I thanked Ned for warning me, but could not remember the last time I had been photographed with a blonde woman, let alone been caught in a compromising position. My agent, Jane Morgan, and I spoke to some friends in the press and discovered the pictures showed me hugging the lady concerned. Our contacts said the photos had been submitted by someone with a digital camera in the club in Brick Lane the previous weekend.

The woman who had invited me to the launch also made enquiries, and discovered that one of the staff there had seen an opportunity, gone out to a nearby petrol station to buy a camera, and caught me off guard. She checked with friends who had also taken pictures that night, and it soon became clear that the female in question was Ricky George's wife, Patricia. Suffice it to say, the newspaper concerned dropped the idea of using the photograph, but it was another warning as to the dangers of being indiscreet in the public domain.

In any walk of life, you produce your best when you feel at peace with yourself. And though setbacks are bound to come along from time to time, your soulmates are there to help you overcome them.

Annie and I met at East Barnet Old Grammarians Football Club in 1974, and were married two years later. I owned a two-bedroom flat in New Barnet, and we decided to keep our home in Hertfordshire. I was fortunate in more ways than one to meet Annie. She was a Newcastle girl who had been to university there, but was living in London while she did her articles as a solicitor at the London Borough of Barnet.

Our first date was a visit to the cinema to see *Papillon*, and we bonded straight away. Annie was sharing a flat in Hendon at the time, but after briefly returning to Newcastle, she moved south permanently and set about tidying up my bachelor flat in New Barnet. Our first house was in St Albans, although we got a scare when the builder went bankrupt the weekend we were due to move in. I was in Montreal at the Olympic Games at the time, but Annie eventually managed to get the house in shape thanks to our NHBC guarantee.

The location was perfect for me, within forty-five minutes of London and the BBC to the south on the nearby M1. Going north, I could be in Birmingham in ninety minutes. The proximity to grounds at which I was working has always been a priority when we have moved. We had seventeen happy years in St Albans, and when Fred grew up and we needed more space, we moved to a new house in nearby Harpenden.

Again, the main consideration was my travelling. Not just at weekends for *Match of the Day*, but also midweek when I wanted to attend matches for background purposes. Had I been living in South London where I was brought up, it would have added at least another hour to my journey in both directions, and some-times more. When I received frequent letters from would-be commentators asking me for advice on how to approach the job, I was often tempted to add 'make sure you live north of the Thames'.

Annie's support in my job is something I could never have done without. Sports reporters lead a largely itinerant life, and my foot-ball commitments more or less ruled out socialising at weekends. Many was the time we received invitations to parties or dinners on a Saturday night, and had to say no. Even if I got back in time to make a late appearance, my priority would always be to watch *Match of the Day*.

Friends frequently found it hard to understand why I didn't record the programme and watch it the following morning – some-thing that is much easier now that there is a repeat scheduled every Sunday. The explanation was simple. I could not relax or sleep until I had seen the edited version of my game and moni-tored my performance. That was a must as far as I was concerned.

Sometimes I would try to turn the tables on our hosts, and suggest they arranged their function on a Sunday or Monday night instead.

'But we have to go to work,' they would say incredulously.

'Well, that's what I do on a Friday and a Saturday,' I would explain.

Where possible, Annie and I would try to fit in trips to the theatre and cinema on midweek evenings when there was no foot-ball. In later years even that became more difficult. Try finding an evening when there *is* no football!

Annie has made a life for herself following her own interests. She also brought up Fred in my long absences, knowing I was likely to be away for several weeks every summer. She even took him to football herself. His early years watching Derby were often in the company of his mum and his grandma, while I was working elsewhere.

We did not discuss it often, but I knew that she and Fred were proud of what I had achieved and were hurt whenever criticism came my way.

As well as coping with the pressure from being in the public eye, my job also brings with it the challenge of keeping yourself fresh over the course of a long season. In that way, we commentators are no different from the teams we are reporting on.

How one deals with this boils down to the individual, and over the years I have tried to come up with a formula that suits me. I know of one commentator who disappears on a two-week holiday halfway through the season, but I would not normally be happy deserting my post to the point of going abroad. By the same token I would not want to find myself churning out routine commentaries that sound tired and tedious, which is what happens when a commentator does too many matches.

Fortunately, I found a handful of hobbies and outlets which took my mind off the job: road running (maybe more like jogging in my case); racing (about which I knew very little); and restaurants (where I ate and drank far too much at times). Over the years, this three-way release valve has helped me unwind, but kept me close enough to the action not to feel out of touch.

My interest in running began when Annie and I moved to St Albans just after we got married in 1976. I was lucky to find myself living on the same road as Tom McNab, a highly respected athletics coach who later made a name for himself as an author with the novel *Flanagan's Run*. Tom took one look at my posture (I was thirty-one) and said: 'If you don't start doing some proper exercise, with your lifestyle you won't see sixty.'

McNab dragged me round the Hertfordshire streets and footpaths until it hurt. I lost a lot of weight and, with his encouragement, began keeping a careful note of my distances and times.

In the same year that we met, I went to the Montreal Olympics and was used as an interviewer. Producer Bob Abrahams took me to the athletics stadium to watch Brendan Foster win a bronze medal in the 10,000 metres. He was the only British athlete to win a track and field medal at those games, and when he finished I pressed forward to grab an interview across the security cordon.

It established a friendship that blossomed when Foster launched his running revolution in the North-East. He started the Great North Run in 1981, and two years later I entered for the first time with two broadcasting colleagues, Alan Parry and Jim Rosenthal. Over the next twenty-three years I managed to take part in the event a dozen times, joining a field that eventually swelled to a staggering 50,000 runners. In 2008, the organisers received their one millionth entry.

I have proudly kept the certificate of my best performance, 1 hour 41 minutes in 1997. When I took part for the last time in 2006, my time had slumped to 2 hours 10 minutes, but by then I was just glad to get round.

Those of us who came from the media world were taken to and from the course on what became known as the 'celebrity bus'. One year, when the race finished at South Shields as usual, the bus took ages to get back to Newcastle, and I was so worn out after the run that I made a polite complaint to race director John Caine.

'What do you expect me to do, lay on a bloody helicopter?' retorted John.

'Well, that would be nice,' I replied, half seriously.

The following year, when Mark Lawrenson and I came out of the hospitality tent at South Shields, we were intercepted by security staff and walked across a nearby field to where a helicopter was waiting to take us back to Newcastle.

Four different teams on the
cover of *Radio Times* © RADIO
TIMES MAGAZINE

Right: Motson and Lynam in the Cup winners' dressing room with Vinnie Jones after Wimbledon had beaten Liverpool at Wembley in 1988 © JOHN MOTSON ARCHIVE

Above: The darkest day. Fans try to escape the crush at Hillsborough © BOB THOMAS/GETTY IMAGES

Right: Still friends after all these years. Hereford hero Ricky George pictured with the author at Tottenham

© RAY PICKARD

Above: The most talented English player of my generation scores against Scotland during Euro 96 © STU FORSTER/ALLSPORT/GETTY IMAGES

Above: On tour with the media as a guest of Premier League sponsors Barclays

© JOHN MOTSON ARCHIVE

Above: Ronaldo out – then in! The two team sheets from the 1998 World Cup final © JOHN MOTSON ARCHIVE

Above: Mrs Motson at Buckingham Palace in 2001 © JOHN MOTSON ARCHIVE

Above: It got better and better and better. Michael Owen celebrates his hat-trick against Germany in Munich in 2001 © BEN RADFORD/ALLSPORT/GETTY IMAGES

Above: Unforgettable! David Beckham's goal against Greece that took England to the 2002 World Cup © SHAUN BOTTERILL/ALLSPORT/GETTY IMAGES

DATE SATURDAY MARCH 8th 2008   **MATCH** F.A.CUP SIXTH ROUND

		BARNSLEY				CHELSEA
		BEAT LIVERPOOL IN INJURY TIME			OVER 5,000 FANS - FREE TRAVEL FROM CLUB	
		BARNSLEY			CHELSEA FAITH COPS!?	
31 ✓		**LUKE** UP TO PONTEFIELD - ON LOAN FROM WBA	23	✓	CARLO 34 YEAR FROM SECOND LONGEST 1999	
		STEELE HEINZ MULLER OUT FOR SEASON			**CUDICINI** SERVING TO TERRY CECH ANKLE	
23 * ✓		**MARCIANO** BROTHER BRUNO AT CHELSEA — JEFFERY	35	✓	JULIANO UPS WON WORLD CUP + ECL	
		VAN HAMEL YTS - SPARTA ROTTERDAM			**BELLETTI** SCORED SPURS (H) WIGAN (A)	
18 ✓		**DENNIS** FROM CHARLEROI LAST SUMMER	26	✓	JOHN LOST CHELSEA GOAL DUE 2006 v MAN U	
		SOUZA 'ITS JUST LIKE WATCHING BRAZIL'			**TERRY** 51 GAMES WITHOUT SCORING	
16 ✓		**STEPHEN** HEADED EQUALISER AT ANFIELD	6	✓	RICARDO MISSED LAST YEAR'S FINAL INJURED	
		FOSTER ALSO SCORED v BLACKPOOL IN RND 3			**CARVALHO** JUST COMPLETED 150 APPS	
5 * ✓		**ROBERT** PEN (AM) v SHEFF WED LAST SAT (YC)	18	✓	WAYNE HANDBALL IN CARLING FINAL FOR	
		KOZLUK SUSP. TUES. BLOCK AT ANFIELD			**BRIDGE** SPURS EQUALISER - WYCOMBE	
25 ✓		**MARTIN** CROSS FOR FOSTER GOAL AT L'POOL	5	✓	MICHAEL LEFT OUT AT WEST HAM AND ON WED	
		DEVANEY EX-CHELTENHAM - EITHER WING			**ESSIEN** LAST GOAL DEC 24th BEFORE PEN	
2 ✓		**BOBBY** SWITCHED FROM RB TS MF-LUNS	10	✓	JOE SUB IN CARLING 100 FINAL	
		HASSELL INJURY THIS SEASON EX MANSFIELD — KNEE			**JOE COLE** EXECUTIONER WITHOUT DROGBA	
10 ✓ C EX CHELSEA		**BRIAN** PENALTY APPEAL BEFORE GOAL	13	✓	MICHAEL ROARED BACK TO FORM WINNER	
		HOWARD 9 YELLOW (AM) SAINTS / SWINDON			**BALLACK** SCORED IN LAST TWO SEMI v BLN	
20 ✓		**JAMAL** WINNER AT OLD CLUB SOUTHEND R4	24	✓	SHAUN SCORED IN R4 AT WIGAN	
		CAMPBELL-RYCE ALSO GOAL ON TUES BLACKPOOL			**WRIGHT-PHILLIPS**	
13 ✓		**ISTVAN** HUNGARIAN INT STRIKER - SUB KEPT	39	✓	NICOLAS SCORED HIS FIRST CHELSEA GOAL DJ	
		FERENCZI — SA — TIED UP LLS DEPUTY KEEPER			**ANELKA** WIGAN IN R4	
9 ✓		**KAYODE** 28 GAMES WITHOUT A GOAL SINCE SEPT	15 OFF		FLORENT NO DOMESTIC GOAL SINCE OPENING	
		ODEJAYI £200,000 HIS CHELTENHAM			**MALOUDA** WEEKEND v BIRMINGHAM	
RYAN KIM KOIL ANION		SIMON DAVEY - 37 (CAREER ENDED AT 27)			AVRAM GRANT - 3 DEFEATS IN 37 GAMES	
		WITH BECKHAM AT PRESTON FREE KICKS!				
		DANIEL ON LOAN FROM QPR IN FOURTH	10-20		DIDIER SPURS GOAL ONLY ONCE SINCE NOV.	
S 11 ✓		**NARDIELLO** SPELL AT BARNSLEY GOAL v WBA			**DROGBA** INJURY + ON BACK FOR LAST FOUR	
S 29 * ✓		**DIEGO** NEDI MADRID JUNIOR SIGNED FROM	* 22		TALL BEN LAST APP v GOAL	
		LEON GRASSHOPPERS IN JAN LEFT WINGER			**HAIM** HUDDERSFIELD RSMB	
S 7 ✓		**SAM** EX PRIDE MIF. PLAYER TUESDAY	S 14 ✓		CLAUDIO MAN DE SAVE MAGPIE	
		TOGWELL GOAL v SAINTS IN 2-2			**PIZARRO** 2 GOALS IN 30 - BOTH v BRUM	
24 ✓		**MICHAEL** SCORED v BLACKPOOL IN R3 (19)	S 40		HILARIO PLAYED v QPR IN R3.	
		COULSON STRIKER ON LOAN AT NORTHWICH				
19 * ✓		**JACOB** BRIEF SUB APP AT NEWCASTLE C/C	PASSION S 21 FOR FAC		SALOMON SCORED v HUDDERSFIELD IN R5	
		BUTTERFIELD CMF. YTS BROOM (17)			**KALOU** FOUR IN LAST SIX STARTS P	
		1912 HARRY TUFNELL	S 12		JON-OBI TWO RED CARDS THIS SEASON	
					MIKEL v MAN UTD AND EVERTON	
		REPLAY WOULD BE A WEEK ON	(DAVE HANCOCK) 2		DR. BRIAN ENGLISH DE STH	
		PHYSIO - RICHARD KAY			JASON PALMER	
STEVE BENNETT (FINAL)		(NEAR) DARREN CANN	(FAR) BARRY SYGMUNTA		PHIL DOWN	
2007						

Still a fan of the felt tip pen! My commentary chart from Barnsley's big day

© JOHN MOTSON ARCHIVE

CHELSEA ARE THE F.A. CUP HOLDERS AND HAVE BEEN IN THE FINAL FIVE TIMES IN 14 YEARS

DURING THE WEEK THEY REACHED THE QUARTER FINALS OF THE CHAMPIONS LEAGUE

TWO WEEKS AGO THEY WERE CRITICISED AFTER LOSING IN THE CARLING CUP FINAL TO TOTTENHAM

CHAMPIONSHIP CLUB BARNSLEY ARE NOT CLEAR OF RELEGATION WORRIES AFTER THREE DRAWS

THEY SPENT ONE SEASON IN THE PREMIER LEAGUE IN 1997-98 UNDER DANNY WILSON

THEY BEAT SPURS AND MAN UTD HERE IN F.A. CUP REPLAYS THAT YEAR – LOST IN 6th RND TO NEWCASTLE

BARNSLEY ALSO REACHED THE 6th ROUND THE FOLLOWING SEASON AND LOST TO TOTTENHAM HERE

CHELSEA LAST LOST AN F.A. CUP TIE TO A LOWER DIVISION TEAM IN 1995 - MILLWALL IN 4th RND REP. PENS.

THEY WON 6-0 HERE (VIALLI 4) AND 2-0 AT STAMFORD BRIDGE WHEN BARNSLEY WERE IN PREM

BUT BARNSLEY WON THE ONLY PREVIOUS F.A. CUP MEETING 4-0 HERE 1989 (BOTH IN OLD DIV 2)

BARNSLEY HAVE 14 DIFFERENT NATIONALITIES ON THEIR BOOKS – BOLTON HAVE A RECORD 17.

CHELSEA BEAT QPR. WIGAN AND HUDDERSFIELD ON THEIR WAY TO THE SIXTH ROUND

BARNSLEY BEAT BLACKPOOL. SOUTHEND AND LIVERPOOL – LAST MINUTE WINNER AT ANFIELD

CARDIFF. BRISTOL ROVERS AND WEST BROM ALL IN ACTION TOMORROW IN SIXTH ROUND

BARNSLEY SCORERS: HOWARD 11. FERENCZI 5. MACKEN 5. DEVANEY 4. McCANN 3.

CAMPBELL-RYCE 3. FOSTER 2. SOUZA 2. COULSON 1. TOGWELL 1. ODEJAYI 1. NARDIELLO 1.

NEXT GAME HERE ON TUESDAY v IPSWICH   SEVEN AHEAD OF SHEFF WED   PLAYED TWO GAMES MORE

CHELSEA SCORERS: LAMPARD 13. DROGBA 10. KALOU 9. J. COLE 7. SHEVCHENKO 7.

BALLACK 5. WRIGHT-PHILLIPS 4. MALOUDA 3. ESSIEN 3. ALEX 3. ANELKA 2 (+11 BOLTON)

PIZARRO 2. BELLETTI 2. SINCLAIR 1. SIDWELL 1. A. COLE 1.

NEXT GAME v DERBY ON WEDNESDAY AT STAMFORD BRIDGE

Above: Sharing a joke with Tony Blair on *Football Focus* © JEFF OVERS/BBC

Above: The Motson family's newest arrival, Motty's Gift © JOHN MOTSON ARCHIVE

Above: Fernando Torres won the European Championship for Spain and then produced one of the goals of the 2008/09 season for Liverpool against Blackburn © CARL DE SOUZA/AFP/GETTY IMAGES

'I hope that suited you,' John Caine said, smiling, when I saw him in the evening.

'Just a bit,' I said, 'it only took four minutes.'

'Well, consider yourselves lucky,' he said, grimacing, 'the celebrity bus took two hours.'

Building up towards the half-marathon distance was painful, but in its way also stimulating. I always took my running shoes on holiday. In later years I found a treadmill in the gym or leisure centre when I stayed in hotels at the World Cup or European Championships.

An old Barnet connection also came up trumps on the fitness front. Roger Thompson, who had played right back at Underhill in my days on the local paper, was youth coach at Arsenal in the late seventies and early eighties. Every Thursday evening Roger would invite a group of us to Highbury to take part in what he called the 'seven doubles'. This routine involved running round the track beside the pitch fourteen times, in seven bursts of two laps each, with a walk in between each repetition. I found it mentally beneficial, as it cleared my mind before a Saturday match.

Not that we were leading a monastic lifestyle or anything like it. After the run Parry, Rosenthal and I would repair to a local hostelry called The Bank of Friendship, just up the road from the Arsenal ground. It is a place where I spent many a jovial Thursday night.

I didn't know at the time, but the author Nick Hornby, whose book *Fever Pitch*, which later became a film, so brilliantly summed up an obsession with Arsenal, also used the pub. One night he saw my business card on the shelf behind the bar, and assumed I had a financial interest in the establishment. When I met him some time later, I reassured him that I had drunk in more pubs than I would care to admit, but had never owned one.

Horse racing was something that left me totally unmoved until 1972, when I received a telephone call from a good friend, Bob

Sims, who owned a media buying company in London. He was helping put together a partnership to buy a horse called Earth Summit, and wanted to know whether I would take the last share. Ownership had never occurred to me. I suggested he would be better off approaching our mutual friend Ricky George.

The rest, as they say, is history. Earth Summit became the first horse to win the English, Scottish and Welsh Grand Nationals. The partnership had the time of their lives watching him make history. The day he won at Aintree in 1998, I was commentating at White Hart Lane on a match between Tottenham and Everton. They delayed the second half so that spectators could watch the race on the jumbo screens, and if there was a pang of regret that I had not bought a stake in the horse, it was offset by the biggest winning bet of my life.

The experience made me start to think about the sport as another potential hobby. Racing, which I could attend on a weekday afternoon, did not conflict with football. Sims organised a partnership in which I was involved with Helen Rollason, the BBC sports presenter so sadly claimed by cancer, and Des Lynam. We had a horse with trainer Jim Old called Out of the Deep, although he never got out far enough to make an impression on the track.

We were more fortunate with the little mare Hannigan's Lodger, in a partnership put together by the then Aintree press officer, Nigel Payne. She won a number of races and gave us a lot of pleasure. Mixed experiences followed with horses called Summit Else, Corroboree and Royal Coburg, but we have high hopes of our latest purchase, Valerius. He is trained in Ireland by Gordon Elliott, who won the Grand National with Silver Birch.

It was Sims who introduced me to the Cheltenham Festival in 1994. Quite apart from the stunning setting of the course in Prestbury, the spiritual home of jump racing made a big impression. The atmosphere in March was something that I had never anticipated, and I was soon booking myself into the Dormy House

Hotel just outside Broadway for the three- and later four-day festival. It didn't stop there. Soon I was going for the whole week, and taking in a meeting at Stratford on the Monday. In November, I was a regular at the Paddy Power meeting.

This would be the only Saturday in the season when I did not go to a football match. Even when I go to Bournemouth in April with my old Sunday football league side, Roving Reporters, I still take the veterans on the tour to a game at Southampton or Portsmouth, while the younger members play a friendly in the area.

It was at Fratton Park that I met George Best for the last time, on Grand National day in 2005. A friend in our local pub had advised me to back Hedgehunter, and while we were having lunch in the Portsmouth boardroom, George enquired where I was putting my money. He casually pulled out his wallet and called across to John Jenkins, the veteran steward who had been at Wembley when Portsmouth played in the 1934 Cup Final. 'Put this on Hedgehunter, could you, please?'

I saw him deliberately count out one thousand pounds in notes.

'The price will be about fourteen to one, so don't you want to do it each way?' I asked him. Bestie, though, never did things by halves.

'On the nose,' he insisted.

By the time we came in at half-time, Hedgehunter had won the National and George was £14,000 better off. My winnings were more modest. Sadly, I never saw him again.

Come the summer, I am usually ready for a rest from football. In the years when there was no World Cup or European Championship, I widened my racing experience by going to meetings at Sandown Park, Kempton Park, Ascot, Towcester and Goodwood. On a couple of family birthdays I sponsored a race at Huntingdon.

The big advantage of a day's racing is the fact that hardly anybody wants to talk football. Racing people are so heavily into their sport that I am able to enjoy a day out in the fresh air without having to think about my next commentary. The same applied to cricket. I normally find time to get to Lord's or The Oval a couple of times each summer. A Test match is something I find absorbing, certainly a more cerebral experience than the wham-bang of Twenty20, which seems to me a cheap-and-cheerful version of a sport I had played to a decent level at school.

I had better address another question I am frequently asked: 'Did you ever play football?' The answer, in one word, is 'badly'.

After I helped form Roving Reporters in 1965, I played for five years in the Barnet Sunday League. The club records show I figured in 165 games and scored 19 goals. I was always left footed as a boy, so I normally played left back or on the left side of midfield. As I got older, my right foot seemingly became as good, or as bad, as my left.

Soon after I got into television, Alan Parry came up with the idea of forming a commentators' team to play friendly and charity matches on Sundays. This continued for the best part of twenty-five years. Parry, Rosenthal, Martin Tyler of Sky and myself were the four regulars, assisted by former professionals such as Gordon Riddick and Roger Smith.

We had four members of the Walford family – Nick, Pete, Chris and Steve – together with Steve Hamer, who ran the National Sporting Club and was for a time chairman of Swansea City. The two Steves also worked for television on a Saturday, Walford as a liaison man for *Match of the Day* and Hamer as an ITV 'fixer' back in the days of Brian Moore.

Our commentators' team enlisted the help of ex-professionals if we were playing for charity. Trevor Brooking, Derek Dougan, Brian Labone, Peter Kitchen, Keith East, Ron Atkinson, Bob Wilson, Don Howe, Bobby Robson, Terry Neill, Ian St John, Ron Yates, Mike England, Andy Gray and John Gorman all turned out for us at one time or another. It made us sound like a Premiership outfit!

There was a good camaraderie between the lads, and our long-suffering wives and girlfriends would lend support. We were grateful for the efforts of Colin Booth, who organised many of the games. Sadly, he died from cancer in 2001.

One of the reasons the team faded away, apart from age and weight, was the proliferation of Sunday football in the Premiership. It seems strange now to think that when we started, only ITV's highlights package was shown on a Sunday.

No longer is it a day off. Even if I have been up until midnight watching *Match of the Day*, I always start my Sunday with Garry Richardson's *Sportsweek* on Five Live, followed by a recording of the BBC's championship highlights if I've been too tired to stay up the night before. Then I go for my Sunday morning run with two neighbours, Pete Hill and Liz Philpott, before settling down to watch two matches on Sky in the afternoon. Somewhere in between I catch up on the Sunday papers, and after a couple of drinks in the local pub in the early evening, I always make sure I am back for *Match of the Day Two*.

Because Sunday is a working day, I try to make Monday as near to a day off as possible. The long lunches with which, for some reason, I have sometimes been associated are normally fitted in here. Occasionally they occur on Tuesdays after I have attended the BBC's *Football Focus* meeting. This is a free-range discussion around a conference-room table between editors, producers, commentators and reporters. We review the previous Saturday's programme and plan the next one.

It is also the morning I collect my postbag from the office. Quite apart from requests for charities and auctions, the letters usually include a few barbed comments about my recent commentaries, polite enquiries about aspects of our programmes and, just occasionally in my case, a request for an autographed photo.

I have always tried to reply to all my correspondents. If they attach a telephone number I sometimes surprise them, and save myself an awful lot of time by ringing and talking over points they have raised.

Even though I usually go into the *Match of the Day* office only once a week, I feel part of the furniture after all these years. We have a committed and enthusiastic team, and I often wonder whether I would have fitted in as comfortably anywhere else. The BBC Sports Department will soon move to Manchester, which is unlikely to affect me towards the end of my career, but which would have given me a difficult decision had it happened earlier.

Although I live a good thirty miles outside the capital in a leafy corner of Hertfordshire, I still regard myself as a Londoner. I would feel cut off if I was more than an hour outside the city. Which brings me to the other pastime in my life. I suppose you could call it my only concession to luxury, but I do enjoy a good meal in a nice restaurant.

Not that I play in the Premier League when it comes to eating out. My squad of favourite chefs and owners would not figure on the list of any restaurant critic, simply because I enjoy plain food. When you cannot stand Japanese, Chinese, Indian or Thai food, it limits your choice considerably. French and Italian are about as far as I go in the overseas market.

I have always had a fairly rich palate and my physician, Dr Newman, would not be happy with my regular selections from the menu. This probably explains why, at the end of each football season, I am invariably a stone heavier. My weight balloons to over thirteen stone after nine or ten months on the road, but with a more careful diet and plenty of running in the summer, I can get down to below twelve stone.

Working as a reporter or commentator – and I am sure this applies in other sections of the media as well as sport – is not conducive to a healthy lifestyle. Attending press conferences, football matches and corporate functions sounds like a great way to earn a living. Few of us complain, but trying to maintain an even eating and drinking pattern is well nigh impossible.

There are some ample girths around in press rooms and television studios, but I don't attribute these to a degenerate lifestyle. For many, the football season means living in hotels and out of suitcases. There is also an enormous amount of time spent waiting around for matches to start, or for transport home. The sandwiches and sausage rolls then become irresistible.

Annie has tried valiantly to offer me a healthy eating pattern at home. I remain conscious of how important it is to watch the calories, and the dangers of over-indulgence. But what is life about if we cannot allow ourselves some latitude? Even the most dedicated of would-be athletes must sometimes crave fish and chips or a gin and tonic. I am tempting fate here, but at the time of writing I have never spent a day in hospital, nor have I ever missed a match through illness. I have been very lucky, and I never take that for granted.

In 2005, just as I was starting to think about the World Cup in Germany, Annie was diagnosed with breast cancer and bravely went through two operations and chemotherapy. Fred was in the first year of a degree course in law and politics at Buckingham University, and it was a testing time for us all.

Head of Football Niall Sloane offered me as much time as I wanted at home, although I preferred to carry on with my *Match of the Day* commitments as much as I could. The BBC football unit was tremendously supportive, scheduling me in London whenever possible and helping with transport if I had to go farther afield.

We came though that worrying period with our strong family ties still intact, and thanks to Annie's stoicism I was able to get through the World Cup and Fred graduated with a first, which made us both extremely proud.

The experience put a lot of things into perspective. I was able to ignore the inconvenience of food poisoning in Germany, and even a blogger's campaign against me seemed unimportant. The newspaper coverage that had emanated from that died down as the tournament progressed. Jane Morgan kept an eye on what was being said and tried to protect me from the worst of the reviews.

One columnist described me as 'the worst broadcaster since Lord Haw-Haw', which seemed strange when the BBC had selected me to commentate on the World Cup final for the sixth time. I did not make it public then, but I was privately aware that this would be my last World Cup as a commentator. I had seen the tournament expand from sixteen to thirty-two teams, and the demands on commentators had grown accordingly. Access to the squads had become increasingly difficult. Public training sessions, into which we had once wandered freely, were now restricted to, at best, fifteen minutes.

The German hosts deservedly took credit for the innovation of 'fan parks', in which hundreds of thousands could watch the matches on huge screens, but in the media section I was disappointed by their organisation. Unlike the Japanese, they seemed to have made little effort in making access to the stadia easy. Car parks and media centres seemed a long way apart, and some of the temporary walkways and staircases seemed to have been constructed with little thought for comfort or appearance.

I mentioned earlier how a commentator dreads making a mistake in a World Cup final, because it would take four years to live it down. I was enormously grateful that highly observant colleagues prevented that happening to me. Few people in the Olympic Stadium in Berlin would have seen Zinedine Zidane butt Marco Materazzi in the chest early in the second period of extra time.

When the referee's attention was drawn to the incident by the fourth official, Luis Medina Cantalejo of Spain, my producer Phil Bigwood came over the headphones to tell me what our director, Sean Hughes, had spotted from one of his isolated cameras.

I repeat that story to emphasise how dependent the commentator is on the people around him, and how I have been extremely fortunate in that respect. That's not to say, though, that on the odd occasion I haven't been put in the firing line. One encounter with a certain Scottish manager springs to mind . . .

Chapter 16

'You know the rules here, John'
Rows with Fergie and other managers

THE FIRST TIME I met Alex Ferguson I didn't have to go to see him. He came to see me.

In October 1980 his Aberdeen side were drawn to play Liverpool in the second round of the European Cup. In those days, prior to the invention of the misnamed European 'Champions' League, the competition was a straight knockout affair, in which only the previous season's champions in each European country, and the cup holders, were allowed to compete.

Aberdeen, where Ferguson took over in May 1978, had broken the monopoly of the 'Old Firm' by lifting the Scottish title in the 1979/80 season – the first time in fifteen years it had not been won by Celtic or Rangers, and the first time Aberdeen had won it since 1954/55. The club from the Granite City, whose Pittodrie Stadium was the first in Britain to go all-seater, were playing in Europe's premier competition for the first time.

Liverpool, of course, were old hands. Back in 1965 they had reached the semi-finals under Bill Shankly, and been dubiously beaten by Inter Milan. When Bob Paisley succeeded Shankly they won the trophy in Rome in 1977 and retained it the following year when they beat Bruges at Wembley.

A year before they went to Aberdeen, Liverpool had lost their grip on the European Cup when they fell to Brian Clough's Nottingham Forest – who won it in 1979 and again in 1980. Liverpool put the record straight by regaining the first-division title from Forest and keeping it the following season. Their first-round opponents in the European Cup were OPS Oulu of Finland, and Liverpool beat them 10–1 at Anfield, with Graeme Souness and Terry McDermott both scoring hat-tricks.

Aberdeen, meanwhile, made a rather less prolific start to their campaign. A goal from Mark McGhee gave them a 1–0 victory over Austria Vienna at Pittodrie and a goalless draw in the away leg sent them through to play Liverpool.

The match was predictably billed as the Battle of Britain, or England versus Scotland, and BBC's *Sportsnight* had the rights to show high-lights of the first leg. They booked me into a hotel called The Tall Trees on the outskirts of Aberdeen, and when I rang Ferguson, whom I had never met before, he could not have been more helpful.

'What time are you checking into The Tall Trees?' he asked, and when I told him he replied, 'I'll be there waiting for you.'

And he was. He was disarmingly frank about his team, which included a number of developing players destined to become house-hold names: Willie Miller, Alex McLeish, Jim Leighton, Gordon Strachan, Mark McGhee – and a brilliant inside forward called John McMaster, whose career was cruelly blighted by injury.

I had never seen Aberdeen play in the flesh, and up to that point had never done a commentary north of the border. In what was called 'marking my card', thirty-eight-year-old Ferguson cut a sharp, self-assured figure. He went through the strengths and weaknesses of his side, but feared that Liverpool might just know a bit too much for them. So it proved.

The night before the match, the Liverpool squad went to the

cinema to see Peter Sellers in *Being There*. When they got back to our hotel they were teasing Terry McDermott about similarities between him and Chance, the gardener – the role played by Sellers. McDermott had the perfect answer. He scored with a delicately placed shot which won the first leg of the tie for Liverpool. Ferguson had no complaints as Aberdeen were clearly on a learning curve.

Two weeks later they were crushed 4–0 in the second leg at Anfield, with Alan Hansen and Kenny Dalglish among the scorers. Liverpool went on to win the European Cup for the third time in five seasons, beating Real Madrid in Paris in the final.

But north of the border Ferguson had Aberdeen on the march. Within two years they, too, were beating Real Madrid in a European final – the Cup Winners' Cup in Gothenburg. They won the Scottish FA Cup in three successive years from 1982. In 1984 they won the championship to complete a double and retained the league title the following year. It was the third time in six seasons the championship pennant had flown over Pittodrie to deny Rangers and Celtic.

So it was no surprise to me that after Ferguson collected his seventh domestic trophy with Aberdeen by winning the Scottish League Cup in 1986, and his eighth by regaining the Scottish Cup a few months later, he was top of Manchester United's shortlist to succeed Ron Atkinson as manager later that year.

His fourth match in charge was away to Wimbledon. I found him sitting alone in a small room off the Plough Lane boardroom less than an hour before kick-off. He told me he liked to get out of the dressing room and let the players settle down after he had given his team talk. The Crazy Gang were buoyant after having won promotion to the first division. They beat United with a goal from former hod carrier Vinnie Jones, playing only his second league game.

For the next nine years my relationship with Alex Ferguson remained cordial. He invited me to lunch with the team a few days before the FA Cup final in 1990, which brought him the first of what would be some thirty-plus trophies at Old Trafford. I had his home number and he gave the nod to any number of requests to film stories at the training ground and interview players. On a Friday, I had a direct line to his office and he invariably helped me with his squad for the following day.

On the morning of 28 November 1992, I was the only English reporter at the Sopwell House Hotel in St Albans, two days after Ferguson had signed Eric Cantona from Leeds United. Manchester United were playing Arsenal at Highbury that afternoon, and I had gone to check out their team. Cantona was not registered in time to play.

Eric was sitting on a sofa, talking to a French journalist.

'Where are you going to play him?' I asked Ferguson.

'At the moment I have no idea,' he replied. I wondered whether he was joking.

United were no great shakes at the time. Earlier that month they had dropped to tenth in the new FA Premier League. Ferguson persevered with Brian McClair and Mark Hughes up front that day, and Hughes scored their goal in a 1–0 win.

The rest, as they say, is history. Cantona made his debut as a substitute against Manchester City the following week and United lost only two matches between the end of November and the rest of the season, finishing up as champions for the first time in twenty-six years.

Things between us blew up quite unexpectedly on 28 October 1995. It was the day Bryan Robson made his first return to Old Trafford as manager of Middlesbrough. Before going to the commentary position I'd had a light lunch with Bryan's wife, Denise, and Michael Edelson, the Manchester United director.

The match itself was fairly uneventful. Robson's team seemed overawed by the occasion, and their former player Gary Pallister put United ahead. Andy Cole added a second for a comfortable 2–0 win. The other incident of note was a red card for Roy Keane – his third in seven months and one of thirteen he received in his turbulent career. Keane had grown frustrated at the antics of Middlesbrough's Norwegian international, Jan Aage Fjortoft, who was pulling his shirt. He'd turned round and plainly struck his opponent in the face.

My first job after the game was a snatched interview with Ferguson for *Grandstand* to ask his views on the sending off. 'No complaints,' he said. 'Rule one says never lift your hands on the football pitch.'

I then had to conduct a more considered interview with the United manager for *Match of the Day*. Des Lynam, the presenter, and Brian Barwick, the editor, had been watching the game in the studio and passed a message down to make sure I pressed Fergie on Keane's disciplinary record.

I said, 'I appreciate you keep your disciplinary action inside the club, but is the Roy Keane situation one that you will have to address?'

'John, you have no right to ask that question,' Fergie replied. 'You're out of order. You know full well my ruling on that. Right, that's the interview finished,' he continued, taking his microphone off the lapel of his jacket. 'I'm going to cancel the interview, the whole fucking lot of it. Cancel it, right?'

As he strode up the tunnel with a face even redder than mine, he turned round and said, 'Fucking make sure that doesn't go out, John, or you'll never get in here again.'

'Well, I was specifically told to ask you, Alex,' I managed to blurt out. Which was true, although I would have been unprofessional not to raise the subject, even without the reminder from the studio.

'You're fucking not getting in again, right?' Fergie blasted. 'You know the rules here.'

The exchange had been witnessed by other television personnel and stewards in the tunnel. I beat a hasty retreat and got on to the studio. There followed a long debate as to whether *Match of the Day* should air the interview. I had little say in the matter as I was rushing for a plane. Lynam, Barwick and others such as Trevor Brooking discussed the issue well into the evening.

Des felt I had been badly treated, and believed the viewers should be shown what had happened. 'It's not as if Motty is Jeremy Paxman,' he said. 'The question was put politely.'

Maybe to protect me, or more likely the *Match of the Day* relationship with managers in general, it was decided not to put it on the air. What had been said in the heat of the moment was not deemed to be an essential part of the match coverage. In hindsight I think we should have run it up to when Ferguson halted the interview, without including the invective that followed. In fact, the whole exchange between us was screened in a BBC1 programme, *The Ferguson Factor*, in May 2002.

Several weeks passed without me having to cover another Manchester United match, until I received a telephone call in my car as I drove into the ground of my local club, Barnet, at Underhill. It was Ned Kelly, United's chief security officer.

'The boss says everything is all right now,' he said.

'How do you mean?' I asked.

Kelly replied: 'You're still welcome here and everything is OK between you.'

I would have preferred the call to have come from the man himself, but it was reassuring to know that the incident had blown over. For the next five years Ferguson was true to Kelly's word. The incident was never referred to again. I did a number of interviews and features with him – including one to mark his first ten years at Old Trafford. Then in March 2000, I commentated on a 1–1 draw between United and arch-rivals Liverpool at Old Trafford. Reading the game as fairly as I could, I thought Liverpool were slightly unlucky to get only a 1–1 draw. Patrik Berger put them ahead and they had two or three other good chances before Ole Gunnar Solskjaer equalised.

Ferguson obviously heard my commentary that night, and in the players' tunnel at Bradford two weeks later he let rip. I won't quote him verbatim this time, except to say the sentiments and abuse were much the same as after the Keane business.

As the years went by, Ferguson's outbursts became colloquially known as 'The Hairdryer Treatment', and bearing in mind I had known him for twenty-five years by then, a few people told me I was lucky to get it only twice. Once again our relationship settled down. On the Friday before the FA Cup final between Manchester United and Millwall at Cardiff in 2004, I phoned him and asked whether he would help me with the team he intended to field.

'I haven't told the players yet, but you can have it as long as it doesn't go any further,' he said.

As this was my twenty-fifth Cup Final and he was about to lift his twenty-fifth trophy, I wished him all the best and assumed we were back to square one. Little did I know what was around the corner.

Just a few days later, BBC3 screened a programme entitled *Fergie and Son*. The documentary raised questions about the business relationship between Manchester United and Alex Ferguson's son Jason, who was a football agent. Certain transfer deals were alluded to, although nothing concrete came out of the programme and no legal action followed.

What *did* follow was another flare-up, but one that put his tiffs with me very much into the also-ran category. Sir Alex Ferguson said he would not countenance any more interviews or cooperation with the BBC unless he received an apology from the top of the organisation. It was made clear he was talking about the director general.

Nobody involved with *Match of the Day* or any other programme produced by the BBC Sports Department had anything to do with this News and Current Affairs production, but Sir Alex blamed the BBC in general and, it seemed, everybody in it.

Mistakenly, I thought he would calm down, as he had done before. We hoped that by the start of the following season he would be prepared to resume relations, at least with our football department. Not a chance. For the five years that have followed, *Match of the Day* has had to talk to his assistant or his players after a match, but never to the manager. The rare exception was a cause dear to his heart – such as the Lifetime Achievement Award he presented to Sir Bobby Robson at the *BBC Sports Personality of the Year* programme in 2007.

Having heard him speak so lucidly at dinners, I still have the utmost respect for the man and his towering achievements as a football manager, but I fear I will never be on the same terms with him as I once enjoyed.

As a working journalist or broadcaster you need to have broad shoulders. Lynam was right – I was never going to be a Jeremy Paxman – but I have the right to proffer an opinion, and I was never prepared to be bullied out of voicing one. Sam Leitch had given me a good grounding. In those early days he sent me to interview managers such as Sir Alf Ramsey, Jock Stein, Bill Shankly, Don Revie and Brian Clough.

Also around at that time was Malcolm Allison, whom I first interviewed in Vienna after Manchester City lifted the Cup Winners' Cup in 1970. With Malcolm as coach, City had already won the championship and the FA Cup. I was a radio reporter then, and so worried about getting an interview that I had timidly knocked on the door of the City manager, Joe Mercer, at the team hotel that afternoon. Dear old Joe was obviously having a nap because he was in his underpants, but he arranged for Malcolm to do the interview.

As soon as I started with *Match of the Day* I was sent to the Baseball Ground to cover Derby County's match with City. Clough's team were 3–0 up in no time, and although City got one back, I said that Derby had outplayed them in my *Grandstand* report on the 3–1 win. Allison stormed into the press room and shouted at me, 'That report was rubbish. You don't know anything about this game.' Then, after he had calmed down a bit, he said with a grin, 'But I'll tell you when you're good!'

It was Allison, when he moved to Crystal Palace, who encouraged the coaching potential he recognised in Terry Venables. Terry was soon fast-tracked into management, and our paths crossed when he was in charge of Queens Park Rangers in the early eighties. During a match at Villa Park I thought Rangers were negative, playing an offside trap and breaking up the game at every opportunity.

Terry was on the phone the next day. 'You're not suggesting that we're cheating, are you?' he said. We've had many conversations since about getting off on the wrong foot, and how later we became firm friends.

I bonded very early with another former England manager, Graham Taylor. When he was boss of Lincoln City in the seventies I put together a two-part series for *Sportsnight* featuring two young managers – Taylor, who soon moved to Watford, and Alan Durban, who was at Shrewsbury and Stoke City.

Watford's rise from the fourth division to the first struck a chord. My home was in Hertfordshire and they were very much the friendly local club. When Elton John was fully involved as chairman, it was a pleasure to see them enjoy their rise through the divisions. I took in many evenings at Vicarage Road, even when I was not working.

Taylor was extremely cooperative with the media, and as far as football matters were concerned, his chairman stayed in the background. On the one occasion Elton was quoted on a topical issue in the game, I expressed surprise. 'I'm over fifty now, John,' he said. 'So I can say what I like.'

After successive promotions on his arrival from the fourth to the second division, Taylor spent the next three years preparing a team good enough to join the big hitters. His methods were straightforward and the football exciting, if a little too 'route one' for some of Watford's critics. Taylor had two attacking wingers in Nigel Callaghan and John Barnes, and big target men like George Reilly, Gerry Armstrong and Ross Jenkins. There were support strikers, Luther Blissett and Mo Johnston, to scoop up the pieces and score goals.

Taylor found the most direct route to goal. In the *Sportsnight* piece he said, 'What supporters want is to see the ball in the penalty area, how we get it there they don't really need to worry about. They want to enjoy the "oohs" and the "aahs".'

The Vicarage Road crowd certainly did that on 8 May 1982, when Watford beat Leicester City 3–1, with Barnes scoring twice and Blissett once, to secure promotion to the top flight for the first time. After the match I interviewed Taylor on the pitch. Having done the congratulations and remarked on what an achievement it had been to win three promotions in double quick time, I put it to him that he might find the football in the first division a bit too sophisticated for Watford.

Graham's face did not go as red as Alex Ferguson's, but for one horrible moment he tossed it so far in the air that I thought it was going to leave his body.

'Sophisticated football?' He almost spat the words out. 'What is sophisticated football? Don't you talk to me about sophisticated football.' Every time he used the word he managed to make it sound more contemptuous.

We have laughed about it since, but not then or the following season, when Watford finished runners-up to Liverpool in the first division playing exactly their own way. I went on to commentate on Taylor's team in Europe and in the FA Cup final when they lost 2–0 to Everton.

What was it with me and England managers? Ron Greenwood, who took over from Don Revie, ended England's exile from major tournaments. He took them to the 1980 European Championships and the 1982 World Cup – but there was one bad period in between.

In the summer of 1981, England played a World Cup qualifier to Switzerland in Basle. It was one of the many occasions when English hooligans wrecked a town. England lost 2–1 and there was a serious danger they might fail to qualify for the World Cup for the third successive time. The match ended about ten minutes before the national news on BBC1, so a live interview was set up with Greenwood at the mouth of the tunnel. In front of an audience of several millions I had to ask him whether, in the light of that result, he would consider his position as manager.

Greenwood brushed aside the question, saying that there was another game in Hungary a week later. When we had finished the interview he called over Bob Abrahams, my producer, and said, 'Tell John to watch his questions.'

A week later, after Keegan and Brooking inspired a 3–1 win over Hungary in Budapest, Greenwood agreed to be interviewed by me only after scolding ITV for keeping his two match winners out on the pitch when he wanted everybody in the dressing room.

I found it strange when he made a point of thanking all his staff by name in our interview, and it was only when he resigned on the plane home that I realised why. *Sunday Grandstand* nearly had their scoop of the year when the late Justin Fashanu, a member of the Under-21 party, whispered to me what had happened.

'Big story for you, John,' he said.

Albeit only for a couple of minutes. The players persuaded Ron to change his mind. England suffered another embarrassing defeat in Norway in the autumn, but they still qualified and came back from the 1982 World Cup unbeaten. Two goalless draws in the second group stage saw them go out.

Ron Greenwood never bore a grudge. He was one of the most honest men I ever met in football. When he stepped upstairs at West Ham prior to taking the England job, he left the Hammers in the capable hands of his assistant, John Lyall, whose playing career as a full back had been prematurely ended by injury.

John had a large, likeable presence. He was affable and polite – until you crossed him, which I did at Goodison Park in February 1982. Everton and West Ham had played out a goalless draw, and in my match report for *Grandstand* I blamed both teams for a lack of spectacle. Philip Carter, the Everton chairman, was so incensed by my comments that he sent word from the boardroom to stop his manager, Howard Kendall, from doing an interview with me for *Match of the Day*.

He was too late. Kendall was already halfway across the pitch with Lyall, and I put it to both of them that this was a poor version of what was supposed to be entertainment. Howard defended Everton's performance by pointing out that they had forced over twenty corners, but John took the criticism person-ally. 'Don't have a go at West Ham about being negative, when you think of the football we have always preached and played down the years,' he said fiercely.

The newspapers all agreed with my assessment, and I forgot all about it until I bumped into John Lyall in the car park at Tottenham a few weeks later. 'Don't ask me for any help,' he spluttered, 'you're a bommeroo.'

Now I had no idea what he meant and the dictionary was of no help, but it was clear that relations with West Ham were suspended until the dust settled.

Reg Drury, the well-connected *News of the World* reporter, came to my rescue. He and his wife, Cepta, had shared many meals out with me and my wife Annie. He was also very close to Lyall, and after a few soothing words the rift was healed. I later had some convivial dealings with John when he took Ipswich into the Premier League. His premature death came as a big shock to all his friends in football.

In his brief spell as manager of Arsenal, Bruce Rioch was a neighbour of mine in the Hertfordshire town of Harpenden. But there was nothing neighbourly about the way he reacted when I asked him a direct question about Ian Wright in a *Football Focus* interview. Bruce walked off in a huff – they clearly weren't getting on. When the game was over Rioch saw me in the car park. 'Do you want a lift home?' he asked. Another example of how a manager's mood can change depending on the moment.

Just across London at Upton Park, I fell foul of Harry Redknapp when he was manager of West Ham. They were at home to Newcastle at the end of October 2000, and were unusually low – eighteenth in fact – in the Premier League table. Redknapp had taken them to eighth, fifth and ninth in the three previous seasons, and I had no reason to believe he was under pressure.

When we were preparing for the *Football Focus* interview I said to Harry that it would be a good idea to mention the 'Kids for a Quid' scheme which the Hammers were introducing to encourage young supporters into the ground. He agreed. But just as I came to my last question I forgot all about the kids and wound up the interview with a mumbled 'So everything is all right with you here at West Ham, Harry?' It was not supposed to be provocative, but I had unintentionally lit a blue touchpaper. 'People just want to remember what I've done for this club,' Harry fumed. 'And I'll be longer in this job than you will be in yours, John.'

It transpired later that a faction on the West Ham board had grown restless with the league position, and Harry went into that game under a bit of a cloud. Once West Ham had beaten Newcastle he looked years younger, and even wished me a cheery farewell when I left the ground.

One of the most hospitable managers I encountered was Ron Atkinson, whom I first met at a tennis tournament while he was in charge at Cambridge United. When he became manager of West Bromwich Albion, he took my old Hereford contact, Colin Addison, as his assistant. I shared many meals with them when their team included 'The Three Degrees' – Brendan Batson, Laurie Cunningham and Cyrille Regis – as well as a young Bryan Robson and the England winger Peter Barnes.

By the time he got to Manchester United, Atkinson had become one of the most flamboyant characters in the game. He was popular with the press, and his office after the match was a hive of activity. There was always an open discussion about the match and other football issues, in which Ron encouraged all his selected friends to have their say.

I once interviewed the great Matt Busby – whom Atkinson and Ferguson were charged to emulate – about his Busby Babes team, which were decimated at Munich. He said, 'It got to the stage where all I had to do was sit in my office and let them go out and play.'

Well, many games *were* played in Ron Atkinson's office, certainly in words, with Ron in the chair correcting anybody who got one of the players' names wrong. His memory for footballers and matches was unbeatable, in my experience. It was the same when he moved to Aston Villa, Sheffield Wednesday and Coventry, but it was those days at Old Trafford that I remember most.

So many people were in and out of Ron's office, it should have had a revolving door. One day a guy walked in while we were having a post-match drink and hung five suits in Ron's wardrobe. I turned to Mick Brown, Atkinson's assistant, and said plaintively, 'Mick, there are people here who I just don't know.'

Mick replied, 'Motty, there are people here who even Ron doesn't know.'

I think this chapter proves that catching managers within minutes of the final whistle is tantamount to meeting them when their stress level is at its highest. Most of them need time to calm down, which is why criticism of the referee in post-match interviews often withers when they have time to look at the video. Give a manager another half-hour or so, and he will have completed a demanding round of television, radio and newspaper interviews. He will then be able to relax in his office with family and friends. At which point, you'll see them for what, by and large, they really are – warm characters with a good sense of humour.

Chapter 17

Grumpy Old Man
Things I couldn't get my head round

WHEN CHELSEA AND Liverpool produced their stirring 4–4 draw in April 2009, people were amazed to know I had never commentated on a European Champions League match. And what is more, until then I had no burning desire to do so.

The last time I held the microphone at what was then a two-leg European Cup tie was when Rangers played Red Star Belgrade in the second round in the 1990/91 season. Then the Yugoslavian side, which went on to win the competition that season, triumphed 3–0 in Belgrade, with Rangers' manager Graeme Souness admitting they were outclassed. The second leg at Ibrox Park ended in a 1–1 draw.

The following season UEFA changed the format. After the first two rounds, the eight remaining teams were split into two groups of four, and played in a league system. The two group winners, Sampdoria and Barcelona, met in the final at Wembley. This method lasted three seasons. In 1994/95, when entry was still limited to clubs that were domestic champions, the sixteen teams were split from the start into four groups of four, playing each other twice. Knockout quarter-finals and semi-finals were reinstated.

England's champions, Manchester United, were eliminated in

the group stage largely because of a 4–0 defeat in Barcelona. The following season, the English entry fared no better. Blackburn Rovers, under Kenny Dalglish, won only one of their six matches. Manchester United survived the group stage in 1996/97, and were eventually beaten in the semi-finals by Borussia Dortmund. That season Newcastle United finished runners-up to Ferguson's team in the Premier League, and now two teams from England were admitted to the Champions League.

With no disrespect to Newcastle in particular, this was when I finally fell out with the new UEFA concept. The European Cup had been strictly for champions. It was a sacrosanct concept that had been the brainchild of Gabriel Hanot when the French sports magazine *L'Equipe* launched the tournament in 1955.

But the Champions League was now becoming a cash cow, and could not resist the lure of television money. In 1999/2000 UEFA expanded the competition to thirty-two clubs – including three from the Premier League – and introduced a second group phase. This meant that each club played six matches in its first-round group, and six more in the second stage. Knockout quarter-finals and semi-finals followed, so to win the European Cup, as Real Madrid did that season, they had to play seventeen matches. The demands on the clubs and on the European football calendar meant that UEFA saw some sense in 2004, when they abandoned the second group stage and went straight to knockout in the round of the last sixteen. That has been the format since.

This has been a long explanation as to how and why an originally elite competition has been watered down. The winners are no longer necessarily champions of their country. I am biased, having written a history of the European Cup with John Rowlinson in 1980. But I am not alone. Before he assumed the UEFA presidency, Michel Platini came up with a revolutionary plan to standardise the two European club competitions.

He suggested that 256 clubs, which would have competed in

either the Champions League or the UEFA Cup, should enter a straight knockout competition, unseeded, and contest five rounds leading to the quarter-finals. Then we could go back to the days when there was no seeding and the losers knew that it was the end of their involvement for another season.

That could never happen now, of course. A careful seeding system means the leading clubs are kept apart, at least until the first knockout round. Quite honestly, when UEFA make the draw at the end of August, you could forecast which sixteen teams will advance from the group stage, and get fourteen right every season. In my view it is a cosmetic exercise to pull in as much television money as possible, and eliminate the champions from Europe's weaker nations.

The revenue the more successful clubs receive from the competition is startling. And it is still growing. In the 2008/09 season, Manchester United made £33.7 million. Chelsea pulled in £27.7 million. Arsenal, the third of the Premier League semi-finalists collected £23.4 million. And Liverpool, beaten by Chelsea in the quarter-final received £20.4 million.

What concerns me about this revenue stream is that it is self-perpetuating, as long as the top four clubs in the Premier League remain the same. So the gap between the 'big four' and the rest of the league gets wider. If the other clubs can't get a crack at the Champions League, they are never going to catch up financially. And if they cannot afford the best players, how can they break the dominance of the 'big four'? It is a vicious circle, completely at odds with what should be a democratic game. If the rich get richer and the poor get poorer, there is no chance for clubs like Nottingham Forest or Ipswich Town to achieve the European success they enjoyed less than thirty years ago. Indeed, this point was echoed by the then Culture Secretary Andy Burnham in May 2009 when he called on the big four clubs to share their winnings in Europe with other Premier League teams.

*   *   *

The Champions League is not solely to blame. There are other reasons why the distribution of wealth has polarised professional football in this and other countries. The main one is the Bosman ruling.

The landmark judgement of the European Court of Justice during the 1995/96 season changed the way football would be for ever. Now, a player can walk away at the end of his contract without his club receiving any compensation. I believe that judgement to be flawed. If I work at a motor car assembly plant, and choose to exercise my freedom of labour by going down the road to work for a rival firm, I leave the cars behind. They are the product belonging to my previous employer.

Surely, in football, the players *are* the product. Their parent club has either employed them or signed them, trained and developed them, improved and incentivised them, and treated them when they have been injured. When the player walks away at the end of his contract, all that investment in 'the product' counts for absolutely nothing.

So too, it seems, do some contracts. I always believed that it was incumbent on two parties to observe a written agreement between them. Nowadays, an unsettled player can almost always get the move he wants, even when his club would prefer to keep him, thanks largely to the influence of agents.

A good example of this was Dimitar Berbatov's move from Tottenham to Manchester United at the beginning of the 2008/09 season. Spurs had brought Berbatov from Bayer Leverkusen for around £11 million and the Bulgarian responded with forty-six goals in two seasons. He then decided he did not want to play for Tottenham any more, and Manchester United made their interest plain. Spurs knew there was no point in keeping an unhappy player, and held out for the £30 million fee they eventually received.

Good business, you might argue, for all three parties. Maybe, but it was not the only transfer to leave a nasty taste in the mouth. I don't necessarily agree with supporters jeering players who come back to play against their own club, but on occasions like this I can understand it.

All this greed and gratification has done football in this country no good. On the surface, the product is a shiny, superbly wrapped package, pulling in an avid audience week after week. In reality, the game is skating on such financially thin ice that in any other business it would be declared bankrupt. Lower-division clubs are flirting with administration on an almost weekly basis, some having already lost points for not coming to terms with their creditors.

What is also disturbing is the way new investors from abroad have heaped a cartload of debt on the club they have acquired. I have serious moral reservations about the way the Glazer family bought Manchester United. Before they arrived the club was virtually solvent. In the spring of 2009 it was reported the club and its associated companies had total debts of some £700 million. Even the £80 million that Manchester United received from Real Madrid for Cristiano Ronaldo in June 2009 has to be set against the enormous amount of annual interest the club are paying on their debts.

And in spite of the largesse of Roman Abramovich, Chelsea are in a not dissimilar position. His personal investment in the club was also said to be in the region of £700 million, until he reportedly converted half of it into equity in February 2009.

As long as these clubs remain in the Champions League, and maintain their worldwide brand, nobody seems too bothered.

The first warning signs of such profligacy came at Liverpool, where the building of a new stadium was put on hold while the two American owners worked out how to extend and service the loans they had taken out on their and the club's behalf. In June 2009, Liverpool's auditors KPMG said when the accounts of the club and their holding company were published: 'There is a material uncertainty which may cast significant doubt upon the Group's ability to continue as a going concern.'

Liverpool's holding company had paid £36.5 million in interest on their debt – more than the club recorded in profit before depreciation and deductions, and three times the club's pre-tax profit of £7.10 million'.

'Debt is fine as long as you can service it,' one club chairman said to me a few years ago. I would add to that, as long as television remains in love with football. Because that is the game's life support, and without it the industry would collapse. The days when gate receipts paid the players' wages are long gone. Television money is their lifeblood, and most clubs keep afloat with the help of commercial income.

In my first season at *Match of the Day* in 1972, I was approached before a match at Bramall Lane by a gentleman called Harold Rumsey. 'Have you got time to see our new restaurant?' he asked.

Thinking he meant that he and some partners had opened a new eating house in Sheffield city centre, I politely declined. Then I realised he meant it was at the ground.

In those days, there was little or no commercial or advertising income. Flicking through my old programmes, I see no mention of replica shirts, marketing departments or sponsors. I remember the little club shop at Highbury, run by the former Arsenal goalkeeper Jack Kelsey. Just about all you could buy there was a scarf and a rattle.

When David Dein and the new wave of commercial operators moved into football, things changed very quickly. Club shops became megastores, and outlets like Arsenal's World of Sport at Finsbury Park, among other sites, took the game into a new wave of consumerism.

Before the movers and shakers saw football as a growth industry, clubs were run by three or four people. My programme on the day I saw my first match at Charlton listed only Jimmy Seed as secretary/manager (like Alf Ramsey at Ipswich, he combined the two jobs), Jimmy Trotter as trainer, and Mr J Phillips as assistant secretary. There were five directors.

The programme for Charlton's first match of the 2008/09 season listed fifteen directors and nine associate directors. There was an assistant to the manager, a reserve team coach, a performance manager, a chief scout, a physiotherapist and a doctor. They have a football secretary, a youth-academy manager with two assistants, an under-18 coach, and an education and welfare officer. That array of staff is just on the playing side.

On the business page, they listed a group chief executive and his deputy, a finance director, an operations director, a commercial director and a commercial centre manager. Added to that there were two development officers, a communications manager, a conference and banqueting manager, a retail manager, a stadium safety officer, and a community trust executive. And Charlton are by no means overstaffed compared to other clubs. They had cut costs that summer after failing to win promotion to the Premier League at the first attempt. Things got worse when they were relegated from the Championship at the end of the 2008/09 season.

This brings us on to the gap between the Premier League and the Championship – bridged for two years by the 'parachute payment', which guarantees relegated clubs £11 million in each of those seasons.

Going up for one year can therefore be worth £60 million – £38 million from one year in the Premier League and £22 million for two years in parachute payments – but not getting back quickly can see funds dissolve. Especially if much of the money has been squandered on unsuccessful transfers and inflated wages.

At the start of the 2009/10 season, fifteen of the twenty-four clubs in the Championship had spent time in the Premier League and were desperate to return. Six had the support of the parachute payment, while the other ten had to try to compensate by shrewd management. But the danger facing a club that does get promoted is that they stretch themselves so far to keep up with the big boys, they find themselves not only back where they started, but without the resources to rejoin the elite.

And it can get even worse. Charlton, Southampton and Norwich – all recently comfortably placed in the Premier League – started the 2009/10 season in League One. Would any of the three have envisaged sliding so quickly from the heady heights of the Premier League to the third tier of English football?

At many clubs, bank loans, directors' guarantees, money borrowed against future income – all have kept the wolf from the door. If you took all these support mechanisms away, would you find an absolutely solvent club anywhere in the league? The fact that most of them operate on a hand-to-mouth policy from week to week means that our overcrowded calendar cannot be trimmed. Nobody is going to vote for a reduction in the fixture list if it means a loss of revenue.

When I was a boy, the only pre-season match my father and I went to was the 'public trial' at Charlton. The week before the season started, the 'probables' (near enough the first team) would play the 'possibles' (the likely reserves) in a gentle precursor at The Valley. Most clubs adopted this style of curtain raiser, but it faded out in the sixties. The big clubs now concentrate on lucrative friendlies and tournaments abroad.

Television has again dictated the agenda. When I started, only the Charity Shield would be in the schedules pre-season – and then only the highlights. In the summer of 2008, the *Sun* came up with an ironic headline: JULY 17TH. 7.08PM. THE FIRST GOAL OF THE SEASON. Martin Petrov had scored for Manchester City against EB Streymur of the Faroe Islands in the first qualifying round of the UEFA Cup.

Not only would I prefer to see football leave the field free for cricket in July, but I wish we would follow the example of

Italy and Spain and delay the start of the league season until September. This would give everybody a longer summer break. It would also make more sense for clubs to complete their spending, with the transfer window closing at the end of August. It seems a contradiction in terms for players to start the season with one club, only to join another two weeks later.

When Huddersfield Town marked their centenary with a match against Arsenal for the Herbert Chapman trophy in August 2008, the excellent souvenir brochure mentioned the club's first Football League match in 1910. 'Football League rules at that time forbade any competitive football to be played before September,' it stated. Not that the game has changed that much. A crowd of 16,000 saw the 1910 match at Bradford, exactly the same number who bought season tickets at Huddersfield in 2008.

When, as kids, we put our cricket bats away in early August and rubbed dubbin on our football boots, it marked a significant seasonal hiatus in our year. Now, the new season starts before the last one has finished.

The 60,000 Arsenal fans who attended a pre-season friendly at the Emirates Stadium in July 2008 will no doubt shout me down. But my fear is that by playing too much football, we shall ultimately destroy the rarity value that used to be attached to live television coverage. The damage may already have been done.

The history, tradition and fabric of the game probably mean very little to the new breed of owners and investors who have moved into the Premier League and the Championship over the last three years. Overseas ownership is all very well if the investors are coming in for the right reasons. By that I mean football reasons, rather than just financial ones.

The Premier League is undoubtedly a gigantic global brand, and nobody can stop the market forces that have seen the big clubs capitalise on their fan base in the Middle and Far East. Which is what prompted the idea of the thirty-ninth game. My fear about that is similar to the one I felt when a European League was touted. If we lose the symmetry of our game, where each club plays the other twice, home and away, we destroy 120 years of history.

It would be unfair to blame the blatant proliferation of football purely on the European Champions League and the Barclays Premier League. The two international events, the World Cup and the European Championship, must share the responsibility for everyone believing that more is necessarily better.

When I first covered the World Cup in 1974, there were sixteen countries in the finals. That increased to twenty-four in Spain in 1982, and thirty-two in France in 1998. The European Championship had just four semi-finalists when I went to Yugoslavia in 1976. Four years later in Italy there were eight nations. When England hosted the finals in 1996, it had expanded to sixteen teams, and now there will be twenty-four nations in the 2012 finals. The only justification for this has to be more money for more countries. But does making something bigger guarantee it will improve in quality?

It may not happen in my lifetime, but I firmly believe that overkill will ultimately affect football, particularly on television, to its detriment. What a pity that nobody with a little foresight at international or domestic level can see beyond the next billion pounds, and call a halt to the relentless pursuit of financial gain which threatens the pleasure and purity of the game. Especially as nearly all the money goes to the players and their agents.

Money isn't the only issue I have with the modern game. Change is not always for the best, and in my view that also applies to video technology. It is fine for cricket and rugby union, where the game has natural breaks and there is time to consult the video referee. But I think it should be resisted by football.

There are those who argue that a decision as to whether the ball has crossed the goal line could affect a team's season. My stance is that if you bring in technology to determine whether a goal should stand, the following week there will be a demand to use it for other disputes, such as offside, penalties, even red or yellow cards. The crowd would grow restless if there were constant referrals and interruptions. As Rick Parry once said to me when he was running the Premier League: 'Part of the fun of going to football is arguing about it on the way home.'

Anything artificial takes away from the natural beauty and simplicity of the game. Having commentated on more of them than I can remember, I have no love of penalty shoot-outs either. This has nothing to do with the fact that the Germans always seem to prevail and the English always lose. I just think it is a wretched, manufactured way of settling a football match.

So with a calendar that affords no time for replays, how else would you settle a drawn game? Roger Ball, my friend whom I met after the Hillsborough disaster, devised the only theory I think would work. In boxing, the next best thing to stopping your opponent is winning on points. These are awarded for punches that hit the target during the bout, but matter only if nobody lands the knockout blow.

Now transfer that theory to football. The nearest thing to scoring a goal is to hit the post or crossbar. Suppose points were awarded for shots or headers that come off the frame of the goal. With five minutes to go (and I am no lover of extra time either) the score could be 0–0, but one team might lead 3–1 on 'points'. The losing side would then have no option but to throw everything into attack, and we would have a far more exciting finish to the game.

I am sure there are ways in which this method would fall short, or be open to abuse, but at least the result would be based on things that happen naturally during the game, rather than a post-match scenario where everybody shakes hands, shrugs their shoulders and leaves it to chance – or the two goalkeepers.

I have seen too many penalty shoot-outs when it would be better for the players to walk off and call it a draw. Take the Community Shield at Wembley, which has been settled that way so often. Why bother? Let the two clubs share the trophy for six months, as used to be the case.

Staying with Wembley, I was unconvinced about the rebuilding of the stadium . . . and even more unconvinced when it reopened.

One music critic who reviewed a George Michael concert for his Sunday newspaper saw it as a 'massive, artless lump of concrete, corridors, glass and grass resembling a gigantic storage hangar in the Dubai desert, dropped into a fairly ghostly, neglected area of north-west London, topped off with an expensive glowing arch – a luminous bangle of branding confidence that can be seen for miles'.

I knew what he meant, especially when they built the television commentary position one tier too high and several yards too far away from the pitch. The fact that the FA did not have the foresight to buy the land that surrounds the stadium meant that when it reopened, it was in a setting that could be described at best as shabby.

There were those who lobbied for the national stadium to be built on the outskirts of Birmingham. I personally wish they had looked more closely at a site bordering the M1 motorway in Bedfordshire. But rather as with the redesigned Ascot racecourse, the more I got used to the new Wembley, the more I moderated my opinion.

Going to a venue as a supporter can sometimes give you a perspective you do not have as a commentator. I enjoyed the experience of watching an international as an England fan, without having to worry about whether the lift was working, or being stopped from going down the players' tunnel by an overzealous steward.

By now the reader will have come to the conclusion that I am at best hard to please, at worst downright intransigent. Over some things, yes, but we all have our standards and values, and one of my faults is expecting everything to be perfect. Perhaps the years of detailed devotion to the commentator's craft have taken their toll and made me irritable when others are less than precise in their attention to detail.

One thing that has changed for the better, for me at least, is that I don't have to go through the sheer tedium and boredom of watching training sessions any more. That part of the job was something I was only too glad to shed when the BBC lost the FA contract and I stopped covering England matches in 2008. It was a necessity to watch training – especially the opposition – in order to identify the players. Just occasionally, a coach would line up his team the way he intended them to play. That was gold dust to a commentator. It made the exercise instantly worthwhile. But it became more and more of a chore to witness their warm-up routine, after which we were often asked to leave.

I started this chapter talking about the European Cup and I'd like to end with something Bob Paisley once said about the competition: 'You curse the hotels, raise hell about training, worry about the food, about the hanging around, about the travel weariness . . . and then the moment you are out of it, you are empty inside. The icing is off the cake. God, you do miss it.'

I feel the same about commentating. I've certainly cursed plenty of hotels in my time. I always seemed to land the room near the lift, or with the window over a busy street. I have lost count of the times I have repacked my bag, gone downstairs to reception and asked for a move. But if I stopped commentating completely, the icing would similarly be off my cake. For all my grumbles and the grumpiness, it must surely be the next best thing to playing.

Chapter 18

'Half a second away from . . .'

'Sad but true, it is for their faux pas they will be remembered'

I F I HAD a pound for every time someone has asked me, 'Where's the sheepskin Motty?' I'd be as rich as the magnates who have bought their way into the Premier League. Although I've been wearing it since the early 1970s, the moment the coat and I became synonymous was actually at Wycombe Wanderers' Adams Park ground in December 1990.

I was there to cover their second-round FA Cup tie against Peterborough United. Wycombe were playing in the then GM Vauxhall Conference under the management of Martin O'Neill, who later that season took them to Wembley, where they won the FA Trophy, and later into the Football League. A shock result seemed quite a possibility when I left home in bright sunshine that morning, preparing to interview O'Neill for *Football Focus*.

As I turned off the M40 in the Thames Valley and started my descent down the hill that leads to Wycombe's ground, it started to snow. So heavily that within five minutes there was a covering on the road. But that was nothing compared with the Adams Park pitch half an hour later. It was deep in three or four inches of snow, and the referee took one look and postponed the game. *Grandstand* told me to forget the interview with O'Neill, and record a piece to camera explaining the sudden change in weather conditions.

I did not know that a photographer called Stuart Clarke was standing a few yards away. The image of me freezing in the sheepskin was to become one of the photographs in his *Homes of Football* postcard series. It was used in a number of books and magazines, and I lose count of the times people ask me: 'Where was that picture taken of you in the snow?'

Many years earlier, at the start of my career, I noticed commentators such as Brian Moore wearing a warm, padded jacket to protect themselves against the cold in exposed positions. I found the *half*-length jacket quite easy to buy, but it was quite by chance that the *full*-length coat came my way.

I had been in the job for only a couple of years when I was invited to a party in West London one Christmas. I was single then, and our hostess invited me to join her in the garage at the back of her property. All sorts of things went through my mind, but I certainly wasn't prepared for what she showed me. A rail of full-length sheepskin coats was standing on one side of the garage, and she invited me to try a few of them. For a small price I bought one, and immediately felt the benefit the next time I went on to the television gantry. It kept me warm more or less down to my feet.

That lady never reappeared in my life, so when the coat wore out I wondered where to get the next one. The big London stores still stocked the half-length jackets, but that was all. Fortunately, Steve Rowley, the scout who had so much to do with Arsenal's successful recruitment of young players, came to my rescue. He knew a man in Hornchurch in Essex who made coats from the skins he kept in his garage. This time there was no guided tour.

I submitted my measurements, and soon a new coat arrived. I must have bought two or three from him.

By now my coats were coming from a variety of sources. I found a firm in Borehamwood, not far from where I lived in Hertfordshire, which made them for export to Russia, but did not sell them in the home market. Then, while on holiday in Cannes, I met a bar owner called Leslie Azoulay, who had been a furrier in Paris. I bought two coats from him. Nearer home, I sat on a table in the sponsors' lounge at Tottenham with two guests who had moved into Savile Row and opened the outfitters William Hunt. My last two coats have come from them.

I normally send my coat away for cleaning in the summer. By the time I have spent nine months climbing up and down ladders and brushing against all sorts of obstacles on my way to the commentary position, there are plenty of dirty marks and patches of oil to be seen and, where possible, removed.

A lot of the affection that seems to have come my way should really be credited to the coat. That lady who took me into her garage in the early seventies would never know what she started – and there was everyone thinking I was a football 'anorak'!

Rarely does a footballer pay a commentator a compliment, but one I remember receiving was particularly welcome. It was the week after my first FA Cup final in 1977, and Northern Ireland were about to play England in the Home International Championship. In the narrow corridor that leads to the dressing rooms at Windsor Park, Belfast, was the imposing figure of the Northern Ireland goal-keeper, Pat Jennings. 'Well done last Saturday,' he murmured in his deep Irish brogue. 'I thought you did really well.'

Five years later, after Jennings had starred in a World Cup tie, somebody asked him whether he had enjoyed the game. 'You never enjoy it as a goalkeeper,' he replied. 'Not until it's over and you know you haven't made a bad mistake.'

I've wondered since whether that was why he took time out to reassure me. There is something of a correlation between goalkeepers and commentators – and referees for that matter. In each of our different roles, every decision has to be made instantly. We do our jobs without a safety net. And what people remember us for, more than anything, is when we make mistakes.

In 1984, I had the opportunity to delve a little deeper into what being a commentator is all about, when I was I asked to appear on Ludovic Kennedy's Sunday night programme *Did You See?* The main part of the show was a critical review of the week's television, but the last item was a feature in which a broadcaster interviewed two of his contemporaries in the same field to get their take on the job.

I was asked to choose two sports commentators to interview. Without hesitation I picked Richie Benaud and Peter O'Sullevan. It was not so much my interest in cricket and racing which swayed the decision, more the contrast between a fast and a slow sport.

I met Benaud in the commentary box at Lord's, sitting behind him and Jim Laker while they covered the morning session. The mood in their camp was relaxed and convivial, with a lot of caustic comment off the microphone between overs. Neither of them missed a thing. It was the first time I witnessed the advantage of having former internationals at the microphone, as long as they could broadcast, of course.

Benaud had enrolled on a BBC Outside Broadcast course one summer while he was still playing, and his focused response to my questions was a trifle chilling. He never looked at me once, preferring to address the camera, his clipped, deliberate delivery telling the viewers exactly how he went about his job.

He was determined to get off his chest his irritation at television viewers who turned down the sound and listened to the radio commentary on *Test Match Special*. 'That's what we fought two world wars for, so that people can make stupid decisions like that,' he said.

A few days later, I was in a much smaller commentary box at Goodwood, although you could hardly call Peter O'Sullevan's position a box. He was perched on a high chair next to a camera in the roof of the grandstand, binoculars at the ready. As he took in the next race, in which there were over twenty runners, I marvelled at his impeccable identification, but even more so at his even delivery and timing. He raised his voice two furlongs out and rattled through the first five past the post in perfect order.

When he took off his headphones, he was just as polished as he had been on the air. We had never met before, but his polite welcome and readiness to cooperate made me warm to him straight away. 'Dear boy, the only commentary we shall ever be remembered for is the one we got wrong,' he said. 'We are always half a second away from disaster.'

I found those words quite welcome. Here was a vastly more experienced commentator calling seven races in an afternoon, yet still plagued by the nagging insecurity that we all feel most of the time.

It's a sad fact that the faux pas Terry Wogan referred to are what we will most likely be remembered for. Although in this case, I think Wogan was referring to the classic commentary bloomers that spawned the *Private Eye* column 'Colemanballs'. Not that David Coleman is by any means responsible for all or even many of those gaffes. 'We all get the blame for each other's,' he once said to me.

It didn't take long for me to get into the column. One Saturday in December 1977 at Roker Park, where Sunderland were playing Tottenham, I fell flat on my face trying to respond to a letter from a viewer in the North-East. 'We live in a poor mining area and we can't afford colour television like all you affluent people in the South,' wrote my critic. 'My son has all the team pictures on his bedroom wall, but how does he know which team it is when you keep referring to red and blue shirts?'

Good question, I thought. Tottenham were playing in their change strip that day, so as the second half started, I thought this was the moment to pacify our angry viewer. 'For the benefit of those watching in black and white,' I said, 'Spurs are in the yellow shirts.'

I have opened my mouth and put my foot in it dozens of times since, but I find that one hard to beat.

But those are not the mistakes that the commentators dread, or the ones that keep me awake at night. The biggest fear is 'calling it wrong', whether it be a goalscorer, a substitute or a referee's decision. It doesn't matter how many cup finals or internationals you have done, the commentator is never immune to that terrifying moment when something happens and you have either missed it, or momentarily don't trust your own eyes.

It happened to me as recently as the 2008 FA Cup final between Portsmouth and Cardiff City, when Kanu scored the only goal. One of my golden rules when the ball hits the net has always been to look at the referee and his assistant. So many times commentators have shouted 'Goal!' and started to praise the scorer before realising that an infringement has been spotted and the effort has been disallowed.

One clue is that the assistant referee, if he is satisfied that there has been no offside or any other offence, will run back towards the halfway line. At Wembley that day, Trevor Massey, the assistant on the far side from me, remained rooted by the corner flag. Mark Lawrenson and I paused before establishing it was a goal. From our position on the other side of the stadium, Kanu's scrambled effort could conceivably have gone in with the help of a hand.

'Yes, Portsmouth have scored,' I confirmed after a few seconds, but I knew the critics would be after me the following day.

'Yes, Motty, of course they have scored,' wrote one columnist. 'The ball was in the net.'

After the match I went down to the officials' room, as was my custom at the Cup Final, to present my commentary notes to the referee. Mike Dean generously told me to give my card to Trevor Massey, who believed at the time that this would be his last match.

'You threw me a bit on the goal,' I said. 'I wondered for a moment if you had seen something wrong with it.'

'I was just monitoring the situation,' replied Trevor, an experienced official who later that summer was given a one-year extension on the line. Bearing in mind there was a cluster of players near the goal line, and Kanu had not wheeled away very far in celebration, he was no doubt keeping an eye out for any 'afters'.

I only use that as an example of where the commentator decides not to dive in and make a mistake, but takes a second or two to make sure he is right. I have seen too many unusual things happen to always commit straight away.

Perhaps the strangest came in an FA Cup fourth-round tie between Tranmere Rovers and Sunderland at Prenton Park in the first month of the millennium. This was the season when Manchester United withdrew from the FA Cup to play in the World Cup Championship in Brazil. It was also the year when the FA decided to play the third-round ties in December. Those decisions did nothing to protect the reputation of the competition, and it took a few years to repair the damage.

Barry Davies and part of our regular commentary team went to South America, and I was left to hold the fort. Tranmere had knocked out West Ham in the third round, and were now after another Premier League scalp. Sunderland, under Peter Reid, fell behind to a first-half goal from Wayne Allison. That was how things stood going into stoppage time.

Then Tranmere's Clint Hill, already on a yellow card, fouled Sunderland's Alex Rae. Referee Rob Harris correctly sent off Hill. Before the free kick could be taken, Tranmere wanted to make a substitution. The fourth official, David Unsworth, held up the board, which fleetingly flashed number six – that of the dismissed

Hill. Tranmere substitute Stephen Frail came on, but nobody went off. Rovers still had eleven players on the pitch, despite the sending off!

Sunderland took their free kick. Frail took up his place in the Tranmere defence, the ball was headed out for a goal kick, and Harris then blew for time. Fortunately I had spotted that for a few seconds Tranmere had played with an extra man, and told the story correctly.

'Thank goodness you didn't go to Brazil, John,' said Bob Shennan, who was acting Head of Sport at BBC Television at the time. 'That was a tricky one. Never happened before.'

Referee Harris and his assistant Tony Green were suspended by the FA, but the result stood.

Another curious incident I had to deal with occurred at Derby County's Baseball Ground many years earlier. The pitch there was notoriously muddy come the end of the season. When Derby played Manchester City at the end of April, with their first-division fate in the balance, there wasn't a blade of grass.

Derby were leading 3–0 and City's Brian Kidd had been sent off, before referee John Yates awarded Derby a penalty late in the game. But nobody could find the penalty spot. It was completely obscured in two or three inches of mud. Derby groundsman Bob Smith was summoned with a pot of paint. Yates paced out the 12 yards from Joe Corrigan's goal line, and Smith solemnly painted a new penalty spot. Gerry Daly promptly scored Derby's fourth goal and they survived relegation. John Yates, whose last match it was as a Football League referee, presented me with his whistle. I still have it today.

The only place I have ever been able to commentate without fear of making a mistake is in Burnaby, Canada, headquarters of the computer giant Electronic Arts. I was the voice on the *FIFA* computer game from its inception in 1995, until 2004. I also played a part in developing the commentary, even though computer technology is, to me, a mystery.

I was in a perfect position to see how far the game advanced from the first year, when I sat in a studio and recorded a few random phrases such as 'what a goal'. Within a year or two the script was running to hundreds of pages. I had to record the names of just about every footballer on the planet, in different tones of voice – excited, unexcited and so on.

Then there were all manner of phrases to cover shots, saves, assists, tackles, passes and refereeing decisions. I was shut in Aquarium Studios in Wardour Street, Soho, for days on end. The tapes then went back to Vancouver, where the high-tech whizz-kids fitted my sound to the images of the players and the 'game play'.

Curiously, the frequent and detailed reviews of *FIFA*, and comparisons with its competitors, rarely mentioned the commentary. But believe me, I put in many hours with Andy Gray, David Pleat, Ally McCoist and Chris Waddle. The chiefs at Electronic Arts must have been pleased with my contribution, however, because in the year 2000 they flew me first class to and from Vancouver and put me up in a five-star hotel for four days.

The idea was for me to mix with the staff who made the game, and give them some insight into how real the action and the surroundings seemed. At one point, I suggested they let me commentate over the pictures of an actual game, rather than just sitting in a studio and reciting names. They were astonished at the result. I had to speak a lot faster than I would at a match, but my flow was that bit more natural and they decided that, in future, this was the way to do the recordings.

So back in London, I looked at the monitor and did an 'off tube' commentary on, say, Chelsea against Manchester United, without naming any of the players. It had to be generic to meet the demands of the game.

Even though I have not been the voice on *FIFA* for the last five years, parents still come up to me and say: 'We've got your voice in our house all the time.' They are not talking about *Match of the Day* or *Five Live*, but about earlier versions of *FIFA* which their sons and daughters are still playing.

It was a great experience for me and a lucrative contract. But I never played the game myself, owing to my reluctance to get tuned in to computers. I don't even have an e-mail address!

My lack of interest in computer technology has a huge bearing on how I carry out my all important pre-match preparation. My homework owes nothing to computers or the Internet, but to paraphrase Paul Simon: 'I have my books to protect me.'

My library at home has shelves of football annuals and year-books going back well before the war. The volume I use most is the *Sky Sports Football Yearbook* – formerly known as 'The Rothmans' after the cigarette company sponsored it from its inception in 1970 until 2003. The *PFA Footballers' Who's Who*, edited by Barry Hugman, and his magnificent volumes of *Premier League* and *Football League Players' Records*, are also invaluable. I also have a complete set of *FA Yearbooks*, *Playfair Football Annuals* and *News of the World* (now Nationwide) annuals.

Being able to rattle off the history of a player or club at a moment's notice is one thing, but researching my next match requires a more topical approach. This can involve watching a DVD of a club's last performance, or better still going to see them play if they have a midweek game. David Coleman said to me when I started that I would always learn more when I was watching and not working. There is nothing like seeing a team in the flesh to familiarise myself with the players' shirt numbers, and mannerisms. Another advantage I found in going to games, rather than sitting at home and watching on television, was that I rarely came back without another contact made, another telephone number collected.

There are the telephone calls commentators make to managers or coaches, hoping to discover who might be in the squad and checking on injuries. A lot depends here on whether the manager trusts the commentator. Some realise that we don't start talking until kick-off, so as long as the line-up is kept under wraps, the manager will sometimes disclose his team. On the other hand, if he feels the commentator or somebody to whom he might pass the information cannot be trusted, the shutters come down.

For my week-to-week statistics and newspaper cuttings, I have my diligent wife Annie to thank. For some thirty years now, she has lovingly kept what we call her 'Black Book', in which she records every result, appearance, goalscorer and attendance.

She also logs every international squad and line-up, a running list of transfers, red and yellow cards, and suspensions. Annie always says you can tell the most successful teams because they use the least number of players over a season. The squads of relegated clubs usually extend to the bottom of the page.

For many years, Albert Sewell was the doyen of football statistics at the BBC. His match notes on a Thursday were an education. If something had happened in the corresponding match the year before, Albert would know. I would regularly ring him on a Friday night with some obscure enquiry. 'Ring you back in a few minutes,' he would say. Moments later the answer would arrive.

Albert remained sprightly up to his retirement at seventy-eight in 2005, whereupon the BBC Sports Assistants, a department formed a few years earlier, inherited his responsibilities. A team of four subeditors working in the *Match of the Day* office service commentators, editors and producers with background material on all the sports covered by the BBC. They produce huge, detailed volumes of information before major events such as the World Cup and Olympic Games, as well as a Premier League annual at the start of the season with pen pictures of every player.

I have always been fascinated by facts and figures from the time

I kept my football records as a boy. When I saw the way commentators such as Barry Davies and Gerald Sinstadt carefully compiled their notes, I made up my mind to be at least as detailed. There have been times when I have overdone it. When Trevor Brooking and Tommy Hutchison scored with rare headers in consecutive cup finals, I was taken to task for pointing out that both were wearing the number-ten shirt.

David Coleman often said I would become a better commentator when I threw my homework away. I knew what he meant, because I would probably have remembered the important things anyway. I was relying on my research as some sort of insurance policy. In later years I cut down considerably on background information. But I knew that if someone scored their 100th goal, or was sent off for the third time that season, the morning papers would mention it and the viewers would wonder why I hadn't.

Sometimes the commentator can't win.

You will have gathered by now that commentators are not short of support. But one thing nobody can do for us is identify the players, and sometimes we have to go to unusual lengths to ensure that we can do that quickly and accurately. A television commentator starting at kick-off has no time to ascertain who is who once the whistle sounds. He has to be able to recognise every player, and potential substitutes.

Overseas teams are obviously more difficult. They are not as easy to watch in advance. Sometimes I have felt like a super-sleuth trying to get a glimpse of players through the strict security cordon now commonplace at internationals. The media are usually admitted only to the first fifteen minutes of a training session. It is hardly long enough to work out who is who, especially as they are probably just loosening up on the far side of the field.

My method when covering international matches in recent years has been to find the hotel where England's opponents are staying, and attempt to catch the players walking around. When Russia played a European Championship qualifier at Wembley in 2007, they were secluded in a separate wing of their Hertfordshire hotel, and protected wherever they went by two heavies, neither of whom spoke English.

I positioned myself outside the dining room and asked one of the medical staff to say the name of each player as he walked in and out. Not a very dignified way of working at the age of sixty-two, but needs must. Had one of their players been earning his living in the Premier League, it would have been a different story.

When Spain came to Old Trafford for a friendly, Cesc Fabregas pointed out each player for me in their hotel. I had similar help from Jurgen Klinsmann with the Germans.

Now we come to the problems of pronunciation. If you saw my postbag after a big tournament – and read the letters in the *Radio Times* – you would think I put no effort into this part of the job. Once the trickle of overseas players in English football became a flood, most of the conscientious commentators decided the only way to settle on the correct pronunciation was to ask the player directly.

Scandinavian and Dutch players always met this request with a smile. 'You will never say it the way we do in our country,' they invariably replied. Then gave us a simple English version. This worked perfectly well with Peter Schmeichel, Jan Molby – what would the Scousers have thought if we'd called him Molbu? – Ole Gunnar Solskjaer and Pierre van Hooijdonk. But then winger Jesper Gronkjaer came over from Ajax to play for Chelsea.

I pronounced his name as 'Gronk-yire', but then the letters started arriving from a Danish lady who rubbished my version. Mind you, hers was almost unreadable, and certainly impossible for me to get my tongue around. In the end I sought the opinion of Peter Schmeichel, who had played with Gronkjaer in the Danish team and was working for the BBC on *Match of the Day* and *Football Focus*.

'Say "Gronk–yire",' said Peter. So I carried on as usual.

While we're on the subject of overseas players, I must make my position clear on the influx of those joining the domestic game – and the Premier League – in recent years. I accept this may have made it harder for academy products and English lads to come through into the first team, but feel that is far outweighed by the value that the foreign imports have added.

Their attitude to training, as exemplified by Eric Cantona at Manchester United and Gianfranco Zola at Chelsea, was a huge eye-opener when they arrived. If it did not rub off on the home-based players, then they were not willing to learn. The lifestyle off the pitch of the Western European players, particularly, also set a good example. There did not seem to be a drinking culture like the one prevalent at most English clubs until more recently, when coaches such as Arsène Wenger have encouraged players to adapt their eating and drinking habits so as to extend their career.

And then there is the compelling entertainment value that they have added to the Premier League. Would we really have been content to have missed out on Thierry Henry, Eric Cantona, Dennis Bergkamp, Fernando Torres, Robinho and so on?

Certainly I would not. The names and pronunciations are a real headache, but not as big a one as the decision in the 2008/09 season to allow Premier League teams to name seven substitutes rather than five. It may seem a moot point, but now the commentator has an extra fourteen names to work on, outside the starting eleven, rather than ten. When I started there were only two substitutes – one for each side!

It is not uncommon, after the change has been made, for a manager to slide a comparatively unknown teenager on to the substitute's bench, largely for the experience. For the commentator arriving at the ground, it may be a seventeen-year-old he has never heard of. A lot of last-minute checking went on last season!

By now the reader is probably thinking that commentators are a peculiar breed who are immersed in detail and rarely come up for air. Before a game, when I find casual conversation a distraction, people often say: 'He's in the zone,' whatever that means.

But for all the hours spent preparing, perfecting and sometimes panicking, there is a great sense of release when you get into your commentary position, your notes on your knee, and the teams come out. The late Brian Moore said to me when he was about to retire: 'If you could spirit me into the stadium with all the travelling and homework done, I could go on for ever.'

I always condense my notes on to two pieces of paper, sticking them to either side of a card. One of my early radio bosses, Bob Hudson, always said, 'Never let your notes blow away!' On one side I list the two squads side by side, using felt-tip pen to distinguish the colours, and blue or red biro to write biographical notes alongside. A star next to the name of a player denotes he has never scored a goal. YC stand for yellow cards. Then I insert Christian names and shirt numbers in different colours.

Over the last few years my 'commentary charts', as I call them, have proved useful items to send to charities and auctions. I must get nearly a hundred requests in a season. When I spoke at a testimonial dinner in Southampton for the cricketer Shaun Udal, my chart for England's 5–1 win in Germany in 2001 fetched £1,900 for his fund.

Mostly, though, my wife Annie keeps a pile on hand so that I can sign them and make them personal items for a worthwhile cause. After Wimbledon beat Liverpool in the 1988 FA Cup final, their owner, Sam Hammam, had the two sides of my chart framed. Others have followed his lead since, sometimes putting the cover of the match programme in between.

However meticulous my preparation, accidents have sometimes happened. Mark Lawrenson spilled a bottle of water over my notes just before the Euro 2000 final in Rotterdam. We are still speaking.

* * *

I started by saying the enjoyment of commentating sometimes comes afterwards, when you have got through the match unscathed. So how did I get to the point where I could enjoy the ninety minutes without squirming on the edge of my seat?

I am far less nervous now than when I started, and for that I have to thank Ron Atkinson and Gordon McQueen. When they reached the 1983 FA Cup final against Brighton and Hove Albion, I went to United's hotel the night before the game. It was the Royal Lancaster in West London, where Sam Leitch had interviewed me twelve years earlier.

As Ron was giving me the United team, McQueen walked past with a big grin on his face. 'Look at him,' said Atkinson, 'he really loves the big games.'

The implication was that if some players suffered from nerves, then big Gordon wasn't one of them.

I also received reassurance from Rod Stewart, whom I first met during the 1986 World Cup when he was supporting Scotland in Mexico. We had a long chat about the games in a hotel in Mexico City, and met again when Scotland came to Wembley for a European Championship qualifier. Rod had his own football team and a beautifully maintained pitch near his house in Essex. He invited the commentators' football team to play there one afternoon, and I found myself on the same side of the pitch as the singer, who was playing right back.

We hardly got the ball for the first twenty minutes, because Rod's team never gave it away. He showed why he might once have gone down a different road to fame and become a professional footballer. After the match, Rod took both teams down to his local pub for drinks and refreshments. I fell into conversation with him and asked whether he ever felt nervous when he went onstage.

He looked at me incredulously. 'Nervous? Why should I be nervous? Singing is what I do.'

His answer was so straightforward, I repeated it under my breath the next time I did an important game. 'Nervous? Why should I be nervous? Commentating is what I do.'

The words of Ron Atkinson and Rod Stewart made me decide that if I was going to be considered good enough to do FA Cup finals and World Cup finals, I was going to enjoy them. That meant developing a thick skin when it came to the inevitable criticism that came my way from press and public, especially during big tournaments.

Columnists who never bother to write about football commentary at any other time come out of the woodwork and think nothing of pulling it to pieces, without the slightest suggestion as to how it could be improved. Nobody pretends commentating is an art form – a craft at best, I would say – but it is spontaneous, unscripted, and often demands that the broadcaster says the first thing that comes into his head.

What chance have we got, when even the great artists and musicians were not beyond reproach? I am always amused by the story of Mozart sending the music for a new opera to the emperor, who sent it back saying it needed improvement. 'Certainly, Your Majesty,' Mozart wrote back. 'But which notes should I take out?'

I also feel for newspaper reporters when an aggrieved reader says, 'He must have been at a different match.' These correspondents are sending over a running match report right up to the final whistle. They then have to edit it into a more considered piece within minutes. Imagine having to change your story completely when somebody scores in the last thirty seconds.

Jim McGrath, who has succeeded Sir Peter O'Sullevan so seamlessly as the BBC's racing commentator, told me at Ascot one day that he thinks the commentator is now more of a target than ever owing to modern technology. 'Our predecessors never had to worry about text messages, e-mails, blogs, chatrooms or message boards,' said Jim. 'You can now start a campaign within seconds.'

I should know. A couple of bloggers launched an anti-Motson site just as the 2006 World Cup opened. Within a week three or four newspapers were on the case. My commentaries were no different from usual. No better. No worse. But suddenly I was a sitting target. Criticism subsided when the BBC audience figure for the final outnumbered ITV's by nearly five to one. If I had been that bad, millions would have switched channels.

I would dearly love to have punctuated my commentaries with better language, nicely rounded phrases, wider vocabulary and memorable lines. Unfortunately there were twenty-two guys out there playing football at a furious pace. Had I stopped for a few seconds to think how to express in well-chosen words what had happened, I would probably have missed a shot, a goal, a yellow card, a substitution or even a crowd disturbance.

That is what makes football commentary an imperfect exercise. If you stop to think for a second the game has moved on. Unlike in the studio, there is no script or autocue to fall back on.

What summed it up for me, and made me laugh at myself, was when I came out of the Estadio de Luz at the end of the 2004 European Championship final, won by Greece against Portugal. Greece had brought on Dimitrios Papadopoulos as an eighty-first minute substitute.

My producer, Mark Demuth, and I were walking towards the car park when my mobile phone rang. It was Alastair Campbell, a keen Burnley supporter. 'John, didn't you know Papadopoulos used to play for Burnley?'

It had never occurred to me.

So finally, what is commentary all about? Yes, it is designed to help the viewer by identifying the players, explaining what is happening, and bringing some excitement into the living room. But first and foremost, despite the pitfalls, I think it is about broadcasting. You can give all sorts of people a microphone and they can call themselves a commentator, but do they have the delivery, the voice and the timing to be easy on the ear and clear in their speech?

It is no coincidence that nearly all today's good football commentators have served an apprenticeship in radio. Without that, many of us would never have made the grade in television. You can put the commentator into the broadcaster, but you can't put the broadcaster into the commentator.

Chapter 19

'Do you fancy jumping ship?'

Staying married to the BBC

I N THE SUMMER of 1995, after I had lost both the World Cup and the FA Cup finals, I received a telephone call from Andy Melvin, the executive producer of football at Sky Sports.

We both lived in Harpenden at the time, and agreed to meet in a local pub. It was the first time we had really spoken. Melvin is a straight-talking Scotsman, and no sooner had I ordered the beers than he came straight to the point. 'Do you fancy jumping ship?' he asked.

Sky were still new boys on the block, having taken over the failed British Satellite Broadcasting, and negotiated an exclusive deal for live coverage of the new Premier League from 1992. Melvin was preparing to revamp their Monday night coverage in the 1995/96 season, and wanted to know whether I would join their commentary team. He and his colleagues at Sky had obviously monitored events at the BBC and concluded that I was destined to play second fiddle to Barry Davies.

To be fair to Andy, he made no promises about where I would fit into the Sky pecking order. Nor did he mention international matches or the FA Cup final. He asked me to go away and think about it, which I did. But as I have previously explained, my main motivation at the time was to try to regain pole position at the BBC.

Looking back, I think it was the right decision not to jump ship. Within a year I was commentating on the European Championship final, and the fact that Sky had no access to that tournament, nor to the World Cup, played a major part in my decision.

Soon after came the approach from ITV, which I mentioned in an earlier chapter. The situation there was different. They were promising the prime position, as Brian Moore's successor, which would have given me first call on all the big games. The fact that the BBC offered me an improved contract was the deciding factor here, but it was flattering to have had an approach from the two other major television football channels in the space of just over twelve months.

Annie and I went to Cyprus on holiday soon afterwards, and while we were debating whether I had done the right thing, one of the factors that came up was how I would have bonded with Andy Gray, Sky's dynamic co-commentator and analyst. Gray rapidly gained a big reputation for his forthright views on the game and the challenging way he put them across. I believed we would have got on well together, on and off the air.

Staying in the same hotel in Paphos was Richard Money, whom I had known as a player at Fulham and Liverpool, and who had been manager at his home-town club, Scunthorpe United. Money had developed a good name as a coach, and in the early part of our holiday confided in me about his next move. He had been lined up to go to Everton as right-hand man to prospective new manager Andy Gray. Joe Royle had just left Goodison Park after three seasons in charge. He had won the FA Cup, but Everton had finished his third campaign in the bottom half of the table.

Gray, however, was regarded by his colleagues and competitors as Sky's trump card in the strong football hand they now held. While Money was rubbing his hands at the promise of an exciting new job, the Sky paymasters made Gray an offer to stay he could not refuse.

I felt sorry for Money. He heard that the deal had fallen through while we were still in Cyprus and his face was a picture of disappointment when I left him at the hotel, but he went on to become a successful coach at a number of clubs and was voted second-division Manager of the Year when he led Walsall to the championship in 2007. He later became Newcastle United's Academy Director.

I have often wondered how Sky's coverage would have been affected had Gray taken up Everton's offer. He had been assistant to Ron Atkinson at Aston Villa, and part of him obviously hankered to get back into the game. Because Sky valued him so highly, we never found out how he would have performed as a manager.

Twelve years later, he has not gone back on his decision. The same applies to my BBC colleagues Gary Lineker and Alan Hansen. Both have said the stress and strain of management hold no appeal for them. Mark Lawrenson tried it briefly, but is far happier making his living as a broadcaster.

For those who make the reverse journey – coming into broadcasting while they are taking a breather from management – it is rather different. Gordon Strachan spent a year working with the BBC after he left Southampton, and made a significant impression on *Match of the Day Two* on Sunday nights. But when Celtic came calling, there was no holding him back. The same thing happened when Newcastle asked Alan Shearer to take charge in the closing weeks of the 2008/09 season.

What cemented my own lifelong employment at the BBC was the departure of Des Lynam to ITV in 1999. It came out of the blue, and I shall never forget the day the announcement was made.

I was on my way into London to do a day's recording on the *FIFA* computer game. Des phoned me in the car and said: 'I have just resigned from the BBC. I am going to ITV to host the Champions League coverage. I am just phoning a few close friends so that you don't hear it first on the television at lunchtime.'

ITV had planned a press conference to announce what, for them, was a major coup. Lynam was the face of BBC Sport, and the Sydney Olympics were only a year away.

'You're winding me up. I thought you were under contract,' I said.

'No, I'm serious. I've taken legal advice and I am assured I am not in breach of contract,' replied Lynam.

The *FIFA* commentary that day was done on the strength of two large gin and tonics. I had worked with Des, in radio and television, for the best part of thirty years. The newspapers, of course, had a field day. It was ITV's new 'Snatch of the Day'. We did not know it then, but a year later they would also steal the Premiership highlights contract from the BBC.

Bob Shennan, Radio Five Head of Sport, who had taken temporary charge of Television Sport following the departure of Brian Barwick and Jonathan Martin, now had to move fast. Newspaper stories were linking Gary Lineker and Alan Hansen with ITV. My name was also thrown into the ring, although a firm offer, such as the one I had received three years earlier, was never made at this time. Shennan sorted out Lineker's and Hansen's contracts, then called me into his office. 'I've signed the top presenter and the top pundit, now I want to secure the top voice,' he said.

I had always been well paid at the BBC, but this deal gave me a great deal of security. I walked out with a new five-year contract at double my original salary, with the rise backdated a year.

'Nice of Des to leave and give us all that money,' joked Lineker.

* * *

In 2001 I marked thirty years with *Match of the Day*, and it was that association which brought me, in the same year, the honour of an OBE for services to broadcasting.

My trip to Buckingham Palace to meet the Queen was not the only surprise to come my way that year. I was also voted number one in a scientific survey to discover which football commentator had the best voice. A panel of speech experts studied the voices of all the leading football commentators in categories such as volume, tone, rhythm and pitch. They came up with the following formula for the perfect commentary voice.

$$P - \frac{OL}{2} + (Lv \times 2) + \frac{Ra}{2} + Rh + (T \times 1.5) - \frac{C}{2}$$

No, I don't know what that means either! Anyway, I scored thirty on their calculations: six for pitch, two for overall loudness, six for loudness variability, four for rate, six for rhythm, four for tone and two for constriction. My total compared to a top score of twenty-two among the other commentators and I was declared the winner.

I had a lot of people to thank for these accolades. Most broadcasters have a modicum of natural talent, but any I possessed was honed by tutors such as Angus Mackay, Alan Hart, Bob Abrahams and another former editor of *Match of the Day*, Mike Murphy.

Mike and I met on a Football Association preliminary badge coaching course at Lilleshall in 1973. He was working for the opposition, having been signed for London Weekend Television by Jimmy Hill. We both had North London connections, and when Murphy followed Hill to the BBC in 1973, we became good friends. Mike was a down-to-earth London boy with a keen editorial brain and a flair for pictures and stories. He became the youngest editor of *Match of the Day* and *Grandstand*, before leaving to run his own production business. Tragically, he died of cancer at the age of fifty-one. Sports broadcasting lost a talented operator who was respected throughout the industry.

After Murphy left the BBC, a succession of new editors came through the system. Brian Barwick was editor of *Sportsnight* and *Match of the Day*, and later Head of Sports Production before leaving for ITV. Niall Sloane succeeded him as the top man in football. Paul Armstrong, Andrew Clement, Lance Hardy, Steve Boulton and Mark Demuth were placed in editorial charge of various strands of the BBC's football output. I was lucky to have their support, and that of producer Phil Bigwood, at a time when the BBC was doing more live football than ever before.

The increased exposure was undoubtedly the reason I received three honorary degrees, one from the University of Suffolk, one from the University of Luton, and finally one from the University of Hertfordshire. Not bad for a sixteen-year-old who had left school with eight O-levels and resisted the opportunity of higher education.

Having the experience of working under pressure certainly had its advantages when I was asked to contribute to outlets other than the BBC. When the film *Bend It Like Beckham* was in production, I was asked to record a few lines of commentary to be used at the start of the film. When I arrived at the studio, the producer told me she had booked four hours for the recording. It took me ten minutes.

Where I was lucky is that football, perhaps more than any other sport, is a universal language. It has taken me to places I would never otherwise have seen, and to around fifty countries where I have broadcast. Not that I saw much more than the airport, the hotel and the stadium in many of them.

Four visits to Downing Street also stand out. Mrs Thatcher entertained the media there before England went to Italy for the European Championships in 1980. Sadly, she had us back a few years later to help tackle the growing problem of football hooliganism.

I was also invited by Tony Blair and Gordon Brown, during their respective periods of office, to go to Number Ten to 'chat about football'. In 2008 the prime minister was accompanied by his namesake, Defence Secretary Des Browne, and their knowledge of the game took me by surprise. A young Gordon had seen Alex Ferguson make his debut for St Johnstone at Aberdeen in the early sixties.

As for Tony Blair, I was invited with Annie to one of his dinner parties at Chequers, thanks to Alastair Campbell, whom I had met when we were both taking part in the Great North Run. When we got there and lined up to be introduced, Mr Blair shook my hand and said: 'You won't believe this, but you are one of my heroes.'

It was a light-hearted reference to his Saturday lunchtime date with *Football Focus*. 'It's the only time in the week when I can sit down and watch television with no distractions,' he explained.

When he and Cherie waved us goodbye at the end of the evening I shouted, 'You should come on *Football Focus* some time.'

Soon afterwards, he took me up on the offer and came to the studio one Saturday to talk about his interest in the game, including watching Newcastle United when he was at university.

Around this time, my marriage to the BBC was once again put to the test. I had lunch with Vic Wakeling, the managing director of Sky Sports, whom I had got to know well on the annual media trip organised by Barclays, the Premier League sponsors. Vic seemed very keen for me to come on board and we had a frank discussion about where my career was going and what might be on offer at Sky. But not for the first time, the move did not quite fit for either party.

Again, the World Cup was a factor, although I remember Vic giving me a bit of good advice. 'If you stay, make sure you get the final. They will want to move a younger commentator in sooner or later.'

There was one more bid to tempt me to move before I started

thinking about winding down. When Setanta came on the scene as serious challengers to Sky, their Director of Sports, Trevor East, came to see me in the summer of 2007. East was a big player in television negotiations and rights, having worked in senior positions for ITV and later for Sky.

Setanta were about to start their first season with two Premier League packages, and a year ahead they had the rights to England matches and the FA Cup. I still had a year to go on my BBC contract, and knew they would not release me. England had seven important internationals to play at Wembley in the coming season, and I was expected to commentate on all of them.

'We would be quite happy to share you with the BBC,' said Trevor, and I left him to make that proposal. Not surprisingly, perhaps, the BBC would not agree.

Things went on as usual until just before Christmas, when East acquired for Setanta a host of World Cup qualifiers involving the home nations – including exclusive rights to England's away games. Since the BBC were about to lose the FA contract, he repeated his request to share my services. Again, the answer was no.

There followed a number of conversations between East and my agent, Jane Morgan, about a stand-alone offer from Setanta. There was a moment when I prepared myself to go, believing I had at least another two years of live broadcasting in the tank. But whether for financial reasons, or the fact that Trevor's board of directors wanted somebody younger, the deal never got off the ground.

On reflection, it was probably for the best and not only because Setanta went out of business a year later. It would have been a wrench to leave the BBC and start all over again at the age of sixty-three, and Setanta signed a talented and well-connected commentator in Jon Champion, who had worked with us at *Match of the Day* from 1995 to 2001 and subsequently for ITV. Nevertheless, it was something of a watershed for me. My last FA Cup final and summer tournament meant my television appearances for the 2008/09 season would be limited to *Match of the Day* highlights, *Football Focus* and *Final Score*.

In the last few days we spent in Vienna for Euro 2008, Niall Sloane called me into the kitchen at the BBC studio and handed me a personal letter from the Director General, Mark Thompson. Thompson had kindly written to wish me luck for the Euro 2008 final, and to thank me for my service to the BBC over the years. 'Your voice has been the defining soundtrack to the great moments in football for over four decades . . .' Thompson wrote. 'I'm delighted to hear that you're planning to continue to work for BBC Television and Radio.'

Perhaps the most significant words were 'and Radio'. Part of my agreement with the BBC, with whom I signed a new contract up to 2010, was that I would take up a more regular role with Five Live. I was already an occasional commentator on the channel, covering six matches a season under my previous deal, but now I was contracted to some forty appearances – a mixture of live commentaries and contributions to other programmes.

The most important of these, as it turned out, was the *Monday Night Football Club* – a discussion programme already well established in the schedules. Its brief was to review the weekend just gone, and to set the agenda for the coming week by discussing the issues of the moment. In short, a football debating chamber. The presenter at the time, Mark Saggers, and his regular contributors, Steve Claridge and Ian McGarry, made me most welcome when I first went into the studio. When I came out, editor Richard Burgess asked me whether I could do it every week.

This brought a new angle to my career. Having been concerned only with the here and now as a reporter and commentator, I was given a platform from which to air some opinions on issues in the game and, from time to time, add a little to what was already on the agenda.

* * *

On 3 January 2009, the FA Cup sat proudly on the table in the Portsmouth boardroom. It was so close to me as I ate my lunch, I could see the names of the winners engraved around the base. Derby County 1946 stood out: not just because I knew my father had listened to the radio commentary while I was in my pram, but because that was the year the BBC resumed broadcasting after the war.

In each and every season, from then until 2008, there had been FA Cup coverage in some shape or form on BBC Television. A sixty-two-year unbroken relationship had now ended, with the FA's decision to award the contract for the next four years to ITV. Even when the commercial channel had exclusive live coverage of the competition between 1998 and 2001, *Match of the Day* still screened highlights in every round, including the final. But this year, nothing. It was only later that evening on third-round weekend that the nation really noticed the change. There was simply no *Match of the Day* in the BBC1 schedule.

The other big change for BBC Television was that we were not covering England's home internationals any more. In the 2007/08 season, I had been at the commentary position for seven live Wembley internationals. Having found that each England game virtually took a week out of my life, I had a big time slot to fill.

The FA kindly invited Annie and me to be guests at the first home game of the season – a friendly against the Czech Republic. At the pre-match dinner, we found ourselves on the same table as the FA chairman, Lord Triesman, and his wife Lucy.

There was a reason. After he had welcomed the officials from the Czech Republic, and their ambassador in London, the chairman had a surprise up his sleeve. He mentioned the arrival of the FA's new broadcasting partners, ITV and Setanta, but then drew attention to the fact that, after 150 games, mine would no longer be a recognisable voice on England matches.

I was presented with a framed shirt signed by Fabio Capello's squad, which now has pride of place in our bar at home. It stands alongside the shirt Graeme Le Saux wore at the 1998 World Cup, which he presented to me when we worked together.

There is also a picture on the wall of me in the England dressing room, although the players are not there. You can see behind me the shirts awaiting the arrival of David Beckham and Paul Scholes, but that night in Slovakia I had been rescued from a potential incident in the corridor by the England back-room team.

An aggressive steward had tried to throw me out (not a unique event in my life) and, having been ushered into the sanctity of the dressing room by the kit men, I had my photograph taken sitting on one of the benches. If nothing else, it made for a good Christmas card.

The Wembley presentation, flattering though it was, was soon overtaken by the events on the night. As I was switching off my phone before going to our seats, Lady Triesman whispered, 'I would leave that on, if I were you.'

A few minutes into the match, I realised what she meant. Word spread like wildfire through the Royal Box that Brian Barwick, the FA's chief executive, had been relieved of his post. The decision had been taken at an FA board meeting earlier in the day.

I had never had to walk out of an England game before, but soon I was answering a succession of calls from BBC colleagues, including Niall Sloane, who was in Spain for the Formula One grand prix. He, Barwick and I had worked together at the BBC for around twenty years. Brian produced a series of videos on the history of famous clubs which I scripted and voiced for BBC Enterprises (which later became BBC Worldwide).

As the news of his departure whistled round the stadium, I sensed he was not terribly surprised. I saw Brian first and foremost as a television man, although he had attacked the FA job with vigour and confidence. He also left them with Fabio Capello.

If Barwick's departure from the FA early in the season had caused me a minor tremor (he was, after all, an old colleague), the telephone call I got in March from the BBC's Head of Football, Niall Sloane, was an even bigger shock.

At the end of February, there was a major reshuffle of management in BBC Sport. Roger Mosey moved out of his director's role to take over responsibility for the London Olympics; and his predecessor, Peter Salmon, was appointed Director, BBC North, ready for the department's move to Manchester in 2011.

Sloane was one of the candidates for the vacant Director of Sport role, but after being interviewed initially, was passed over in favour of Barbara Slater, the former Olympic gymnast who had worked in the department since 1983. To the disappointment of many of his colleagues in the football unit, Niall elected to take an offer of redundancy and leave the BBC. Within a matter of weeks he had been appointed Controller of Sport at ITV.

He and I had quite a lot in common. After being voted Young Footballer of the Year in Northern Ireland while playing for Portadown, Sloane was offered a professional contract with Sheffield Wednesday, but chose instead to do a university law degree and train in journalism on the *Herts Advertiser* – the neighbouring weekly paper to mine in Barnet. He spent twenty-six years in the BBC Sports Department, rising from assistant producer to Head of Football, and piloting the BBC through three World Cups and four European Championships.

Sloane was largely responsible for the success of the BBC's live football coverage, led by Gary Lineker and Alan Hansen between 2000 and 2008. His football responsibilities were taken over by another stalwart BBC servant, Philip Bernie, in his new role as Head of BBC Television Sport.

The fact that I wasn't covering England internationals any more meant that for the first time in many years I had some time on my hands. Away from the travel, the preparation and the perspiration of covering England, I was able to take up invitations and opportunities that in seasons past I would have had to turn down.

School reunions were a good example. I had lost touch with Culford, my old boarding school near Bury St Edmunds. When they organised a lunch for pupils who had left in the early sixties, Annie and I spent a pleasant day retracing steps I had taken nearly half a century earlier. I had forgotten how close we were then to the end of the war. We kept our tuck boxes in a cellar, which had been a bomb shelter, among a maze of underground tunnels.

I did have a furtive glance at the junior school's solitary football pitch, where I scored on my debut as an eleven-year-old. Not much had changed. The boys still played hockey and rugby when they moved up to the senior school.

Another nostalgic throwback to my childhood came when I was invited to speak in the Boston Stump, the church with the tallest tower in the country. The occasion was a fund-raising dinner in aid of this great Lincolnshire landmark, but it gave me the chance to catch up on the fortunes of Boston United, the club I had watched with my uncles as a boy.

I had kept up a dialogue down the years with the secretary, John Blackwell, who had seen thirty years' service with United, but the last two years had been the most difficult. After going into administration on the day they were relegated from the Football League in 2007, the club failed to meet the deadlines for coming out of that condition and were relegated two divisions as a punishment. Boston United were days away from liquidation when they were rescued by a Lincolnshire businessman, David Newton. But their perilous position signified troubled times for football at all levels.

At the turn of the year my local club, Berkhamsted Town, were in so much debt that the electricity supply at their stadium was turned off and they were no longer able to fulfil their home fixtures in the Spartan South Midlands League. I rang Bill Hamilton, who was refereeing in his fifty-first season in the middle, and asked him how serious their plight was. I was expecting him to say they owed £20,000 or £30,000. Imagine my amazement when he told me their liabilities were ten times those figures.

It was a stark reminder to all levels of the game that banks would not be so forgiving in what was now a severe economic downturn. Berkhamsted folded a few days later.

As the season continued, I also found time to pursue my growing interest in racing, and to experience for the first time the phenomenon that professional darts had become. I had met Barry Hearn a couple of times in his role as chairman of Leyton Orient, and knew of his success as a snooker and boxing promoter, but when he said to me at Goodwood in the summer that I would not have seen an event quite like the World Darts Championship he was right on the money, so to speak.

Ricky George and I turned up at Alexandra Palace one evening between Christmas and New Year, and could not believe the crowds. The famous old building, from where the BBC first broadcast before the war, was disgorging its afternoon audience and a boisterous full house was waiting to take their seats for the evening session.

We were shown into a VIP bar away from the already cheering throng, and within five minutes Barry Hearn breezed into the room holding three glasses of champagne.

'Motsy,' he opened up (nobody had ever called me Motsy before: Motty or Mots, perhaps, but never Motsy). 'Motsy, I never really wanted to get involved in darts, but the Professional Darts Corporation' – of which Hearn is now chairman – 'were struggling to get a sponsor or any television coverage in 1994, and they dragged me down to the Circus Tavern in Purfleet to try to get me involved.

'As soon as I walked in, Motsy, I smelt money,' Hearn went on, crooking his fingers into the palm of his hand to make his point. 'Booze, gambling, it was ready made for a take-off.'

When play started later that evening, I saw what he meant.

Football crowds had nothing on this. The welcome given to the competitors, the placards bearing their nicknames, the raucous shouting that preceded the match, left Ricky and me speechless. No wonder Sky Television had signed a lucrative contract with Hearn to cover the event from start to finish. TV ratings for darts are second to those for Premiership football in Sky Sports's audience figures.

And that wasn't the only place where I broke new ground at Christmas. Having only taken an interest in jump racing up to now, I decided to buy Annie a once-in-a-lifetime present in the shape of a flat horse. Walter Swinburn trains in the village of Aldbury, just a few miles from our home, and with the help of Ladbrokes' Mike Dillon we bought a yearling ready to run in the 2009 season. My driver of many years, former professional foot-baller Russell Townsend, came up with the name 'Motty's Gift'.

We also maintained our partnership in two National Hunt horses, Valerius and Oscar's Ballad, as part of the 'Our Friends in the North' syndicate, run by Newcastle businessman Ian Robinson.

Football, and the way it is presented on television and radio, have changed enormously since I joined the BBC in 1968. In 2008, I celebrated my fortieth anniversary in the corporation with the Director General, Mark Thompson, and his assistant, Mark Byford, and they struggled to think of anybody who had been a regular on BBC1 as long as I had.

When I joined *Match of the Day* in 1971, many people thought I had won the 'Commentators' competition' held by the *Sportsnight with Coleman* programme two years earlier. The prize was a trip to Mexico for the World Cup the following year, and was won by Idwal Robling – a Cardiff-based broadcaster who was given Sir Alf Ramsey's casting vote ahead of Ian St John and briefly joined the BBC commentary team.

There were nothing like the number of football commentators

around then compared with the number that crop up regularly on our screens today. In a busy week in the current season, *Match of the Day* would regularly use ten commentators to cover the Barclays Premier League fixtures. Sky would have a panel of eight for their two busy Champions League nights. ITV, covering the Champions League and the FA Cup, augmented their regular team to field five commentators at least. To those, add two from Channel Five, and a handful from other broadcasters, and you have a list of about thirty different voices covering televised football on a national basis.

Now compare that to when I started. The BBC team was David Coleman (not always a regular), Barry Davies and myself, with the occasional appearance of Alan Weeks. ITV majored on Brian Moore, who fronted all their nationwide games, while the regional commentators generally cropped up only on Sunday afternoon or the Wednesday night highlights. We all became quite well known and our voices recognisable because there were so few of us.

I am not suggesting one system was better than the other, merely that it is much harder these days for a commentator to push himself ahead of the pack because a lot of the voices merge into one, and viewers would sometimes struggle to name the individual they are listening to.

Maybe that is one reason why the keen rivalry between Barry and me attracted such national interest. I was reminded of it when Nigel Clough, having just taken over at Derby County as manager, told me he had received a letter of good wishes from 'your old colleague'. It had to be Barry, of course.

As well as keeping his two Derby season tickets with his girl-friend Beth, my son Fred by now had been called to the bar, and was teaching law at the University of Westminster. That didn't stop us making a number of trips to Pride Park, to monitor Derby's improvement under their new manager.

The fact that Nigel was the second Clough to have managed Derby during my career was another sign of time passing. So too was the mistaken assumption that the final of Euro 2008 was my last ever commentary. Gary Lineker's generous introduction to the final in Vienna, when to my surprise he listed all the major finals I had done, led a lot of people to assume that I was stepping down not just from international football, but from commentary altogether.

I spent much of the summer and the first half of the 2008/09 season trying to convince them that was not the case. But even on the morning after I had commentated on the FA Cup third round for Five Live, the postman delivering to our flat in Bournemouth greeted me with 'So what are you doing these days?'

He was by no means alone. Had I been sensitive to the many comments like 'How is retirement treating you?' I would probably have suggested that people were not watching or listening too closely. After all, I was comfortably fulfilling my usual quota of forty commentaries and was also figuring in at least as many radio programmes.

Faith in my generation was restored when I went with a coach party from a local pub, the Rose and Crown at Flamstead, to see Joe Brown in concert at the Royal Albert Hall. Now I know my knowledge of popular music got lost somewhere in the early seventies, but Joe and his Bruvvers were very much part of my teenage years. He had rocked with the early pioneers, such as Gene Vincent, Eddie Cochran, Bill Haley, Little Richard and Jerry Lee Lewis.

Fifty years on, I was amazed at his vitality. I knew Joe Brown could play a wide variety of instruments, but I never expected to see him on stage for three hours without a break. At sixty-seven, he had more energy than some performers half his age. Here was a guy who clearly still loved doing what he does best. There was a generous manner about him, as he seemed to get as much pleasure from his supporting acts as he did from singing his own songs. To still be touring twice a year at his time of life to packed audiences across the country is a tribute to Joe Brown's talent and enthusiasm.

Rather like the celebrities quoted at the beginning of the book, Joe Brown obviously saw no reason to retire. And as I entered the sixty-fifth year of my life, and my forty-second in broadcasting, neither did I.

The four things I treasure most – family, friends, football and fun – all came together one glorious weekend in April 2009.

Annie and my mother-in-law Marion came down to our apartment in Bournemouth, enabling me to join my old football club, Roving Reporters, on their annual tour. The team we started in 1965 is still flourishing, largely thanks to the efforts of Gary King, who organises the trip every year.

Four older stalwarts – John Watts, Clive Townsend, Vince Penn and my friend of over forty-five years Roger Jones, have formed a veterans' group for whom I always organise a visit to a local league match – in this case Southampton v. Charlton.

Sadly, both these once stable clubs have been snared by the financial problems I mentioned earlier. I found myself sitting next to Mark Fry of Begbies Traynor, the administrators trying to keep the Saints alive. How could a club whom, like Charlton, had been in the top half of the Premiership six years ago, now be struggling for survival?

Most of all, it makes you feel sorry for the supporters, who have seen so much of their money wasted and their dreams destroyed. But then again, where the fans are concerned, loyalty never wavers.

That same weekend, Luton Town took over forty thousand supporters to Wembley to see them lift the Johnstons Paint Trophy. This in spite of the fact that a thirty-point deduction at the start of the season meant they were about to drop out of the Football League.

A few days later, I was sharing the concern of Newcastle United followers, themselves fearing the prospect of relegation, and wondering whether my erstwhile BBC colleague Alan Shearer could turn things round in their last eight games.

I was in the North-East to make a presentation to Ray Scott, the Gateshead Harrier who had run so dutifully alongside me to help me through the Great North Run on a number of occasions.

Ray and Sir Jimmy Savile, along with three other worthy recipients, were being inducted into the GNR Hall of Fame and I was delighted to take him by surprise by presenting him with his statuette.

The end of that busy week found me in Liverpool, sitting on the same television gantry on the roof of the main stand at Anfield where I had made my television commentating debut nearly thirty-eight years earlier.

The occasion marked the twentieth anniversary of the Hillsborough disaster. I was part of a *Football Focus* team presenting the Saturday lunchtime programme direct from the ground, before commentating on the match against Blackburn Rovers.

The weather was identical to that on the day of the tragedy, and we all had our private thoughts as a minute's silence was impeccably observed in a city which had mourned ninety-six lives for two decades.

I tried to gently make the point on the air that they did not die in vain. The sparkling all-seater stadiums in which we now enjoy our football are a direct result of Lord Justice Taylor's report into the cause of the disaster in 1989.

If that was the lowest point of my forty years in the business, the game has given me as much pleasure and more than I had any right to expect.

Within a few weeks, the BBC opened discussions with me about a new role at the 2010 World Cup in South Africa. They also raised the subject of the London Olympics in 2012, suggesting mine was one of the voices they felt should be heard.

The prospect of three more years of front-line broadcasting does not faze me one bit. On the contrary. My enthusiasm and health are as strong as ever, as is the feeling of satisfaction that I have been privileged to do something for a living that brings excitement and enjoyment nearly every day.

Appendix 1:

Motty's Forty Year Favourites

World Cup

1982	Italy 3, W. Germany 1	(Madrid)
1986	Argentina 3, W. Germany 2	(Mexico City)
1990	W. Germany 1, Argentina 0	(Rome)
1998	France 3, Brazil 0	(Paris)
2002	Brazil 2, Germany 0	(Yokohama)
2006	Italy 1, France 1	(Berlin)
		(Italy won 5–3, on penalties)

European Championship

1980	W. Germany 2, Belgium 1	(Rome)
1984	France 2, Spain 0	(Paris)
1988	Holland 2, USSR 0	(Munich)
1992	Denmark 2, Germany 0	(Gothenburg)
1996	Germany 2, Czech Republic 1	(Wembley)
		(Germany won on Golden goal)
2000	France 2, Italy 1	(Rotterdam)
		(France won on Golden Goal)
2004	Greece 1, Portugal 0	(Lisbon)
2008	Spain 1, Germany 0	(Vienna)

TOP FIVE GAMES (IN DATE ORDER)

1	Tottenham 3, Manchester City 2	(FA Cup Final, replay 1981)
2	Brazil 2, Italy 3	(World Cup 1982)
3	France 3, Portugal 2	(European Championship 1984)
4	Liverpool 5, Nottingham Forest 0	(Division One 1988)
5	Germany 1, England 5	(World Cup qualifier 2001)

TOP TEN GOALS (IN DATE ORDER)

1   Ronnie Radford (Hereford v. Newcastle 1972)

2   Alan Mullery (Fulham v. Leicester 1974)

3   Ricky Villa (Tottenham v. Man. City 1981)

4   Falcão (Brazil v. Italy 1982)

5   Michel Platini (France v. Portugal 1984)

6   Keith Houchen (Coventry v. Tottenham 1987)

7   Paul Gascoigne (England v. Scotland 1996)

8   David Beckham (England v. Greece 2001)

9   Thierry Henry (Arsenal v. Charlton 2004)

10   Fernando Torres (Liverpool v. Blackburn 2009)

TOP FIVE TEAMS (IN DATE ORDER)

1.	Liverpool 1977–86	Four European Cups and seven League titles
2.	Nottingham Forest 1978–1980	Two European Cups and one League title
3.	Manchester Utd 1999	The Treble winners
4.	Arsenal 2004	The Invincibles
5.	Chelsea 2005–2006	The Mourinho years

BEST ENGLAND TEAM SINCE 1974

Peter Shilton

Mick Mills	John Terry	Roy McFarland	Stuart Pearce

Wayne Rooney	Bryan Robson	Paul Gascoigne	Steven Gerrard

Alan Shearer   Gary Lineker

Subs: Glenn Hoddle, Michael Owen, Ray Clemence, Tony Adams, John Barnes, Frank Lampard, Gary Neville.

TOP FIVE GIANTKILLERS (IN DATE ORDER)

1. Hereford United 1972
2. Leatherhead 1975
3. York City 1985
4. Sutton United 1989
5. Barnsley 2008

BEST TEAM OF OVERSEAS PREMIERSHIP/DIV 1 PLAYERS

Jaaskelainen (Bolton)

Golac	Stam	Hyypia	Gallas
(Southampton)	(Manchester Utd)	(Liverpool)	(Chelsea/Arsenal)

Bergkamp	Makélélé	Ardiles	Zola
(Arsenal)	(Chelsea)	(Tottenham)	(Chelsea)

Henry   Cantona
(Arsenal)   (Manchester Utd)

Subs: Juninho (Middlesbrough), Di Canio (West Ham).

John Motson's Seasonal Totals for BBC Football Commentaries

1971/72	21	
1972/73	30	
1973/74	46	(inc. World Cup)
1974/75	35	
1975/76	38	
1976/77	48	
1977/78	50	(inc. World Cup)
1978/79	44	
1979/80	51	(inc. Euro Champ)
1980/81	48	
1981/82	55	(inc. World Cup)
1982/83	43	
1983/84	44	(inc. Euro Champ)

1984/85	47	
1985/86	33	(inc. World Cup)
1986/87	21	
1987/88	33	(inc. Euro Champ)
1988/89	24	
1989/90	39	(inc. World Cup)
1990/91	29	
1991/92	40	(inc. World Cup)
1992/93	45	
1993/94	56	(inc. World Cup)
1994/95	40	
1995/96	45	(inc. Euro Champ)
1996/97	41	
1997/98	51	(inc. World Cup)
1998/99	33	
1999/2000	46	(inc. Euro Champ)
2000/01	40	(inc. Radio Five Live games)
2001/02	41	(inc. World Cup)
2002/03	31	(inc. Radio Five Live games)
2003/04	38	(inc. Euro Champ and Radio Five Live games)
2004/05	48	(inc. World Cup and Radio Five Live games)
2005/06	56	(inc. World Cup and Radio Five Live games)
2006/07	45	(inc. Radio Five Live games)
2007/08	53	(inc. Euro Champ and Radio Five Live games)
2008/09	41	(inc. Radio Five Live games)

Total 1,569

1971/72

9 Oct	Liverpool 0, Chelsea 0
23 Oct	Blackpool 1, QPR 1
13 Nov	Manchester Utd 3, Tottenham 1
27 Nov	Burnley 1, Swindon 2
4 Dec	Derby 3, Manchester City 1
11 Dec	Chelsea 0, Leeds 0
18 Dec	Arsenal 2, West Brom. 0
1 Jan	Arsenal 1, Everton 1
15 Jan	Blackpool 0, Chelsea 1 (FA Cup 3rd round)
22 Jan	Sheffield Wed. 1, Millwall 1
29 Jan	West Brom. 2, Manchester Utd 1
5 Feb	Hereford 2, Newcastle 1 (FA Cup 3rd round replay)
12 Feb	Sheffield Utd 3, Manchester City 3
19 Feb	Coventry 0, Wolverhampton 0
26 Feb	Manchester Utd 0, Middlesbrough 0 (FA Cup 5th round)
4 Mar	Tottenham 2, Manchester Utd 0
11 Mar	Norwich 1, Sunderland 1
25 Mar	Newcastle 0, Manchester City 0
8 Apr	Arsenal 2, Wolverhampton 1
22 Apr	Birmingham 1, Middlesbrough 1
20 May	Scotland 2, N. Ireland 0 (Home Int. Championship)

Total: 21 commentaries

1972/73

29 Jul	Bristol Rovers 2, Wolverhampton 0 (Watney Cup)
12 Aug	Leicester 0, Arsenal 1
19 Aug	Sheffield Utd 1, Newcastle 2
26 Aug	Norwich 1, Derby 0
2 Sep	Blackpool 2, Millwall 0
9 Sep	Manchester Utd 0, Coventry 1
16 Sep	Ipswich 2, Stoke 0

7 Oct	Fulham 2, Aston Villa 0
14 Oct	Sheffield Wed. 0, Burnley 1
21 Oct	Tottenham 0, Chelsea 1
28 Oct	Manchester Utd 1, Tottenham 4
4 Nov	Southampton 1, Norwich 0
18 Nov	Wolverhampton 0, Ipswich 1
25 Nov	West Brom. 2, Stoke 1
9 Dec	Derby 2, Coventry 0
16 Dec	Wolverhampton 1, Chelsea 0
23 Dec	West Brom. 2, Ipswich 0
30 Dec	Liverpool 1, Crystal Palace 0
6 Jan	Derby 1, Norwich 0
13 Jan	Leyton Orient 1, Coventry 4 (FA Cup 3rd round)
27 Jan	Leeds 1, Stoke 0
3 Feb	Sheffield Wed. 1, Crystal Palace 1 (FA Cup 4th round)
17 Feb	Ipswich 4, Manchester Utd 1
24 Feb	Wolverhampton 1, Millwall 0 (FA Cup 5th round)
10 Mar	QPR 1, Aston Villa 0
24 Mar	West Brom. 1, Southampton 1
31 Mar	Nottingham Forest 3, Burnley 0
21 Apr	Everton 0, Arsenal 0
28 Apr	Chelsea 1, Manchester Utd 0
12 May	Wales 0, Scotland 2 (Home International)

Total: 30 commentaries

1973/74

11 Aug	Plymouth 0, Stoke 1 (Watney Cup)
14 Aug	Bristol Rovers 0, Hull 1 (Watney Cup)
25 Aug	Manchester City 3, Birmingham 1
1 Sept	Everton 3, Ipswich 0
8 Sept	Coventry 2, Southampton 0

15 Sept	Newcastle 2, Wolverhampton 0
22 Sept	Nottingham Forest 1, Preston 1
29 Sept	West Brom. 1, Sunderland 1
6 Oct	Leeds 1, Stoke 1
13 Oct	Hereford 0, Cambridge 0
20 Oct	Derby 2, Leicester 1
27 Oct	QPR 2, Arsenal 0
3 Nov	Norwich 1, Leicester 0
10 Nov	Bristol City 0, Crystal Palace 1
17 Nov	Wolverhampton 0, West Ham 0
24 Nov	Everton 1, Newcastle 1
1 Dec	Arsenal 2, Coventry 2
8 Dec	QPR 0, Sheffield Utd 0
15 Dec	Newcastle 0, Derby 2
22 Dec	Arsenal 1, Everton 0
29 Dec	Birmingham 1, Leeds 1
5 Jan	Manchester Utd 1, Plymouth 0 (FA Cup 3rd round)
9 Jan	Hereford 2, West Ham 1 (FA Cup 3rd round replay)
12 Jan	Ipswich 1, Stoke 1
19 Jan	Everton 0, Leeds 0
26 Jan	Fulham 1, Leicester 1 (FA Cup 4th round)
2 Feb	Carlisle 3, Leyton Orient 0
16 Feb	Bristol City 1, Leeds 1 (FA Cup 5th round)
23 Feb	Tottenham 1, Ipswich 1
2 Mar	QPR 3, Tottenham 1
9 Mar	Derby 1, West Ham 1
16 Mar	Leicester 0, Derby 1
13 Mar	England 2, Scotland 0 (Under-23 Int.)
23 Mar	Manchester Utd 0, Tottenham 1
6 Apr	Leeds 2, Derby 0
20 Apr	Leyton Orient 1, Notts Co. 1
27 Apr	Everton 0, Southampton 3

1974 WORLD CUP FINALS

14 Jun	E. Germany 2, Australia 0	(Hamburg)
15 Jun	Poland 3, Argentina 2	(Stuttgart)
18 Jun	Yugoslavia 9, Zaire 0	(Gelsenkirchen)
19 Jun	Uruguay 1, Bulgaria 1	(Hanover)
22 Jun	Brazil 3, Zaire 0	(Gelsenkirchen)
23 Jun	Sweden 3, Uruguay 0	(Düsseldorf)
26 Jun	W. Germany 2, Yugoslavia 0	(Düsseldorf)
30 Jun	Holland 2, E. Germany 0	(Gelsenkirchen)
3 Jul	E. Germany 1, Argentina	(Gelsenkirchen)

Total: 46 commentaries

1974/75

17 Aug	Luton 1, Liverpool 2
24 Aug	Leeds 1, Birmingham 0
31 Aug	Stoke 1, Middlesbrough 1
7 Sep	Wolverhampton 1, Leicester 1
14 Sep	Manchester City 2, Liverpool 0
21 Sep	Peterborough 0, Preston 0
28 Sep	Everton 3, Leeds 2
5 Oct	QPR 1, Ipswich 0
12 Oct	Newcastle 2, Stoke 2
19 Oct	Sunderland 0, Aston Villa 0
26 Oct	Burnley 1, Everton 1
2 Nov	Crystal Palace 1, Peterborough 1
9 Nov	Middlesborough 0, Newcastle 0
16 Nov	Everton 0, Liverpool 0
23 Nov	Manchester City 4, Leicester 1
30 Nov	Leeds 2, Chelsea 0
7 Dec	Norwich 1, Cardiff 1

14 Dec	Coventry 2, Newcastle 0
21 Dec	Tottenham 1, QPR 2
28 Dec	Leicester 0, Leeds 2
4 Jan	Leyton Orient 2, Derby 2 (FA Cup 3rd round)
11 Jan	Leeds 2, West Ham 1
18 Jan	Tottenham 1, Sheffield Utd 3
25 Jan	Leicester 3, Leatherhead 2 (FA Cup 4th round)
1 Feb	West Ham 2, Carlisle 0
8 Feb	Oxford Utd 1, Manchester Utd 0
15 Feb	Mansfield 0, Carlisle 1 (FA Cup 5th round)
1 Mar	Sunderland 3, West Brom. 0
15 Mar	Plymouth 0, Wrexham 3
22 Mar	Sheffield Utd 3, West Ham 2
29 Mar	Liverpool 1, Birmingham 0
13 Apr	Burnley 3, Tottenham 2
20 Apr	Blackpool 0, Aston Villa 3
27 Apr	Chelsea 1, Everton 1
23 May	N. Ireland 1, Wales 0 (Home Int.)

Total: 35 commentaries

1975/76

16 Aug	QPR 2, Liverpool 0
23 Aug	Arsenal 0, Stoke 1
30 Aug	Everton 2, Derby 0
6 Sep	Newcastle 3, Aston Villa 0
13 Sep	Charlton 1, Blackpool 1
20 Sep	Manchester Utd 1, Ipswich 0
27 Sep	Crystal Palace 1, Sheffield Wed. 1
4 Oct	Leeds 2, QPR 1
11 Oct	West Ham 2, Newcastle 1
18 Oct	Sheffield Utd 0, Stoke 2

25 Oct	Manchester City 1, Ipswich 1	
1 Nov	Derby 3, Leeds 2	
8 Nov	Fulham 1, Charlton 1	
15 Nov	Burnley 1, Wolverhampton 5	
22 Nov	Norwich 1, Newcastle 2	
26 Nov	Middlesbrough 0, Fulham 0	(Anglo-Scottish Cup Final – 1st leg)
29 Nov	QPR 3, Stoke 2	
6 Dec	Middlesbrough 0, Manchester Utd 0	
13 Dec	Ipswich 2, Leeds 1	
20 Dec	Liverpool 2, QPR 0	
27 Dec	Manchester Utd 2, Burnley 1	
3 Jan	West Ham 0, Liverpool 2	(FA Cup 3rd round)
10 Jan	Cardiff 0, Brighton 1	
17 Jan	Wolverhampton 1, Leeds 1	
24 Jan	Coventry 1, Newcastle 1	(FA Cup 4th round)
31 Jan	West Ham 0, Liverpool 4	
7 Feb	Bristol City 1, Southampton 1	
14 Feb	Chelsea 2, Crystal Palace 3	(FA Cup 5th round)
18 Feb	Newcastle 0, Bolton 0	(FA Cup 5th round replay)
21 Feb	Sunderland 4, Charlton 1	
6 Mar	Bradford City 0, Southampton 1	(FA Cup 5th round)
20 Mar	Middlesbrough 0, Derby 2	
27 Mar	Hereford 1, Brighton 1	
10 Apr	Bristol City 2, Chelsea 2	
17 Apr	Liverpool 5, Stoke 3	
24 Apr	Oldham 0, West Brom. 1	
8 May	Scotland 3, N. Ireland 0	
17 Jun	Yugoslavia 2, West Germany 4	(European Championship semi-final – Belgrade)

Total: 38 commentaries

1976/77

21 Aug	QPR 0, Everton 4
28 Aug	Bolton 3, Millwall 1
4 Sep	Manchester Utd 3, Tottenham 2
11 Sep	Fulham 0, Wolverhampton 0
15 Sep	Manchester City 1, Juventus 0 (UEFA Cup – 1st round, 1st leg)
18 Sep	Stoke 2, Ipswich 1
25 Sep	West Ham 1, Sunderland 1
2 Oct	Chelsea 2, Cardiff 1
9 Oct	Blackpool 0, Plymouth 2
16 Oct	West Brom. 4, Manchester Utd 0
23 Oct	Crystal Palace 2, Rotherham 1
27 Oct	West Ham 0, QPR 2
30 Oct	Birmingham 2, QPR 1
6 Nov	Aston Villa 3, Manchester Utd 2
13 Nov	Oldham 4, Carlisle 1
20 Nov	Nottingham Forest 1, Chelsea 1
27 Nov	Middlesbrough 0, Ipswich 2
4 Dec	Arsenal 5, Newcastle 3
11 Dec	Tottenham 2, Manchester City 2
18 Dec	Bristol City 1, Middlesbrough 2
1 Jan	Chelsea 5, Hereford 1
8 Jan	Southampton 1, Chelsea 1 (FA Cup 3rd round)
15 Jan	Liverpool 1, West Brom. 1
19 Jan	Derby 3, Blackpool 2 (FA Cup 3rd round replay)
22 Jan	Sheffield Utd 0, Luton 3
29 Jan	Colchester 1, Derby 1 (FA Cup 4th round)
5 Feb	Arsenal 0, Sunderland 0
12 Feb	Manchester City 1, Arsenal 0
19 Feb	Bristol City 1, Manchester City 0
26 Feb	Leeds 1, Manchester City 0 (FA Cup 5th round)

2 Mar	St Etienne 1, Liverpool 0	(European Cup quarter-final, 1st leg)
5 Mar	Arsenal 1, Ipswich 4	
12 Mar	West Ham 1, Manchester City 0	
19 Mar	Manchester Utd 2, Aston Villa 1	(FA Cup 6th round)
26 Mar	Leicester 0, Bristol City 0	
2 Apr	Chelsea 3, Blackburn 1	
9 Apr	Norwich 0, Ipswich 1	
13 Apr	Aston Villa 3, Everton 2	(League Cup final 2nd replay)
16 Apr	Liverpool 2, Arsenal 0	
23 Apr	Liverpool 2, Everton 2	(FA Cup semi-final)
27 Apr	Liverpool 3, Everton 0	(FA Cup semi-final replay)
30 Apr	Derby 4, Manchester City 0	
7 May	QPR 1, Liverpool 1	
14 May	Liverpool 0, West Ham 0	
21 May	Manchester Utd 2, Liverpool 1	(FA Cup final)
28 May	N. Ireland 1, England 2	(Home Int.)
4 Jun	England 1, Scotland 2	(Home Int.)
12 Jun	Argentina 1, England 1	(Int. friendly)

Total: 48 commentaries

1977/78

13 Aug	Liverpool 0, Manchester Utd 0	(Charity Shield)
20 Aug	Ipswich 1, Arsenal 0	
27 Aug	West Ham 0, Manchester City 1	
3 Sep	Derby 0, Manchester Utd 1	
10 Sep	Wolverhampton 2, Nottingham Forest 3	
17 Sep	Blackpool 0, Tottenham 2	
24 Sep	West Brom. 3, Birmingham 1	
1 Oct	Arsenal 3, West Ham 0	

8 Oct	Newcastle 1, Derby 2
12 Oct	Luxembourg 0, England 2 (World Cup qualifier)
22 Oct	Tottenham 9, Bristol Rovers 0
29 Oct	Derby 2, Norwich 2
2 Nov	Manchester Utd 5, FC Porto 2 (European Cup Winners' Cup, 2nd round, 2nd leg)
5 Nov	Liverpool 1, Aston Villa 2
12 Nov	Southampton 2, Blackpool 0
19 Nov	Wrexham 2, Colchester 1
26 Nov	Bolton 1, Tottenham 0
3 Dec	Leeds 3, QPR 0
10 Dec	Sunderland 1, Tottenham 2
17 Dec	Birmingham 0, Everton 0
31 Dec	Luton 1, Brighton 0
7 Jan	Carlisle 1, Manchester Utd 1 (FA Cup 3rd round)
11 Jan	Manchester Utd 4, Carlisle 2 (FA Cup 3rd round replay)
21 Jan	Norwich 1, Manchester City 3
28 Jan	Newcastle 2, Wrexham 2 (FA Cup 4th round)
4 Feb	Coventry 1, Liverpool 0
18 Feb	QPR 1, Nottingham Forest 1 (FA Cup 5th round)
25 Feb	Liverpool 3, Manchester Utd 1
8 Mar	England 1, Italy 1 (UEFA Under-21, quarter-final, 1st leg)
11 Mar	Millwall 1, Ipswich 6 (FA Cup 6th round)
15 Mar	Liverpool 4, Benfica 1 (European Cup, quarter-final, 2nd leg)
18 Mar	Derby 1, Birmingham 3
25 Mar	West Ham 3, Chelsea 1
1 Apr	Arsenal 3, Manchester Utd 1
15 Apr	Everton 1, Ipswich 0
22 Apr	Coventry 0, Nottingham Forest 0
29 Apr	Southampton 0, Tottenham 0
13 May	Wales 1, England 3 (Home Int.)

| 16 May | England 1, N. Ireland 0 | (Home Int.) |
| 20 May | Scotland 0, England 1 | (Home Int.) |

WORLD CUP IN ARGENTINA

2 Jun	Argentina 2, Hungary 1	(Buenos Aires)
3 Jun	Austria 2, Spain 1	(Buenos Aires)
6 Jun	W. Germany 6, Mexico 0	(Córdoba)
7 Jun	Scotland 1, Iran 1	(Córdoba)
10 Jun	France 3, Hungary 1	(Mar del Plata)
11 Jun	Spain 1, Sweden 0	(Buenos Aires)
14 Jun	West Germany 0, Italy 0	(Buenos Aires)
18 Jun	Argentina 0, Brazil 0	(Rosario)
21 Jun	Holland 2, Italy 1	(Buenos Aires)
24 Jun	Brazil 2, Italy 1	(Buenos Aires)

Total: 50 commentaries

1978/79

19 Aug	Chelsea 0, Everton 1	
26 Aug	Brighton 2, Sunderland 0	
2 Sep	Manchester Utd 1, Everton 1	
9 Sep	Burnley 3, West Ham 2	
16 Sep	Arsenal 1, Bolton 0	
23 Sep	Coventry 0, Leeds 0	
27 Sep	Liverpool 0, Nottingham Forest 0	(European Cup, 1st round, 2nd leg)
30 Sep	Norwich 3, Derby 0	
7 Oct	Sheffield Utd 3, Sunderland 2	
14 Oct	Southampton 1, QPR 1	
21 Oct	Nottingham Forest 1, Ipswich 0	

28 Oct	Everton 1, Liverpool 0
1 Nov	Nottingham Forest 5, AEK Athens 1 (European Cup, 2nd round, 2nd leg)
4 Nov	West Brom. 1, Birmingham 0
11 Nov	Bristol City 4, Bolton 1
18 Nov	West Ham 1, Crystal Palace 1
25 Nov	Chelsea 0, Manchester Utd 1
9 Dec	Coventry 1, QPR 0
16 Dec	Manchester Utd 2, Spurs 0
23 Dec	Tottenham 0, Arsenal 5
30 Dec	Ipswich 5, Chelsea 1
10 Jan	Southend 0, Liverpool 0 (FA Cup 3rd round)
13 Jan	Norwich 1, West Brom. 1
20 Jan	Brighton 1, Stoke 1
3 Feb	Liverpool 2, West Brom. 1
10 Feb	Arsenal 0, Middlesbrough 0
17 Feb	Southampton 3, Everton 0
24 Feb	Derby 0, Liverpool 2
3 Mar	Stoke 2, West Ham 0
7 Mar	Nottingham Forest 4, Grasshoppers 1 (European Cup, quarter-final, 1st leg)
17 Mar	Bristol City 1, Middlesbrough 1
24 Mar	Sunderland 1, Leyton Orient 0
31 Mar	Arsenal 2, Wolverhampton 0 (FA Cup semi-final)
4 Apr	Manchester Utd 1, Liverpool 0 (FA Cup semi-final replay)
7 Apr	Leeds 1, Ipswich 1
14 Apr	Liverpool 2, Manchester Utd 0
21 Apr	Derby 2, Arsenal 0
28 Apr	Nottingham Forest 0, Liverpool 0
2 May	Wales 0, W. Germany 2 (Euro Championship qualifier)
5 May	Plymouth 2, Swansea 2
12 May	Arsenal 3, Manchester Utd 2 (FA Cup final)

| 23 May | England 0, Wales 0 | (Home Int.) |

6 Jun   Bulgaria 0, England 3   (European Championship qualifier)

10 Jun   Sweden 0, England 0   (Int. friendly)

Total: 44 commentaries

1979/80

1 Aug   West Brom. 4, China 0   (friendly)

11 Aug   Liverpool 3, Arsenal 1   (Charity Shield)

18 Aug   Manchester City 0, Crystal Palace 0

25 Aug   Derby 0, Everton 1

1 Sep   Leicester 1, Luton 3

8 Sep   Liverpool 4, Coventry 0

15 Sep   West Ham 2, Sunderland 0

22 Sep   Stoke 1, Crystal Palace 2

26 Sep   Manchester City 1, Sunderland 1   (League Cup, 3rd round)

29 Sep   Nottingham Forest 1, Liverpool 0

6 Oct   Coventry 2, Everton 1

13 Oct   Luton 2, Sunderland 0

20 Oct   Manchester Utd 1, Ipswich 0

27 Oct   Southampton 1, Leeds 2

31 Oct   West Brom. 0, Norwich 0   (League Cup, 4th round)

3 Nov   Middlesbrough 0, Tottenham 0

10 Nov   Manchester City 2, Manchester Utd 0

24 Nov   Ipswich 3, Southampton 1

1 Dec   Liverpool 4, Middlesbrough 0

8 Dec   Manchester Utd 1, Leeds 1

15 Dec   Tottenham 1, Aston Villa 2

22 Dec   Notts Co. 2, Newcastle 2

29 Dec   Wrexham 2, Chelsea 0

5 Jan   Cardiff 0, Arsenal 0   (FA Cup 3rd round)

12 Jan	Bolton 0, Brighton 2	
16 Jan	Nottingham Forest 1, Liverpool 0	(League Cup semi-final, 1st leg)
19 Jan	West Ham 2, Preston 0	
26 Jan	Watford 4, Harlow 3	(FA Cup 4th round)
2 Feb	Manchester City 1, West Brom. 3	
9 Feb	Swindon 1, Sheffield Wed. 2	
16 Feb	Everton 5, Wrexham 2	(FA Cup 5th round)
23 Feb	Manchester Utd 4, Bristol City 0	
1 Mar	Southampton 1, West Brom. 1	
8 Mar	Tottenham 0, Liverpool 1	(FA Cup 6th round)
15 Mar	Grimsby 2, Millwall 0	
19 Mar	Dynamo Berlin 1, Nottingham Forest 3	(European Cup, quarter-final, 2nd leg)
22 Mar	QPR 2, Luton 2	
29 Mar	Brighton 1, Nottingham Forest 0	
5 Apr	Wolverhampton 1, Spurs 2	
12 Apr	Everton 1, West Ham 1	(FA Cup semi-final)
9 Apr	Arsenal 1, Juventus 1	(European Cup Winners' Cup, semi-final, 1st leg)
16 Apr	Liverpool 1, Arsenal 1	(FA Cup semi-final replay)
26 Apr	Manchester Utd 2, Coventry 1	
3 May	Liverpool 4, Aston Villa 1	
10 May	West Ham 1, Arsenal 0	(FA Cup final)
14 May	Arsenal 0, Valencia 0	(European Cup Winners' Cup final; Valencia won on penalties)

EUROPEAN CHAMPIONSHIP FINALS

| 11 Jun | W. Germany 1, Czechoslovakia 0 | (Rome) |
| 12 Jun | England 1, Belgium 1 | (Turin) |

15 Jun	Italy 1, England 0	(Turin)
18 Jun	Belgium 0, Italy 0	(Rome)
22 Jun	W. Germany 2, Belgium 1	(Rome)

Total: 51 commentaries

1980/81

16 Aug	Leicester 0, Ipswich 1
23 Aug	Sunderland 1, Southampton 2
30 Aug	Liverpool 4, Norwich 1
6 Sep	Coventry 3, Crystal Palace 2
13 Sep	QPR 1, Newcastle 2
17 Sep	Manchester Utd 1, Widzew Lodz 1	(UEFA Cup, 1st round, 1st leg)
20 Sep	Southampton 2, Liverpool 2
27 Sep	Manchester Utd 2, Manchester City 2
4 Oct	Middlesbrough 6, Norwich 1
8 Oct	Norwich 1, Ipswich 3	(League Cup, 3rd round replay)
11 Oct	Liverpool 1, Ipswich 1
18 Oct	Manchester City 0, Birmingham 1
22 Oct	Aberdeen 0, Liverpool 1	(European Cup, 2nd round, 1st leg)
25 Oct	Chelsea 6, Newcastle 0
1 Nov	Everton 2, Spurs 2
8 Nov	West Brom. 0, Aston Villa 0
15 Nov	Plymouth 1, Colchester 1
22 Nov	Stoke 0, Crystal Palace 0
29 Nov	Tottenham 1, West Brom. 3
6 Dec	Norwich 2, Manchester Utd 2
13 Dec	Swansea 4, Newcastle 0
20 Dec	Nottingham Forest 3, Sunderland 0

GOLD CUP (IN URUGUAY)

30 Dec	Uruguay 2, Holland 0	
1 Jan	Argentina 2, West Germany 1	
3 Jan	Uruguay 2, Italy 0	
4 Jan	Argentina 1, Brazil 1	
6 Jan	Holland 1, Italy 1	
7 Jan	West Germany 1, Brazil 4	
10 Jan	Uruguay 2, Brazil 1	(Gold Cup final)
24 Jan	Watford 1, Wolverhampton 1	(FA Cup 4th round)
31 Jan	Derby 2, Luton 2	
7 Feb	Everton 1, Aston Villa 3	
14 Feb	Tottenham 3, Coventry 1	(FA Cup 5th round)
18 Feb	Exeter 4, Newcastle 0	(FA Cup 5th round replay)
28 Mar	Huddersfield 0, Chester 0	
11 Apr	Manchester City 1, Ipswich 0	(FA Cup semi-final)
15 Apr	Tottenham 3, Wolverhampton 0	(FA Cup semi-final replay)
18 Apr	Ipswich 0, Arsenal 2	
22 Apr	Cologne 0, Ipswich 1	(UEFA Cup, semi-final, 2nd leg)
25 Apr	Aston Villa 3, Middlesbrough 0	
29 Apr	England 0, Romania 0	(World Cup qualifier)
2 May	Arsenal 2, Aston Villa 0	
9 May	Tottenham 1, Manchester City 1	(FA Cup final)
14 May	Tottenham 3, Manchester City 2	(FA Cup final replay)
16 May	Wales 2, Scotland 0	(Home Int.)
20 May	Az Alkmaar 4, Ipswich 2	(UEFA Cup final, 2nd leg)
23 May	England 0, Scotland 1	(Home Int.)
30 May	Switzerland 2, England 1	(Home Int.)

Total: 48 commentaries

1981/82

22 Aug	Tottenham 2, Aston Villa 2 (Charity Shield)
29 Aug	Manchester City 2, West Brom. 1
5 Sep	Manchester Utd 1, Ipswich 2
12 Sep	Luton 0, Sheffield Wed. 3
19 Sep	Liverpool 0, Aston Villa 0
26 Sep	Manchester City 0, Tottenham 1
3 Oct	QPR 2, Blackburn 0
10 Oct	Ipswich 1, Wolverhampton 0
24 Oct	Wolverhampton 0, Aston Villa 3
31 Oct	Leicester 0, Sheffield Wed. 0
7 Nov	Liverpool 3, Everton 1
14 Nov	Watford 0, Cardiff 0
18 Nov	England 1, Hungary 0 (World Cup qualifier)
21 Nov	Birmingham 0, Wolverhampton 3
28 Nov	Aston Villa 3, Nottingham Forest 1
5 Dec	West Ham 1, Arsenal 2
12 Dec	Swansea 1, Nottingham Forest 2
19 Dec	Everton 2, Aston Villa 0
2 Jan	Barnet 0, Brighton 0 (FA Cup 3rd round)
9 Jan	Huddersfield 2, Oxford 0
16 Jan	Liverpool 2, Wolverhampton 1
23 Jan	Watford 2, West Ham 0 (FA Cup 4th round)
3 Feb	West Brom. 0, Tottenham 0 (League Cup semi-final, 1st leg)
6 Feb	Colchester 5, Sheffield Utd 2
13 Feb	Tottenham 1, Aston Villa 0 (FA Cup 5th round)
27 Feb	Everton 0, West Ham 0
6 Mar	Chelsea 2, Tottenham 3 (FA Cup 6th round)
13 Mar	Oldham 0, Sheffield Wed. 3
20 Mar	Notts Co. 1, Manchester Utd 3
24 Mar	France 4, N. Ireland 0 (Int. friendly)

27 Mar	Sheffield Wed. 2, Leyton Orient 0
3 Apr	QPR 1, West Brom. 0 (FA Cup semi-final)
7 Apr	Tottenham 1, Barcelona 1 (European Cup Winners' Cup semi-final, 1st leg)
10 Apr	Gillingham 2, Fulham 0
17 Apr	Blackburn 1, Watford 2
24 Apr	Brighton 0, Manchester Utd 1
1 May	Ipswich 3, Middlesbrough 1
8 May	Watford 3, Leicester 1
15 May	Liverpool 3, Tottenham 1
22 May	Tottenham 1, QPR 1 (FA Cup final)
27 May	Tottenham 1, QPR 0 (FA Cup final replay)

WORLD CUP IN SPAIN

13 Jun	Belgium 1, Argentina 0 (Barcelona)
16 Jun	England 3, France 1 (Bilbao)
18 Jun	Brazil 4, Scotland 1 (Seville)
19 Jun	USSR 3, New Zealand 0 (Malaga)
20 Jun	Spain 2, Yugoslavia 1 (Valencia)
21 Jun	France 4, Kuwait 1 (Valladolid)
23 Jun	Brazil 4, New Zealand 0 (Seville)
25 Jun	N. Ireland 1, Spain 0 (Valencia)
29 Jun	England 0, W. Germany 0 (Madrid)
1 Jul	N. Ireland 2, Austria 2 (Madrid)
2 Jul	Argentina 3, Brazil 1 (Barcelona)
5 Jul	Brazil 2, Italy 3 (Barcelona)
8 Jul	Italy 2, Poland 2 (Barcelona)
11 Jul	Italy 3, West Germany 1 (Madrid)

Total: 55 commentaries

1982/83

28 Aug	Wolverhampton 2, Blackburn 1
4 Sep	Ipswich 1, Coventry City 1
11 Sep	Manchester Utd 3, Ipswich 1
15 Sep	Manchester Utd 0, Valencia 0 (UEFA Cup, 1st round, 1st leg)
18 Sep	Swansea City 0, Liverpool 3
25 Sep	Tottenham 4, Nottingham Forest 1
2 Oct	Ipswich 1, Liverpool 0
6 Oct	Stoke 1, West Ham 1 (Milk Cup, 2nd round, 1st leg)
9 Oct	Chelsea 0, Leeds 0
13 Oct	England 1, West Germany 2 (Int. friendly)
16 Oct	Newcastle 1, Fulham 4
23 Oct	Watford 0, Coventry 0
27 Oct	Newcastle 1, Leeds 4 (Milk Cup, 2nd round, 2nd leg)
30 Oct	Aston Villa 4, Tottenham 0
6 Nov	Everton 0, Liverpool 5
13 Nov	Manchester Utd 1, Tottenham 0
17 Nov	Greece 0, England 3 (European Championship qualifier)
20 Nov	Watford 4, Brighton 1
27 Nov	Luton 3, Southampton 3
11 Dec	Brighton 3, Norwich City 0
18 Dec	Tottenham 2, Birmingham 1 (500th match for BBC TV)
1 Jan	Manchester Utd 3, Aston Villa 1
8 Jan	Manchester Utd 2, West Ham 0 (FA Cup 3rd round)
15 Jan	West Brom. 0, Liverpool 1
22 Jan	Watford 2, Southampton 0
29 Jan	Aston Villa 1, Wolverhampton 0 (FA Cup 4th round)
5 Feb	Luton 1, Liverpool 3
8 Feb	Liverpool 3, Burnley 0 (Milk Cup semi-final, 1st leg)

12 Feb	Tottenham 1, Swansea 0	
19 Feb	Norwich 1, Ipswich 0	(FA Cup 5th round)
12 Mar	Arsenal 2, Aston Villa 0	(FA Cup 6th round)
19 Mar	Liverpool 0, Everton 0	
26 Mar	Liverpool 2, Manchester Utd 1	(aet – Milk Cup final)
30 Mar	England 0, Greece 0	(European Championship qualifier)
2 Apr	Fulham 1, Chelsea 1	
9 Apr	Nottingham Forest 2, Tottenham 2	
16 Apr	Manchester Utd 2, Arsenal 1	(FA Cup semi-final)
23 Apr	Manchester Utd 2, Watford 0	
7 May	Brighton 0, Manchester City 1	
14 May	Manchester City 0, Luton 1	
21 May	Manchester Utd 2, Brighton 2	(FA Cup final)
26 May	Manchester Utd 4, Brighton 0	(FA Cup final replay)
1 Jun	England 2, Scotland 0	

Total: 43 commentaries

1983/84

20 Aug	Manchester Utd 2, Liverpool 0	(Charity Shield)
27 Aug	Aston Villa 4, West Brom. 3	
3 Sep	Fulham 0, Portsmouth 2	
10 Sep	Arsenal 0, Liverpool 2	
17 Sep	Tottenham 1, Everton 2	
24 Sep	Manchester Utd 1, Liverpool 0	
28 Sep	Watford 3, Kaiserslautern 0	(UEFA Cup, 1st round, 2nd leg)
8 Oct	Newcastle 2, Charlton 1	
12 Oct	Hungary 0, England 3	(European Championship qualifier)

| 15 Oct | Leicester 0, Southampton 0 | (match abandoned) |
| 19 Oct | Tottenham 4, Feyenoord 2 | (UEFA Cup, 2nd round, 1st leg) |

BBC strike in this period meant we missed four Saturdays.

19 Nov	Luton 2, Tottenham 4	
26 Nov	Ipswich 1, Liverpool 1	
30 Nov	Oxford 1, Manchester Utd 1	(Milk Cup, 4th round)
3 Dec	Chelsea 0, Manchester City 1	
10 Dec	Coventry 4, Liverpool 0	
16 Dec	Manchester Utd 4, Tottenham 2	
31 Dec	Aston Villa 2, QPR 1	
6 Jan	Liverpool 4, Newcastle 0	(FA Cup 3rd round)
20 Jan	Aston Villa 1, Liverpool 3	
25 Jan	Oxford 1, Everton 1	(Milk Cup, 5th round)
28 Jan	Portsmouth 0, Southampton 1	(FA Cup 4th round)
4 Feb	Blackpool 3, York 0	
7 Feb	Liverpool 2, Walsall 2	(Milk Cup semi-final, 1st leg)
11 Feb	Notts Co. 3, Watford 5	
17 Feb	Blackburn 0, Southampton 1	(FA Cup 5th round)
25 Feb	Nottingham Forest 0, Arsenal 1	
3 Mar	Chelsea 3, Oldham 0	
7 Mar	Liverpool 1, Benfica 0	(European Cup quarter-final, 1st leg)
10 Mar	Notts Co. 1, Everton 2	(FA Cup 6th round)
24 Mar	Wimbledon 2, Walsall 0	
31 Mar	Leeds Utd 1, Sheffield Wed. 1	
14 Apr	Watford 1, Plymouth 0	(FA Cup semi-final)
18 Apr	France 1, W. Germany 0	(Int. friendly)
21 Apr	Sheffield Wed. 1, Grimsby 0	

28 Apr	Liverpool 2, Ipswich 2
12 May	Notts County 0, Liverpool 0
19 May	Everton 2, Watford 0 (FA Cup final – my 7th)
2 Jun	England 0, Soviet Union 2 (Int. friendly)

EUROPEAN CHAMPIONSHIP FINALS

14 Jun	W. Germany 0, Portugal 0 (Strasbourg)
17 Jun	W. Germany 2, Romania 1 (Lens)
20 Jun	W. Germany 0, Spain 1 (Paris)
23 Jun	France 3, Portugal 2 (aet) (Marseilles)
27 Jun	France 2, Spain 0 (Paris final – my 2nd)

Total: 44 commentaries

1984/85

25 Aug	Manchester Utd 1, Watford 1
31 Aug	Chelsea 0, Everton 1
8 Sep	Arsenal 3, Liverpool 1
12 Sep	England 1, E. Germany 0 (Int. friendly)
15 Sep	Southampton 2, Norwich 1
22 Sep	Aston Villa 0, Tottenham 1
29 Sep	Newcastle 1, West Ham 1
6 Oct	Aston Villa 3, Manchester Utd 0
20 Oct	Liverpool 0, Everton 1
24 Oct	Liverpool 3, Benfica 1 (European Cup, 2nd round, 1st leg)
27 Oct	West Ham 3, Arsenal 1
10 Nov	Nottingham Forest 1, Tottenham 2
17 Nov	Watford 1, Sheffield Wed. 0
21 Nov	Sunderland 0, Tottenham 1 (Milk Cup, 4th round)
24 Nov	Oxford 5, Leeds 2
1 Dec	Arsenal 3, Luton 1

5 Dec	Tottenham 1, Sunderland 2 (Milk Cup, 4th round replay)
8 Dec	Nottingham Forest 3, Manchester Utd 2
12 Dec	Dundee 2, Manchester Utd 3 (UEFA Cup, 3rd round, 2nd leg)
15 Dec	West Ham 0, Sheffield Wed. 0
29 Dec	Ipswich 0, Everton 2
4 Jan	Leeds 0, Everton 2 (FA Cup 3rd round)
12 Jan	QPR 2, Tottenham 2
19 Jan	Chelsea 1, Arsenal 1
26 Jan	York 1, Arsenal 0 (FA Cup 4th round)
30 Jan	Wimbledon 1, Nottingham Forest 0 (FA Cup 4th round replay)
2 Feb	Luton 2, Tottenham 2
9 Feb	Manchester City 1, Carlisle 3
23 Feb	Blackburn 1, Oxford 1
27 Feb	N. Ireland 0, England 1 (World Cup qualifier)
2 Mar	Manchester Utd 1, Everton 1
9 Mar	Manchester Utd 4, West Ham 2 (FA Cup 6th round)
13 Mar	Luton 1, Millwall 0 (FA Cup 6th round)
15 Mar	West Ham 2, Manchester Utd 2
20 Mar	Liverpool 4, FK Austria 1 (European Cup, quarter-final, 2nd leg)
30 Mar	Southampton 1, Everton 2
6 Apr	Everton 4, Sunderland 1
10 Apr	Bayern Munich 0, Everton 0 (European Cup Winners' Cup, semi-final, 1st leg)
13 Apr	Everton 2, Luton 1 (FA Cup semi-final)
27 Apr	Chelsea 1, Tottenham 1
1 May	Romania 0, England 0 (World Cup qualifier)
4 May	Blackburn 0, Portsmouth 1
11 May	Southampton 2, Coventry 1
18 May	Manchester 1, Everton 0 (FA Cup final)
25 May	Scotland 1, England 0 (Home Int.)

| 9 Jun | Mexico 1, England 0 | (Rous Cup) |
| 16 Jun | USA 0, England 5 | (pre-World Cup tour) |

Total: 47 commentaries

1985/86

| 10 Aug | Everton 2, Manchester Utd 0 | (Charity Shield) |
| 13 Nov | England 0, N. Ireland 0 | (World Cup qualifier) |

(TV dispute with the league meant that there were no league or League Cup matches televised before Christmas)

5 Jan	Charlton 0, West Ham 1	(FA Cup 3rd round)
18 Jan	Manchester Utd 2, Nottingham Forest 3	
22 Jan	QPR 1, Chelsea 1	(Milk Cup, quarter-final)
25 Jan	Manchester City 1, Watford 1	(FA Cup 4th round)
9 Feb	Liverpool 1, Manchester Utd 1	
26 Feb	Derby 1, Sheffield Wed. 1	(FA Cup 5th round)
2 Mar	Tottenham 1, Liverpool 2	
5 Mar	Tottenham 1, Everton 2	(FA Cup 5th round)
8 Mar	Luton 2, Everton 2	(FA Cup 6th round)
12 Mar	Sheffield Wed. 2, West Ham 1	(FA Cup 6th round)
22 Mar	Manchester Utd 2, Manchester City 2	
5 Apr	Everton 2, Sheffield Wed. 1	(FA Cup semi-final)
19 Apr	Watford 0, West Ham 2	
3 May	Chelsea 0, Liverpool 1	
10 May	Liverpool 3, Everton 1	(FA Cup final)

WORLD CUP FINALS IN MEXICO

| 31 May | Italy 1, Bulgaria 1 | (Mexico City) |
| 1 Jun | Brazil 1, Spain 0 | (Guadalajara) |

3 Jun	England 0, Portugal 1 (Monterrey)
5 Jun	France 1, Soviet Union 1 (Leon)
6 Jun	Brazil 1, Algeria 0 (Guadalajara)
8 Jun	W. Germany 2, Scotland 1 (Querétaro)
10 Jun	Argentina 2, Bulgaria 0 (Mexico City)
11 Jun	Morocco 3, Portugal 1 (Guadalajara)
12 Jun	Brazil 3, N. Ireland 0 (Guadalajara)
16 Jun	Argentina 1, Uruguay 0 (Puebla)
17 Jun	France 2, Italy 0 (Mexico City)
18 Jun	England 3, Paraguay 0 (Mexico City)
21 Jun	France 1, Brazil 1 (pens) (Guadalajara)
22 Jun	Belgium 1, Spain 1 (pens) (Puebla)
25 Jun	Argentina 2, Belgium 0 (Mexico City)
29 Jun	Argentina 3, W. Germany 2 (Mexico City)

Total: 33 commentaries

1986/87

10 Sep	Sweden 1, England 0 (Int. friendly)
21 Sep	Everton 3, Manchester Utd 1
15 Oct	England 3, N. Ireland 0 (Euro Championship qualifier)
23 Nov	Everton 0, Liverpool 0
7 Dec	Manchester Utd 3, Tottenham 3
4 Jan	Tottenham 1, Arsenal 2
11 Jan	Luton 0, Liverpool 0 (FA Cup 3rd round)
21 Jan	Arsenal 2, Nottingham Forest 0 (League Cup quarter-final)
31 Jan	Wimbledon 4, Portsmouth 0 (FA Cup 4th round)
4 Feb	QPR 2, Luton 1 (FA Cup 4th round replay)
18 Feb	Spain 2, England 4 (Int. friendly)
22 Feb	Wimbledon 3, Everton 1 (FA Cup 5th round)
8 Mar	Watford 2, Everton 1

10 Mar	Arsenal 0, Liverpool 1
14 Mar	Arsenal 1, Watford 3 (FA Cup 6th round)
22 Mar	Tottenham 1, Liverpool 0
15 Apr	Manchester City 1, Tottenham 1
29 Apr	Turkey 0, England 0 (European Championship qualifier)
6 May	Coventry 1, Manchester Utd 1
16 May	Coventry 3, Tottenham 2 (FA Cup final)
26 May	Scotland 0, Brazil 2 (Rous Cup)

Total: 21 commentaries

1987/88

20 Sep	Newcastle 1, Liverpool 4
7 Oct	Tottenham 3, Torquay 0 (League Cup, 2nd round, 2nd leg)
14 Oct	England 8, Turkey 0 (Euro Championship Qualifier)
17 Oct	Liverpool 4, QPR 0
17 Nov	Manchester City 3, Watford 1 (League Cup, 4th round)
22 Nov	Derby 2, Chelsea 0
28 Dec	Manchester Utd 2, Everton 1
3 Jan	Everton 1, Nottingham Forest 0
10 Jan	Ipswich 1, Manchester Utd 2 (FA Cup 3rd round)
16 Jan	Liverpool 2, Arsenal 0
20 Jan	Sheffield Wed. 0, Arsenal 1 (League Cup, quarter-final)
30 Jan	Leyton Orient 1, Nottingham Forest 2 (FA Cup 4th round)
10 Feb	Oxford 1, Luton 1 (League Cup semi-final, 1st leg)
17 Feb	Israel 0, England 0 (Int. friendly)
21 Feb	Everton 0, Liverpool 1 (FA Cup 5th round)
28 Feb	Luton 2, Oxford 0 (League Cup semi-final, 2nd leg)
13 Mar	Arsenal 1, Nottingham Forest 2 (FA Cup 6th round)
16 Mar	Derby 1, Liverpool 1

23 Mar	England 2, Holland 2	(Int. friendly)
4 Apr	Liverpool 3, Manchester Utd 3	
9 Apr	Liverpool 2, Nottingham Forest 1	(FA Cup semi-final)
13 Apr	Liverpool 5, Nottingham Forest 0	
14 May	Liverpool 0, Wimbledon 1	(FA Cup final)
24 May	England 1, Colombia 1	(Rous Cup)

EUROPEAN CHAMPIONSHIP FINALS (WEST GERMANY)

10 Jun	W. Germany 1, Italy 1	(Düsseldorf)
12 Jun	Holland 0, Soviet Union 1	(Cologne)
14 Jun	Italy 1, Spain 0	(Frankfurt)
15 Jun	England 1, Holland 3	(Düsseldorf)
17 Jun	W. Germany 2, Spain 0	(Munich)
18 Jun	Holland 1, Republic of Ireland 0	(Gelsenkirchen)
21 Jun	Holland 2, W. Germany 1	(Hamburg)
22 Jun	Italy 0, Soviet Union 2	(Stuttgart)
25 Jun	Holland 2, Soviet Union 0	(Munich)

Total: 33 commentaries

1988/89

20 Aug	Liverpool 2, Wimbledon 1	(Charity Shield)
14 Sep	England 1, Denmark 0	(Int. friendly)
7 Sep	Glasgow Rangers 1, Katowice 0	(UEFA Cup, 1st round, 1st leg)
19 Oct	England 0, Sweden 0	(World Cup qualifier)
19 Nov	Enfield 1, Leyton Orient 1	(FA Cup 1st round)
23 Nov	Leyton Orient 2, Enfield 2	(FA Cup 1st round replay)
10 Dec	Altrincham 0, Halifax 3	(FA Cup 2nd round)
7 Jan	Sutton 2, Coventry 1	(FA Cup 3rd round)
8 Jan	West Ham 2, Arsenal 2	(FA Cup 3rd round)

11 Jan	Arsenal 0, West Ham 1	(FA Cup 3rd round replay)
18 Jan	Watford 1, Newcastle 0	(FA Cup 3rd round 3rd replay)
28 Jan	Norwich 8, Sutton 0	(FA Cup 4th round)
1 Feb	West Ham 1, Swindon 0	(FA Cup 4th round replay)
8 Feb	Greece 1, England 2	(Int. friendly)
18 Feb	Bournemouth 1, Manchester Utd 1	(FA Cup 5th round)
19 Feb	Watford 0, Nottingham Forest 3	(FA Cup 5th round)
22 Feb	Manchester Utd 1, Bournemouth 0	(FA Cup 5th round replay)
18 Mar	Manchester Utd 0, Nottingham Forest 1	(FA Cup 6th round)
19 Mar	Everton 1, Wimbledon 0	(FA Cup 6th round)
26 Apr	England 5, Albania 0	(World Cup qualifier)
7 May	Liverpool 3, Nottingham Forest 1	(FA Cup semi-final)
20 May	Liverpool 3, Everton 2	(FA Cup final)
23 May	England 0, Chile 0	(Rous Cup)
3 Jun	England 3, Poland 0	(World Cup qualifier)

Total: 24 commentaries

1989/90

12 Aug	Liverpool 1, Arsenal 0	(Charity Shield)
6 Sep	Sweden 0, England 0	(World Cup qualifier)
13 Sep	Rangers 1, Bayern Munich 3	(European Cup, 1st round, 1st leg)
11 Oct	Wales 1, Holland 2	(World Cup qualifier)
18 Oct	A C Milan 2, Real Madrid 0	(European Cup)
18 Nov	Blackpool 2, Bolton 1	(FA Cup 1st round)
22 Nov	Torquay 4, Sutton 0	(FA Cup 1st round replay)
9 Dec	Whitley Bay 2, Preston 0	(FA Cup 2nd round)
13 Dec	England 2, Yugoslavia 1	(Int. friendly)
6 Jan	Blackburn 2, Aston Villa 2	(FA Cup 3rd round)
10 Jan	Aston Villa 3, Blackburn 1	(FA Cup 3rd round replay)
27 Jan	Arsenal 0, QPR 0	(FA Cup 4th round)

28 Jan	Norwich 0, Liverpool 0	(FA Cup 4th round)
1 Feb	Liverpool 3, Norwich 1	(FA Cup 4th round replay)
18 Feb	Liverpool 3, Southampton 0	(FA Cup 5th round)
21 Feb	Holland 0, Italy 0	(Int. friendly)
10 Mar	Cambridge 0, Crystal Palace 1	(FA Cup 6th round)
11 Mar	QPR 2, Liverpool 2	(FA Cup 6th round)
14 Mar	Liverpool 1, QPR 0	(FA Cup 6th round replay)
28 Mar	England 1, Brazil 0	(Int. friendly)
8 Apr	Crystal Palace 4, Liverpool 3	(FA Cup semi-final)
12 May	Manchester Utd 3, Crystal Palace 3	(FA Cup final – my 13th)
17 May	Manchester Utd 1, Crystal Palace 0	(FA Cup final replay – my 4th)
22 May	England 1, Uruguay 2	(Int. friendly)

WORLD CUP

9 Jun	Romania 2, Soviet Union 0	(Bari)
10 Jun	W. Germany 4, Yugoslavia 1	(Milan)
11 Jun	England 1, Republic of Ireland 1	(Cagliari)
13 Jun	Uruguay 0, Spain 0	(Udine)
14 Jun	Italy 1, USA 0	(Rome)
16 Jun	England 0, Holland 0	(Cagliari)
18 Jun	Argentina 1, Romania 1	(Naples)
19 Jun	Italy 2, Czechoslovakia 0	(Rome)
20 Jun	Brazil 1, Scotland 0	(Turin)
21 Jun	Republic of Ireland 1, Holland 1	(Palermo)
23 Jun	Czechoslovakia 4, Costa Rica 1	(Bari)
26 Jun	England 1, Belgium 0	(Bologna)
30 Jun	Italy 1, Republic of Ireland 0	(Rome)
4 Jul	England 1, W. Germany 1	(Turin)
8 Jul	W. Germany 1, Argentina 0	(Rome)

Total: 39 commentaries

1990/91

18 Aug	Liverpool 1, Manchester Utd 1	(Charity Shield – my 8th)
12 Sep	England 1, Hungary 0	(Int. friendly)
2 Oct	Rangers 6, Valletta 0	(European Cup, 1st round, 2nd leg)
17 Oct	England 2, Poland 0	(Euro Championship qualifier)
24 Oct	Red Star Belgrade 3, Rangers 0	(European Cup, 2nd round, 1st leg)
7 Nov	Rangers 1, Red Star 1	(European Cup, 2nd round, 2nd leg)
17 Nov	Telford 0, Stoke 0	(FA Cup 1st round)
21 Nov	Stoke 1, Telford 0	(FA Cup 1st round replay)
12 Dec	Wycombe 1, Peterborough 1	(FA Cup 2nd round)
5 Jan	Blackburn 1, Liverpool 1	(FA Cup 3rd round)
7 Jan	Manchester Utd 2, QPR 1	(FA Cup 3rd round)
9 Jan	Wigan 0, Coventry 1	(FA Cup 3rd round replay)
21 Jan	Nottingham Forest 2, Crystal Palace 2	(FA Cup 3rd round replay)
26 Jan	Tottenham 4, Oxford 2	(FA Cup 4th round)
27 Jan	Arsenal 0, Leeds 0	(FA Cup 4th round)
30 Jan	Leeds 1, Arsenal 1	(FA Cup 4th round replay)
13 Feb	Arsenal 0, Leeds 0	(FA Cup 4th round, 2nd replay)
16 Feb	Portsmouth 1, Tottenham 2	(FA Cup 5th round)
18 Feb	Norwich 2, Manchester Utd 1	(FA Cup 5th round)
10 Mar	Tottenham 2, Notts Co. 1	(FA Cup 6th round)
11 Mar	West Ham 2, Everton 1	(FA Cup 6th round)
27 Mar	England 1, Republic of Ireland 1	(Euro Championship qualifier)
14 Apr	Nottingham Forest 4, West Ham 0	(FA Cup semi-final)
18 May	Tottenham 2, Nottingham Forest 1	(FA Cup final)
25 May	England 2, Argentina 2	(Int. friendly)
1 Jun	Australia 0, England 1	(Sydney – tour match)
3 Jun	New Zealand 0, England 1	(Auckland – tour match)
8 Jun	New Zealand 0, England 2	(Wellington – tour match)
12 Jun	Malaysia 2, England 4	(Kuala Lumpur – tour match)

Total: 29 commentaries

1991/92

10 Aug	Arsenal 0, Tottenham 0	(Charity Shield – my 9th)
11 Sep	England 0, Germany 1	(Int. friendly)
18 Sep	Liverpool 6, K. Lahti 1	(UEFA Cup, 1st round, 1st leg)
2 Oct	K. Lahti 1, Liverpool 0	(UEFA Cup, 1st round, 2nd leg)
16 Oct	England 1, Turkey 0	(Euro Championship qualifiers)
13 Nov	Poland 1, England 1	(Euro Championship qualifiers)
16 Nov	Colchester 0, Exeter 0	(FA Cup 1st round)
27 Nov	Swarowski Tirol 0, Liverpool 2	(UEFA Cup, 3rd round, 1st leg)
7 Dec	Enfield 1, Barnet 4	(FA Cup 2nd round)
11 Dec	Liverpool 4, Swarowski Tirol 0	(UEFA Cup, 3rd round, 2nd leg)
4 Jan	Middlesbrough 2, Manchester City 1	(FA Cup 3rd round)
5 Jan	Aston Villa 0, Tottenham 0	(FA Cup 3rd round)
14 Jan	Tottenham 0, Aston Villa 1	(FA Cup 3rd round replay)
25 Jan	Leicester 1, Bristol City 2	(FA Cup 4th round)
26 Jan	Chelsea 1, Everton 0	(FA Cup 4th round)
4 Feb	Sheffield Wed. 1, Middlesbrough 2	(FA Cup 4th round replay)
5 Feb	Bristol Rovers 1, Liverpool 1	(FA Cup 4th round)
11 Feb	Liverpool 2, Bristol Rovers 1	(FA Cup 4th round replay)
15 Feb	Chelsea 1, Sheffield Utd 0	(FA Cup 5th round)
16 Feb	Swindon 1, Aston Villa 2	(FA Cup 5th round)
19 Feb	England 2, France 0	(Int. friendly)
26 Feb	Liverpool 3, Ipswich 2	(FA Cup 5th round replay)
8 Mar	Liverpool 1, Aston Villa 0	(FA Cup 6th round)
18 Mar	Norwich City 2, Southampton 1	(FA Cup 6th round replay)
25 Mar	Czechoslovakia 2, England 2	(Int. friendly)
5 Apr	Portsmouth 1, Liverpool 1	(FA Cup semi-final)
13 Apr	Portsmouth 0, Liverpool 0	(FA Cup semi-final replay – Liverpool won on penalties)

29 Apr	CIS 2, England 2	(Int. friendly – Moscow)
9 May	Liverpool 2, Sunderland 0	(FA Cup final)
17 May	England 1, Brazil 1	(Int. friendly)
3 Jun	Finland 1, England 2	(Int. friendly)

EUROPEAN CHAMPIONSHIPS IN SWEDEN

11 Jun	England 0, Denmark 0	(Malmö)
12 Jun	Holland 1, Scotland 0	(Gothenburg)
14 Jun	Sweden 1, Denmark 0	(Stockholm)
15 Jun	Holland 0, CIS 0	(Gothenburg)
17 Jun	France 1, Denmark 2	(Malmö)
18 Jun	Scotland 3, CIS 0	(Norrköping)
21 Jun	Germany 3, Sweden 2	(Stockholm semi-final)
22 Jun	Denmark 2, Holland 2 (pens)	(Gothenburg semi-final)
26 Jun	Denmark 2, Germany 0	(Gothenburg final)

Total: 40 commentaries

1992/93

All matches in the FA Premier League unless otherwise stated

8 Aug	Leeds 4, Liverpool 3	(Charity Shield – my 10th)
15 Aug	Leeds 2, Wimbledon 1	
22 Aug	Sheffield Wed. 3, Chelsea 3	
29 Aug	Coventry 0, Blackburn 2	
5 Sep	Tottenham 2, Everton 1	
9 Sep	Spain 1, England 0	(Int. friendly)
12 Sep	Arsenal 0, Blackburn 1	
16 Sep	Liverpool 6, Apollon Cyprus 1	(European Cup Winners' Cup, 1st round, 1st leg)
26 Sep	Manchester Utd 0, QPR 0	

3 Oct	Ipswich 4, Leeds 2
14 Oct	England 1, Norway 1 (World Cup qualifier)
17 Oct	Everton 1, Coventry 1
24 Oct	QPR 2, Leeds 1
7 Nov	Aston Villa 1, Manchester Utd 0
14 Nov	Kingstonian 1, Peterborough 1 (FA Cup 1st round)
18 Nov	Scotland 0, Italy 0 (World Cup qualifier)
21 Nov	Crystal Palace 1, Nottingham Forest 1
28 Nov	Arsenal 0, Manchester Utd 1
5 Dec	Sheffield Wed. 1, Aston Villa 2
3 Jan	Nottingham Forest 2, Southampton 1 (FA Cup 3rd round)
9 Jan	Manchester Utd 4, Tottenham 1
16 Jan	Southampton 1, Crystal Palace 0
23 Jan	QPR 1, Manchester City 2 (FA Cup 4th round)
27 Jan	Aston Villa 3, Sheffield Utd 1
30 Jan	Chelsea 0, Sheffield Wed. 2
3 Feb	Wimbledon 0, Aston Villa 0 (FA Cup 4th round replay – after extra time Wimbledon won on penalties)
6 Feb	Aston Villa 2, Ipswich 0
13 Feb	Arsenal 2, Nottingham Forest 0 (FA Cup 5th round)
14 Feb	Sheffield 2, Manchester Utd 1 (FA Cup 5th round)
17 Feb	England 6, San Marino 0 (World Cup qualifier)
20 Feb	Aston Villa 2, Everton 1
6 Mar	Ipswich 2, Arsenal 4 (FA Cup 6th round)
8 Mar	Derby 3, Sheffield Wed. 3 (FA Cup 6th round)
10 Mar	Aston Villa 0, Tottenham 0
13 Mar	Norwich 1, Oldham 0
17 Mar	Sheffield Wed. 1, Derby 0 (FA Cup 6th round replay)
24 Mar	Manchester Utd 0, Arsenal 0
4 Apr	Arsenal 1, Tottenham 0 (FA Cup semi-final)
17 Apr	Manchester Utd 3, Chelsea 0
21 Apr	Crystal Palace 0, Manchester Utd 2

28 Apr	England 2, Holland 2	(World Cup qualifier)
3 May	Manchester Utd 3, Blackburn 1	
15 May	Arsenal 1, Sheffield Wed. 1	(FA Cup final – my 16th)
20 May	Arsenal 2, Sheffield Wed. 1	(FA Cup final replay – my 5th)
2 Jun	Norway 2, England 0	(World Cup qualifier)

Total: 45 commentaries

1993/94

All matches in the FA Carling Premiership unless otherwise stated

7 Aug	Manchester Utd 1, Arsenal 1	(Charity Shield – my 11th)
14 Aug	Liverpool 2, Sheffield Wed. 0	
21 Aug	Leeds 0, Norwich 4	
28 Aug	Aston Villa 1, Tottenham Hotspur 0	
8 Sep	Wales 2, RCS 2	(World Cup qualifier)
11 Sep	Chelsea 1, Manchester Utd 0	
15 Sep	Norwich 3, Vitesse Arnhem 0	(UEFA Cup, 1st round, 1st leg)
29 Sep	Vitesse Arnhem 0, Norwich 0	(UEFA Cup, 1st round, 2nd leg)
2 Oct	Liverpool 0, Arsenal 0	
16 Oct	Newcastle 1, QPR 2	
19 Oct	Bayern Munich 1, Norwich 2	(UEFA Cup, 2nd round, 1st leg)
23 Oct	Sheffield Utd 1, Sheffield Wed. 1	
3 Nov	Norwich 1, Bayern Munich 1	(UEFA Cup, 2nd round, 2nd leg)
6 Nov	Arsenal 1, Aston Villa 2	
13 Nov	Marlow 0, Plymouth 2	(FA Cup 1st round)
17 Nov	San Marino 1, England 7	(World Cup qualifier)
4 Dec	Manchester Utd 2, Norwich 2	

18 Dec	Leeds 2, Arsenal 1
29 Dec	Norwich 1, Aston Villa 2
1 Jan	Aston Villa 0, Blackburn 1
8 Jan	Bristol City 1 Liverpool 1 (FA Cup 3rd round – abandoned)
9 Jan	Sheffield Utd 0, Manchester Utd 1 (FA Cup 3rd round)
15 Jan	Tottenham 0, Manchester Utd 1
19 Jan	Bristol City 1, Liverpool 1 (FA Cup 3rd round)
22 Jan	Chelsea 1, Aston Villa 1
29 Jan	Charlton 0, Blackburn 0 (FA Cup 4th round)
31 Jan	Bolton 2, Arsenal 2 (FA Cup 4th round)
9 Feb	Arsenal 1, Bolton 3 (FA Cup 4th round replay)
12 Feb	Tottenham 0, Blackburn 2
19 Feb	Wolverhampton 1, Ipswich 1 (FA Cup 5th round)
20 Feb	Bolton 1, Aston Villa 0 (FA Cup 5th round)
26 Feb	West Ham 2, Manchester Utd 2
2 Mar	Charlton 2, Bristol City 0 (FA Cup 5th round replay)
5 Mar	Tottenham 2, Sheffield Utd 2
9 Mar	England 1, Denmark 0 (Int. friendly)
12 Mar	Manchester Utd 3, Charlton 1 (FA Cup 6th round)
26 Mar	Wimbledon 1, Leeds 0
30 Mar	Manchester Utd 1, Liverpool 0
4 Apr	Manchester Utd 3, Oldham 2
10 Apr	Manchester Utd 1, Oldham 1 (FA Cup semi-final)
13 Apr	Manchester Utd 4, Oldham 1 (FA Cup semi-final replay)
30 Apr	Liverpool 0, Norwich 1
4 May	Manchester Utd 4, Southampton 0
14 May	Manchester Utd 4, Chelsea 0 (FA Cup final – my 17th)
17 May	England 5, Greece 0 (Int. friendly)

WORLD CUP IN USA

18 Jun	USA 1, Switzerland 1	(Detroit)
20 Jun	Brazil 2, Russia 0	(San Francisco)
21 Jun	Germany 1, Spain 1	(Chicago)
23 Jun	Italy 1, Norway 0	(New York)
25 Jun	Argentina 2, Nigeria 1	(Boston)
28 Jun	Ireland 0, Norway 0	(New York)
30 Jun	Greece 0, Nigeria 2	(Boston)
3 Jul	Romania 3, Argentina 2	(Los Angeles)
5 Jul	Bulgaria 1, Mexico 1 (pens)	(New York)
10 Jul	Germany 1, Bulgaria 2	(New York)
13 Jul	Italy 3, Bulgaria 1	(New York)

Total: 56 commentaries

1994/95

All matches in FA Carling Premiership unless otherwise stated

14 Aug	Manchester Utd 2, Blackburn 0	(Charity Shield – my 12th)
20 Aug	Manchester Utd 2, QPR 0	
27 Aug	Tottenham 0, Manchester Utd 1	
7 Sep	England 2, USA 0	(Int. friendly)
13 Sep	Blackburn 0, Trelleborg 1	(UEFA Cup, 1st round, 1st leg)
24 Sep	Blackburn 3, Aston Villa 1	
27 Sep	Trelleborg 2, Blackburn 2	(UEFA Cup, 1st round, 2nd leg)
8 Oct	Southampton 2, Everton 0	
15 Oct	Crystal Palace 0, Newcastle 1	
22 Oct	Manchester City 5, Tottenham 2	
12 Nov	Kidderminster 1, Torquay 1	(FA Cup 1st round)
16 Nov	England 1, Nigeria 0	(Int. friendly)
19 Nov	Wimbledon 3, Newcastle 2	
26 Nov	Chelsea 0, Everton 1	

3 Dec	Tottenham 4, Newcastle 2
28 Dec	Manchester Utd 1, Leicester 1
2 Jan	Tottenham 1, Arsenal 0
7 Jan	Walsall 1, Leeds 1 (FA Cup 3rd round)
8 Jan	Newcastle 1, Blackburn 1 (FA Cup 3rd round)
14 Jan	Blackburn 3, Nottingham Forest 0
28 Jan	Luton 1, Southampton 1 (FA Cup 4th round)
30 Jan	Sheffield Wed. 0, Wolverhampton 0 (FA Cup 4th round)
4 Feb	Manchester Utd 1, Aston Villa 0
8 Feb	Southampton 6, Luton 0 (FA Cup 4th round replay)
11 Feb	Manchester City 0, Manchester Utd 3
18 Feb	Wolverhampton 1, Leicester 0 (FA Cup 5th round)
19 Feb	Manchester Utd 3, Leeds 1 (FA Cup 5th round)
1 Mar	Southampton 2, Tottenham 6 (FA Cup 5th round replay)
4 Mar	Aston Villa 0, Blackburn 2
8 Mar	Blackburn 3, Arsenal 1
11 Mar	Liverpool 1, Tottenham 2 (FA Cup 6th round)
1 Apr	Everton 1, Blackburn 2
9 Apr	Everton 4, Tottenham 1 (FA Cup semi-final)
15 Apr	Leicester 0, Manchester Utd 4
29 Apr	Arsenal 1, Tottenham 1
6 May	Crystal Palace 1, West Ham 0
10 May	West Ham 3, Liverpool 0
14 May	Liverpool 2, Blackburn 1
6 June	Brazil 3, Japan 0 (Umbro Cup)
8 June	England 3, Sweden 3 (Umbro Cup)

Total: 40 Commentaries

1995/96

In August and September, I took a two month 'sabbatical' and did not start work again until October. Matches are in Premiership unless otherwise stated.

11 Oct	Norway 0, England 0 (Int. friendly)
14 Oct	Manchester Utd 0, Manchester City 0
17 Oct	Brondby 0, Liverpool 0 (UEFA Cup, 2nd round, 1st leg)
21 Oct	West Ham 1, Blackburn 1
28 Oct	Manchester Utd 2, Middlesbrough 0
31 Oct	Liverpool 0, Brondby 1 (UEFA Cup, 2nd round, 2nd leg)
4 Nov	Newcastle 2, Liverpool 1
15 Nov	England 3, Switzerland 1 (Int. friendly)
18 Nov	Tottenham 2, Arsenal 1
21 Nov	Nottingham Forest 1, Lyon 0 (UEFA Cup, 3rd round, 1st leg)
25 Nov	Newcastle 2, Leeds Utd 1
5 Dec	Lyon 0, Nottingham Forest 0 (UEFA Cup 3rd round, 2nd leg)
13 Dec	Holland 2, Republic of Ireland 0 (Euro Championship play-off)
16 Dec	Arsenal 1, Chelsea 1
30 Dec	Chelsea 2, Liverpool 2
6 Jan	Tranmere 0, QPR 2 (FA Cup 3rd round)
13 Jan	Tottenham 1, Manchester City 0
27 Jan	Reading 0, Manchester Utd 3 (FA Cup 4th round)
31 Jan	Aston Villa 0, Liverpool 2 (my 1,000th game)
3 Feb	Newcastle 2, Sheffield Wed. 0
7 Feb	Wolverhampton 0, Tottenham 2 (FA Cup 4th round replay)
18 Feb	Manchester Utd 2, Manchester City 1 (FA Cup 5th round)
24 Feb	Southampton 2, Chelsea 3
28 Feb	Chelsea 4, Grimsby 1 (FA Cup 5th round replay)
5 Mar	Bayern Munich 2, Nottingham Forest 1 (UEFA Cup quarter-final, 1st leg)

9 Mar	Chelsea 2, Wimbledon 2	(FA Cup 6th round)
19 Mar	Nottingham Forest 1, Bayern Munich 5	(UEFA Cup quarter-final, second leg)
20 Mar	Wimbledon 1, Chelsea 3	(FA Cup 6th round replay)
23 Mar	Arsenal 2, Newcastle 0	
27 Mar	England 1, Bulgaria 0	(Int. friendly)
31 Mar	Manchester Utd 2, Chelsea 1	(FA Cup semi-final)
6 Apr	Manchester City 2, Manchester Utd 3	
13 Apr	Southampton 3, Manchester Utd 1	
17 Apr	Newcastle 1, Manchester Utd 0	
27 Apr	Bolton 0, Southampton 1	
5 May	Middlesbrough 0, Manchester Utd 3	

EUROPEAN CHAMPIONSHIP

9 Jun	Germany 2, Czech Republic 0	(Manchester)
10 Jun	Holland 0, Scotland 0	(Villa Park)
11 Jun	Italy 2, Russia 1	(Liverpool)
15 Jun	England 2, Scotland 0	(Wembley)
18 Jun	France 3, Bulgaria 1	(Newcastle)
19 Jun	Croatia 0, Portugal 3	(Nottingham)
23 Jun	Czech Republic 1, Portugal 0	(Villa Park)
26 Jun	France 0, Czech Republic 0 (Czech won on pens)	(Manchester)
30 June	Germany 2, Czech Republic 1 (Germany won on the 'golden goal' in extra time.)	(Wembley)

Total: 45 commentaries

1996/97

17 Aug	Wimbledon 0, Manchester Utd 3
21 Aug	Chelsea 1, Middlesbrough 0
24 Aug	West Ham 2, Southampton 1
1 Sep	Moldova 0, England 3 (World Cup qualifier)
7 Sep	Leeds 0, Manchester Utd 4
14 Sep	Newcastle 2, Blackburn 1
21 Sep	Liverpool 5, Chelsea 1
28 Sep	Everton 2, Sheffield Wed. 0
9 Oct	Republic of Ireland 3, Macedonia 0 (World Cup qualifier)
15 Oct	Ferencvaros 3, Newcastle 2 (UEFA Cup, 2nd round, 1st leg)
19 Oct	Nottingham Forest 1, Derby 1 (25 years with MOTD)
29 Oct	Newcastle 4, Ferencvaros 0 (UEFA Cup, 2nd round, 2nd leg)
2 Nov	Manchester Utd 1, Chelsea 2
9 Nov	Georgia 0, England 2 (World Cup qualifier)
20 Nov	Liverpool 1, Everton 1
23 Nov	Coventry 1, Aston Villa 2
3 Dec	Newcastle 2, Metz 0 (UEFA Cup, 3rd round, 2nd leg)
7 Dec	Arsenal 2, Derby 2
14 Dec	Liverpool 5, Middlesbrough 1
4 Jan	Birmingham 2, Stevenage 0 (FA Cup 3rd round)
11 Jan	Aston Villa 2, Newcastle 2
25 Jan	Coventry 1, Woking 1 (FA Cup 3rd round)
26 Jan	Chelsea 4, Liverpool 2 (FA Cup 4th round)
1 Feb	Leeds 0, Arsenal 0
4 Feb	Woking 1, Coventry 2 (FA Cup 3rd round replay)
12 Feb	England 0, Italy 1 (World Cup qualifier)
15 Feb	Chesterfield 1, Nottingham Forest 0 (FA Cup 5th round)
19 Feb	Arsenal 1, Manchester Utd 2
26 Feb	Derby 3, Coventry 2 (FA Cup 5th round)
4 Mar	Newcastle 0, Monaco 1 (UEFA Cup, quarter-final, 1st leg)

8 Mar	Derby 0, Middlesbrough 2	(FA Cup 6th round)
18 Mar	Monaco 3, Newcastle 0	(UEFA Cup, quarter-final, 2nd leg)
22 Mar	Coventry 1, West Ham 3	
29 Mar	England 2, Mexico 0	(Int. friendly)
5 Apr	Manchester Utd 2, Derby 3	
12 Apr	Arsenal 2, Leicester City 0	
13 Apr	Chelsea 3, Wimbledon 0	(FA Cup semi-final)
3 May	Liverpool 2, Tottenham 1	
5 May	Manchester Utd 3, Middlesbrough 3	
11 May	Wimbledon 1, Sunderland 0	
17 May	Chelsea 2, Middlesborough 0	(FA Cup final)

Total: 41 commentaries

1997/98

9 Aug	Wimbledon 1, Liverpool 1	
13 Aug	Manchester Utd 1, Southampton 0	
23 Aug	Newcastle 1, Aston Villa 0	
30 Aug	Chelsea 4, Southampton 2	
13 Sep	Newcastle 1, Wimbledon 3	
16 Sep	Celtic 2, Liverpool 2	(UEFA Cup, 1st round, 1st leg)
20 Sep	Bolton 0, Manchester Utd 0	
27 Sep	Chelsea 1, Newcastle 0	
30 Sep	Liverpool 0, Celtic 0	(UEFA Cup, 1st round, 2nd leg)
18 Oct	Everton 2, Liverpool 0	
25 Oct	Coventry 0, Everton 0	
8 Nov	Liverpool 4, Tottenham 0	
22 Nov	Sheffield Wed. 2, Arsenal 0	
29 Nov	West Ham 2, Aston Villa 1	
6 Dec	Liverpool 1, Manchester Utd 3	
13 Dec	Chelsea 0, Leeds 0	
3 Jan	Watford 1, Sheffield Wed. 1	(FA Cup 3rd round)

17 Jan	Leicester 0, Liverpool 0	
24 Jan	Middlesbrough 1, Arsenal 2	(FA Cup 4th round)
26 Jan	Sheffield Wed. 0, Blackburn 3	(FA Cup 4th round)
31 Jan	Liverpool 0, Blackburn 0	
7 Feb	Derby 0, Aston Villa 1	
14 Feb	West Ham 2, Blackburn 2	(FA Cup 5th round)
15 Feb	Manchester Utd 1, Barnsley 1	(FA Cup 5th round)
21 Feb	Leicester 2, Chelsea 0	
3 Mar	Atletico Madrid 1, Aston Villa 0	(UEFA Cup quarter-final, 1st leg)
7 Mar	Coventry 1, Sheffield Utd 1	(FA Cup 6th round)
28 Mar	Crystal Palace 1, Tottenham 3	
4 Apr	Tottenham 1, Everton 1	
5 Apr	Newcastle 1, Sheffield Utd 0	(FA Cup semi-final)
11 Apr	Bolton 2, Blackburn 1	
13 Apr	Blackburn 1, Arsenal 4	
2 May	Wimbledon 2, Tottenham 6	
3 May	Arsenal 4, Everton 0	
10 May	Everton 1, Coventry 1	
16 May	Arsenal 2, Newcastle 0	(FA Cup final – my 19th)

WORLD CUP IN FRANCE

11 Jun	Austria 1, Cameroon 1	(Toulouse)
13 Jun	Holland 0, Belgium 0	(Paris)
15 Jun	Germany 2, USA 0	(Paris)
16 Jun	Scotland 1, Norway 1	(Bordeaux)
18 Jun	France 4, Saudi Arabia 0	(Paris)
20 Jun	Belgium 2, Mexico 2	(Bordeaux)
22 Jun	Colombia 0, Tunisia 0	(Montpellier)
23 Jun	Norway 2, Brazil 1	(Marseilles)

24 Jun	France 2, Denmark 1	(Lyon)
26 Jun	England 2, Colombia 0	(Lens)
27 Jun	Brazil 4, Chile 1	(Paris)
30 Jun	Croatia 1, Romania 0	(Bordeaux)
4 Jul	Croatia 3, Germany 0	(Lyon)
8 Jul	France 2, Croatia 1	(Paris)
12 Jul	France 3, Brazil 0	(Paris)

Total: 51 commentaries

1998/99

15 Aug	Newcastle 0, Charlton 0	
28 Aug	Chelsea 1, Real Madrid 0	(European Super Cup)
9 Sep	Liverpool 2, Coventry 0	
12 Sep	West Ham 2, Liverpool 1	
15 Sep	Blackburn 0, Olympique Lyon 1	(UEFA Cup, 1st round, 1st leg)
19 Sep	Olympique Lyon 2, Blackburn 2	(UEFA Cup, 1st round, 2nd leg)
3 Oct	Southampton 0, Manchester Utd 3	
14 Oct	Luxembourg 0, England 3	(Euro Championship qualifier)
17 Oct	West Ham 0, Aston Villa 0	
24 Oct	Tottenham 2, Newcastle 0	
7 Nov	Aston Villa 3, Tottenham 2	
21 Nov	Aston Villa 2, Liverpool 4	
28 Nov	Chelsea 1, Sheffield Wed. 1	
5 Dec	Aston Villa 1, Manchester Utd 1	
28 Dec	Liverpool 4, Newcastle 2	
2 Jan	Bristol City 0, Everton 2	(FA Cup 3rd round)
16 Jan	Tottenham 0, Wimbledon 0	

23 Jan	Portsmouth 1, Leeds 5	(FA Cup 4th round)
30 Jan	Coventry 2, Liverpool 1	
6 Feb	Aston Villa 1, Blackburn 3	
13 Feb	Sheffield Wed. 0, Chelsea 1	(FA Cup 5th round)
27 Feb	Chelsea 2, Liverpool 1	
6 Mar	Arsenal 1, Derby 0	(FA Cup 6th round)
13 Mar	Chelsea 0, West Ham 1	
3 Apr	Wimbledon 1, Manchester Utd 1	
5 Apr	West Ham 0, Charlton 1	
10 Apr	Aston Villa 3, Southampton 0	
22 Apr	Real Mallorca 1, Chelsea 0	(European Cup Winners' Cup, 2nd leg)
1 May	Chelsea 3, Everton 1	
5 May	Tottenham 1, Arsenal 3	
16 May	Arsenal 1, Aston Villa 0	
19 May	Real Mallorca 1, Lazio 2	(European Cup Winners' Cup final)
22 May	Manchester Utd 2, Newcastle 0	(FA Cup final – my 20th)

Total: 33 commentaries

1999/2000

7 Aug	Chelsea 4, Sunderland 0	
14 Aug	Tottenham 3, Everton 2	
21 Aug	Coventry 2, Derby 0	
25 Aug	Newcastle 1, Sunderland 2	
28 Aug	Tottenham 1, Leeds 2	
8 Sep	Poland 0, England 0	(Euro Championship qualifier)
18 Sep	Leicester 2, Liverpool 2	
25 Sep	Manchester Utd 3, Southampton 3	

2 Oct	Aston Villa 0, Liverpool 0	
16 Oct	Leicester 2, Southampton 1	
23 Oct	Tottenham 3, Manchester Utd 1	
13 Nov	Scotland 0, England 2	(Euro Championship play-off)
20 Nov	Everton 1, Chelsea 1	
27 Nov	West Ham 1, Liverpool 0	
4 Dec	Manchester Utd 5, Everton 1	
11 Dec	Hereford 0, Leicester 0	(FA Cup 3rd round)
14 Dec	Arsenal 3, Nantes 0	(UEFA Cup, 3rd round, 1st leg)
26 Dec	Newcastle 2, Liverpool 2	
28 Dec	West Ham 1, Derby 1	
3 Jan	Wimbledon 1, Sunderland 0	
8 Jan	Tranmere 1, Sunderland 0	(FA Cup 4th round)
15 Jan	Watford 1, Liverpool 2	
22 Jan	Aston Villa 0, Chelsea 0	
29 Jan	Gillingham 3, Sheffield Wed. 1	(FA Cup 5th round)
12 Feb	Leeds 1, Tottenham 0	
20 Feb	Chelsea 5, Gillingham 0	(FA Cup 6th round)
26 Feb	Middlesbrough 0, Leeds 0	
4 Mar	Manchester Utd 1, Liverpool 1	
11 Mar	Liverpool 1, Sunderland 1	
25 Mar	Bradford 0, Manchester Utd 4	
1 Apr	Leeds 0, Chelsea 1	
9 Apr	Chelsea 2, Newcastle 1	(FA Cup semi-final)
22 Apr	Tottenham 2, Wimbledon 0	
29 Apr	Chelsea 2, Liverpool 0	
6 May	Leicester 3, Bradford 0	
14 May	Southampton 2, Wimbledon 0	
20 May	Chelsea 1, Aston Villa 0	(FA Cup final – my 21st)

EURO 2000 IN HOLLAND & BELGIUM

11 Jun	Holland 1, Czech Republic 0
12 Jun	Germany 1, Romania 1
13 Jun	Yugoslavia 3, Slovenia 3
17 Jun	England 1, Germany 0
19 Jun	Italy 2, Sweden 1
21 Jun	Spain 4, Yugoslavia 3
25 Jun	France 2, Spain 1 (quarter-final)
28 Jun	France 2, Portugal 1 (semi-final – Golden Goal in extra time)
2 Jul	France 2, Italy 1 (Final – Golden Goal in extra time)

Total: 46 commentaries

2000/01

19 Aug	Charlton 4, Manchester City 0
23 Aug	Newcastle 3, Derby 2
26 Aug	Middlesbrough 1, Leeds 2
6 Sep	Liverpool 3, Aston Villa 1
9 Sep	Coventry 0, Leeds 0
16 Sep	Everton 1, Manchester Utd 3
23 Sep	Ipswich 1, Arsenal 1
28 Sep	Liverpool 0, Rapid Bucharest 0 (UEFA Cup, 1st round, 2nd leg)
30 Sep	Manchester City 0, Newcastle 1
11 Oct	Finland 0, England 0 (World Cup qualifier)
14 Oct	Leicester 0, Manchester Utd 3
21 Oct	Liverpool 1, Leicester 0
26 Oct	Liverpool 1, Slovan Liberec 0 (UEFA Cup, 2nd Round, 1st leg)
28 Oct	West Ham 1, Newcastle 0
4 Nov	Coventry 1, Manchester Utd 2

18 Nov	Leeds 0, West Ham 1
25 Nov	Everton 2, Chelsea 1
2 Dec	Leicester 3, Leeds 1
9 Dec	Southampton 1, Leeds 0
30 Dec	Newcastle 1, Manchester Utd 1
1 Jan	Liverpool 2, Southampton 1
6 Jan	Leyton Orient 0, Tottenham 1 (FA Cup 3rd round)
13 Jan	Arsenal 1, Chelsea 1
27 Jan	QPR 0, Arsenal 6 (FA Cup 4th round)
31 Jan	Sunderland 0, Manchester Utd 1
3 Feb	Coventry 0, Arsenal 1
10 Feb	Chelsea 1, Manchester Utd 1
15 Feb	Roma 0, Liverpool 2 (UEFA Cup, 4th round, 1st leg)
17 Feb	Wycombe 2, Wimbledon 2 (FA Cup 5th round)
22 Feb	Liverpool 0, Roma 1 (UEFA Cup, 4th round, 2nd leg)
3 Mar	Leicester 2, Liverpool 0
10 Mar	Arsenal 3, Blackburn 0 (FA Cup 6th round)
31 Mar	Arsenal 2, Tottenham 0
7 Apr	Leicester 1, Coventry 3
14 Apr	Arsenal 0, Middlesbrough 3
16 Apr	Coventry 1, Sunderland 0
28 Apr	Coventry 0, Liverpool 2
12 May	Liverpool 2, Arsenal 1 (FA Cup final – my 22nd)
19 May	Derby 1, Ipswich 1
6 Jun	Greece 0, England 2 (World Cup qualifier)

Total: 40 commentaries

2001/2002

12 Aug	Liverpool 2, Manchester Utd 1 (Charity Shield)
15 Aug	England 0, Holland 2 (Int. friendly)
1 Sep	Germany 1, England 5 (World Cup qualifier)

| 15 Sep | Newcastle 4, Manchester Utd 3 | (Radio Five Live) |

15 Sep   Newcastle 4, Manchester Utd 3   (Radio Five Live)

22 Sep   Arsenal 1, Bolton 1   (Radio Five Live)

29 Sep   Tottenham 3, Manchester Utd 5   (Radio Five Live)

6 Oct   England 2, Greece 2   (World Cup qualifier)

18 Oct   Ipswich 0, Helsingborg 0   (UEFA Cup, 2nd round, 1st leg)

1 Nov   Helsingborg 1, lpswich 3   (UEFA Cup, 2nd round, 2nd leg)

4 Nov   Arsenal 2, Charlton 4   (Radio Five Live)

10 Nov   England 1, Sweden 1   (Int. friendly)

18 Nov   Hereford 1, Wrexham 0   (FA Cup 1st round)

24 Nov   Chelsea 0, Blackburn 0   (Radio Five Live)

5 Jan   Dagenham & Redbridge 1, lpswich 4   (FA Cup 3rd round)

6 Jan   Aston Villa 2, Manchester Utd 3   (FA Cup 3rd round)

13 Jan   Southampton 1, Manchester Utd 3   (Radio Five Live)

16 Jan   Coventry 0, Tottenham 2   (FA Cup 3rd round)

26 Jan   Chelsea 1, West Ham 1   (FA Cup 4th round)

27 Jan   Ipswich 1, Manchester City 4   (FA Cup 4th round)

6 Feb   West Ham 2, Chelsea 3   (FA Cup 4th round replay)

13 Feb   Holland 1, England 1   (Int. friendly)

16 Feb   Arsenal 5, Gillingham 2   (FA Cup 5th round)

17 Feb   Newcastle 1, Manchester City 0   (FA Cup 5th round)

10 Mar   Middlesbrough 3, Everton 0   (FA Cup 6th round)

14 Apr   Chelsea 1, Fulham 0   (FA Cup semi-final)

17 Apr   England 4, Paraguay 0   (Int. friendly)

4 May   Arsenal 2, Chelsea 0   (FA Cup Final – my 23rd)

26 May   England 2, Cameroon 2   (Int. friendly)

WORLD CUP FINALS

31 May   France 0, Senegal 1   (Seoul)

2 Jun   Argentina 1, Nigeria 0   (Ibaraki)

3 Jun   Mexico 1, Croatia 0   (Niigata)

5 Jun   Ireland 1, Germany 1   (Ibaraki)

7 Jun   England 1, Argentina 0   (Sapporo)

9 Jun	Mexico 2, Ecuador 1	(Miyagi)
12 Jun	England 0, Nigeria 0	(Osaka)
13 Jun	Mexico 1, Italy 1	(Ouita)
15 Jun	England 3, Denmark 0	(Niigata)
17 Jun	Brazil 2, Belgium 0	(Kobe)
21 Jun	Brazil 2, England 1	(Shizuoka)
26 Jun	Brazil 1, Turkey 0	(Saitama)
30 Jun	Brazil 2, Germany 0	(Yokohama)

Total: 41 commentaries

2002/03

14 Aug	Zalaegerszeg 1, Manchester Utd 0	(Champions League qualifier, 1st leg)
18 Aug	Aston Villa 0, Liverpool 1	(Radio Five Live)
28 Aug	Manchester Utd 5, Zalaegerszeg 0	(Champions League qualifier, 2nd leg)
14 Sep	Chelsea 3, Newcastle 0	(Radio Five Live)
23 Sep	Fulham 0, Chelsea 0	(Radio Five Live)
12 Oct	Slovakia 1, England 2	(Euro Championship qualifier)
16 Oct	England 2, Macedonia 2	(Euro Championship qualifier)
20 Oct	Charlton 1, Middlesbrough 0	(Radio Five Live)
31 Oct	Celtic 1, Blackburn 0	(UEFA Cup, 2nd round, 1st leg)
3 Nov	Fulham 0, Arsenal 1	(Radio Five Live)
14 Nov	Blackburn 0, Celtic 2	(UEFA Cup, 2nd round, 2nd leg)
17 Nov	Forest Green 0, Exeter 0	(FA Cup 1st round)
24 Nov	Tottenham 2, Leeds 0	(Radio Five Live)
7 Dec	Margate 0, Cardiff 3	(FA Cup 2nd round)
15 Dec	Tottenham 1, Arsenal 1	(Radio Five Live)
4 Jan	Southampton 4, Tottenham 0	(FA Cup 3rd round)
12 Jan	Tottenham 4, Everton 3	(Radio Five Live)
19 Jan	Fulham 1, Middlesbrough 0	(Radio Five Live)

26 Jan	Manchester Utd 6, West Ham 0	(FA Cup 4th round)
2 Feb	West Ham 0, Liverpool 3	(Radio Five Live)
5 Feb	Millwall 1, Southampton 2	(FA Cup 4th round replay)
15 Feb	Manchester Utd 0, Arsenal 2	(FA Cup 5th round)
27 Feb	Liverpool 2, Auxerre 0	(UEFA Cup, 4th round, 2nd leg)
2 Mar	Arsenal 2, Charlton 0	(Radio Five Live)
9 Mar	Watford 2, Burnley 0	(FA Cup 6th round)
22 Mar	West Ham 2, Sunderland 0	(Radio Five Live)
2 Apr	England 2, Turkey 0	(Euro Championship qualifier)
13 Apr	Arsenal 1, Sheffield United 0	(FA Cup semi-final)
3 May	Southampton 0, Bolton 0	(Radio Five Live)
17 May	Arsenal 1, Southampton 0	(FA Cup final – my 24th)
11 Jun	England 2, Slovakia 1	(Euro Championship qualifier)

Total: 31 commentaries

2003/2004

16 Aug	Portsmouth 2, Aston Villa 1	(Radio Five Live)
20 Aug	England 3, Croatia 1	(Int. friendly)
30 Aug	Wolverhampton 0, Portsmouth 0	(Radio Five Live)
6 Sep	Macedonia 1, England 2	(Euro Championship qualifier)
10 Sep	England 2, Liechtenstein 0	(Euro Championship qualifier)
15 Sep	Leicester 4, Leeds 0	(Radio Five Live)
28 Sep	Charlton 3, Liverpool 2	(Radio Five Live)
9 Nov	Chelsea 5, Newcastle 0	(Radio Five Live)
16 Nov	England 2, Denmark 3	(Int. friendly)
23 Nov	Tottenham 2, Aston Villa 1	(Radio Five Live)
7 Dec	Southampton 3, Charlton 2	(Radio Five Live)
3 Jan	Southampton 0, Newcastle 3	(FA Cup 3rd round)
11 Jan	Leicester 0, Chelsea 4	(Radio Five Live)
14 Jan	Leicester 1, Manchester City 3	(FA Cup 3rd round replay)
24 Jan	Arsenal 4, Middlesbrough 1	(FA Cup 4th round)

25 Jan	Manchester City 1, Tottenham 1	(FA Cup 4th round)
1 Feb	Arsenal 2, Manchester City 1	(Radio Five Live)
8 Feb	Chelsea 1, Charlton 0	(Radio Five Live)
14 Feb	Fulham 0, West Ham 0	(FA Cup 5th round)
15 Feb	Arsenal 2, Chelsea 1	(FA Cup 5th round)
18 Feb	Portugal 1, England 1	(Int. Friendly)
24 Feb	West Ham 0, Fulham 3	(FA Cup 5th round replay)
7 Mar	Millwall 0, Tranmere 0	(FA Cup 6th round)
31 Mar	Sweden 1, England 0	(Int. Friendly)
3 Apr	Manchester Utd 1, Arsenal 0	(FA Cup semi-final)
12 Apr	Tottenham 1, Manchester City 1	(Radio Five Live)
1 May	Arsenal 0, Birmingham 0	(Radio Five Live)
22 May	Manchester Utd 3, Millwall 0	(FA Cup final – my 25th)

2004 EUROPEAN CHAMPIONSHIPS

12 Jun	Spain 1, Russia 0	(Faro)
13 Jun	England 1, France 2	(Lisbon)
15 Jun	Holland 1, Germany 1	(Porto)
17 Jun	England 3, Switzerland 0	(Coimbra)
19 Jun	Holland 2, Czech Republic 3	(Aveire)
21 Jun	England 4, Croatia 2	(Lisbon)
24 Jun	England 2, Portugal 2 at extra time	
	Portugal on penalties	quarter-final (Lisbon)
26 Jun	Sweden 0, Holland 0 at extra time	
	Holland on penalties	quarter-final (Faro)
30 Jun	Portugal 2, Holland 1	semi-final (Lisbon)
4 Jul	Greece 1, Portugal 0	final (Lisbon) – (my 7th)

Total: 38 commentaries

2004/05

Match of the Day returned to the BBC after a three-year absence. All games are in Barclays Premiership unless otherwise stated

14 Aug	Tottenham 1, Liverpool 1
18 Aug	England 3, Ukraine 1 (Int. friendly)
21 Aug	Birmingham 0, Chelsea 1
25 Aug	Arsenal 3, Blackburn 0
28 Aug	Aston Villa 4, Newcastle 2
30 Aug	Portsmouth 4, Fulham 3 (Radio Five Live)
11 Sep	Fulham 0, Arsenal 3
13 Sep	Charlton 0, Southampton 0 (Radio Five Live)
25 Sep	Tottenham 0, Manchester Utd 1
2 Oct	Arsenal 4, Charlton 0
9 Oct	England 2, Wales 0 (World Cup qualifier)
16 Oct	Fulham 2, Liverpool 4
18 Oct	Portsmouth 1, Tottenham 0 (Radio Five Live)
24 Oct	Manchester Utd 2, Arsenal 0
30 Oct	West Brom. 1, Chelsea 4
6 Nov	Tottenham 2, Charlton 3
17 Nov	Spain 1, England 0 (Int. friendly)
22 Nov	Aston Villa 1, Tottenham 0 (Radio Five Live)
27 Nov	West Brom. 0, Manchester Utd 3
4 Dec	Aston Villa 1, Liverpool 1
12 Dec	Arsenal 2, Chelsea 2
26 Dec	Arsenal 2, Fulham 0
28 Dec	Portsmouth 0, Chelsea 2
1 Jan	Tottenham 5, Everton 2
4 Jan	Chelsea 2, Middlesbrough 0
8 Jan	Plymouth 1, Everton 3 (FA Cup 3rd round)
15 Jan	Tottenham 0, Chelsea 2
19 Jan	Exeter 0, Manchester Utd 2 (FA Cup 3rd round replay)
29 Jan	Manchester Utd 3, Middlesbrough 0 (FA Cup 4th round)
5 Feb	Liverpool 3, Fulham 1
9 Feb	England 0, Holland 0 (Int. friendly)

12 Feb	Tottenham 3, West Brom. 1	(FA Cup 4th round replay)
14 Feb	Arsenal 5, Crystal Palace 1	(Radio Five Live)
19 Feb	Everton 0, Manchester Utd 2	(FA Cup 5th round)
5 Mar	Crystal Palace 0, Manchester Utd 0	
12 Mar	Southampton 0, Manchester Utd 4	(FA Cup 6th round)
26 Mar	England 4, N. Ireland 0	(World Cup qualifier)
30 Mar	England 2, Azerbaijan 0	(World Cup qualifier)
2 Apr	Southampton 1, Chelsea 3	
17 Apr	Manchester Utd 4, Newcastle 1	(FA Cup semi-final)
20 Apr	Chelsea 0, Arsenal 0	
23 Apr	Chelsea 3, Fulham 1	
1 May	Charlton 0, Manchester Utd 4	(Radio Five Live)
7 May	Chelsea 0, Charlton 0	
15 May	Fulham 6, Norwich 0	
21 May	Arsenal 0, Manchester Utd 0	(FA Cup final – my 26th)
	Arsenal 5–4 on penalties	
28 May	USA 1, England 2	(Int. friendly)
31 May	Colombia 2, England 3	(Int. friendly)

Total: 48 commentaries

2005/06

All games are in Barclays Premiership unless otherwise stated.

13 Aug	West Ham 3, Blackburn 1	
17 Aug	Denmark 4, England 1	(Int. friendly)
21 Aug	Chelsea 1, Arsenal 0	
27 Aug	Tottenham 0, Chelsea 2	
7 Sep	N. Ireland 1, England 0	(World Cup qualifier)
12 Sep	West Ham 4, Aston Villa 0	(Radio Five Live)
17 Sep	Charlton 0, Chelsea 2	
24 Sep	West Ham 0, Arsenal 0	

1 Oct	Fulham 2, Manchester Utd 3
8 Oct	England 1, Austria 0 (World Cup qualifier)
12 Oct	England 2, Poland 1 (World Cup qualifier)
17 Oct	Charlton 1, Fulham 1 (Radio Five Live)
22 Oct	Arsenal 1, Manchester City 0
29 Oct	Tottenham 1, Arsenal 1
12 Nov	England 3, Argentina 2 (Int. friendly)
19 Nov	Charlton 1, Manchester Utd 3
26 Nov	Manchester City 0, Liverpool 1
12 Dec	Tottenham 3, Portsmouth 1 (Radio Five Live)
17 Dec	Aston Villa 0, Manchester Utd 3
18 Dec	Arsenal 0, Chelsea 2
26 Dec	Charlton 0, Arsenal 1
31 Dec	Tottenham 2, Newcastle 0
2 Jan	West Ham 1, Chelsea 3
7 Jan	Luton 3, Liverpool 5 (FA Cup 3rd round)
21 Jan	Birmingham 5, Portsmouth 0
29 Jan	Portsmouth 1, Liverpool 2 (FA Cup 4th round)
1 Feb	Aston Villa 1, Chelsea 1
11 Feb	Portsmouth 1, Manchester Utd 3
18 Feb	Liverpool 1, Manchester Utd 3 (FA Cup 5th round)
25 Feb	Birmingham 1, Sunderland 0
1 Mar	England 2, Uruguay 1 (Int. friendly)
4 Mar	Fulham 0, Arsenal 4
11 Mar	Chelsea 2, Tottenham 1
22 Mar	Chelsea 1, Newcastle 0 (FA Cup 6th round)
25 Mar	Chelsea 2, Manchester City 0
1 Apr	West Brom. 0, Liverpool 2
15 Apr	Arsenal 3, West Brom. 1
17 Apr	Tottenham 1, Manchester Utd 2
22 Apr	Liverpool 2, Chelsea 1 (FA Cup semi-final)
29 Apr	Chelsea 3, Manchester Utd 0
7 May	West Ham 2, Tottenham 1

| 13 May | Liverpool 3, West Ham 3 | (FA Cup final – my 27th; Liverpool won on penalties) |

13 May	Liverpool 3, West Ham 3	(FA Cup final – my 27th;
		Liverpool won on penalties)
30 May	England 3, Hungary 1	(Int. friendly)
3 Jun	England 6, Jamaica 0	(Int. friendly)

2006 WORLD CUP FINALS

10 Jun	England 1, Paraguay 0	(Frankfurt)
12 Jun	Italy 2, Ghana 0	(Hanover)
13 Jun	Brazil 1, Croatia 0	(Berlin)
15 Jun	England 2, Trinidad & Tobago 0	(Nuremberg)
16 Jun	Holland 2, Ivory Coast 1	(Stuttgart)
20 Jun	England 2, Sweden 2	(Cologne)
21 Jun	Portugal 2, Mexico 1	(Gelsenkirchen)
22 Jun	Italy 2, Czech Republic 0	(Hamburg)
25 Jun	England 1, Ecuador 0	(Stuttgart)
1 Jul	England 0, Portugal 0	(Gelsenkirchen – Portugal won on penalties)
5 Jul	France 1, Portugal 0	(Munich)
9 Jul	Italy 1, France 1	(Berlin – Italy won on penalties)

Total: 56 commentaries

2006/2007

All games are in Barclays Premiership unless otherwise stated.

2 Sep	England 5, Andorra 0	(Euro Championship qualifier)
9 Sep	Arsenal 1, Middlesbrough 1	
17 Sep	Chelsea 1, Liverpool 0	
23 Sep	Reading 1, Manchester Utd 1	
25 Sep	Portsmouth 0, Bolton 1	(Radio Five Live)
1 Oct	Everton 1, Manchester City 1	

7 Oct	England 0, Macedonia 0	(Euro Championship qualifier)
14 Oct	Portsmouth 2, West Ham 0	
21 Oct	Aston Villa 1, Fulham 1	
28 Oct	Watford 0, Tottenham 0	
29 Oct	West Ham 2, Blackburn 1	(Radio Five Live)
5 Nov	West Ham 1, Arsenal 0	
18 Nov	Chelsea 1, West Ham 0	
25 Nov	Liverpool 1, Manchester City 0	
2 Dec	Reading 1, Bolton 0	
10 Dec	Chelsea 1, Arsenal 1	
17 Dec	West Ham 1, Manchester Utd 0	(Radio Five Live)
23 Dec	Aston Villa 0, Manchester Utd 3	
26 Dec	West Ham 1, Portsmouth 2	
30 Dec	Chelsea 2, Fulham 2	
1 Jan	Reading 6, West Ham 0	
6 Jan	Liverpool 1, Arsenal 3	(FA Cup 3rd round)
13 Jan	Watford 0, Liverpool 3	
21 Jan	Arsenal 2, Manchester Utd 1	
27 Jan	Manchester Utd 2, Portsmouth 1	(FA Cup 4th round)
31 Jan	Chelsea 3, Blackburn 0	
3 Feb	Charlton 0, Chelsea 1	
7 Feb	England 0, Spain 1	(Int. friendly)
17 Feb	Manchester Utd 1, Reading 1	(FA Cup 5th round)
27 Feb	Reading 2, Manchester Utd 3	(FA Cup 5th round replay)
3 Mar	Portsmouth 0, Chelsea 2	
4 Mar	West Ham 3, Tottenham 4	(Radio Five Live)
11 Mar	Chelsea 3, Tottenham 3	(FA Cup 6th round)
19 Mar	Tottenham 1, Chelsea 2	(FA Cup 6th round replay)
31 Mar	Charlton 1, Wigan 0	
1 Apr	Tottenham 1, Reading 0	(Radio Five Live)
7 Apr	Reading 1, Liverpool 2	

9 Apr	Watford 4, Portsmouth 2
14 Apr	Manchester Utd 4, Watford 1 (FA Cup semi-final)
28 Apr	Chelsea 2, Bolton 2
6 May	Arsenal 1, Chelsea 1
7 May	Charlton 0, Tottenham 2 (Radio Five Live)
13 May	Tottenham 2, Manchester City 1
19 May	Chelsea 1, Manchester Utd 0 (FA Cup Final – my 28th)
31 May	England 1, Brazil 1 (Int. friendly)

Total: 45 commentaries

2007/08

All games are in Barclays Premiership unless otherwise stated.

11 Aug	Derby 2, Portsmouth 2
15 Aug	Reading 1, Chelsea 2
21 Aug	England 1, Germany 2 (Int. friendly)
25 Aug	Arsenal 1, Manchester City 0
8 Sep	England 3, Israel 0 (Euro Championship qualifier)
12 Sep	England 3, Russia 0 (Euro Championship qualifier)
15 Sep	Tottenham 1, Arsenal 3
23 Sep	Manchester Utd 2, Chelsea 0
29 Sep	Chelsea 0, Fulham 0
1 Oct	Tottenham 4, Aston Villa 4 (Radio Five Live)
6 Oct	Aston Villa 1, West Ham 0
13 Oct	England 3, Estonia 0 (Euro Championship qualifier)
27 Oct	Portsmouth 0, West Ham 0
3 Nov	Arsenal 2, Manchester Utd 2
11 Nov	Chelsea 1, Everton 1
21 Nov	England 2, Croatia 3 (Euro Championship qualifier)
24 Nov	Arsenal 2, Wigan 0

25 Nov	West Ham 1, Tottenham 1	(Radio Five Live)
1 Dec	Portsmouth 0, Everton 0	
15 Dec	Fulham 0, Newcastle 1	(Radio Five Live)
16 Dec	Arsenal 1, Chelsea 0	
26 Dec	Derby 1, Liverpool 2	
29 Dec	West Ham 2, Manchester Utd 1	
1 Jan	Fulham 1, Chelsea 2	
5 Jan	Aston Villa 0, Manchester Utd 2	(FA Cup 3rd round)
19 Jan	Reading 0, Manchester Utd 2	
26 Jan	Wigan 1, Chelsea 2	(FA Cup 4th round)
30 Jan	West Ham 1, Liverpool 0	
6 Feb	England 2, Switzerland 1	(Int. friendly)
10 Feb	Manchester Utd 1, Manchester City 2	
16 Feb	Manchester Utd 4, Arsenal 0	(FA Cup 5th round)
23 Feb	Fulham 0, West Ham 1	
8 Mar	Barnsley 1, Chelsea 0	(FA Cup 6th round)
23 Mar	Chelsea 2, Arsenal 1	
29 Mar	Reading 0, Blackburn 0	
5 Apr	Portsmouth 1, West Brom. 0	(FA Cup semi-final)
13 Apr	Manchester Utd 2, Arsenal 1	
14 Apr	Chelsea 1, Wigan 1	(Radio Five Live)
26 Apr	Birmingham 2, Liverpool 2	
28 Apr	West Brom. 1, Southampton 1	(Radio Five Live)
3 May	Fulham 2, Birmingham 0	
11 May	Chelsea 1, Bolton 1	
17 May	Cardiff 0, Portsmouth 1	(FA Cup final – my 29th)
28 May	England 2, USA 0	(Int. friendly)

EUROPEAN CHAMPIONSHIP FINALS

7 Jun	Switzerland 0, Czech Republic 1
9 Jun	Holland 3, Italy 0
11 Jun	Czech Republic 1, Portugal 3
13 Jun	Holland 4, France 1
15 Jun	Switzerland 2, Portugal 0
17 Jun	France 0, Italy 2
22 Jun	Spain 0, Italy 0 (quarter-final – Spain won on penalties)
25 Jun	Germany 3, Turkey 2 (semi-final)
29 Jun	Spain 1, Germany 0 (final)

Total: 53 commentaries

2008/09

All games are in Barclays Premiership unless otherwise stated.

23 Aug	Fulham 1, Arsenal 0
25 Aug	Portsmouth 0, Manchester Utd 1 (Radio Five Live)
30 Aug	West Ham 4, Blackburn 1
15 Sep	Tottenham 1, Aston Villa 2 (Radio Five Live)
21 Sep	Tottenham 0, Wigan 0
27 Sep	Aston Villa 2, Sunderland 1
5 Oct	Chelsea 2, Aston Villa 0
18 Oct	Arsenal 3, Everton 1
25 Oct	West Brom. 0, Hull 3
26 Oct	Tottenham 2, Bolton 0 (Radio Five Live)
29 Oct	Arsenal 4, Tottenham 4
1 Nov	Chelsea 5, Sunderland 0
8 Nov	West Ham 1, Everton 3
9 Nov	Fulham 2, Newcastle 1 (Radio Five Live)
22 Nov	Manchester City 3, Arsenal 0

29 Nov	Aston Villa 0, Fulham 0
8 Dec	West Ham 0, Tottenham 2 (Radio Five Live)
13 Dec	Tottenham 0, Manchester Utd 0
26 Dec	Aston Villa 2, Arsenal 2
28 Dec	Fulham 2, Chelsea 2
4 Jan	Southampton 0, Manchester Utd 3 (FA Cup 3rd round – Radio Five Live)
18 Jan	West Ham 3, Fulham 1 (Radio Five Live)
23 Jan	Derby 1, Nottingham Forest 1 (FA Cup 4th round – Radio Five Live)
28 Jan	Chelsea 2, Middlesbrough 0
31 Jan	Arsenal 0, West Ham 0
7 Feb	West Brom. 2, Newcastle 3
16 Feb	Arsenal 4, Cardiff 0 (FA Cup 5th round – Radio Five Live)
21 Feb	Aston Villa 0, Chelsea 1
22 Feb	Fulham 2, West Brom. 0 (Radio Five Live)
28 Feb	Arsenal 0, Fulham 0
4 Mar	Tottenham 4, Middlesbrough 0
7 Mar	Fulham 0, Manchester Utd 4 (FA Cup 6th round – Radio Five Live)
16 Mar	West Ham 0, West Brom. 0 (Radio Five Live)
21 Mar	Tottenham 1, Chelsea 0
8 Apr	Liverpool 4, Blackburn 0
18 Apr	Portsmouth 1, Bolton 0
25 Apr	Fulham 1, Stoke 0
2 May	Chelsea 3, Fulham 1
9 May	Fulham 3, Aston Villa 1
18 May	Portsmouth 3, Sunderland 1 (Radio Five Live)
24 May	Fulham 0, Everton 2

Total: 41 commentaries

MOTTY BY NUMBERS:

All stats up to the end of the 2008/09 season

Total games: 1,569

Clubs covered most often:

195 – Manchester Utd

189 – Liverpool

151 – Arsenal

147 – Tottenham

138 – Chelsea

Clubs never covered:

Aldershot, Brentford, Bury, Cheltenham, Crewe, Darlington, Doncaster, Hartlepool, Lincoln, Rochdale, Port Vale, Scunthorpe, Stockport, Yeovil and . . . Inter Milan.

Club Motty has seen win the most: Manchester Utd (108)
Club Motty has seen lose the most: Tottenham (52)

Stadia commentated at the most (including international matches and FA Cup semi-finals):

96 – Wembley

95 – Old Trafford

International teams covered most often:

157 – England

47 – Germany (including West and East Germany)

34 – Italy

33 – Holland

Motty's England record:

87 wins

41 draws

30 defeats (including penalty shoot-outs)

Biggest England win Motty has commentated on:

14 Oct 1987   England 8, Turkey 0

Penalty shoot-outs covered by Motty; the first was Arsenal's defeat to Valencia in 1980: 17

Penalty shoot-outs won by England when Motty was commentating: 0

Biggest wins:

18 Jun 1974   Yugoslavia 9, Zaire 0

22 Oct 1977   Tottenham 9, Bristol Rovers 0

Index